MW00571522

The Dunning School

The Dunning School

*Historians, Race,
and the
Meaning of Reconstruction*

Edited by
John David Smith and J. Vincent Lowery

Foreword by
Eric Foner

UNIVERSITY PRESS OF KENTUCKY

Scholarly publisher for the Commonwealth,
serving Bellarmine University, Berea College, Centre College of Kentucky,
Eastern Kentucky University, The Filson Historical Society, Georgetown
College, Kentucky Historical Society, Kentucky State University, Morehead State
University, Murray State University, Northern Kentucky University, Transylvania
University, University of Kentucky, University of Louisville,
and Western Kentucky University.
All rights reserved.

Editorial and Sales Offices: The University Press of Kentucky
663 South Limestone Street, Lexington, Kentucky 40508-4008
www.kentuckypress.com

17 16 15 14 13   5 4 3 2 1

Library of Congress Cataloging-in-Publication Data

The Dunning school : historians, race, and the meaning of reconstruction /
edited by John David Smith and J. Vincent Lowery ; foreword by Eric Foner.
     pages cm
  Includes bibliographical references and index.
  ISBN 978-0-8131-4225-8 (hardcover : acid-free paper) —
  ISBN 978-0-8131-4273-9 (pdf) — ISBN 978-0-8131-4272-2 (epub)
  1. Reconstruction (U.S. history, 1865-1877)—Historiography. 2. Historians
—United States—Biography. 3. United States—History—Civil War, 1861-1865
—Historiography. 4. United States—Race relations—Historiography.
5. Dunning, William Archibald, 1857-1922. I. Smith, John David, 1949-
II. Lowery, J. Vincent, 1978-
  E468.5D86 2013
  973.8—dc23   2013026580

This book is printed on acid-free paper meeting
the requirements of the American National Standard
for Permanence in Paper for Printed Library Materials.

Manufactured in the United States of America.

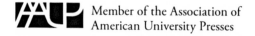 Member of the Association of
American University Presses

To Eckart and Luitgarde Schlemm—J.D.S.
To Bridgett and John—J.V.L.

Contents

Foreword

It is a peculiarity of the historical profession that it displays remarkably little interest in its own history. For this reason alone, a volume on the Dunning School—the first generation of university-trained historians to study the Reconstruction era—is extremely welcome. These essays offer fascinating insights into not only their scholarly writings but also their intellectual formation, social backgrounds, personal experiences, research methods, and the overall trajectories of their careers. The book provides an introduction to an important group of historians, as well as a sad reminder of the price paid when racial prejudice shapes historical judgment.

The term *Dunning School* is a shorthand for the interpretation of Reconstruction that dominated historical writing and public consciousness for much of the twentieth century. It takes its name from William A. Dunning, the Columbia University historian who early in the century supervised a group of graduate students who produced dissertations, subsequently published as books, narrating the history of Reconstruction in the various southern states. (As more than one essay notes, however, the label is a bit of a misnomer, as both Dunning and his students were strongly influenced by the outlook of John W. Burgess, another Columbia professor and a founder of the modern discipline of political science.)

All these scholars viewed the granting of political rights to former slaves as a serious mistake (a "monstrous thing," in Burgess's words), which brought on the South an orgy of corruption and misgovernment. Reconstruction, as John David Smith writes in his introductory essay, was to them a "twelve-year-long nightmare of debauchery, exploitation, and plunder." Nearly all the books took as a given black inferiority. But, as the essays emphasize, these historians differed among themselves in many ways, including their accounts of class relations among white Southerners, the degree of corruption in Reconstruction governments, and the extent of violence in the postwar South. James W. Garner, in his book on Mississippi, adopted a far more

balanced approach to the era than did Walter L. Fleming, whose study of
Alabama offered a vigorous defense of the Ku Klux Klan. These historians
also differed in their personal backgrounds and outlooks. Most of Dunning's students were Southerners, many of them devotees of the Lost Cause.
But Paul Haworth was from Indiana, and the family of Mildred Thompson did not move to Georgia until after the Civil War. Most were socially
and politically conservative, but Thompson, the only woman in the group,
became a New Deal liberal, a friend of Franklin D. Roosevelt and his family, and an advocate of racial fairness in admission to Vassar, where she long
served as dean.

All these writers developed insights still valuable to current historians—for example, that slavery was the fundamental cause of the Civil
War, and that regional and class differences within white society helped
shape Reconstruction politics. Anticipating recent scholarship, Dunning
and Burgess insisted that Reconstruction must be understood in a national
context, as part of the nineteenth century's nation-building process. The
Dunning scholars also pioneered in the use of primary sources to tell the
story of Reconstruction. J. G. de Roulhac Hamilton scoured the South for
documents, helping build the remarkable Southern Historical Collection of
the University of North Carolina. Mildred Thompson conducted in-depth
research in public documents, newspaper archives, and the personal papers
of Georgia leaders such as the Reconstruction governor Joseph E. Brown.
The Dunning School narratives included material that could be used for
very different purposes—for example, by W. E. B. Du Bois, whose account
of Reconstruction in individual states in *Black Reconstruction* relied heavily
for factual information on these studies. A century after they were written,
some of these works remain the only full-length accounts of Reconstruction
in individual southern states.

Of course, the fundamental flaw in the Dunning School was the
authors' deep racism. (Haworth, not always included in accounts of the
group because he studied the election of 1876, not a southern state, was an
exception; he insisted that the South's racial problems arose from white racism, not black incapacity.) As some of the essays make clear, the Dunning
School's racism cannot simply be bracketed, leaving the rest of their volumes intact, for racism shaped not only their interpretations of history but
their research methods and use of historical evidence. William W. Davis
pioneered in the use of oral history to study the Klan but interviewed only
white Floridians—the experience of Klan victims was not worth investi-

gating. Fleming closely read testimony before congressional committees, but he discounted statements by Republicans while accepting at face value Democratic claims, such as one that the extent of violence had been grossly exaggerated. A number of Dunning studies recycle overblown Democratic charges, originating in the Reconstruction era, about political corruption and the ignorance and poverty of black officeholders, without actually investigating them. As Paul Ortiz notes of Davis—a comment applicable to most of the Dunning studies—his historical imagination could not encompass black Southerners. To these scholars the South meant the white South. Thus, while they merit praise for raising the level of historical scholarship by intensive research in the documentary record, their use of that research was seriously flawed by ingrained racist assumptions.

As most of these essays note, the Dunning School's views regarding race reflected prevailing sentiments of the time. These scholars did not invent the portrait of Reconstruction as a disastrous mistake—that originated in Democratic propaganda of the postwar years. Of course, past actors should not be expected to live up to the standards and outlook of the present. But alternative views of Reconstruction were, in fact, available in the early twentieth century. In 1910 the *American Historical Review* published Du Bois's classic essay "Reconstruction and Its Benefits." Three years later the black veteran of Reconstruction politics John R. Lynch published *The Facts of Reconstruction,* a devastating critique of Dunning School scholarship. But there is no evidence that most of these scholars ever rethought their racism or how it had affected their account of history. The one exception is Mildred Thompson, who, William H. Bragg points out, suggested at a session of the Southern Historical Association in 1940 that scholars ought to investigate "the part of the Negroes themselves in securing and maintaining their freedom" (perhaps a bow, without naming him, to Du Bois, whose *Black Reconstruction* had made precisely this point five years earlier).

In any event, the writings of the Dunning School did more than reflect prevailing prejudices—they strengthened and helped perpetuate them. They offered scholarly legitimacy to the disenfranchisement of southern blacks and to the Jim Crow system that was becoming entrenched as they were writing. Well into the twentieth century, as Francis B. Simkins pointed out in a remarkable paper at a historical conference in 1937, the alleged horrors of Reconstruction helped freeze the mind of the white South in bitter opposition to any change in the region's racial system.[1]

All the essays note that the Dunning School has fallen completely out of favor among historians (although it enjoys a remarkable staying power among the public at large). Scholars now view Reconstruction as a praiseworthy attempt to create an interracial democracy from the ashes of slavery and emphasize its accomplishments as much as its failings. Most of the writers in this volume attribute the eclipse of the Dunning School to the declining legitimacy of racism and the effect on historians of the modern civil rights revolution (sometimes called the Second Reconstruction). Bragg, however, explains the evolution of historical interpretation as having been brought about not by the inadequacies of the Dunning School but by the infiltration of the academy by "the campus student radicals of the 1960s" and the triumph of the "politically correct"—as if the Dunning School itself had not been deeply political.

Interpretations of Reconstruction always reflect, in part, contemporary race relations. So long as racial equality remains a divisive question in American society, the Dunning School will not be entirely forgotten.

Eric Foner

Note

1. Francis B. Simkins, "New Viewpoints of Southern Reconstruction," *Journal of Southern History* 5 (February 1939): 49–61.

Introduction

John David Smith

In 1916 the historian Arthur C. Cole of the University of Illinois noted the emergence of what he termed the new "southern school of historians." The pupils, largely "historical students of southern birth and breeding" and "representatives of the new south," had "migrated northward to the class room of a northern guide and philosopher to receive words of wisdom and inspiration."[1] Their school was Columbia University in New York City, and their teacher was Professor William Archibald Dunning (1857–1922), one of the most important figures in developing and legitimizing southern history and the Reconstruction era as research fields. During the first half of the twentieth century Dunning reigned as the foremost authority on Reconstruction.

In 1922 the *Independent* reported, "No other American has ever so exhaustively studied the period of reconstruction as professor Dunning did, and no other writer, historian or publicist, has so deeply or so sanely influenced later American thinking upon the rights and wrongs of that unhappy time."[2] According to the historian John Higham, Dunning "maintained such Olympian aloofness from the northern bias of previous scholars that Southerners flocked to Columbia to study with him."[3] More recently and more critically, the historian David Levering Lewis dubbed Dunning "high priest of the regnant dogma in Reconstruction writing—the Dunning School, whose successive generations of historians deplored the decade of federal intervention in the South as the 'tragic era' of Negro misrule."[4]

In 1930 the Vanderbilt University historian Frank Lawrence Owsley singled out Dunning and the "Dunning School" of southern historians for repelling what Owsley considered the arrogant, condescending, and smug intellectual and spiritual victory that northern intellectuals had held over Southerners since Appomattox. Complimenting his "tough-mindedness," Owsley applauded Dunning for how his disciples "scorned the injustice and hypocrisy of the condemnation of the South" and credited them with prefiguring the 1930s "Southern renascence" and for challenging "the holiness of the Northern legend," especially its concomitant ideology of southern war guilt.⁵ Eight years later Henry Steele Commager, no hardened "Southern Agrarian" but, rather, one of the deans of the American historical profession, also heaped praise on Dunning: "To immense learning and admirable impartiality he added versatility, originality, discrimination and balance, independence of thought and a style lucid and pungent if rarely brilliant."⁶

Dunning and his students, according to the historian Glenda Gilmore, "completely rewrote the history of the conflict." He taught his students "that the Civil War had been a tragic misunderstanding and that Reconstruction had been a scurrilous punishment foisted upon helpless white Southerners by arrogant Yankees who exploited African Americans by giving them citizenship rights."⁷ This interpretation, with its accompanying stereotypes of corrupt and incompetent black rule facilitated by devilish, mischievous carpetbaggers and scalawags, took on a life of its own. For decades it dominated the popular understanding of Reconstruction thanks to its dissemination in David W. Griffith's film *The Birth of the Nation* (1915), Claude G. Bowers's *The Tragic Era: The Revolution after Lincoln* (1929), George Fort Milton's *The Age of Hate: Andrew Johnson and the Radicals* (1930), and Margaret Mitchell's novel *Gone with the Wind* (1936) and the film of the same title that appeared three years later. In 1965 the historian Kenneth M. Stampp, a leading revisionist historian of Reconstruction, framed the Dunningites' influential and powerful story as a tragedy involving "sordid motives and human depravity" in four acts.

First, following President Abraham Lincoln's death and against his plans for quickly and mildly restoring the Union, the Radical wing of his Republican Party, for reasons of economic greed and political gain, grasped control of Reconstruction, eager to prolong the process and to humiliate the former southern insurgents. Second, after Southerners willingly accepted emancipation and the war's outcome, Lincoln's successor, President Andrew Johnson, expeditiously organized new state governments, supervised elections, and proclaimed the nation restored. The Radicals, however, accepted none of this, repudiating the southern state governments, refusing to seat the Southerners' elected representatives to Congress, and launching a vituperative campaign against Johnson that garnered an overwhelming victory in the 1866 congressional elections.⁸

Congressional Radicals, in the third phase of the Dunning story of Reconstruction, took control of Reconstruction by overriding Johnson's vetoes, placing the southern states under military rule, disfranchising whites and enfranchising the freedmen. Under Radical and military rule they formed new southern state governments led by corrupt, despicable, and vindictive whites and blacks and, in a brazen act of political malice, impeached Johnson, coming within one vote of removing him from office. Under President Ulysses S. Grant's two administrations (1869–77), the Dunningites maintained, the Radical Republicans committed all manner of financial extravagance and personal venality in the state and federal governments. Finally, during the 1870s, Democrats in one former Confederate state after another, peacefully or by force, wrested control from the freedmen and their carpetbag and scalawag allies. Once redeemed, the southern states again had honest government under their natural leaders. After the disputed presidential election of 1876, the Reconstruction tragedy finally drew to a close. "But," Stampp added when concluding his summation of Reconstruction according to the Dunning School authors, "the legacy of radical reconstruction remained in the form of a solidly Democratic South, and embittered relations between the races."[9]

With the start of the 1950s civil rights movement, revisionist historians began to dismiss, if not vilify, Dunning and his Columbia University students as outright racists, branding their works as relics of an unfortunate earlier era, a time when elite whites dominated southern historical scholarship and Jim Crow defined the status of African Americans. According to the historian Fletcher M. Green, after midcentury a new Revisionist School of historians "conducted a veritable crusade for the cause" of repudiating the Dunningites.[10] In 1957, for example, William M. Brewer, editor of the *Journal of Negro History,* blasted two of the leading Dunning historians, Walter Lynwood Fleming and Ulrich B. Phillips, as having "trained under [John W.] Burgess and Dunning in the nostalgic mecca which these historians developed at Columbia University for Southern historical students." Brewer charged the "unreconstructed" Dunning historians, "tarnished by inheritance and bitterness from slavery," with distorting the history of Reconstruction by portraying "Negroes as the malefactors who were chiefly responsible for Southern woes."[11]

As late as 1982 the historian Howard N. Rabinowitz held the Dunning School responsible for what he termed "the negative image of Reconstruction still shared by most Americans today." In his widely popular *The Tragic Era* Claude G. Bowers embedded "the most condemnatory sections of [the] Dunningite works, ignoring most of the qualifications present in even the least balanced studies."[12] George Fort Milton's *The Age of Hate* similarly propounded Dunning's interpretation of Reconstruction as a direful moment in southern history. The Dunning studies directly influenced not only journalistic accounts but also textbook treatments, thus shaping generations of students at all levels of education.

Like Rabinowitz, most mainstream late twentieth-century scholars relegated the Dunning School to the dustbin of American historiography, dismissing its historians' partisan, reactionary, antiblack, prosouthern condemnation of Reconstruction. Many in fact marginalized this corpus of early scholarship either by selective reading of the Dunning historians' books or without even reading them. Indeed, the literary historian Brook Thomas has recently noted that Dunning is "more often derisively cited as an apologist for the southern stand on Reconstruction than actually read."[13] A close student of Dunning's influence and work states correctly that because critics have charged Dunning with being a racist so frequently, the term *racist* "has become Dunning's epigrammatic fate."[14]

Despite the almost universal revulsion of twenty-first-century historical sensibilities to their writings, the work of the Dunning School nonetheless is important. The Columbia dissertations on Reconstruction appeared at a pivotal transitional moment in American graduate-level education and the training of professional historians—what Dunning termed the emergence of "the Germanified universities that took form out of the academic void about 1880."[15] Historians at Columbia, Johns Hopkins, and other pioneer graduate schools of the day found themselves bombarded by influential ideas—notions of "scientific" scholarship imported from Germany, pseudoscientific racism and folklore from home and abroad, post–Civil War sympathy for white Southerners, a romanticized view of the South and the Lost Cause, and American imperialism and experiences with "subject" peoples. These ideas shaped their view of Reconstruction generally and of African Americans particularly. As Vernon L. Wharton, a revisionist historian of Reconstruction in Mississippi, explained in 1965, the longevity of the Dunningites' interpretation "may be attributed to the fact that it was compatible with the practices, principles, beliefs, and prejudices that justified domination of the world by people whose origins were in northern and western Europe."[16]

Though historians remember the Dunningites for their racist descriptions of Reconstruction, they accomplished much more than that, setting forth basic facts mobilized by later scholars and investigating aspects of Reconstruction ignored by previous polemicists and historians. These included uncovering divisions within southern churches before, during, and after the Civil War, and identifying the suffering and hardships experienced by Southerners during the entire era. Their research documented the severe economic dislocation—railroads wrecked and farms left in shambles by the tramping of soldiers, and whites left without labor following Appomattox. In 1906, reviewing one of the Dunning dissertations, the historian David Y. Thomas noted what he considered the insolence the typical freedman exhibited—"testing his freedom by fishing, going to meeting[s], and lounging about the towns and military camps only to become the victim of disease and destitution while waiting for his forty acres and a mule."[17]

Like Thomas, white historians at the turn of the century almost uniformly believed in what they termed Anglo-Saxon superiority, a mythic belief in Aryanism that they found confirmed through respected science of their day and the social philosophy of Scientific Darwinism. Employing a circular logic, most white Americans of the Jim Crow era believed that the depressed economic condition of contemporary African Americans—a product of their discrimination and proscription by whites—proved their innate inferiority.[18] For example, in 1895 a North Carolina newspaper documented what its editor considered to be the alarming mortality rate of African Americans since emancipation and Reconstruction. Freedom, the journalist explained, unleashed "a loose rein to their passions and indulging, without any consideration of prudence and moderation, in every sort of debauchery open to them." Freedom did not suddenly "create virtue and self control." He blamed the Civil War–era abolitionists and the Radical Republicans of Reconstruction for believing naively that simply freeing the blacks would civilize them.[19]

Not only did German-inspired American intellectuals focus on empirical, fact-driven "scientific" studies, but they worked at a time when even nonracists employed Darwinian science to justify racial hierarchies and classifications of people by ethnicity. After the 1880s American historians, following what they considered the German model, compared the development of institutions, casually employing biological analogies and metaphors to underscore the *Wissenschaftlich* quality of their analyses. Scholars almost uniformly positioned persons of African descent at the bottom of their racial classifications.[20] Africans had been enslaved and brought to the New World as chattel, and, scholars believed, they were retrogressing as freedmen and freedwomen. "Scientific" historians of Dunning's day prided themselves on striving for objectivity, sorting the facts, and letting them "speak for themselves." As the historian Trent A. Watts has observed, Progressive-era historians "perhaps felt that black inferiority was one of those self-spoken facts."[21]

Not surprisingly, then, most fin de siècle historians of Reconstruction voiced little objection to the 1896 *Plessy v. Ferguson* decision and the avalanche of state-level statutory and customary discrimination that followed in its wake, proscribing and circumscribing the civil and political rights of persons of African descent. It was a period, the historian Harold M. Hyman has explained, when " 'Proofs' of the Negro's ineradicable inferiority quieted the consciences of men of good will. American society lost its penchant for reform—or reduced its awareness of distress—less out of a hardening of the nation's heart than from rigidity in the nation's brains. Because white men would no longer look at the Negro's declining condition, Negroes by the 1890s were on their way to becoming America's invisible men. The neglect was in striking contrast to the century-long concern over their plight that had culminated in the Reconstruction effort."[22]

The products of Dunning's famous Columbia seminar largely shaped historians' understandings of Reconstruction for the first half of the twentieth century. The Dunningites' interpretation of Reconstruction squared perfectly with turn-of-the-century white Americans' emerging historical memory of the Civil War, their belief in racial hierarchies, their fears of integrating nonwhite minorities at home and abroad, and new social problems and questions posed by modernizing trends resulting from urbanization and industrialization. As cultural and political battles raged among businessmen, farmers, laborers, imperialists, and Progressives, among others, Dunning and his students provided Americans an understanding of the past to ease the uncertainties of the present.[23] In 1912 two of Dunning's former students, Walter Lynwood Fleming of Louisiana State University and J. G. de Roulhac Hamilton of the University of North Carolina, corresponded about Reconstruction's contemporary meaning. "I agree with you," Fleming wrote, "that reconstruction is not a delightful period for study and work. If I were teaching in a Northern school it would not be so unpleasant, but down South where we see so much of the remnants of the thing the work is quite unpleasant."[24]

"The Dunning warning," Hyman explains, "was that the real danger to democracy was not in the loss of Negro rights but in the lessening of states' rights and in the sinister secret links of big business to corrupt and demagogic public officials."[25] In his glowing review of Dunning's *Essays on the Civil War and Reconstruction and Related Topics* (1898), Henry James pinpointed what Dunning considered "the full front-face of the question at issue—the fond old figment of the Sovereign State. This romantic idea," James wrote, "becomes for us a living, conscious figure, the protagonist of the epic." James shared Dunning's regret over the demise of states' rights and the rise of African American civil rights during Reconstruction. He found Dunning's book "irresistible to read," so intriguing that James found himself "sometimes holding my breath."[26]

For decades Dunning-inspired historians did much to shape contemporary understandings of the South and its history inside and outside the academy and above and below the Mason-Dixon Line. Dunning's students elevated southern and Civil War–era history "beyond earlier filiopietistic treatments of the south's past at the hands of Confederate veterans and other guardians of the Lost Cause."[27] Even Rabinowitz acknowledged that the Dunning dissertations first "provided the scholarly apparatus that seemed to raise Reconstruction history above the level of mere emotion and partisanship." Though the Dunning dissertations "shared an overall condemnation of Reconstruction," Rabinowitz admitted that "they vary greatly in tone, emphasis, and objectivity."[28] As the historian Adam Fairclough has argued recently, "Burgess, Dunning and Dunning's Ph.D. students believed that they were honest scholars. If one reads them with an open mind, treating them as individuals rather than as a 'school,' he will find that they often rose above their limitations."[29]

Dunning and his students in fact considered themselves revisionists. Whereas previous writers had focused on Civil War military history, or launched partisan sectional polemics championing or denouncing Reconstruction, the Dunning School historians provided constitutional and political histories of the southern states in the postwar years. But to a certain degree Dunning and his followers deceived themselves. In most respects the Dunning historians virtually adopted a prosouthern view, one that exaggerated so-called Negro rule and the sufferings of white Southerners under alleged Yankee misrule. "Loosely attributed to the Dunning school," C. Vann Woodward explained, "the prevailing and all but universally received interpretation" actually "preceded Dunning and was more the product of a regional white consensus than of a school or of a scholar."[30] To a certain degree, then, Dunning and his students documented and then propagated the myths and legends of a "tragic" Reconstruction rather than creating them.

In 1898 Dunning remarked that most persons equated Reconstruction with "bad government," when actually it involved "profound problems of statecraft that had to be solved between 1865 and 1870."[31] Writing to the historian Frederic Bancroft in 1901, Dunning joked about how Columbia's historians of Reconstruction were establishing a new consensus interpretation. "Lord," Dunning exclaimed, "how the reconstructors have been reconstructed! I'm going to . . . take the ground that the whole [Reconstruction] business was ethically, socially, and politically right; that's the only way in which a man can attract any attention now."[32] In 1927 the University of Chicago political scientist Charles E. Merriam, one of Dunning's foremost protégés, remarked that his fellow Columbia students "presented the period of the Reconstruction in a wholly different light from that in which it had commonly been viewed." He added, "No one did more than Dunning to rewrite the history of the generation following the Civil War."[33]

Dunning viewed Reconstruction broadly, from a northern and national perspective. Unlike earlier writers, he appreciated Reconstruction as "one of the most remarkable achievements in the history of government."[34] A close student of political administration, he admired the Reconstruction era's political achievements. No mindless defender of former Confederates and the Lost Cause, Dunning never considered himself a southern historian, a defender of the region, or a student of race. An elite mugwump northern intellectual, he concerned himself with national questions, including foreign policy and economic development.

Dunning even maintained that longer military occupation of the defeated Confederacy, not shorter, would have been appropriate following Appomattox. As for the alleged corruption of the southern Republican carpetbag and scalawag governments, Dunning was careful to frame them within the pattern of rampant national corruption of the era, most often identified with New York's Tweed Ring. He also noted that the South's Republican Reconstruction governments, by necessity, spent considerable amounts of money to rebuild bridges, levees, and roads destroyed during the war and to provide basic humanitarian relief to the destitute. Dunning credited the southern state governments with establishing the region's first system of universal public education, singling out South Carolina's Reconstruction state constitution as especially commendable.[35] The historian David Donald observed the degree to which in his writings Dunning foreshadowed C. Vann Woodward's thesis that Reconstruction ended not in 1877, but rather during the Populist revolt of the 1890s, when one southern state after another disfranchised its African American male electorate.[36]

In 1965 Donald reminded readers prone to dismiss Dunning as partisan and racist that "only forty years ago W. A. Dunning was considered a model of historical excellence." His students based their dissertations on primary sources, strove for factual accuracy, and considered themselves objective and fair.[37] Ironically, by identifying, collecting, editing, and publishing primary sources on Reconstruction and the history of the South generally, the Dunning scholars paved the way for future historians to discredit their pioneering interpretations. They and their admirers also unwittingly helped sow the seeds of the Dunningites' historiographical demise through the creation of such institutions as the Walter Lynwood Fleming lecture series at Louisiana State University, the Southern Historical Collection at the University of North Carolina, and the Dunning Fund for travel and research at Columbia.

Donald reminds us that contemporaries judged the Dunning studies "triumphs of the application of the scientific method to historiography, and indeed they still provide our best knowledge of the political history of the South during the postwar years." Donald argued that, to a certain degree, Dunning's interpretation of Reconstruction foreshadowed later works, viewing the era from the perspective of national growth, especially in terms of constitutional, legislative, and political change. Though acknowledging obvious defects in Dunning's work, Donald insisted in 1965 that his *Essays on the Civil War and Reconstruction* "remains the best account of the constitutional and legislative history of the Reconstruction period."[38]

Wharton also underscored the importance of positioning the Dunning volumes on Reconstruction between what preceded and followed their publication. He noted that in the years 1875–1910 most writers, influenced by notions of laissez-faire capitalism and Anglo-Saxonism, commonly condemned Reconstruction as an evil. Though "this interpretation of Reconstruction is commonly attributed to Professor William Archibald Dunning . . . the Dunning School merely gave elaborate and expert documentation to a story already generally accepted." Not only did the Columbia University students offer "an interpretation that already was familiar and that suited the spirit of the time," but given "that spirit and of their own cultural heritage, most of the historians of the Dunning School were remarkably temperate and factual." Beyond this, Wharton cautioned against treating the products of Dunning's seminar as a monolith. In his opinion, "in temperament, emphasis, and quality they differed widely among themselves."[39]

More recently the historian Laura F. Edwards acknowledged that Dun-

ning and his disciples were pioneers. "While drawing on Lost Cause narratives," they "also revised them in important ways. They tended to downplay
the conflicts that led to the Civil War and focused instead on Reconstruction as the pivotal moment of sectional discord. Rather than casting asper-
sion on the North generally, they blamed radical elements within the North
for the South's woes. Specifically, northern radicals gave African Americans
too much power during Reconstruction. A race not ready for freedom, African Americans supposedly abused their new privileges and threw the entire
region into political chaos, corruption, and economic despair." According
to Edwards, "The South's post–Civil War brand of white supremacy," built
atop pseudoscientific racial theories that defined African Americans as bio-
logically inferior to Caucasians, "became the means of sectional reunion in
the narratives of Dunning School historians."[40]

This book seeks to provide a fair-minded, rounded view of the Dunning group of historians, contextualizing its contributions and framing
its strengths and weaknesses within the arc of past and current historical scholarship on the history of the South and Reconstruction. Describing a recent panel discussion on the 150th anniversary of the preliminary
Emancipation Proclamation, a reporter mentioned that the historians had
discussed the difficulties of engaging "with the existing historiography,
including the infamous 'Dunning School.'" During the exchange Edward
L. Ayers stated a truism: "The only way to have command over it [history]
is to understand it."[41]

The historians' work assessed in these pages revised previous writings
on Reconstruction and signified a generational and intellectual response to
Reconstruction's aftermath, Bourbon ascendancy in the South during the
Gilded Age, and the rise of Jim Crow and Progressivism. Whereas most
historians dismiss the Dunning School historians as conservatives and racists, the authors included in this anthology consider them within the context of early twentieth-century American historical practice, Progressivism,
and social theory. In doing so the authors have kept in mind Arthur M.
Schlesinger Jr.'s advice that historians "judge men of the past with the same
forbearance and charity which we hope the future will apply toward us."[42]

Following the history education researcher Sam Wineburg's admoni-
tions about misreading the past, they resist the common tendency of decon-
textualizing history and, in this case, historians. "Judging past actors by
present standards," Wineburg insists, "wrests them from their own context
and subjects them to ways of thinking that we, not they, have developed.

Presentism, the act of viewing the past through the lens of the present, is a psychological default state that must be overcome before one achieves mature historical understanding."[43] Or, as the Lincoln scholar Harold Holzer recently explained, viewing the past "from the vantage point of the twenty-first century . . . encourages our looking at history from the comparatively enlightened future backward, not from the past forward. And diagnoses from ever-widening distances unavoidably distort history."[44]

To understand Dunning and his students, one must comprehend how Americans generally, and historians in particular, interpreted Reconstruction in late nineteenth- and early twentieth-century America. Before, during, and after Reconstruction writers cast the entire period in unabashedly partisan terms. "For many years," explained the historian Howard Kennedy Beale, "both Northerners and Southerners who wrote on Reconstruction were dominated by sectional feelings still embittered by the Civil War. Men of the postwar decades were more concerned with justifying their own position than they were with painstaking search for truth." Northerners extolled the Republicans for saving the Union, condemned Southerners as traitors, and dismissed President Johnson as an incompetent drunk.[45] The first wave of post–Civil War scholarship, according to the historian Don E. Fehrenbacher, was "a literary continuation of the hostilities. Bristling with vindication, it fastened the blame for disaster upon individual villains and treated the sectional conflict in narrow constitutional and moralistic terms."[46]

In 1864, for example, the Massachusetts Radical Republican politician-turned-historian Henry Wilson, later Ulysses S. Grant's vice president, made clear his abolitionist sympathies. "I present this volume to the public," Wilson wrote in the preface to his *History of the Antislavery Measures of the Thirty-Seventh and Thirty-Eighth United-States Congresses, 1861–64* (1864), "in the hope that it will be of some little interest, especially to those who, amid years of obloquy and reproach, have labored and hoped for the dawning of that day, when, in all the wide circuit of our land, 'the sun will not rise upon a master, or set upon a slave.' "[47]

Between 1872 and 1877 Wilson published his dense three-volume, undocumented *History of the Rise and Fall of the Slave Power in America*, totaling over two thousand pages, written unabashedly from the perspective of an abolitionist politician and with the method of a fact collector. His fellow abolitionist James Freeman Clarke judged Wilson's work fair-minded and definitive. "The defenders of slavery at the North and South are regarded, not as bad men, but as the outcome of a bad system," he wrote.[48] W. E. Church, reviewing Wilson's volumes in the *Galaxy*, disagreed strongly, describing the tedious volumes as "the dullest, most unthoughtful and unsuggestive historical books ever written."[49]

Wilson devoted surprisingly little attention to Reconstruction. Volume 3 of *History of the Rise and Fall of the Slave Power in America* contains seven chapters and fewer than two hundred pages devoted to postwar Reconstruction. Reaffirming that the war had been an "irrepressible conflict," Wilson criticized Democrats and clergymen, north and south, for not caring for the needs of the freedpeople. White Southerners continued to yearn for the Lost Cause and considered slavery the natural condition of Negroes. "The demon of slavery has indeed been exorcised and cast out of the body politic," he concluded, "but other evil spirits remain to torment, if not destroy." Its stilted writing, thin and haphazard coverage, and awkward structure garnered Wilson's final volume little praise from or influence on later historians.[50]

So too for his fellow Republican politician James G. Blaine's two-volume *Twenty Years of Congress: From Lincoln to Garfield, with a Review of the Events Which Led to the Political Revolution of 1860*, which appeared in 1884 and 1893. A founder of the Republican Party, Blaine was an influential member of the House of Representatives and the Senate, and he later served as secretary of state. Generally a moderate on Reconstruction, Blaine, as a student of contemporary history, sharply criticized slavery and disunion and underscored the unwillingness of white Southerners to accept the true freedom of African Americans and national sovereignty.

In Blaine's opinion, the secessionists' project betrayed "the spirit of loyalty to the Republic, . . . carried with it a challenge to the progress of civilization, and was a fight against the nineteenth century." As for Reconstruction, Blaine remarked, "History and the just judgment of mankind will vindicate the wisdom and the righteousness of the Republican policy, and that vindication will always carry with it the condemnation of Andrew Johnson." "The elevation of a race, the stamping out of the last vestige of caste, the obliteration of cruel wrongs, were the objects aimed at by the Republicans," Blaine concluded. "If they remain unaccomplished, or only partially accomplished, no discredit can attach to the great political organization which entertained lofty conceptions of human rights, and projected complete measures for their realization."[51]

Perhaps not surprisingly, others launched a counteroffensive to Wilson's and Blaine's partisanship. For example, in 1874 the northern journalist James Shepherd Pike condemned Reconstruction generally and in South Carolina in particular, describing it as an orgy of corruption by former slaves who threatened to "Africanize" the state. South Carolina "lies prostrate in the dust," Pike wrote, "ruled over by this strange conglomerate, gathered from the ranks of its own servile population. It is a spectacle of a society turned bottom-side up. . . . It is the slave rioting in the halls of his master, putting that master under his feet."[52]

In 1890, in *Why the Solid South? or, Reconstruction and Its Results,* Alabama Democratic congressman Hilary A. Herbert, a former Confederate officer and secretary of the navy under Grover Cleveland, edited and contributed to a collection of essays on Reconstruction in each of the former Rebel states, in addition to Missouri, Washington, D.C., and West Virginia. C. Vann Woodward credited Herbert with crafting "the leading apology for the ultraconservative Redeemer regime."[53] According to Herbert's biographer, Hugh B. Hammett, the hastily assembled *Why the Solid South?* was Democratic propaganda against the Lodge Election Bill of 1890. Like other Bourbon Democrats, Herbert likened the supervision of southern elections by federal officials proposed by Massachusetts Republican congressman Henry Cabot Lodge to the hated military rule of Radical Reconstruction. Four chapters from *Why the Solid South?* appeared in the *Congressional Record* as testimony against the act's passage. Hammett considers Herbert's book "the most comprehensive and articulate statement of the southern point of view of Reconstruction that had yet appeared."[54]

Herbert considered "the days during which the reconstruction governments ruled in the several Southern states . . . the darkest that ever shrouded any portion of our country." Though mindful of the challenges posed by writing about events that occurred only two and one-half decades earlier, Herbert nonetheless assured readers that the authors in his anthology, including a number of influential southern politicians, wrote unprejudiced history. "This work has not been undertaken with any such impracticable purpose as agitating for the repeal of the Fifteenth Amendment, or for the deportation of the negro."[55]

Having vouched for the anthology's authors' open-mindedness, Herbert next explained that their goal was "to show to the public, and more especially to those business men of the North, who have made investments in the South . . . the consequences which once followed an interference in the domestic affairs of certain states by those, who either did not understand the situation or were reckless of results." In what Hammett termed "the siren song of reconciliation," Herbert dedicated his book to "The Business Men of the North." He considered his anthology a primer for Americans "in deciding what ought not to be done by the Federal Government" regarding the South. Reconstruction had proven true the adage "that sins of commission are generally more fatal than sins of omission." Herbert believed that the excesses committed by the federal government during Reconstruction underscored the importance of "home rule." Local officials, not distant federal officeholders, were best positioned to answer local questions. "It is sincerely to be hoped that the American people may not need to take another lesson in the school of Reconstruction," he added.[56]

The authors in Herbert's collection sketched a gloomy portrait of Reconstruction in their states. Military rule in Virginia, according to Robert Stiles, was a system of "absolute despotism," whereas Mississippians, Ethelbert Barksdale complained, suffered under the thumb of "two objectionable elements . . . the negro and the carpet-bagger." Freedmen's Bureau agents in Texas, Charles Stewart charged, "were, for the most part, a set of unmitigated rascals. Sent to protect the negro against the cruelty and rapacity of his employer, they managed to pluck from him his hard-earned dollars, and not unfrequently they were in the pay of the employer, who, from necessity, submitted to be blackmailed, rather than be subjected to constant and unnecessary annoyance."[57]

North Carolina's former governor Zebulon B. Vance condemned the Republicans' program of enfranchising the freedmen while disfranchising North Carolina's "leading citizens." Federal policy following Appomattox reminded Vance of Great Britain's administration in India following the Indian Rebellion of 1857. "As the Sepoy troops were commanded by British officers, so these ignorant negroes were officered by a trained corps of expert thieves and scoundrels who showed them how to plunder the helpless whites." G. G. Vest complained that even Missouri, a state that never seceded from the Union, experienced misrule during Reconstruction. Vest hoped "that never again will be witnessed upon this continent the reign of fraud and outrage to which the people of Missouri were subjected during these years of Republican supremacy. They are to-day paying the fraudulent debts then created and from which they cannot escape."[58]

The partisan writings on Reconstruction of Wilson and Blaine on the one hand, and of Herbert and his collaborators on the other, gave way in the 1890s and afterward to a sustained interest in Reconstruction as a research field by serious historians. James Ford Rhodes, the industrialist–turned–amateur historian, and Dunning and his students dominated this new, largely revisionist historiography. According to Beale, "Rhodes and the Dunning group drew a picture of a South that—but for outside inter-ference—might have made a happy and practical readjustment suited to the new social, economic, and political order."[59] Historians found Reconstruc-tion attractive as a research field because it enabled them to understand the constitutional, economic, political, and social implications of the war and its aftermath in shaping federalism, the role of the states, and sovereignty in the early twentieth-century nation-state. For them Reconstruction was the past, but the not-too-distant past.

Turn-of-the century historians often remarked that understanding the two complex decades following Appomattox posed serious interpretive problems. "Indeed," wrote the Alabama historian William Garrott Brown in 1902,

> there is probably no more difficult subject to be found anywhere in modern history. To arrive at any fixed opinion of one's own concern-ing the main things that were done is hard enough. It is conceivable that a really intelligent student possessed of all the important facts, and not without the power of sympathetic comprehension, might fail all together in this initial part of his work. He might never achieve a view, a theory, a judgment, on which his own mind would rest with any degree of satisfaction, which he could with reasonable conscience and assurance commend to his readers.[60]

Six years later L. S. Rowe of the University of Pennsylvania wrote that Reconstruction had "been so generally neglected, but [remained a topic] which is fraught with lessons of the deepest import." He added, "Although we are but a quarter of a century removed from the reconstruction era, it seems very much further from us, both in thought and feeling, than the earlier decades of the nineteenth century."[61] Another scholar, Roy F. Nich-ols, who earned his doctorate at Columbia after Dunning's death, wrote that historians did not seriously consider Reconstruction as a subject of inquiry until the 1880s, "and no judgment was rendered in book form until the early years of the twentieth century." Historians of this era, including Rhodes and Dunning, waited "until the elapse of quite an interval after their occurrence" to discuss what twenty-first century scholars would term "contemporary history."[62]

Rhodes launched the revisionist Reconstruction project through a sweeping multivolume history, *History of the United States from the Compromise of 1850 to the Final Restoration of Home Rule at the South in 1877* (1893–1920), and Dunning disseminated it through two books, *Essays on the Civil War and Reconstruction* and *Reconstruction, Political and Economic, 1865–1877* (1907), and then over two decades through the writings of his Columbia graduate students. According to Beale, both scholars brought "meticulous and thorough research" to the study of Reconstruction, essentially concluding that Radical Reconstruction harmed the South and that the former Confederate states could have reentered the Union smoothly without federal interference.[63]

Rhodes's and Dunning's histories were only slightly less partisan than Herbert's in defending the South and indicting northern policies during Reconstruction. "The primary difference," explains Hammett, "was in tone of presentation rather than in substance or interpretation; it was revisionism all right—southern style." Herbert's imprint appeared not only in Rhodes's and Dunning's works, but throughout those of the Dunning School.[64] To an important degree, then, the Dunning School interpretation of Reconstruction was neither new nor the brainchild of the Columbia historians. The historian Anne M. Chapman writes: "Its members did, however, lend academic credibility and expert documentation to an already familiar story."[65]

Though Rhodes was a self-taught amateur, his nine-volume *History of the United States from the Compromise of 1850* ranked as one of America's most influential historical works at the fin de siècle. His *History* remained widely popular with lay readers and proved influential to scholars well into the interwar years. Northerners welcomed Rhodes's unequivocal condemnation of slavery as *the* cause of the Civil War. He considered the "peculiar institution" a national blight and disunion a detour to American greatness. But unlike Henry Wilson, Rhodes apportioned blame for the sectional crisis equally among Northerners and Southerners and condemned Reconstruction. Contemporaries credited him with writing with balance and fairness. As a result, Rhodes won friends north and south.

White Southerners appreciated Rhodes's work because he openly sympathized with the plight of their forebears during Reconstruction, especially their resistance to military rule and determination to attain local control.

His treatment of Reconstruction appealed to the prejudices of southern readers. For example, he denounced Reconstruction in Louisiana as "a sickening tale of extravagance, waste, corruption and fraud," and he considered Negroes "one of the most inferior races of mankind"—mentally and morally backward—and hence unprepared for citizenship and the suffrage. Rhodes blamed unprincipled native scalawags, lecherous carpetbag adventurers, and northern reformers for foisting black suffrage on Southerners, unmindful of what Rhodes termed "the great fact of race, that between none of the important races of mankind was there a difference so wide as between the Caucasian and the Negro."[66]

"The worst feature about the Reconstruction Acts," Rhodes explained, "was not the military government. Honest government by American soldiers would have been better than negro rule forced upon the South at the point of the bayonet." After researching conflicting accounts of violence directed at blacks and Unionists, for instance, Rhodes concluded that "violence was indeed practiced at the South, but was sporadic and not universal." He also charged southern state Republican governments with financial waste and corruption. For example, Rhodes judged the Democrats' 1870 electoral triumph in North Carolina as "a victory of righteousness." In his opinion, "Congressional reconstruction had built up a corrupt party which deserved to be overthrown; any observer who had an opportunity to contrast the constituents of the two parties could not fail to see that the cause of good government had won."[67]

Rhodes branded southern Republicans' governments as mere "usurpatory rule" and their "redemption" by Democrats "the re-establishment of the control of intelligence and property." Regarding the freedman, he wrote:

> At last, owing to a great moral movement, he gained the long-wished-for boon of freedom; and then when in intellect still a child, instead of being treated as a child, taught gradually the use of his liberty and given rights in the order of his development, he, without any demand of his own, was raised at once to the white man's political estate, partly for the partisan designs of those who had freed him. His old masters, who understood him best and who, chastened by defeat and by adversity, were really his best friends, were alienated. He fell into the hands of rascals who through his vote fattened on the spoils of office.[68]

Not surprisingly, unreconstructed Southerners welcomed Rhodes's "balanced" view. In 1906 the Mississippi historian and archivist Dunbar Rowland wrote to Rhodes, informing him he hoped that his *History* "could be placed in every Southern home for it would impress the truth that justice finally prevails. We have all along felt that the time would come when a Northern historian, with the ability to ascertain the truth and the courage to write it, would give a true picture of the Reconstruction in the South."[69] A year later in a review essay, Dunning greeted Rhodes's first seven volumes enthusiastically. "The reader may readily sympathize with the historian in his aversion from the repulsive aftermath of the war," he wrote.[70] In the preface to his *Reconstruction, Political and Economic, 1865–1877,* Dunning acknowledged his intellectual debt to Rhodes. "The appearance of Dr. James Ford Rhodes's last two volumes, covering the years 1866–1877, in time to be used in the final revision of my manuscript, is a mercy the greatness of which in a preface cannot be adequately expressed."[71] Years before, Rhodes, when writing about Reconstruction, noted with gratitude his dependence on Dunning's *Essays on the Civil War and Reconstruction.*[72]

Rhodes's writings on Reconstruction proved helpful not only to Dunning, but also to his *Doktorvater,* the renowned Columbia University political scientist and historian John W. Burgess (1844–1931). Burgess, one of the founders of the field of political science in the United States, sought to balance "a science of politics which history would continue to serve and a history which could benefit from the methodological refinements which a rigorous political science could produce."[73] He shaped Columbia's graduate curriculum and mentored Dunning (thirteen years his junior) and in turn his generations of students and their disciples. The connectedness of the sovereignty of the state, liberty, and government shaped Burgess's understanding of history and political science. According to his former student William R. Shepherd, Burgess was sui generis: a "Southerner by birth, Northerner by adoption, and American by devotion to a common country."[74]

Burgess grew up in a Whig slaveholding family in war-torn Tennessee. Confederates persecuted his family for their loyalty to the Union. After serving in the Union Army and attending college and reading law in Massachusetts, Burgess studied history in Göttingen, Leipzig, and Berlin, 1871–73, and, like Johns Hopkins University's Herbert Baxter Adams, he imported the German historical method, especially the quest for objectivity and the use of primary sources to test hypotheses, to the American university. In 1876 Burgess joined Columbia's law faculty and four years later organized that university's School of Political Science, structuring the school into three departments—Public Law and Comparative Jurisprudence, Economics and Social Science, and History and Political Philosophy.[75] In 1890 Burgess became the school's first dean. At Columbia Burgess, and later Dunning, assembled an outstanding social science faculty, including Frank Goodnow in administrative law, Munroe Smith in jurisprudence, Richmond Mayo-Smith in statistics, E. R. A. Seligman in public finance and economic history, Franklin H. Giddings in sociology, John Bates Clark in economics, and Herbert L. Osgood and William M. Sloane in history.

In addition to creating the institutional framework later embraced by Dunning and his students, Burgess published an important work in political theory, *Political Science and Comparative Constitutional Law* (two volumes, 1890–91), and three influential works in American history: *The Middle Period, 1817–1858* (1897), *The Civil War and the Constitution, 1859–1865* (two volumes, 1901), and *Reconstruction and the Constitution* (1902).[76]

Burgess approached the subject of the Civil War and Reconstruction sympathetically toward both the victors and the vanquished. He interpreted the conflict as an unfortunate case study in disunion—one with deeply painful personal memories—but as a necessary step in the hammering out of a true American nationality. When the smoke of battle had cleared, secession played a constructive part in what Burgess termed "the hastening of emancipation and nationalization. The United States were lagging in the march of modern civilization. Slavery and 'State sovereignty' were the fetters which held them back, and these fetters had to be screwed down tight in order to provoke the Nation to strike them off at one fell blow, and free itself, and assert its supremacy, forevermore."[77] Much as he considered the 1871 unification of the German states a progressive, divinely inspired move, Burgess interpreted Radical Reconstruction as necessary to restore civil governments in the formerly rebellious states.[78] He believed that constitutionally the seceded states became territories until Congress readmitted them to the Union. That said, Burgess argued that congressional Radicals went too far, that Reconstruction in fact undid much of the good that Union victory in the war had achieved. In the historian Harvey Wish's opinion, Burgess, much like Rhodes, "contributed to the new 'revisionist' and racist interpretation of Reconstruction, which assumed that the biracial legislatures [of the southern states] failed because Negroes were inherently inferior and incapable of understanding their true interests."[79]

In his *Reconstruction and the Constitution* Burgess wrote that in enfranchising blacks "Congress did a monstrous thing, and committed a great political error, if not a sin." He considered it "a great wrong to civilization to put the white race of the South under the domination of the negro race. The claim that there is nothing in the color of the skin from the point of view of political ethics is a great sophism. A black skin means membership in a race of men which has never of itself succeeded in subjecting passion to reason, has never, therefore, created any civilization of any kind." Burgess regretted that the freedmen served in southern state governments—a policy that constituted "a great wrong to the negroes themselves. It made the white men among whom they must live their most bitter enemies, when they most needed them for friends, and it made the negroes trifling and corrupt politicians, when they should have been devoting themselves exclusively to the acquirement of property and education."[80]

Burgess believed that Reconstruction "was a punishment so far in excess of the crime that it extinguished every sense of culpability upon the part of those whom it sought to convict and convert."[81] Like Rhodes, he faulted the Radical Republicans for enfranchising African Americans generally and as a means to control southern state governments. Burgess judged the granting of universal black suffrage "one of the 'blunder-crimes' of the century." He maintained that "there is something natural in the subordination of an inferior race to a superior race, even to the point of the enslavement of the inferior race, but there is nothing natural in the opposite. It is entirely unnatural, ruinous, and utterly demoralizing and barbarizing to both races." The entire Reconstruction experiment, Burgess concluded, was a "terrible mistake of the North," one that ushered in the "terrible degradation of the South." He added: "It was the most soul-sickening spectacle that Americans have ever been called upon to behold. Every principle of the American polity was here reversed. In place of government by the most intelligent and virtuous part of the people for the benefit of the governed, here was government by the most ignorant and vicious part of the population for the benefit, the vulgar, materialistic, brutal benefit of the governing set." Burgess's belief that Reconstruction constituted "the dark night of domination by the negro and adventurer" influenced Dunning's understanding of the period and so too that of his students.[82]

The Dunning School generally refers to the corps of Dunning's disciples who wrote pioneering dissertations and later books on Reconstruction on the state level, many appearing in Columbia University's Studies in History, Economics and Public Law series, established in 1890.[83] During his long career at Columbia, then located on Forty-ninth and Fiftieth streets, between Madison and Fourth avenues, Dunning served as a magnet for students, especially Southerners, interested in studying the Civil War era and history of the American South. David Y. Thomas, who came from Arkansas in 1901 to study with Dunning, believed that "the history of reconstruction must be written by Southerners, who were the ultimate victors in that life-and-death struggle. It is for that work, now one of the richest fields for investigation in American history, that the younger generation is being trained. The scientific spirit of the universities has largely divested them of inherited passions and prejudices, and they are going at the task of writing history with a simple desire to discover and tell the truth."[84]

Dunning directed eight dissertations on Reconstruction in individual states, ten theses on aspects of the Civil War or Reconstruction, several others on other topics in southern history, and numerous dissertations in political theory.[85] Most of these theses were the first scholarly discussions of their topics, especially on the state level. The most important members of the Dunning School (and their state studies) assessed in this book are William W. Davis (Florida), Walter Lynwood Fleming (Alabama), James W. Garner (Mississippi), J. G. de Roulhac Hamilton (North Carolina), Charles W. Ramsdell (Texas), and C. Mildred Thompson (Georgia). Ulrich B. Phillips, the historian most often identified with the Dunning School, studied with Dunning at Columbia but wrote his dissertation on pre–Civil War Georgia politics. A number of other scholars, rarely identified with the Dunning School per se, also studied Reconstruction-era topics under the man whom his Columbia students dubbed their "Old Chief."[86] Still others, most notably E. Merton Coulter, who published general and state studies on Reconstruction that historians consider "Dunningite" in tone, had no direct association with Dunning or Columbia.[87]

Paul L. Haworth, the least known and most politically and socially progressive of Dunning's protégés (and the member of the school most commonly shunned by the Dunningites themselves), wrote his dissertation at Columbia on the disputed 1876 presidential election and another general work, *Reconstruction and Union, 1865–1912* (1912). In 1904 Fleming advised Hamilton: "You needn't find so much fault with Haworth's notions of negro equality. If he thinks Cuffy and himself are about equal I guess he is about right. . . . To my mind, H. is the embodiment of most of the things that a history man should not be. He will have to be born again before he knows how to feel & act as a gentleman." Dunning's students joked among themselves that Haworth, an Indiana native, was a "Black Republican."[88]

Henry Watterson, the fiery Democratic editor of the *Louisville Courier-Journal,* found nothing humorous in Haworth's published dissertation, *The Hayes-Tilden Disputed Presidential Election of 1876* (1906). In an editorial titled "A Partisan Dissertation," Watterson subjected the young historian's doctoral thesis to a withering attack, charging him with naïveté, pro-Republican leanings, and selective, sloppy scholarship that justified the election of Rutherford B. Hayes over Samuel J. Tilden. According to the editor, Haworth was "one of those mousing and industrious literary persons who have every aptitude for writing history except the breadth to understand the truth and the will to tell it." Watterson ended his review by taking a swipe at Columbia's Department of History. If, the editor wrote, the university could do no better than producing a scholar like Haworth, then "it should shut up shop and turn to shoemaking."[89]

No one could have accused the Alabamian Walter Lynwood Fleming, who moved to New York City in 1900 to work with Dunning, of Yankee sympathies. Upon enrolling at Columbia, Fleming explained to George Petrie, his former mentor at Alabama Polytechnic Institute (later Auburn University), that he was taking classes with Herbert Osgood and Burgess in American political history, English constitutional history with Osgood, Continental history (Middle Ages) with James Harvey Robinson, and international law with John B. Moore. Fleming expected to write his master's thesis on American colonial history and hoped to write his doctoral dissertation under Dunning on either southern or Alabama history. Fleming informed Petrie that Columbia's library holdings on the South were weak, except for material on Virginia and the Carolinas. He complained that retrieving books at Columbia's library was cumbersome. "Sent in a list of ten books this afternoon & got three of them that I didn't want." Despite his complaints, Fleming informed Petrie that at Columbia he stumbled on a series of public documents unavailable at Auburn.[90]

Fleming also commented on the social composition of his classes at Columbia. "There is a Jap in one of my history classes & a big black nigger in the Int. Law class," Fleming wrote Petrie. "There are several negroes in the university," he added. Fleming went on to comment on his female classmates from Barnard and Columbia Teacher's College. "They are the driest looking lot the sun ever shone upon. It is a fact I haven't seen a single good looking one yet. I can now understand why the Northern college woman seldom marries. She is not asked." Fleming continued: "The women here in college (Columbia) are not as good as the girls that Auburn has had. They can't see a thing unless knocked down with it. They are so ugly they ought to study well, too." Fleming also remarked that quite a few Southerners, "more than ever before," had come to Columbia to study history. "[Ulrich B.] Phillips—a young man from U. of Ga.—is one of the Fellows in History," he added. Fleming commented on what he considered the "queer habit the history men have here of criticizing the work of each other. Prof. Robinson says that Prof. Burgess's theories on some subjects are all wrong, etc. & Profs. Osgood & Dunning pay left-handed compliments to one another. Not in a spirit of fault finding but of fact stating. It is funny sometimes." Fleming found the Columbia graduate program satisfying, but he nevertheless informed Petrie that "a person with any sense could do all this work by himself."[91]

As the historian Philip R. Muller has made clear, Dunning never imposed a unitary view, most notably his own, on his graduate students.[92] Still, Fleming and his fellow Columbia students shared a common set of assumptions and crafted a more or less similar narrative.

They considered Reconstruction a conspiracy by vindictive and power-hungry northern Republicans determined to have white Southerners, who genuinely accepted military defeat and emancipation, "pay" for their apostasy of disunion. In 1903 Fleming wrote to Hamilton: "The more I work on reconstruction the more firmly I believe in h—l—for Thad. Stevens etc. It will be hard for them to get their just deserts, no matter how hot it may be."[93] The Columbia students described Reconstruction as a twelve-year-long nightmare of debauchery, exploitation, and plunder of native white Southerners by dishonest and greedy outsiders, the northern carpetbaggers, rogue and shiftless insiders, the scalawags, corrupt federal officials, despotic U.S. Army personnel, and aggressive, brutal freedmen bent on revenge and social and political equality. Eric Foner observes that according to the Dunning School historians, "Reconstruction was the darkest page in the saga of American history."[94]

Dunning's pupils argued that in their quest for power, Republicans

overturned the provisional southern state governments Johnson had established, instituted black suffrage, and placed the Reconstruction process
under military rule. This was Radical Reconstruction. The Dunningites
reasoned that unscrupulous whites, both on the ground in the South and
in Congress, manipulated ignorant and inferior Negroes for political control and economic gain. They ignored evidence that during Reconstruction
many prominent white Southerners had in fact collaborated with southern Republicans. Not surprisingly, Dunning's students justified the Black
Codes, denounced the Civil Rights Act of 1866, opposed the military governments established in 1867, and condemned the Radical governments as
controlled by self-interested politicians who manipulated the South's former slaves.

The Dunning historians objected most loudly to what they considered
the unnatural elevation of African American males to civil and political
equality. They charged that the Radical Republicans enfranchised blacks
to humiliate the defeated Confederates. This move proved futile, they
explained, first, because the freedmen were unqualified to hold office and
vote and, second, because white Southerners never would accept blacks
as their political and social equals. Dunning's students underscored what
they considered the indignities of "Negro rule," a concept that for them
signified a saturnalia of corruption and fiscal excess by black, carpetbag,
and scalawag state governments and the tyranny of U.S. Army occupation
forces.

Criticism of the freedpeople ran through the Dunning studies like a
leitmotif. The authors emphasized black inferiority generally, describing
the former slaves as barbarous, childlike, often criminal, deluded, ignorant, and controlled by their white friends. Members of the Dunning
School generally found little to praise in either the African Americans'
participation in the southern state constitutional conventions or their
service in the Reconstruction state governments. They viewed the overthrow of the Republican regimes as a necessary reform, so too the control of black Southerners by relegating them to a permanent second-class
citizenship.

Dunning's students sympathized with native white Southerners, characterizing them as courageous, decent, and determined to be reintegrated
into the American body politic. They credited President Andrew Johnson,
a former Tennessee slaveholder, with attempting to implement Abraham
Lincoln's mild restoration program and then bravely attempting to fore-

stall Radical control. The president's overthrow ushered in what Dunning's postgraduates described as a dangerous cyclic pattern in each former Confederate state. First, Radicals enfranchised blacks, who in turn established corrupt black-led governments. Native white Southerners by necessity had to overthrow these governments by whatever means necessary (the Dunningites even condoned white terrorist organizations such as the Ku Klux Klan) to return their states to "normalcy" and "good government." Dunning's students equated "normalcy" and "good government" with white supremacy and, later, Jim Crow. As Don E. Fehrenbacher observed, the Dunning School historians interpreted "the restoration of white supremacy as the happy ending of Reconstruction."[95]

William A. Dunning was born in Plainfield, New Jersey, in 1857, and the Civil War and its aftermath had less of an effect on his sense of nationalism than it had on Burgess's. Dunning moved quickly up the academic ladder at Columbia, earning his bachelor's degree in 1881, his master's in 1884, and his doctorate in 1885.[96] Dunning's dissertation, "The Constitution of the United States in Civil War and Reconstruction" (1885), according to David Donald, "made the post–Civil War period a respectable field for academic historical investigation." In this study Dunning explained how the unprecedented circumstances of the war finally settled the debate over national versus state sovereignty, which had threatened to destroy the Union. Dunning set the tone for his later writings, categorizing the Radicals' project of punishing the Confederates by elevating blacks as revolutionary—the "passionate fancies of fanatics more extreme than the Southern fire-eaters who had precipitated the Civil War."[97]

Dunning joined Columbia's political science faculty in 1885, and, aside from studying briefly with Heinrich von Treitschke in Berlin, he spent his entire academic career there. In 1904 the university named Dunning the first Lieber Professor of History and Political Philosophy. The historian Barry Karl suggests that as a Columbia mentor, Dunning was broader intellectually and less committed to Hegelian process, Teutonicism, and the hierarchical ordering of societies than Burgess. Dunning privileged the social sciences over political science and proved more flexible and less dogmatic regarding research topics and dissertation supervision than his mentor. His political theory was more descriptive than Burgess's, involving the collection and classification of information for historical analysis.[98] Dunning, one of the early twentieth century's foremost social scientists, served as president of both the American Historical Association (AHA) (1913) and the American Political Science Association (1922).

Dunning was a curious blend of deep intelligence, wide intellectual curiosity, intense seriousness, effervescence, and youthful mischievousness. He prided himself in his scholarly detachment, objectivity, maturity of thought, nuance, and precision of argument and exposition. In 1900, for example, he found absent in the historian James Schouler's *History of the Civil War* (1899) "the note of qualification that marks the unbiased historical temper."[99] Seven years later he quipped that the writings of Hermann von Holst constituted "a prose epic on the wrath of the slavocracy, tempering a blend of Homer and William Lloyd Garrison by occasional lapses into the method of German jurisprudence."[100] About a year before his death, Dunning informed a former student about his maladies, including a thrombosis in his leg. "Thrombosis is a plug in the circulation," he explained, "and I'm told that if it had located in my head instead of my leg, it would have made a noise like Woodrow Wilson."[101]

Dunning premised his philosophy of history on amassing an accurate record of past events, shunning romanticism, and overcoming presentism. In 1898 Dunning admonished his former Columbia classmate Frederic Bancroft, prone to cynicism and conspiracy theories, to move from Washington, D.C., in order to gain some perspective on his work. "What kind of history of reconstruction will you write," Dunning asked, "if you are going to judge things by the petty, selfish, mean motives that always play a part in a big movement, instead of by the great continental heart throbs of a mighty people."[102] In his 1913 AHA presidential address, "Truth in History," Dunning warned historians to judge the past on its own terms, not by current standards. "The crying need in the study of history to-day is humility. The realities of the past will never be scientifically apprehended so long as the student of history stands contemplating in a stupor of admiration the reversals of ancient beliefs effected in our own age. Contempt for those who lacked our light is the worst of equipments for understanding their deeds."[103]

Recently the historian Christopher Waldrep remarked: "Although Dunning is known today chiefly for his racial prejudice, his scholarship included values some now still find appealing, contempt for idealism, idealists, and higher-law principles as a source for governmental reform programs. It was this skepticism that led him to look behind reformers for their true motivations." Unlike his mentor, Burgess, who believed in a Hegelian higher law and the Constitution, Dunning shared the sociologist William Graham Sumner's belief in fact over sentiment and in laissez-faire. Dunning doubted that governments could control cultural practices, what Waldrep terms "his theory of state helplessness." Dunning's writings on Reconstruction, according to Waldrep, reflected Sumner's belief that governments proved incapable of changing culture. Thus, "Dunning silently rejected Lincoln's argument that the Civil War gave the nation an opportunity for 'a new birth of freedom' rooted in its original founding 'dedicated to the proposition that all men are created equal.' "[104]

Though the mere mention of Dunning's name among late twentieth-century and early twenty-first-century scholars elicits images of a villainous racist, his contemporaries and students found him charming and gracious, encouraging and generous. Dunning's cadre of devoted former graduate students considered their "Old Chief" a demanding but committed mentor and friend. "Dunning's wit and warm intelligence," Karl writes, "attracted students and kept his relationships with them alive. His criticisms were sharp and incisive, but helpful always, and delivered with a light humor to assuage the pain of the barb without dulling the point. Students stood in awe of his reception of their work long after they had left the tutelage of his classroom and long after their own reputations had been established. And they were more often than not surprised by the way in which his mind would open to welcome the companionship of their most revolutionary doctrines."[105] According to one of his prize students, Dunning's "humor and his logic were likely to be disconcerting to the unwary, or the wary too, for that matter."[106]

Dunning interpreted Reconstruction as a dangerous period in American history, a political and social revolution whereby African Americans, radical northern whites, and their southern white sympathizers overthrew orthodox white southern racial control and political power. Radical Reconstruction, Dunning believed, pitted two rival philosophies regarding reuniting the nation. The Radicals, influenced by abolitionists and other reformers, sought to overhaul the South in the wake of emancipation. They based their *reconstruction* of the South on the ideology of the common rights of all men. The three Reconstruction amendments to the U.S. Constitution signified their hope for the future equal rights of all Americans. In contrast, conservatives who, following President Lincoln's assassination, claimed him as one of their own favored a *restoration* and the continuity of the old Union after the Civil War. They sought stability and favored replacing slavery not with the equality of the races, but with a new racial order incorporating paternalism and white supremacy.[107]

Dunning considered slavery the *"modus vivendi* through which social life was possible; . . . after its disappearance, its place must be taken by some set of conditions which, if more humane and beneficent in accidents, must in essence express the same fact of racial inequality." By the mid-1870s the conservatives undid what they considered the dangerous measures of the congressional radicals. Dunning believed that late nineteenth-century imperialism generally, and the United States' experiences with indigenous peoples in its own colonial forays, validated the conservatives' belief in the folly of racial equality. "The progress in the acceptance of this idea in the North has measured the progress in the South of the undoing of reconstruction. In view of the questions which have been raised by our lately established relations with other races it seems most improbable that historians will soon, or ever, have to record a reversal of the conditions which this process has established."[108]

In *Essays on the Civil War and Reconstruction,* Dunning dismissed Reconstruction as the nadir of American history. He judged the two decades following Appomattox a phase in the nation's history that stood "the social pyramid on its apex" and that positioned the freed people "on the necks of their former masters." Dunning complained that during Congressional Reconstruction, blacks "exercised an influence in political affairs out of all relation to their intelligence or property." The blacks who came to power, Dunning regretted, "were very frequently of a type which acquired and practiced the tricks and knavery rather than the usual arts of politics, and the vicious courses of these negroes strongly confirmed the prejudices of the whites."[109]

Southern whites who joined the Radicals in usurping control of the reconstructed South, the so-called scalawags, according to Dunning, were little better. As a group they were a disgraceful lot who "lacked the moral authority to conduct government in the Southern states." "The enfranchisement of the freedmen and their enthronement in political power," Dunning wrote, "was as reckless a species of statecraft as that which marked 'the blind hysterics of the Celt' in 1789–95." After native white conservatives overthrew the Radicals' state governments, politicians began to "reform" their state constitutions by launching the disfranchisement and proscription campaigns of the 1890s. Dunning termed the disfranchisement of black voters "the undoing of reconstruction." He judged it a necessary reform, at once eliminating class conflict among whites and controlling blacks.[110]

Dunning's general synthesis, *Reconstruction, Political and Economic, 1865–1877,* appeared in the influential American Nation series, edited by Harvard University's Albert Bushnell Hart. This work, heavily influenced by Rhodes's *History,* as well as by his students' research, has received the brunt of the criticism directed at Dunning. Though scholars often credit this book as the first scholarly overview of Reconstruction, they also concur that Dunning wrote the book hastily and consider it "the quintessential 'racist' interpretation" of the period.[111] In 1962 a reviewer in the *Nation* nevertheless described the book as "the standard conservative account [of Reconstruction] after fifty-five years."[112]

Dunning's *Reconstruction, Political and Economic* contextualizes the postwar period nationally, whereas his students examined Reconstruction in the individual southern states. Dunning viewed Lincoln's and Johnson's restoration plans favorably and considered their redirection by the Radicals, especially under Thaddeus Stevens ("truculent, vindictive, and cynical") and Charles Sumner ("the perfect type of that narrow fanaticism which erudition and egotism combine to produce"), deleterious. The Radicals, aided by renegade white Southerners and predatory Northerners, condemned the South to a period that Dunning described as a carnival of misrule and corruption led by ignorant, recently enfranchised freedmen and the venal federal leadership of President Grant. Gradually Negro domination succumbed to a coalition of right-minded white Northerners and oppressed white Southerners. The overthrow of Reconstruction ushered in so-called home rule, a euphemism conservative white Southerners of Dunning's day used for white supremacy.[113]

Like his students, Dunning indulged in numerous clichés, including that of ignorant former slaves unsure of slavery's meaning, freedmen too lazy to work without compulsion, and exploitative black leaders who manipulated their black constituencies and stole money entrusted to them as state officeholders. Assessing what he considered the black American's behavior and abilities during Reconstruction, Dunning wrote:

> The negro had no pride of race and no aspiration save to be like the whites. With civil rights and political power, not won, but almost forced upon him, he came gradually to understand and crave those more elusive privileges that constitute social equality.

A more intimate association with the other race than that which business and politics involved was the end toward which the ambition of the blacks tended consciously or unconsciously to direct itself. The manifestations of this ambition were infinite on their diversity. It played a part in the demand for mixed schools, in the legislative prohibition of discrimination between the races in hotels and theaters, and even in the hideous crime against white womanhood which . . . assumed new meaning in the annals of outrage.

In Dunning's opinion, violent clashes between the races that punctuated the 1870s "displayed to the people of the North the *reducio ad absurdum* of reconstruction through negro suffrage and a régime of carpet-baggers."[114]

The Dunning School's "chamber of horrors" or "tragic era" interpretation of Reconstruction influenced Americans' understandings of that age in popular culture, in textbooks, and in professional scholarship until after World War II. Writing two years before the United States declared war on Germany and Japan, the southern revisionist historian Francis B. Simkins, himself a former graduate student of Dunning's, explained how "the successful historian of Reconstruction, by revealing early phases of the still burning race question, arouses more attention among the reading public than is usually accorded historical works." In Simkins's opinion, "Conservative scholars have described the follies and rascalities of Negro politicians and their Carpetbagger friends so as to make the reader thankful that such knavery cannot be repeated in his time." Simkins explained that what he considered the "extremely partisan," "biased," "one-sided and unhistorical" interpretation of Reconstruction remained alive and "like Banquo's ghost it will not down." He drew a direct relationship between white Southerners' interpretation of Reconstruction and the disfranchisement of African Americans. "White Southerners will argue the issues of the Civil War and even the merits of the Democratic party," Simkins added, "but there is scarcely one in a position of authority who will debate Negro suffrage and the related issues of Reconstruction."[115]

Despite the Dunning School's influence and longevity, its interpretation of Reconstruction did not go unchallenged. As early as 1909 James R. L. Diggs, the African American president of the Virginia Theological Seminary and College in Lynchburg, Virginia, and a founder of the

Niagara Movement, proposed a multivolume series on Reconstruction in all the former Confederate states as well as the District of Columbia. "The educated Negro owes the world a history of reconstruction," Diggs wrote, and he assumed that leading African Americans, including John W. Cromwell, John R. Lynch, Robert Smalls, and Theophilus G. Steward, would contribute volumes to such a project. "No subject has been treated in a way more harmful to our race than this one subject," he added. "We must get our views of that period before the public. The series of works by southern writers present our white brothers' side of the question but I do not find the proper credit given our people for what of good they really did in those trying days. . . . Should we not have both sides of reconstruction?"[116]

Four years later, in his *Facts of Reconstruction* (1913), John R. Lynch, an African American from Mississippi who during Reconstruction had served in the state's legislature and in the U.S. House of Representatives, confronted the Columbia students' interpretation head-on, arguing that contrary to their writings, the enfranchising of southern blacks was a positive step for American democracy, that the Republican state governments established after the war were successes, not failures, and that the Fifteenth Amendment benefited all Americans. Specifically, Lynch defended the administrations of Mississippi's Republican governors, Adelbert Ames and James L. Alcorn, as "among the best with which that State was ever blessed."[117]

Lynch aimed his ire at Rhodes, but indirectly at the Dunning studies as well, in an influential article in the *Journal of Negro History* in 1917. He expressed his "hope that a fair, just and impartial historian will, someday, write a history covering the Reconstruction period, in which an accurate account based upon actual facts of what took place at the time will be given, instead of a compilation and condensation of untrue, unreliable and grossly exaggerated statements taken from political campaign literature."[118] The white liberal historian John Spencer Bassett, who taught at Smith College, found Lynch's article encouraging, a positive step toward informing blacks "that the period of reconstruction was less a failure than has been said in the histories. If they can see in what respect the best representatives of the race served well and unselfishly, it will be an incentive to [do] the best that they can do in the future. It will also have a good effect on the whites."[119] Norman P. Andrews, a Howard University student, made much the same point in 1920 in the *Journal of Negro History*. Andrews argued that in his

1914 study of Reconstruction in North Carolina, J. G. de Roulhac Hamilton exaggerated the extent of Negro political control and attempts to "Africanize" the state. Andrews also chided Burgess for faulting Republicans in establishing blacks in positions of authority over whites. "Burgess sees justice in subjecting the inferior to the superior class but none in subjecting the superior to the inferior."[120]

In 1924 Andrews's Howard University mentor, the Harvard-trained black scholar Carter G. Woodson, lamented the absence of "scientific studies of the nation-wide reconstruction in which the Negroes took a part." He denounced the works of Rhodes and several of the Dunning group, including Burgess, Dunning himself, and Fleming, as "biased and inadequate." The extant state studies on Reconstruction, Woodson further charged, "merely try to make a case for the white man's side of the question as to whether the reduction of the Negro to serfdom was just."[121]

Four years later Woodson, founding editor of the *Journal of Negro History,* took aim at one of the Dunning authors, Walter Lynwood Fleming, but cast his net broadly to malign what he termed "a good many writers on the reconstruction." Fleming and the others, Woodson complained, disparaged "the freedmen's general roving," an allegation that, following emancipation, black Southerners failed to work and instead "undertook to make a living by preying upon the public." According to Woodson, such arguments resulted from racist stereotypes based on limited observation and a failure to question why the freedmen seemed to be transient during Reconstruction. Woodson explained that Fleming failed to understand "that many Negroes in order to make good their freedom had to refuse to work for their former masters when the latter endeavored to handle them roughly as they did before the Negroes were emancipated. It was natural for the freedmen to feel that they could secure better treatment from someone who had never known them as slaves."[122]

No scholar, however, did more to refute the Dunning School than the Harvard-trained African American activist, historian, and sociologist William Edward Burghardt Du Bois. As early as December 1909, at the AHA's annual meeting in New York City, Du Bois took up the gauntlet to challenge white historians' interpretations of Reconstruction, appearing at a session along with Dunning and attended by his former student Ulrich B. Phillips.[123] According to David Levering Lewis, Du Bois's biographer, the forty-one-year-old Atlanta University professor considered the invitation to speak before the leading white historians in the nation "a personal honor and a racial challenge."[124]

In his oral presentation, "Some Actual Benefits of Reconstruction," Du Bois acknowledged corruption among some black politicians and admitted that many ex-slaves were ignorant and easily deceived. But previous historians, Du Bois insisted, had missed the essential point. The former slaves generally learned quickly, acted responsibly, and received pitifully little support from the U.S. government. Du Bois defended the freedpeople from allegations of misrule and responsibility for Reconstruction's failure. He underscored three long-term contributions black voters and black legislators had made by enacting landmark legislation and reforming southern state constitutions: "1. Democratic government. 2. Free public schools. 3. New social legislation." "Practically the whole new growth of the South has been accomplished under the laws which black men helped to frame thirty years ago," Du Bois averred. "I know of no greater compliment to negro suffrage."[125]

Days after the AHA meeting, word reached Du Bois that "Professor Dunning . . . had spoken of the paper in high terms."[126] In his autobiography Du Bois recalled with seeming delight how thirty years earlier Phillips had become "greatly exercised" upon listening to his revisionist talk at the AHA meeting. Du Bois argued that white historians considered Reconstruction a "tragic" era because it signified a movement "to make American democracy and the tenets of the Declaration of Independence apply not only to white men, but to black men."[127] Alas, for all its brilliance and methodological and interpretive prescience, Du Bois's paper, later published in the *American Historical Review*, Lewis writes, "virtually failed to have any impact upon the mainstream historical scholarship of the day."[128]

In 1935, twenty-five years after his appearance at the AHA, Du Bois put into book form the substance of his paper. His monumental *Black Reconstruction: An Essay towards a History of the Part Which Black Folk Played in the Attempt to Reconstruct Democracy in America, 1860–1880* subjected the work of Dunning and his pupils to withering criticism and established the modern critique of their interpretation and place in American historiography. Du Bois's book signified both a head-on assault of the Dunningites and a new departure in both Reconstruction and African American studies. Unlike previous works, Du Bois informed his readers, his book would "tell and interpret these twenty years of fateful history with especial reference to the efforts and experiences of . . . Negroes themselves." He charged previous historians with intellectual dishonesty and lamented that he worked "in a field devastated by passion and belief."[129] Du Bois faulted the conclusions, method, and tone of the Dunningites' work on Reconstruction while placing the slaves and the freedpeople at the center of the emancipation process. As the historian Clarence E. Walker has noted, Du Bois rendered "them actors in the nation's past rather than passive, malleable clowns."[130]

Du Bois positioned blacks as active participants in the Civil War and Reconstruction, rather than as bystanders caught in the path of social and political change. Unlike Rhodes, Burgess, and Dunning and his disciples, Du Bois assumed "that the Negro in America and in general is an average and ordinary human being, who under given environment develops like other human beings," not an inferior, an outcast from evolution and human development. In a chapter titled "The Propaganda of History," Du Bois wrote that partisan historians like the Dunningites characterized the freedpeople as ignorant, lazy, dishonest, extravagant, and responsible for Reconstruction-era "bad government." To counter this Du Bois wrote creatively, passionately, and powerfully that during the Civil War era African Americans worked to tear down the edifice of slavery in order to build a new structure built on the foundation of democracy. "The legislation of this period was not bad," Du Bois explained in response to those like the Dunningites who debunked Reconstruction, "as is proven by the fact that it was retained for long periods after 1876, and much of it still stands."[131]

Whereas the Dunning authors portrayed blacks during Reconstruction as dupes of northern Republicans and industrialists, Du Bois emphasized the constructive contributions blacks and their white allies made to social legislation in state governments across the South. In his opinion, black legislators "were not primarily responsible for the exceeding waste and corruption in the South any more than the laboring class was to blame for the greater waste and dishonesty in the North. They were not proven incapable of self-government. On the contrary, they took decisive and encouraging steps toward the widening and strengthening of human democracy." In contrast to the Dunningites, who dismissed Freedmen's Bureau officials as interlopers and poachers, Du Bois praised them, describing their agency as "the most extraordinary and far-reaching institution of social uplift that America has ever attempted."[132]

Du Bois consigned the works of the Dunning School to the realm of "propaganda," an insidious force that had polluted popular understandings and textbook treatments of Reconstruction by categorizing blacks as ignorant, lazy, corrupt, and culpable for the so-called bad government during Reconstruction. After dismissing Rhodes, who, Du Bois charged, approached his research "convinced, without admitting any necessity of investigation, that Negroes are an inferior race" and then selected his sources to prove this assumption, Du Bois described what he considered "the real frontal attack on Reconstruction" as emanating "from the universities and particularly from Columbia and Johns Hopkins." Du Bois singled out Burgess and Dunning, whose antiblack bias led them to distort African Americans' "ability, work, honesty, patience, learning and efficiency . . . into cunning, brute toil, shrewd evasion, cowardice, and imitation— a stupid effort to transcend nature's law." Du Bois remarked that "Burgess was a slaveholder, Dunning a Copperhead and Rhodes an exploiter of wage labor. Not one of them apparently ever met an educated Negro of force and ability."[133]

Du Bois charged that the Dunning School authors, with the exception of Haworth, found it impossible to "conceive of Negroes as men" and dismissed their books as "one-sided and partisan to the last degree." Their books fell into the category of "Standard—Anti-Negro" which, according to Du Bois, meant that their "authors believe the Negro to be sub-human and congenitally unfitted for citizenship and the suffrage." The works followed a similar template "based on the same thesis and all done according to the same method: first, endless sympathy with the white South; second, ridicule, contempt or silence for the Negro; third, a judicial attitude towards the North, which concludes that the North under great misapprehension did a grievous wrong, but eventually saw its mistake and retreated." Du Bois singled out Fleming, whose works he considered "anti-Negro in spirit, but, nevertheless, they have a certain fairness and sense of historic honesty." Du Bois judged Fleming's *Documentary History of Reconstruction* (two volumes, 1906–7) the product of "a man who has a thesis to support, and his selection of documents supports the thesis," and he described Fleming's Columbia dissertation, "Civil War and Reconstruction in Alabama" (1905), as "pure propaganda."[134] According to the Howard University poet and folklorist Sterling A. Brown, Du Bois's *Black Reconstruction* pointed out "the true tragedies of Reconstruction—and the real lost cause—which wasn't that of planters but of the people, poor people whether black or white."[135]

Despite Du Bois's brilliant critique, the Dunning volumes on Reconstruction continued to dominate the historiography of the post–Civil War

era until the onset of the modern civil rights movement. In 1940 J. G. de
Roulhac Hamilton wrote, "Today it is difficult to find among intelligent
and informed people a defender of the congressional policy of Reconstruction."[136] Yet that same year the historian Howard Kennedy Beale, signaling
the rise of revisionists who challenged the Dunning interpretation, asked,
"Is it not time that we studied the history of Reconstruction without first
assuming, at least subconsciously, that carpetbaggers and Southern white
Republicans were wicked, that Negroes were illiterate incompetents, and
the whole white South owed a debt of gratitude to the restoration of 'white
supremacy'?"[137] Most historians in fact point to E. Merton Coulter's reactionary *The South during Reconstruction* (1947) as the last major Dunningite
study. John Hope Franklin charged that Coulter, like Dunning, interpreted
Radical Reconstruction as "a social and political system in which all the
forces that made for civilization were dominated by a mass of barbarous
freedmen."[138]

The essays commissioned for this volume include assessments of the founders of the Dunning School, Burgess and Dunning themselves, as well as
eight of Dunning's foremost Columbia doctoral students. The editors
selected historians for inclusion who best represented the range and importance of Dunning's disciples who (with the exception of Phillips) completed
dissertations on Reconstruction, not on the Civil War or other topics. The
essays follow the chapters on Burgess and Dunning, appearing in chronological order by the date when their subjects completed their Columbia
dissertations.

　　Close reading of these essays suggests that their differing attitudes
toward class, race, and the role of the state, more so than their sources
or methods, separate Dunning and his disciples from later revisionist historians of Reconstruction. Whereas the Dunning dissertations underscore
black degeneracy and the heavy hand of the federal government in tram-
pling states' rights, post–World War II revisionist historians emphasized
the positive contributions of the Radical Republicans and blacks during
the Civil War and from the long African American freedom struggle of the
First Reconstruction of the mid-1860s through the Second Reconstruction of the mid-1960s. According to Foner, the demise of the influence of
the Dunning School was inevitable. "It required, however, not simply the
evolution of scholarship but a profound change in the nation's politics and
racial attitudes to deal the final blow to the Dunning School."[139]

By the 1960s mainstream scholars identified serious weaknesses in the contributions of the Dunning School. Generally they overemphasized the deleterious effect of Reconstruction on the South and focused too narrowly on the local or sectional and ignored the larger national picture. More specifically, the Dunning students magnified the tax burdens, the size of state debts, and extravagant expenditures of the Reconstruction state governments, and they overstated the fraud and corruption allegedly perpetrated by blacks and their white friends. The Dunningites exhibited bias against blacks, carpetbaggers, scalawags, Republicans, and Freedmen's Bureau officials, while glorifying former Confederates and Democrats. They exaggerated the nefarious motives of the Radicals and overemphasized the role of blacks as voters and as elected officials in southern state governments. Finally, Dunning's protégés paid short shrift to the positive social and economic reforms those governments accomplished. As Alan D. Harper explained in 1964, in his zeal to revise pro-Republican writers, to set the Reconstruction record straight, Dunning overstepped "and he turned his hand to the work of Nemesis," and thereby shaped Reconstruction historiography for decades.[140]

Though virtually all critics of the Dunning School identify racism as the group's foremost characteristic, they commonly ignore how the Dunningites' analyses mirrored Jim Crow–era perceptions of blacks dominant in America until the 1960s. As Harper noted, "It would have been a greater wonder if Dunning had *not* been some sort of racist," given the racial climate of fin de siècle America.[141] According to the legal scholar Randall Kennedy, the Dunningites' interpretation of Reconstruction triumphed because "it fitted well with the racist presuppositions of white scholars and their audiences. It served an important ideological function by helping to rationalize the relegation of blacks to a separate and unequal status in every aspect of social and political life." Beyond this, the writings of Dunning and his students "also rationalized the federal government's laissez-faire attitude towards local racial practices that betrayed the Reconstruction Amendments."[142]

Dunning's students also noted internal class and social divisions among whites generally and Democrats in particular—differences that tended to evaporate once blacks became enfranchised. Their explication—rather their denunciation—of Reconstruction helped Dunning's students and their readers understand and rationalize the world in which they lived—the era of Jim Crow and the first New South. Reconstruction's fall ushered in a "Solid South"—a region, as Dunning's foremost student, Ulrich B. Phillips, explained in 1928, where no matter their differences on other questions, white residents shared "a common resolve indomitably maintained—that it shall be and remain a white man's country."[143]

The Dunning historians' writings on Reconstruction contributed to a national consensus on the meaning of Reconstruction and, indirectly, to a new American nationalism in the early twentieth century. The Dunning School shaped not only historical scholarship, but popular culture too, as the popularity of Griffith's *The Birth of a Nation* attests. For decades, Foner writes, "nearly all white Americans embraced the Dunning version of [Reconstruction] history."[144] Dwelling on the evils of Radical Reconstruction, the benefits of Redemption for Northerners and Southerners, and the inferiority of people of color implicitly endorsed the Jim Crow racial status quo of their day. As Foner wrote recently, "The abandonment of the nation's commitment to equal rights for the former slaves was one basis on which former white antagonists could reunite."[145] By the early twentieth century, notes the historian Steven Hahn, most white Americans considered "Reconstruction's democratic impulses as a violation of white decency." In their opinion, "black people did not belong in American political society and had no business wielding power over white people."[146]

Like all historians of every age, the Dunning scholars engaged with and explained history from the vantage point of their day, not ours. Consequently they focused on national unity and expansion, constitutional and racial reform, and reconciliation. Their "interests and interpretations" were to a significant degree shaped "by the emotional and psychological needs of the 'New South,'" explains the historian Larry Kincaid, and they sought to show how deleterious Reconstruction had been in devastating their native states and their beloved region.[147] Disillusioned by the Civil War's outcome, Dunning and his followers interpreted Reconstruction as a struggle to overthrow the subjugation of white Southerners by their former slaves and oppressive federal controls. The Dunning students considered Radical Reconstruction an aberration, an interregnum, an extreme between the normal Zeitgeist of the antebellum period, the destructive Civil War, and the restoration of the Union following 1877. Not surprisingly, the Dunningites' histories rejected the key elements of Reconstruction—centralization, increased role of government, newfound citizenship rights for blacks, and the rise of the Republican party.

The Dunningites' repudiation of Radical Reconstruction and its reforms proved attractive to early twentieth-century white Americans who welcomed racial restrictions, whether of Asians, southern and eastern Europeans, Native Americans, or African Americans, including immigration quotas for foreigners, tribal segregation for Indians, and Jim Crow laws for blacks. Perhaps it is unsurprising that Dunning's students dominated historical scholarship on the Civil War and Reconstruction within this political and social climate—during the age of brutal lynchings and racial violence and the founding of the National Association for the Advancement of Colored People in 1909. Just as the revisionists of the 1960s and the "postrevisionists" of the 1970s sought a "relevant" past, so too did the Dunning historians seek to square the past with the present.[148]

Notes

J. Vincent Lowery and Brook Thomas generously provided me with research materials for the introduction.

1. Arthur C. Cole, review of [James W. Garner, ed.], *Studies in Southern History and Politics Inscribed to William Archibald Dunning . . . by His Former Pupils the Authors,* in *Mississippi Valley Historical Review* 3 (June 1916): 108.

2. Typescript obituary from the *Independent,* in J. G. de Roulhac Hamilton Papers, Southern Historical Collection, Louis Round Wilson Special Collections Library, University of North Carolina at Chapel Hill.

3. John Higham, *History* (Englewood Cliffs, N.J.: Prentice-Hall, 1965), 167.

4. David Levering Lewis, *W. E. B. Du Bois: Biography of a Race, 1868–1919* (New York: Henry Holt, 1993), 384.

5. Frank Lawrence Owsley, "The Irrepressible Conflict," in Twelve Southerners, *I'll Take My Stand: The South and the Agrarian Tradition* (1930; reprint, New York: Harper & Row, 1962), 66–67.

6. Henry Steele Commager, "Truth, History and William Dunning," *New York Times,* February 13, 1938, 104.

7. Glenda Gilmore, "Which Southerners? Which Southern Historians? A Century of Southern History at Yale," *Yale Review* 99 (January 2011): 60.

8. Kenneth M. Stampp, "The Tragic Legend of Reconstruction," *Commentary* 39 (January 1965): 45.

9. Ibid., 45–46.

10. Fletcher M. Green, introduction to William Watson Davis, *The Civil War and Reconstruction in Florida* (1913; reprint, Gainesville: University of Florida Press, 1964), xxix, xxxi.

11. William M. Brewer, review of Wendell H. Stephenson, *The South Lives in History,* in *Journal of Negro History* 42 (January 1957): 70, 71.

12. Howard N. Rabinowitz, "Introduction: The Changing Image of Black Reconstructionists," in *Southern Black Leaders of the Reconstruction Era,* ed. Rabinowitz (Urbana: University of Illinois Press, 1982), xi, viii.

13. Brook Thomas, "Reconstructing State and Federal Jurisdiction in *A Fool's Errand* and *The Clansman,*" *English Language Notes* 48 (Winter 2010): 77.

14. Philip R. Muller, "Look Back without Anger: A Reappraisal of William A. Dunning," *Journal of American History* 61 (September 1974): 337.

15. William A. Dunning, "A Generation of American Historiography," in *Annual Report of the American Historical Association for the Year 1917* (Washington, D.C.: Government Printing Office, 1920), 352.

16. Vernon L. Wharton, "Reconstruction," in *Writing Southern History: Essays in Historiography in Honor of Fletcher M. Green,* ed. Arthur S. Link and Rembert W. Patrick (Baton Rouge: Louisiana State University Press, 1965), 308.

17. David Y. Thomas, review of Walter Lynwood Fleming, *Civil War and Reconstruction in Alabama,* in *Publications of the Southern History Association* 10 (January 1906): 50.

18. Anne W. Chapman, "William A. Dunning," in *Dictionary of Literary Biography,* vol. 17, *Twentieth-Century American Historians,* ed. Clyde N. Wilson (Detroit: Gale Research, 1983), 149.

19. "Mortality among Negroes," *Raleigh News & Observer,* October 18, 1895, clipping in John Spencer Bassett Papers, Rare Book, Manuscript, and Special Collections Library, Duke University.

20. Clarence E. Walker, *Deromanticizing Black History: Critical Essays and Reappraisals* (Knoxville: University of Tennessee Press, 1991), 100.

21. Trent A. Watts, *One Homogeneous People: Narratives of White Southern Identity, 1890–1920* (Knoxville: University of Tennessee Press, 2010), 113.

22. Harold M. Hyman, introduction to *The Radical Republicans and Reconstruction, 1861–1870,* ed. Hyman (Indianapolis: Bobbs-Merrill, 1967), xxviii–xxix.

23. Michael A. Ross and Leslie S. Rowland, "Adam Fairclough, John Burgess, and the Nettlesome Legacy of the 'Dunning School,'" *Journal of the Historical Society* 12 (September 2012): 249, 252.

24. Walter Lynwood Fleming to J. G. de Roulhac Hamilton, April 6, 1912, Hamilton Papers.

25. Hyman, introduction, xxxii.

26. Henry James, "Democracy and Theodore Roosevelt," *Literature* (April 23, 1898), reprinted in Henry James, *The American Essays,* ed. Leon Edel (New York: Vintage Books, 1956), 214–15; Andrew Delbanco, *The Abolitionist Imagination* (Cambridge: Harvard University Press, 2012), 65.

27. Watts, *One Homogeneous People,* 106, 108.

28. Rabinowitz, "Introduction: The Changing Image of Black Reconstructionists," xii.

29. Adam Fairclough, "Was the Grant of Black Suffrage a Political Error? Reconsidering the Views of John W. Burgess, William A. Dunning, and Eric

Foner on Congressional Reconstruction," *Journal of the Historical Society* 12 (June 2012): 187–88.

30. C. Vann Woodward, *Thinking Back: The Perils of Writing History* (Baton Rouge: Louisiana State University Press, 1986), 24.

31. William A. Dunning, *Essays on the Civil War and Reconstruction and Related Topics* (1898; reprint, New York: Harper & Row, 1965), xx.

32. William A. Dunning to Frederic Bancroft, April 5, 1901, quoted in Hyman, introduction, xxx. Bancroft completed his dissertation, "A Sketch of the Negro in Politics, Especially in South Carolina and Mississippi," at Columbia in 1885. See John David Smith, "Frederic Bancroft's 'Notes Among the Negroes': Writing Contemporary History in Bourbon-Era Mississippi," *Journal of Mississippi History* 66 (Fall 2004): 227–64.

33. Charles Edward Merriam, "William Archibald Dunning," in *American Masters of Social Science*, ed. Howard W. Odum (New York: Henry Holt, 1927), 139.

34. Dunning, *Essays on the Civil War and Reconstruction*, 247.

35. Hugh Tulloch, *The Debate on the American Civil War Era* (Manchester, U.K.: Manchester University Press, 1999), 217.

36. David Donald, "Introduction to the Torchbook Edition," in William A. Dunning, *Essays on the Civil War and Reconstruction* (1898; reprint, New York: Harper & Row, 1965), xv–xvi.

37. Ibid., vii.

38. Ibid., x, xiii–xiv, xvi.

39. Wharton, "Reconstruction," 298, 300, 304.

40. Laura F. Edwards, "Southern History as U.S. History," *Journal of Southern History* 75 (August 2009): 547–48.

41. Vanessa Varin, "The Emancipation Proclamation and America," *Perspectives on History* 50 (November 2012): 10.

42. Arthur M. Schlesinger Jr., "The Causes of the American Civil War: A Note on Historical Sentimentalism," *Partisan Review* 16 (1949): 981.

43. Sam Wineburg, *Historical Thinking and Other Unnatural Acts: Charting the Future of Teaching the Past* (Philadelphia: Temple University Press, 2001), 90.

44. Harold Holzer, *Emancipating Lincoln: The Proclamation in Text, Context, and Memory* (Cambridge: Harvard University Press, 2012), 125.

45. Howard K. Beale, "On Rewriting Reconstruction History," *American Historical Review* 45 (July 1940): 807.

46. Don E. Fehrenbacher, "Disunion and Reunion," in *The Reconstruction of American History*, ed. John Higham (New York: Harper & Row, 1962), 106.

47. Henry Wilson, *History of the Antislavery Measures of the Thirty-Seventh and Thirty-Eighth United-States Congresses, 1861–64* (1864; reprint, New York: Negro Universities Press, 1969), vi.

48. James Freeman Clarke, review of Henry Wilson, *History of the Rise and Fall of the Slave Power in America*, in *North American Review* 120 (January 1875): 50.

49. [W. E. Church], review of Henry Wilson, *History of the Rise and Fall of the Slave Power in America,* in *Galaxy* 21 (January 1876): 144.

50. Henry Wilson, *History of the Rise and Fall of the Slave Power in America,* 3 vols. (Boston: James R. Osgood, 1872–77), 3:684, 737, 738.

51. James G. Blaine, *Twenty Years of Congress: From Lincoln to Garfield, with a Review of the Events Which Led to the Political Revolution of 1860,* 2 vols. (Norwich, Conn.: Henry Bill Publishing, 1884, 1893), 1:177; 2:304, 475.

52. James S. Pike, *The Prostrate State: South Carolina under Negro Government* (1874; reprint, New York: Harper Torchbooks, 1968), 12.

53. C. Vann Woodward, *Origins of the New South, 1877–1913* (Baton Rouge: Louisiana State University Press, 1951), 271.

54. Hugh B. Hammett, "Reconstruction History before Dunning: Hilary Herbert and the South's Victory of the Books," *Alabama Review* 27 (July 1974): 185–96; Hugh B. Hammett, *Hilary Abner Herbert: A Southerner Returns to the Union* (Philadelphia: American Philosophical Society, 1976), 87–88, 52; Thomas Adams Upchurch, *Legislating Racism: The Billion Dollar Congress and the Birth of Jim Crow* (Lexington: University Press of Kentucky, 2004), 104–5; and Gordon B. McKinney, *Henry W. Blair's Campaign to Reform America: From the Civil War to the U.S. Senate* (Lexington: University Press of Kentucky, 2013), 125–26. In 1890 Lodge introduced the Federal Elections Bill in the House of Representatives; it was designed to enforce the provisions of the Fourteenth and Fifteenth amendments, especially the voting rights of black Southerners. The Senate defeated Lodge's bill.

55. Hilary A. Herbert, ed., *Why the Solid South? or, Reconstruction and Its Results* (Baltimore: R. H. Woodward, 1890), 430, xv, xvii.

56. Ibid., xvii, 442; Hammett, *Hilary Abner Herbert,* 55.

57. Herbert, *Why the Solid South?* 250, 345, 356.

58. Ibid., 75, 293.

59. Beale, "On Rewriting Reconstruction History," 807.

60. William G. Brown, review of John W. Burgess, *Reconstruction and the Constitution, 1866–1876,* in *American Historical Review* 8 (October 1902): 150.

61. L. S. Rowe, review of William A. Dunning, *Reconstruction, Political and Economic, 1865–1877,* in *Annals of the American Academy of Political and Social Science* 32 (September 1908): 189 [453].

62. Roy F. Nichols, review of Eric L. McKitrick, *Andrew Johnson and Reconstruction,* in *Pennsylvania Magazine of History and Biography* 85 (April 1961): 243.

63. Beale, "On Rewriting Reconstruction History," 807.

64. Hammett, *Hilary Abner Herbert,* 56.

65. Chapman, "William A. Dunning," 152.

66. James Ford Rhodes, *History of the United States from the Compromise of 1850 to the Final Restoration of Home Rule at the South in 1877,* 9 vols. (New York: Macmillan, 1920), 7:168; 5:556; 7:95. On Rhodes, see Robert Cruden, *James Ford*

Rhodes, the Man, the Historian, and His Work (Cleveland: Press of Western Reserve University, 1961).

67. Rhodes, *History of the United States,* 6:140, 308, 420–21.

68. Ibid., 7:138, 234.

69. Dunbar Rowland to James Ford Rhodes, November 28, 1906, James Ford Rhodes Papers, Massachusetts Historical Society, Boston.

70. William A. Dunning, "Rhodes's History of the United States," *Educational Review* 34 (September 1907): 113.

71. William A. Dunning, *Reconstruction, Political and Economic, 1865–1877* (New York: Harper & Brothers, 1907), xvi. Rhodes received honorary doctoral degrees from Oxford University and many American universities.

72. Rhodes wrote, "I take this occasion to say that my obligations to Dunning's book are much greater than even my many references would seem to indicate." See Rhodes, *History of the United States,* 6:408n1.

73. Barry D. Karl, *Charles E. Merriam and the Study of Politics* (Chicago: University of Chicago Press, 1974), 25.

74. William R. Shepherd, "John William Burgess," in *American Masters of Social Science,* 50.

75. For a description of the curriculum, see "Columbia University Faculty of Political Science," *Studies in History, Economics, and Public Law* 20 (1904), unpaginated back matter. On the evolution of Columbia's History Department, see Richard Hofstadter, "The Department of History," in *A History of the Faculty of Political Science, Columbia University* (New York: Columbia University Press, 1955), 207–49 and Appendix B.

76. On Burgess, see John Braeman, "John W. Burgess," in *Dictionary of Literary Biography,* vol. 47, *American Historians, 1866–1912,* ed. Clyde N. Wilson (Detroit: Gale Research, 1986), 69–75; Wilfred M. McClay, "John W. Burgess & the Search for Cohesion in American Political Thought," *Polity* 26 (Fall 1993): 51–73; and Wilfred M. McClay, "Introduction to the Transaction Edition," in John W. Burgess, *The Foundations of Political Science* (1933; reprint, New Brunswick, N.J.: Transaction, 1994), vii–xxxvii.

77. John W. Burgess, *The Civil War and the Constitution, 1858–1865,* 2 vols. (New York: Charles Scribner's Sons, 1901), 1:135.

78. John W. Burgess, *Reminiscences of an American Scholar: The Beginnings of Columbia University* (New York: Columbia University Press, 1934), 372; Braeman, "John W. Burgess," 74.

79. Harvey Wish, *The American Historian: A Social-Intellectual History of the Writing of the American Past* (New York: Oxford University Press, 1960), 226.

80. John W. Burgess, *Reconstruction and the Constitution, 1866–1876* (New York: Charles Scribner's Sons, 1902), 133, 134.

81. Ibid., 297.

82. Ibid., 245, 246, 263–64, 296.

83. On the pre-1917 Columbia Studies in History, Economics and Public Law

series, see *A Catalogue of the Publications of the Columbia Studies in History, Economics and Public Law* (New York: Longmans, Green, 1917).

84. David Y. Thomas, "The South and Her History," *American Review of Reviews* 26 (October 1902): 464. Thomas completed his dissertation, "A History of the Military Governments in Newly Acquired Territory of the United States," at Columbia in 1903, and he later published *Arkansas in War and Reconstruction, 1861–1874* (1926). On Thomas, see Mary Elizabeth Massey, "David Yancey Thomas, Historian," *Arkansas Historical Quarterly* 7 (Autumn 1948): 221–26, and Fred Arthur Bailey, "Free Speech and the 'Lost Cause' in Arkansas," *Arkansas Historical Quarterly* 55 (Summer 1996): 143–66.

85. J. G. de Roulhac Hamilton, introduction to William A. Dunning, *Truth in History and Other Essays by William A. Dunning* (New York: Columbia University Press, 1937), xvi.

86. They include Charles E. Chadsey on the contest between President Andrew Johnson and Congress over Reconstruction (1896), Edwin C. Woolley on Reconstruction in Georgia (1901), Sidney D. Brummer on the political history of New York State (1911), George H. Porter on Ohio during the Civil War era (1911), Harriette M. Dilla on the political history of Michigan during Reconstruction (1912), Benjamin B. Kendrick on the journal of the Joint Committee of Fifteen on Reconstruction (1915), and Thomas S. Staples on Reconstruction in Arkansas (1923). With the exceptions of Haworth, Chadsey, and Woolley, all of Dunning's doctoral students were Southerners. Chadsey came from Nebraska; Woolley was a native of Illinois. In 1921 Mary Scrugham completed her Columbia dissertation, "The Peaceable Americans of 1860–61: A Study in Public Opinion," a work that prefigured important revisionist scholarship on the coming of the Civil War published in the 1930s by James G. Randall and Avery O. Craven.

87. Coulter received his Ph.D. from the University of Wisconsin in 1917. See John David Smith, "E. Merton Coulter, the 'Dunning School,' and the *Civil War and Readjustment in Kentucky*," *Register of the Kentucky Historical Society* 86 (Winter 1988): 52–69. Others include the following historians and the subjects of their Reconstruction state studies: James W. Fertig (Tennessee), who earned his Ph.D. at the University of Chicago; Hamilton J. Eckenrode (Virginia), John P. Hollis (South Carolina), and William S. Myers (Maryland), who took their doctorates at Johns Hopkins University; Ella Lonn (Louisiana), who trained at the University of Pennsylvania; John S. Reynolds (South Carolina), who possessed no training as a historian and served as librarian of South Carolina's Supreme Court; and John R. Ficklin (Louisiana), who had no historical training and taught rhetoric and history at Tulane University.

88. Charles W. Ramsdell, review of Paul Leland Haworth, *America in Ferment*, in *Southwestern Historical Quarterly* 19 (October 1915): 207; Walter Lynwood Fleming to J. G. de Roulhac Hamilton, March 3, 1904, and W. W. Davis to Hamilton, November 25, 1913, both in Hamilton Papers.

89. "A Partisan Dissertation," *Louisville Courier-Journal*, August 9, 1906, 4.

90. Walter L. Fleming to George Petrie, October 6, 1900, George Petrie Papers, Special Collections and Archives, Auburn University.

91. Ibid.

92. Muller, "Look Back without Anger," 334–35.

93. Walter Lynwood Fleming to J. G. de Roulhac Hamilton, October 22, 1903, Hamilton Papers.

94. Eric Foner, *Reconstruction: America's Unfinished Revolution, 1863–1877* (New York: Harper and Row, 1988), xx.

95. Fehrenbacher, "Disunion and Reunion," 116.

96. On Dunning, see "Prof. Wm. A. Dunning of Columbia Dead," *New York Times*, August 26, 1922, 7; "Personal," *American Historical Review* 28 (October 1922): 174; Wendell Holmes Stephenson, *The South Lives in History: Southern Historians and Their Legacy* (Baton Rouge: Louisiana State University Press, 1955); Wendell Holmes Stephenson, *Southern History in the Making: Pioneer Historians of the South* (Baton Rouge: Louisiana State University Press, 1964); John H. Hosmer, "The Dunning School and Reconstruction according to Jim Crow" (Ph.D. diss., University of Arizona, 1983); John Harelson Hosmer, "William A. Dunning: 'The Greatest Historian,'" *Mid-America* 68 (April–June 1986): 57–78; Kathleen P. Barsalou, "William A. Dunning Revisited: The Mind or Malice of Reconstruction?" (master's thesis, Florida Atlantic University, 2001); and Kathleen P. Barsalou, "The Age of William A. Dunning: The Realm of Myth Meets the Yellow Brick Road" (Ph.D. diss., Florida Atlantic University, 2008).

97. William Archibald Dunning, *The Constitution of the United States in Civil War and Reconstruction, 1860–1867* (New York: J. F. Pearson, 1885), 95.

98. Karl, *Charles E. Merriam and the Study of Politics*, 34, 39–40.

99. William A. Dunning, review of James Schouler, *The Civil War*, in *American Historical Review* 5 (July 1900): 773.

100. Dunning, "Rhodes's History of the United States," 109.

101. William A. Dunning to J. G. de Roulhac Hamilton, January 14, 1921, Hamilton Papers.

102. William A. Dunning to Frederic Bancroft, January 22, 1898, quoted in Jacob E. Cooke, *Frederic Bancroft, Historian* (Norman: University of Oklahoma Press, 1957), 129.

103. William A. Dunning, "Truth in History," *American Historical Review* 19 (January 1914): 228.

104. Christopher Waldrep, *Jury Discrimination: The Supreme Court, Public Opinion, and a Grassroots Fight for Racial Equality in Mississippi* (Athens: University of Georgia Press, 2010), 208.

105. Karl, *Charles E. Merriam and the Study of Politics*, 34.

106. Merriam, "William Archibald Dunning," 135.

107. Thomas J. Pressly, "Racial Attitudes, Scholarship, and Reconstruction: A Review Essay," *Journal of Southern History* 32 (February 1966): 89, 90, 91.

108. Dunning, *Essays on the Civil War and Reconstruction*, 384–85.

109. Ibid., 250, 252, 354, 355.

110. Ibid., 186, 252, 250–51, 252, 383; James Oakes, *Slavery and Freedom: An Interpretation of the Old South* (New York: Alfred A. Knopf, 1990), 205.

111. Muller, "Look Back without Anger," 337–38. Muller charges that historians have overvalued and overcited Dunning's *Reconstruction, Political and Economic.* He considers the book largely derivative, poorly conceived, poorly argued, and less racist than its critics have alleged.

112. Robert M. Wallace, "Second Impressions: Review of Paperbacks," *Nation,* November 3, 1962, 293.

113. Dunning, *Reconstruction, Political and Economic,* 86, 87.

114. Ibid., 213–14, 219.

115. Francis B. Simkins, "New Viewpoints of Southern Reconstruction," *Journal of Southern History* 5 (February 1939): 49, 50, 51.

116. J. R. L. Diggs to W. E. B. Du Bois, July 12, 1909, in *The Correspondence of W. E. B. Du Bois,* ed. Herbert Aptheker, 3 vols. (Amherst: University of Massachusetts Press, 1973–97), 1:150–51.

117. John R. Lynch, *The Facts of Reconstruction* (New York: Neale, 1913), 10–11, 83.

118. John R. Lynch, "Some Historical Errors of James Ford Rhodes," *Journal of Negro History* 2 (October 1917): 367–68.

119. John S. Bassett to Carter G. Woodson, October 20, 1917, Carter G. Woodson Collection, Manuscript Division, Library of Congress.

120. Norman P. Andrews, "The Negro in Politics," *Journal of Negro History* 5 (October 1920): 421–22.

121. Carter G. Woodson, *The Negro in Our History,* 3rd ed. (Washington, D.C.: Associated Publishers, 1924), 239n.

122. [Carter G. Woodson], review of Walter Lynwood Fleming, *The Freedmen's Savings Bank,* in *Journal of Negro History* 13 (January 1928): 107.

123. "The Meeting of the American Historical Association at New York," *American Historical Review* 15 (April 1910): 488–89.

124. Lewis, *W. E. B. Du Bois,* 383.

125. W. E. Burghardt Du Bois, "Reconstruction and Its Benefits," *American Historical Review* 15 (July 1910): 795, 799.

126. Albert Bushnell Hart to W. E. B. Du Bois, January 2, 1910, quoted in Lewis, *W. E. B. Du Bois,* 384.

127. W. E. Burghardt Du Bois, *Dusk of Dawn: An Essay toward an Autobiography of a Race Concept* (1940; reprint, New York: Schocken, 1968), 318–19; John David Smith, "Du Bois and Phillips: Symbolic Antagonists of the Progressive Era," *Centennial Review* 24 (Winter 1980): 99.

128. Lewis, *W. E. B. Du Bois,* 385.

129. W. E. Burghardt Du Bois, *Black Reconstruction: An Essay towards a History of the Part Which Black Folk Played in the Attempt to Reconstruct Democracy*

in America, 1860–1880 (1935; reprint, New York: Atheneum, 1973), "To the Reader," n.p., 725.

130. Walker, *Deromanticizing Black History,* 82.

131. Du Bois, *Black Reconstruction,* "To the Reader," n.p., 382, 711–16.

132. Ibid., 577, 219.

133. Ibid., 718, 726.

134. Ibid., 732, 726, 731, 719, 720.

135. Sterling A. Brown to W. E. B. Du Bois, January 29, 1935, in *The Correspondence of W. E. B. Du Bois,* 2:22–23.

136. J. G. de Roulhac Hamilton, foreword to Samuel Denny Smith, *The Negro in Congress, 1870–1901* (Chapel Hill: University of North Carolina Press, 1940), viii.

137. Beale, "On Rewriting Reconstruction History," 808.

138. John Hope Franklin, "Whither Reconstruction Historiography?" *Journal of Negro Education* 17 (Autumn 1948): 448

139. Foner, *Reconstruction,* xxi.

140. Alan D. Harper, "William A. Dunning: The Historian as Nemesis," *Civil War History* 10 (March 1964): 62–63, 65, 66.

141. Ibid., 64.

142. Randall Kennedy, "Reconstruction and the Politics of Scholarship," *Yale Law Journal* 98 (January 1989): 524, 525.

143. Ulrich B. Phillips, "The Central Theme of Southern History," *American Historical Review* 34 (October 1928): 31.

144. Eric Foner, *Forever Free: The Story of Emancipation and Reconstruction* (New York: Alfred A. Knopf, 2005), xxii–xxiii.

145. Eric Foner, "The Civil War in 'Postracial' America," *Nation,* October 10, 2011, 24–25.

146. Steven Hahn, "Political Racism in the Age of Obama," *New York Times,* November 11, 2012, 6.

147. Larry Kincaid, "Victims of Circumstance: An Interpretation of Changing Attitudes toward Republican Policy Makers and Reconstruction," *Journal of American History* 57 (June 1970): 50, 51.

148. On postrevisionism, see Eric Foner, "Reconstruction Revisited," *Reviews in American History* 10 (December 1982): 82–100.

1

John W. Burgess, Godfather of the Dunning School

Shepherd W. McKinley

One cannot fully understand the Dunning School without a working knowledge of John W. Burgess's life, career, and publications. Part of an earlier generation, he taught William A. Dunning and helped build the foundations on which the school stood. Burgess published "scientific" scholarship that was in line with the highest international standards, and his views on the Teutonic "race" not only supported but gave intellectual credibility to a wide variety of racist views in Reconstruction histories. Hardly obsessed with race, however, he was interested in topics as diverse as international political science, national reunification, Hegelian philosophy, Germany, and educational reform. His reputation was impressive. Burgess was a founding father of graduate education in the United States and led the transformation of Columbia University into a leading institution in political science and history. Bolstered by a German pedigree, he set the standard for academic rigor at Columbia, and his scholarship was at the cutting edge in Western academia. His theories of political capability, governmental responsibility and limits, social progress, the process of civilization, and world history, and his validations of colonialism, scientific racism, immigration limits, and restricted voting, had a wide following. More specifically, Burgess contributed a number of works in political science and history that profoundly influenced the Dunning School scholars, elevating both their level of scholarship as well as their racist rhetoric.

Born in 1844 in middle Tennessee to a Presbyterian, Whig, and Unionist slave owner originally from Rhode Island, Burgess remembered "intelligent, proud, and courageous slave barons," "ignorant, slovenly, poor white trash," and the "vast mass of African slaves." His was an explicitly rosy view of slavery, dimmed only by the rare brutality of overseers and common whites. Masters fed and clothed their property well, and slaves "worked short hours and never knew what a strenuous effort meant." Like his father, Burgess grew to view slavery as an untenable institution and blacks as an inferior race. The state's "insane secessionists" brought on a violent "reign of universal hate born of misunderstanding and jealousy" under which the Burgess family suffered the Confederacy's "tyranny over opinion" and "reign of terror." These searing experiences led Burgess to lose "faith in the wisdom and goodness of the mass of men" and gain a fierce nationalism, an appreciation of constitutional law, and a fear of the "democratizing of society." The desires to promote domestic peace, stave off mob rule, and promote reconciliation would become driving forces in his career. After a brief stay at nearby Cumberland University, Burgess joined the United States Army in 1862. His harrowing military service inspired his "life's work"—"teaching men how to live by reason and compromise instead of by bloodshed and destruction." War's footprint inspired Burgess to teach nationalism over states' rights, and order and constitutional law over chaos and revolution. Burgess fled the South in the fall of 1864 and followed friends to Amherst, Massachusetts.[1]

Amherst College offered another formative experience. The Hegelian L. Clark Seelye shaped Burgess's appreciation for "universal reason as the real substance of all things," and his duty to promote rationality in "the rules of thought and conduct, law and policy." Edward P. Crowell related ancient Rome's politics and law to "the present," and Burgess later declared, "I laid the groundwork of my study of history in the reading of Tacitus with him."[2] This reference to the Roman historian is especially significant in light of Burgess's subsequent worship of all things German, his belief in the Teutonic germ theory, and his views on race in America. Burgess subscribed to the nineteenth-century vogue of using Tacitus and his *Germania* to create and justify racial and national hierarchies. In addition, he seems to have reinforced the lessons of his Civil War experiences—as a southern Unionist and federal soldier—with Tacitus's references to the allegedly free and orderly society within Teutonic tribes.

After graduating from Amherst in 1867, Burgess passed the Massachusetts bar in 1869. He believed legal knowledge to be a prerequisite to mastering political science. Without such a foundation for America's leaders, he later wrote, society would tend toward "systems of absolutism in government" and the "undervaluation of individual liberty." Following a

brief stint teaching at Knox College in Galesburg, Illinois, Burgess visited
Reconstruction Tennessee before leaving for an academic tour of Germany
in 1871. He found his family and friends in a state of "distress and poverty," suffering in an era in which "respectable and intelligent white people" had lost status and the vote while blacks and carpetbaggers "ruled and
plundered the land." Although Tennessee's experience was hardly the most
severe for slaveholding whites, Burgess concluded that during Reconstruction "neither property nor life nor chastity was safe, and men and women of
the better sort longed to be laid at rest." Burgess's brush with Congressional
Reconstruction inspired rededication to "the work of substituting reason
for passion" in politics and diplomacy, but it also left him with a lasting
negative perspective of the era.[3]

The newly united Germany made a lasting positive impression on Burgess. Drawn to German universities by their notions of *Lehrfreiheit* (the
freedom to pursue research) and *Lernfreiheit* (the freedom to attend multiple universities), Burgess took classes for two years at the University of Göttingen, the University of Leipzig, and Berlin University before returning to
join Amherst's faculty in the summer of 1873. At Berlin, Burgess was taken
with the teaching style and the scientific method of the historian The-
odor Mommsen. The German model of political science, *Staatswissenschaft,*
encouraged skepticism and criticism and aspired to scientific accuracy; for
Burgess this was an inspiring contrast to the ethically and didactically
anchored version taught to American undergraduates. Soon to become one
of the leading American educators of the late nineteenth century, he made
study in Europe a recommended part of his students' education. Burgess
also fell in love with German culture, geography, history, and government.
His visit coincided with an exceptionally exciting time in German history,
but also a time with an undercurrent of intense racial nationalism. His German tour was a seminal experience, one to which he would often refer and
that shaped his intellectual development.[4]

Unable to form a permanent graduate school at Amherst, Burgess reluc-
tantly allowed himself to be lured to Columbia College in 1876 to teach
political science, international law, and history. He soon began to transform
the "small old-fashioned college" into a true university and himself into an
educational reformer and a founding father of political science in America.
Borrowing from French and German models, he became the driving force
behind Columbia's School of Political Science, the *Political Science Quarterly* (*PSQ*), the Academy of Political Science, and a monograph series. He

was a crusader for the "scientific" method, what he described as "free and untrammeled individual research and complete freedom of instruction" for scholars who questioned "what was considered the established truth" in order to foster the "progressive development of truth." He also sought to prepare men for public service in what he believed was the superior form of government, the democratic nation.[5]

Burgess enjoyed an impressive academic career, but his reputation began to decline with the creation of the American Political Science Association in late 1903. He had no role in its creation, and although he continued to publish in *PSQ*, he lost relevance in a discipline shifting away from its European heritage and undergoing a thorough process of "Americanization." The new generation had multiple excuses to regard Burgess as a relic, and he, in turn, had ample reasons to regard the younger scholars as parochial. As his career faded, he maintained a strong bond with Germany and sought to encourage good relations between the United States and Germany throughout the rest of his life. As the Roosevelt Professor at the University of Berlin during 1906–7, Burgess gave several lectures to, and socialized with, the emperor and other influential officials. Teutonic unity between the people of Germany and America was a consistent theme in these lectures, and he was "disturbed and distressed" by the United States' entrance into World War I against his adopted nation. With his reputation already fading, but his scholarly significance well entrenched, Burgess died in 1931.[6]

Burgess's scholarly career included a twenty-six-year span that produced numerous books and articles. In his most important scholarly work, the two-volume *Political Science and Comparative Constitutional Law* (1890, 1893), Burgess attempted a comprehensive and "scientific" analysis of sovereignty, liberty, and government, and he emphasized the most "civilized" nations—the United States, Germany, Great Britain, and France. Friends later published a consolidated version titled *The Foundations of Political Science* (1933). Though Burgess's struggles to discover and define universal truths about nations, states, governments, and their peoples were heroic if ultimately futile, his biases for "Teutonic" nations and peoples are glaring to the modern reader. Burgess assumed that only "Teutonic political genius" could "solve the problem of political civilization" and that the "manifest incapacity" of non-Teutonic peoples rendered them all but helpless in this pursuit. Teutonic nations, Burgess argued, needed to restrict non-Teutonic immigration and have active colonial policies for the good of "civilization." When analyzing the Fourteenth Amendment and the Slaughterhouse Cases, Burgess largely ignored the latter's negative effect on African American civil rights. The nationalist Burgess concluded the first volume with the judgment that the United States was "far ahead of Europe in the domain of civil liberty."[7]

Burgess's most important historical endeavor was a four-volume constitutional analysis of America between 1817 and 1876. Born and raised in the South during slavery and war, and a political science and constitutional law professor at a northern university, Burgess believed that the time was right for "a more complete reconciliation" and a "juster appreciation of the views on both sides." He took up the task of writing the "correct scientific point of view" as "a sacred duty to my country." In *The Middle Period, 1817–1858* (1897), he avoided secondary sources, indulged his own "Northern point of view," and declared that the South needed to admit its "error" in order to restore "national cordiality." In this "truthful record, connection, and interpretation," he analyzed the period chronologically by political subject. Chapters on various topics such as nullification reveal Burgess's political approach, and chapters on slavery, abolition, the Fugitive Slave Law, and Dred Scott offer examples of his opinions on race. Burgess's next book, the two-volume *Civil War and the Constitution, 1859–1865* (1901), begins with profiles of Jefferson Davis, Stephen Douglas, and Abraham Lincoln, ends with the last battles and "international complications," and focuses on analysis of the Constitution. Admiring Lincoln's "real conservatism," Burgess believed the president to be "the master both of Davis and of Douglas upon the ground of positive law and constitutional history, as well as upon the ground of public morality." Like his antebellum work, the war books reveal Burgess's views on racial hierarchies. Concluding a chapter on southern feelings about slave revolts and Harper's Ferry, Burgess declared that though a "sound philosophy will undoubtedly hold that there is a plan of world civilization," the ends of John Brown's raid did not justify the means. Burgess's *Reconstruction and the Constitution, 1866–1876* (1902) completed the trilogy by blazing the trail of "scientific" history on Reconstruction. Seeking to balance his analysis of this still-controversial era, Burgess argued that, just as he had in *The Middle Period* called on the South to admit its "error" and "failure" in seceding, so too should the North acknowledge the same for Reconstruction. Giving freedpeople political power was a colossal mistake, which the Rutherford B. Hayes administration rightfully, according to Burgess, began to reverse.[8] As will be discussed later, Burgess's *Reconstruction* had a significant effect on the development of the Dunning School.

After his retirement in 1912 and despite a declining reputation, Burgess continued to publish. In 1915 he produced *The Reconciliation of Government with Liberty,* an effort to analyze the development of all known governments in the world, focusing on "Germania," the "Anglo Saxon State" in England, the United States up to 1898, and then the "New" United States—a response to recent political developments. Clearly an admirer of Rutherford B. Hayes, Burgess extended his analysis begun in *Reconstruction* in *The Administration of President Hayes* (1916). He more fully developed his concerns about the state of American government in his final book, *Recent Changes in American Constitutional Theory* (1923).[9]

Burgess also published numerous articles, book reviews, and speeches, most of which were devoted to the latest political skirmishes. His interests were wide-ranging, from the United States' ongoing relations with Germany to the popular election of U.S. senators, and he saw himself as an authority on contemporary world issues such as colonialism and Germany's intentions. Burgess occasionally veered into the realm of history, but he always emphasized the philosophic, comparative, and political aspects. In the pages of *PSQ* and other journals he pushed for a more interdisciplinary, and therefore a more "scientific," approach to scholarship. In an article entitled "Political Science and History," published in the *American Historical Review* (*AHR*), Burgess attempted to compare and clarify his views on both disciplines, but he drew tortured distinctions. Notably, he compared history and especially political science to mathematics, chemistry, physics, and other "scientific" disciplines, indicating his plans to bring similar "clearness and exactness" to his disciplines. He also displayed an unflagging belief in "human progress" toward "ultimate perfection." He concluded with the article's least-muddled distinction between history and political science: "while there are parts of history which are not political science, and while there is an element in political science which is not strictly history, yet the two spheres so lap over one another and interpenetrate each other that they cannot be distinctly separated. Political science must be studied historically, and history must be studied politically, in order to

[form] a correct comprehension of either. Separate them, and the one becomes a cripple, if not a corpse, the other a will-o'-the-wisp."[10]

Analyzing Burgess's academic career requires an understanding of his motivations, methods, and assumptions. His education in Civil War–era America, at Amherst, and in Germany strongly informed his approach to scholarly method, philosophy, and race. Burgess came to believe that one could study society objectively using the methods already employed in the natural sciences.[11] The contemporary debate about "scientific" history played a key role in shaping Burgess's scholarship and his legacy for the Dunning School. He sought to advance the writing of political science and history with scientific accuracy, rationality, and comprehensiveness. Thus, when Burgess deemed Teutons superior to people of color, he did so from a self-proclaimed position of scientific exactness, and this gave additional heft to his writings; it was a scientifically derived truth and therefore correct.

Georg W. F. Hegel's influence is central to understanding Burgess's approach to history. He borrowed from Hegel a belief in the existence of a single truth, absolute and ultimate, that became evident through the evolution of ideas and that could help mankind find alternatives to fundamental contradictions like war. From his Amherst professor L. Clark Seelye, Burgess realized his duty, through "objective" scientific method, to advance the human understanding of society and to make reason paramount in law and government. Bert James Loewenberg explained that though both Hegel and Burgess believed that one had to subordinate thought to fact, "ultimate categories of thought, demonstrable by reason, existed." They felt that history generated "general laws and principles, deductible from the facts, but, unless prompted by thought, laws or principles" could not be created. History revealed to Burgess, for example, that democracy was not far removed from mob rule, and he feared the power of public opinion and special interests in the United States. This led Burgess to assess the extent to which different ethnic groups had evolved toward "civilization" and to classify each group, or race, in terms of desirability. Burgess did not invent late nineteenth-century scientific racism, but his Hegelian belief system reinforced what was developing in academia and elsewhere.[12]

Burgess's approach was simultaneously unique and trendy. Loewenberg argued that Burgess's Hegelianism led to biased assumptions and often convoluted definitions that left him out of the mainstream of historians professing scientific accuracy; his "scientific" hypotheses so resembled preconceived notions that even those in the noticeably unscientific "scientific" school cringed. But Burgess's efforts to define and promote "scientific" history were part of the discipline's professionalization. Other historians who studied in Germany anointed Leopold von Ranke "the father" of a scientific method that did not actually exist. Burgess and the others embraced Ranke's critical use of sources, but Burgess differed from Americans of the scientific school and the "new historians" emerging in the 1890s. Hegel and Ranke disagreed on numerous points, and it is likely that Burgess concurred with Hegel's judgment of Ranke as "just an ordinary historian."[13] Professing to write scientific history but straying from the unreachable ideal, Burgess had a better understanding of the German system than did the Americans, but he stayed on the Hegelian path.

Despite his idiosyncratic scientific method, Burgess had clout as a scientific scholar during a U.S. "crisis of intellectual authority" in which science became a virtual cult. Historians proclaimed themselves dispassionate experts and pursued professionalism through "the authority of science." "Under the guise of science," Loewenberg argued, Burgess "propagated a body of social and political ideas which have lastingly conditioned American attitudes." One such idea was a notion of Teutonic racial supremacy that explained the beginnings and evolution of civilized society in which Anglo-Saxons, and especially Germans, played a starring role. Scholars including Burgess joined developing ideas about racial supremacy in Europe and America to this Teutonic germ theory to form the scientific racism that would soon dominate histories of the U.S. South. Burgess's Hegelian elitism, fear of mob rule, approval of colonialism, and low estimation of certain ethnic groups complemented the Teutonic hypothesis and made for a comprehensive worldview.[14]

Burgess's exposure while at Amherst to Tacitus's *Germania* compounded his German experience to form an important influence on his views of race, nationality, and civilization. In *Germania*, Tacitus praised Germanic tribes in an effort to reform Rome, but nineteenth-century German nationalists embraced and exaggerated Tacitus's comments on the superiority of racially pure peoples and applied selected excerpts from *Germania* to German peasants. Even before 1871, Germans seeking a national identity equated Teutons of antiquity with Aryans, the mythic race that allegedly colonized and civilized the earth. For Burgess the lessons learned in the newly unified Germany were all too clear for Americans still seeking national reunification. Peter Novick argues that the nation's first professional historians viewed reconciliation as "the great task" for their generation, and that the key was racism. Burgess agreed with the scholarly consensus that blacks were inferior, a view that conveniently matched the increasing racial repression of American blacks in Jim Crow America and U.S. expansionism in the 1890s. Sharing similar backgrounds, patriotic beliefs, and "ideological homogeneity," the era's historians believed that U.S. history "represented unity, stability, and continuity." In their quest to nationalize what had previously been a collection of more regional histories, scientific racism formed a common assumption in their scholarship.[15] But the "fact" of racial hierarchies was not Burgess's obsession; it was a core belief that provided Dunning and his students the "scientific" backing to proclaim race as the key to understanding Reconstruction.

Beyond his racism, Burgess was one of several during the late nineteenth century who lifted American higher education above the realm of the amateur and toward standards of the modern and professional. He was a political scientist, but he also wrote history, and in joining in the debate about the boundaries, methods, and meanings of both disciplines, Burgess helped define them for all who would follow. He advocated scientism in order to discover basic laws governing political behavior, and he promoted German methods of inquiry, including historical comparative analysis of the most original documents. For Burgess, *scientific method* included all related academic disciplines, so faculty from five other departments taught in Columbia's School of Political Science. And he believed that history and political science were intimately linked because the former was the latter's "foundation."[16] With his interdisciplinary approach, Burgess pulled Columbia and both his disciplines into the twentieth century.

Probably his most influential book among political scientists and historians, *Political Science and Comparative Constitutional Law* demonstrated Burgess's faith in interdisciplinary and comparative analysis. Translated into five languages, the work nonetheless, according to its author, "aroused a great deal of criticism." In it he emphasized the political, geographic, and cultural over the racial in unifying a nation, but some critics accused him of advocating imperialism. This criticism understandably stemmed from his assertions, repeated in his memoirs, that the "Teutonic nations" were the "bearers of modern political civilization" and that their various "colonial systems" (in areas where "savages or semi-savages or races politically incompetent" dwelled) aided the "development and perfection of the national State," helped these areas become part of "the civilized world," and pre-

pared them for "self-government." Other critics accused Burgess of advocating tyranny with his often-incomprehensible definitions of the State,
with unlimited power, and the government, with constitutionally limited
power.[17]

Burgess included several references to U.S. race relations in *Political
Science and Comparative Constitutional Law,* as well as in its condensed version, *Foundations of Political Science.* Within North America, he argued,
English Teutons were most important, and the white races, both pure and
mixed (with other white "elements"), did not "amalgamate" with "the negro
race," a group "destined to maintain a separate race existence." He believed
that Teutons should seize and hold power and should restrict political participation by inferior races. Burgess declared that "under certain circumstances, some of which will readily suggest themselves to the mind of any
observing American, the participation of other ethnical elements in the
exercise of political power has resulted . . . in corruption and confusion
most deleterious and dangerous to the rights of all, and to the civilization of society." He concluded that "the Teutonic nations can never regard
the exercise of political power as a right of man." His references to African Americans' widespread voting during Reconstruction and the advent
of Jim Crow in the 1890s were unmistakable. Obsessed with the Teuton
"duty" to civilize, Burgess was focused not just on southern race relations.[18]
His goal was no less than the scientific analysis and advancement of world
civilization.

Despite the confusion and criticism it generated, *Political Science and
Comparative Constitutional Law* grew in scholarly stature, becoming a classic over the ensuing decades. It received generally favorable reviews, but
with reservations. Summarizing its reception within the discipline of political science, one reviewer compared it favorably to the works of such luminaries as Francis Lieber, Theodore Woolsey, and Woodrow Wilson, and he
declared, "This is one of the works over whose appearance the student of
political science may well rejoice, however one may disagree with positions
and tendencies." The qualified praise probably alluded to Burgess's extreme
positions on immigration and colonialism. The often dogmatic Wilson
was more critical, praising the work for "excellences both of method and
of thought," but finding fault with "a mechanical and incorrect style, a
dogmatic spirit, and a lack of insight into institutions." Another historian
lauded the book for its "novel and startling statements," voiced concern
over its racial theories and confusing terminology, but pronounced the

entire work a "great value." Scholars reviewing *Foundations of Political Science* declared Burgess's analysis applicable to political developments in the 1920s and 1930s. More recent reviewers agree that *Political Science and Comparative Constitutional Law* was a classic, finding it still relevant as late as the 1950s and 1960s. Bernard Edward Brown argued that the work made Burgess widely recognized as a founding father of political science and one of the nation's foremost "political thinkers" before World War I. His efforts to perfect scientific method and professional rigor for political science and history led to the pursuit of higher standards as the disciplines developed. Albert Somit and Joseph Tanenhaus argued that the book made Burgess the "most outstanding advocate of scientism" because it established the "historical-comparative method" as cutting-edge political science.[19]

Published between 1897 and 1902, Burgess's historical trilogy of the antebellum, Civil War, and Reconstruction eras was a strong but not unique statement for national reconciliation. The books, especially the Reconstruction volume, also put into practice Burgess's theories of political science, philosophy, scientific method, and race. Written at the birth of the Jim Crow era, the books were products of a racially biased age. The trilogy carried a great deal of weight because the author had sterling credentials and claimed to be writing "scientific" history. His interpretation of these most sensitive of topics—slavery, secession, the war, and Reconstruction—was highly influential among historians and the public. Advertisements for the trilogy trumpeted its author as "a writer of eminence and of special authority" creating "the best scholarship" and a high level of "literary value." Students could expect "a comprehensive history," and general readers could enjoy an "authentic" and "impartial" description.[20]

Some reviewers thought the title *The Middle Period, 1817–1858* and Burgess's preface promised an overall history of the period, including all social, economic, and political developments. The expert in constitutional law and political science, however, had a narrower project in mind. Confessing his own biases, Burgess resolved to avoid consulting all secondary sources and to avoid "passionate onesidedness." He argued that the period's history had to be written from "the correct view," that of the North. While acknowledging southern leaders' sincerity, Burgess sought to prove the South wrong in order to foster national reconciliation. Reviews were mixed. Blurbs for the book praised it as well suited for the general reader and applauded its "excellence." Others complained about its limited scope.

In generally favorable comments in the *AHR,* a reviewer noted that "this is a history of politics only." Another reviewer took a harsher stance, labeling the book "disappointing," the product of yet another "conventional literary, legalistic, and essentially parliamentary frame of mind" that "adds practically nothing" to understanding the era. Both critics complained that Burgess consulted only legislative documents and that his history had the "tone and manner of a constitutional lawyer." In an eighteen-page review, a third complained that the study had "serious" flaws because Burgess approached the subject with preconceived notions.[21] The reviews exposed Burgess's failure to situate properly his work in the discipline as a narrowly focused constitutional study.

In *The Middle Period* Burgess analyzed most of the antebellum period's political highpoints and divisive issues in chronological order. Although his racial views of early slavery escaped the reviewers' wrath, his analysis clearly extended the views in *Political Science and Comparative Constitutional Law.* Noting parallels between early Christians enslaving infidels and English Americans enslaving Africans, Burgess declared that slavery was "vastly beneficial" to infidels and blacks, and that it was "a principle of modern political science and practical politics . . . that civilized people have the right and duty to impose civilization upon uncivilized populations." Slaves "were, in general, entirely contented" under the "superior intelligence" of the "white race." Ever the reconciliationist, Burgess emphasized the northern origins of slavery in the colonies, and he concluded that the "peculiar institution" was the result of sincere Northerners and Southerners attempting to resolve the labor needs of "the highly civilized Anglo-American race" and the abilities of "the grossly barbaric negro race." As for abolition, he was highly critical of William Lloyd Garrison and John Brown while being what a reviewer labeled "unusually lenient" when discussing the proslavery activists who murdered Elijah Lovejoy.[22]

Reviewers continued to be confused with the trilogy's next volume. Burgess's editors proclaimed that although *The Civil War and the Constitution, 1859–1865* was "eminently a constitutional history" for political and legal topics, it was "also a stirring and graphic account of the events of the war." The result was that some reviewers still expected a history instead of the author's more narrowly focused study. One complained that though Burgess was "a good constitutional lawyer . . . we doubt his capacity to enter upon the difficult field of military history." He praised Burgess for good "descriptions" of nonbattle situations and avoiding "sectional rancor and American bombast," but he recommended the book for popular readers only. A reviewer for the *American Historical Review* commended the constitutional and political analysis, but faulted it as a "scientific" work, probably of interest to political scientists only.[23]

His critics were justifiably confused: Burgess began the book with biographical sketches of Jefferson Davis, Stephen Douglas, and Abraham Lincoln and eschewed significant constitutional analysis until page 17. Burgess generally focused on constitutional and political issues, but his detours to military history were awkward. As he had in *The Middle Period*, he occasionally commented on racial issues. Preferring that only "the white race" fight the war, he lamented that Confederate Native Americans (with their "savage methods of warfare") fought Union blacks ("more or less barbarians, but . . . not savages") at Pea Ridge. Responding to claims that with the Emancipation Proclamation President Abraham Lincoln set a "barbarous race against a civilized race," Burgess argued that "the negro race in the South was not exactly a barbarous race. It was an uneducated race" and "simply a subject race sunken in ignorance."[24] Such explicit racial analysis, however, was the exception, not the rule, up to this point in the trilogy. In the end, Burgess's *Civil War* was not popular with critics because the political scientist and constitutional lawyer ignored previous historians' interpretations and waded blindly, as an outsider, into the most contentious subfield in American history.

Together with his political science classic, Burgess's *Reconstruction and the Constitution, 1866–1876* is the most significant work in understanding his relationship to the Dunning School because the era afforded the best use of his legal and constitutional talents as a political scientist. He effectively mixed in scientific racism to create an influential book, one that buttressed the developing historical consensus. Like the previous two books, this final volume of the trilogy garnered a mixed reception. A reviewer in the *American Historical Review* lamented that what Burgess touted as "sound political science" more closely resembled "the gathering of dry bones together." He admired Burgess's "courage" in "boldly" stating his opinions, but the lack of footnotes and selective use of evidence did not meet standards for sound history. Reconstruction, the reviewer argued, was no place for a political scientist. But a political scientist approvingly noted that Burgess judged events and politicians and prescribed solutions. Similarly, a reviewer from a southern literary journal labeled the work "very scholarly," and he agreed that national reconciliation was a priority and that Radical Reconstruction was a disaster. Two of the reviewers approved of Burgess's explicit racial comments and quoted them extensively.[25]

The reviewers correctly identified Burgess's priorities and sensed a change in his previously "scientific" demeanor. What had been, in the first two parts of the trilogy, only occasional comments about race degenerated into increasingly frequent and virulent affirmations of white supremacy. His relatively detached and pro-North voice often descended, in *Reconstruction,* into passionate denunciations of Republican policies. Characteristically, Burgess viewed himself as an agent, or perhaps the only agent, of reconciliation. It was time, he argued, for the North to acknowledge that Reconstruction was just as wrong as secession. He approved of Congress's "nationalization of civil liberty," but he disagreed vehemently with giving former slaves the vote. It was "the white man's mission, his duty and his right, to hold the reins of political power" for the good of "civilization." Burgess was relieved that under the less confrontational Hayes administration policies in the South and because of recent U.S. imperialism, "the North" had begun to acknowledge that there existed "vast differences in political capacity between the races." Having confessed his motives, Burgess presented a chronological and thematic summary and analysis of the era. He began with "The Theory of Reconstruction," evaluated in ten chapters Abraham Lincoln, Andrew Johnson, Congress, and Ulysses S. Grant, and ended the book discussing " 'Carpet-Bag' and Negro Domination," the 1876 election, and international events.[26]

Burgess began the first chapter with a characteristically confusing discourse on "the state" and the powers of each federal branch. By narrowly delineating congressional powers to reconstruct a state once the state government had been restored, Burgess built the foundation on which to crucify activist Republican policies. He sought to project scientific impartiality and a balanced perspective, however, and he voiced few objections to the early stages of Reconstruction, frequently awarding presidential and congressional actions his stamp of approval as "sound political science." He approved of Andrew Johnson's Reconstruction plan, supported Congress's initial plans for Reconstruction as "true political theory," objected to the Freedmen's Bureau, and defended the Black Codes. Burgess believed the first civil rights bill to be "a great change," Johnson's veto of it a "monumental blunder," and the ensuing Fourteenth Amendment appropriate. With most southern states refusing ratification, there was "no question in the mind of any sound political scientist and constitutional lawyer," he declared, "that Congress was in the right, logically, morally, and legally," to take control of Reconstruction. It was, however, "simply astounding" that Congress "made such a mess of it."[27] Burgess's method to this point had been to explain the merits of both sides, draw distinctions between the legally correct and the morally wrong, and assess whether the action was "sound political science." Some of his constitutional and legal judgments appeared to be well-reasoned and were probably helpful to those trying to make sense of the period.

Burgess abandoned all pretense of impartiality, however, when northern Republicans introduced black suffrage in the South. It was "a monstrous thing," "a great political error," "a sin," "a great wrong to civilization," the placement of "barbarism . . . over civilization," "one of the 'blunder-crimes' of the century," and the surrender of "reason, . . . prudence, . . . and . . . decency" to "passions." He declared—in one of the book's most widely quoted passages—that "a black skin means membership in a race of men which has never of itself succeeded in subjecting passion to reason, has never, therefore, created any civilization of any kind." Disloyalty did not justify "domination" of black over white, the results of which were racial hatred and corruption. An electorate largely composed of "negroes, 'poor white trash,' 'carpet-baggers'" and others made "horrible results" inevitable.[28] The excessive enthusiasm with which Burgess condemned black suffrage and his applying a patina of science to racist theory is crucial to understanding his influence with the American public and the Dunning School. Again, coming from an eminent scholar and an alleged "scientific" authority at a leading university, Burgess's language in this book added credibility to, and possibly encouraged the use of excessively racist rhetoric in, other histories of Reconstruction.

Believing his analysis to be objective, detached, and self-evident science, Burgess declared that it was best to treat the North's "terrible mistake" and the South's "terrible degradation" "briefly and impersonally," merely drawing "lessons of warning" from the period instead of continuing the cycle of blame. But in a chapter titled "'Carpet-Bag' and Negro Domination in the Southern States between 1868 and 1876," he railed against the horrors of black suffrage and sympathized with white Southerners of his class. He also justified the process of Redemption as a messy but necessary expedient. As Republican state governments engaged in "corruption, shame and vulgarity" by "plundering the treasury, increasing the taxes, selling franchises, issuing bonds, and celebrating high carnival everywhere and all the time," "the gentlemen and political leaders of the old school" were understandably outraged, and, not surprisingly, "hotspurs and desperados were stirred to deeds of intimidation and violence." He declared it "natural, though not praiseworthy" that whites formed the Ku Klux Klan, which he equated with the Union Leagues. Defending states' rights, Burgess argued that Klan obstruction of black voting was not a federal concern, and that Congress undoubtedly "overstepped its constitutional powers" with subsequent acts. With "life, property, and female honor insecure," "it was absolutely necessary" for South Carolina's whites "in self-defense" to "take the law into their own hands." Since the law in Mississippi "would not yield, it had to be broken."[29]

Throughout *Reconstruction,* Burgess sympathized especially with former slave owners and other whites who, like his father, assumed that they were the South's natural leaders. The era was tragic because, he argued, the "most intelligent and virtuous" were out of power, and "the most ignorant and vicious" ruled the South in a "vulgar, materialistic, brutal" way. "No sane mind" could fail to understand why the white South coalesced behind the Democratic Party because "life, property, happiness, honor, civilization," and all else "demanded" that the South's "decent white men" unite to defend "their families, their homes and their communities." Similarly, well-heeled Republican moderates and conservatives were repelled by their party's excesses in the South, and they began to push the party toward an emphasis on "sound money" financial policies. Burgess saw Hayes's steering away from bayonet rule in the South and toward sound money as the key to ending the horrors of Reconstruction. Hayes brought "order and peace" to "the plundered and impoverished South." Burgess concluded that after a "dark night of domination by the negro and adventurer," the Spanish American War had begun the process of reunion. "White men of the South" could rest assured that Republicans, with their recent experience in "imposing the sovereignty" of the United States on "eight millions of Asiatics," would "never again give themselves over to the vain imagination of the political equality of man." Reconciliation was finally at hand.[30]

Largely forgotten in the late twentieth-century rush to condemn Burgess, Dunning, and their contemporaries and students is the fact that they did raise the level of historical scholarship. Following Ranke's lead, these scholars examined more sources, cited them in a consistent manner, exposed their works to vigorous peer review, and in many other ways improved the way mankind examined its past. Burgess's contributions to political science were monumental, and he was an important and pathbreaking historian as well; his influence on Dunning and the latter's students was fundamental. It is, of course, the racial biases of these scholars that are so conspicuous to the modern reader, and historians have rightfully targeted that racism. Unlike Dunning, however, Burgess has ceased even to be a target for condemnation. Despite substantial differences among historians of this era, "the Dunning School" has become shorthand for the racist interpretations of the Civil War and Reconstruction eras written in the late nineteenth and early twentieth centuries. Historians including Burgess have, over time, become subsumed and therefore lost under the Dunning School brand. Burgess's scholarly reputation among historians persisted until about 1950, but he then gradually, and with some exceptions, disappeared from scholars' bibliographies. But Burgess was a significant historian and scholar. His positive accomplishments in history and political science ought not to be forgotten, and his racism and its origins should not be ignored.

In a revealing comment from 1967 on Burgess's vanishing scholarly reputation, the political scientists Somit and Tanenhaus asked, "How many persons remember [Burgess] as other than a ridiculously fanatical Germanophile?" The question sets up the authors' main argument, that although Burgess's scholarship had long ceased to be relevant, he remains the "Father" of political science in America and "among the truly great figures in its history." They then lauded his "grasp of scientific method," his passion for "broad interdisciplinary training" and "systemic theory," and his lofty goals for the study of politics.[31] Burgess's long-term effect on the historical profession rests largely on his *Reconstruction,* but the sum of his works, including those devoted solely to political science, had a large influence on Dunning and his students. Burgess was one of the first to write interdisciplinary history, from which much of his claim of being a "scientific" scholar came. As Burgess grew in stature as a writer, teacher, and administrator, so too did the prominence of his scholarship, including his racial pronouncements, and this shaped the development of the Dunning School. So, though Burgess was a generation removed from that historiographic school, he was the, or a, godfather to it.

Assessing Burgess's place in Reconstruction historiography begins with his professional relationship with Dunning. The two worked closely together over thirty years, but their roles evolved from teacher-student to older mentor–younger colleague, to equals and competitors, and finally to fading elder–rising star. Dunning earned a Ph.D. in history in 1885 under Burgess's direction and then taught at Columbia in the History and Political Science departments, outlasting Burgess by seven years. The scholars worked closely on the *PSQ* for twenty-two years, serving together on the editorial board from 1890 to 1912 (including Dunning's terms as managing editor, 1894–97 and 1899–1903). Given this close working relationship and consistent friendship, it should not be surprising that their interpretations of Reconstruction and its racial effect were similar. Burgess and Dunning agreed with James Ford Rhodes that Congress was right to take control of Reconstruction but wrong to support black suffrage. They differed on smaller points, but the centrality of race formed the key to their interpretations. Burgess and Dunning wrote and taught political science and history, and the similarities in their approaches to the era's history are striking. Dunning titled his dissertation "The Constitution in the Civil War and Reconstruction," and his 1898 book *Essays on the Civil War and Reconstruction and Related Topics* included chapters titled "The Constitution of the United States in Civil War" and "The Constitution of the United States in Reconstruction." Burgess followed with *The Civil War and the Constitution, 1859–1865* and *Reconstruction and the Constitution, 1866–1876.* Dunning then published *Reconstruction, Political and Economic, 1865–1877,* covering much of the same ground as Burgess's book.[32]

By the early 1900s the two prominent scholars from one of America's leading universities appeared to be locked in an academic and retail competition, writing on identical topics for competing series while ignoring each other in their books. Burgess's *Reconstruction and the Constitution* was part of Charles Scribner's Sons' American History series, and Dunning's *Reconstruction Political and Economic* was part of Harper and Brothers' series The American Nation: A History. Burgess's 1902 work ignored Dunning's previous book, and Dunning returned the favor in 1907, failing to mention Burgess in his text. He did, however, include Burgess's book in the bibliographic essay, admitting blandly that it "deals incisively with the legal and political aspects of the period." Dunning saved his biggest compliment for Rhodes, whose recent volumes he declared to be "the only comprehensive narrative covering the years of reconstruction in a scientific spirit." Burgess could not have been pleased that his former student deemed his book so insignificant, and he continued to all but ignore Dunning, even in his memoirs. That Dunning was eclipsing Burgess in scholarly reputation during this time only added to the competition.[33]

Despite the textual silence, Burgess and Dunning strongly influenced each other. The similarities in their interpretations of the Reconstruction era rested on the fashionable concepts of racism and reconciliation, and their proximity as Columbia colleagues suggests ample cross-fertilization of ideas. More important, it is likely that Burgess's well-developed racial theories, rooted in his southern upbringing, and his strong desire for national reconciliation, stemming from his war experiences, influenced Dunning. In addition, Dunning probably was impressed by his colleague's stature in the political science and history disciplines and, consciously or not, accepted Burgess's scientific racism as accurate. Both men zealously asserted that the price of national reconciliation was the acceptance of the white South's version of the solution to "the race problem." Their similar and increasingly shrill emphasis on the two concepts brings to mind questions about each author's motivations. Did their competition spur them toward increasing the rhetoric of racism? Did both men perceive an American public eager to read lurid details about Reconstruction and a scholarly community that welcomed the link of race to reconciliation? Perhaps unanswerable, the questions suggest a causal link between the men and their works.[34]

Other historians have noticed Burgess's influence on Dunning. Vernon L. Wharton noted Dunning's move from "mild discussions" on race in his 1897 work toward "severer judgments" in his 1907 book, and he pointed to the significance of Burgess's 1902 work. Burgess was probably "one of the more important influences on Dunning and his students," although Wharton admitted that they did not adopt all Burgess's theories. Burgess's tendency to lurch from dry analysis of legal and political issues to "emotional attack" when discussing race seems to have inspired change in Dunning's later book. Wharton argued that Burgess and his students, including Dunning, reacted to intellectual currents of social Darwinism and helped establish a general interpretational scheme for the history of Reconstruction, especially the part played by African Americans. Members of the Dunning School "merely gave elaborate and expert documentation to a story already generally accepted."[35]

Philip R. Muller added that Dunning wrote the "flawed" *Reconstruction, Political and Economic* quickly and from secondary sources, relying heavily on his students' dissertations. It seems likely, however, that Burgess's *Reconstruction and the Constitution* was equally accessible to the harried Dunning, and that Dunning adopted Burgess's more strident timbre. Muller dismissed Dunning's often unfortunate language in the book on the basis of his refusal "to take the project seriously," but the changes in tone from *Essays* and the parallels to Burgess's structure and language, especially with regard to race, are noticeable. Muller emphasized Dunning's focus in *Reconstruction, Political and Economic* on a national viewpoint, foreign policy, and constitutional considerations, as well as an intensified sense of disgust for carpetbaggers, scalawags, and blacks. Indeed, Muller argued that although Dunning's great reputation as a racist historian derives almost completely from his 1907 work, the sloppy and racist generalizations therein represent not Dunning's beliefs but "those of others." Seeking to vindicate Dunning, Muller reminded the reader that Dunning did not dictate analytical conclusions to his students and that it was Burgess, not Dunning, who developed "a systematic theory of race." Dunning also portrayed Reconstruction as the product of democracy run rampant, a fundamental theme in Burgess's *Reconstruction and the Constitution*. It seems likely, then, that Dunning's students relied on the works of Burgess and others for the racism they applied to individual states, and that Dunning borrowed these ideas from his students and from Burgess for his hastily written classic.[36] While perhaps too soft on Dunning's racism, Muller astutely identified the racist theory in Dunning's best-known work as Burgess's, thus indicating the direct effect of Burgess on Dunning and his school.

Though Burgess was a significant influence on the Dunning School, especially with regard to racial theory, a glance at scholarly works on Reconstruction over the twentieth century reveals the Burgess name gradually receding in importance under the weight of the Dunning School brand. Many historians writing before the civil rights movement recognized Burgess's effect on the prevailing interpretation of Reconstruction as well as his significance in the disciplines of political science and history, but more recent historians began to distance themselves from, and eventually ignore, Burgess and his racist theories. Some, including Mark M. Krug, Herman Belz, and Joe W. Trotter, correctly associated Burgess's name with the historiographic interpretation; each historian labeled the racist view of Reconstruction an element of "the Burgess-Dunning school."[37] Most historians, however, have left Burgess and his accomplishments, both negative and positive, behind in the dustbin of historiography.

While the Dunning School remained in vogue, Burgess's legacy retained a degree of prominence. In his 1924 presidential address to the American Historical Association, Charles M. Andrews acknowledged Burgess's place as one of the founding fathers of graduate history study in the

United States. Burgess's obituary in the *American Political Science Review* described his similar place in modern political science. In 1937 Dunning's student Charles W. Ramsdell referred to Burgess's more evenhanded approach to the North and the South in *Middle Period* and *Civil War* as an example of the maturing of the profession. E. Merton Coulter's *The South during Reconstruction, 1865–1877* (1947) echoed Burgess's racial theories. And as late as 1969, the cautious Avery Craven recommended Burgess's *Reconstruction* as "an older 'traditional' interpretation useful for comparison" to recent scholarship.[38]

Revisionist black historians exposed Burgess as one of the most prominent early historians to insert racism into the study of Reconstruction. Writing in 1920, Norman P. Andrews grouped Burgess with Dunning's student J. G. de R. Hamilton as "biased historians" whose "radical utterances" were of no importance other than demonstrating "the lack of scientific Reconstruction history." In 1935 W. E. B. Du Bois staged a more thorough attack on "the Columbia school of historians" in *Black Reconstruction*. Du Bois judged Burgess and Dunning as "Standard—Anti-Negro," but he distinguished between Burgess's "frank and determined" racism and Dunning's "less dogmatic" biases. Du Bois devoted more than twice as much space to condemning Burgess as he did to denouncing Dunning, whose primary sin was, according to the black scholar, nurturing racist students. Du Bois viewed Burgess as "a Tory and open apostle of reaction" whose views on "Nordic supremacy" and blacks "as essentially property" dominated his writing. Du Bois implied that Burgess, not Dunning, was the force behind Columbia's racist classrooms and scholarship and thus the racism in historiography at the time. A. A. Taylor reviewed the historiography of Reconstruction in 1938 from the black perspective, and, with extensive quotes from Burgess's *Reconstruction*, characterized his attitude toward Reconstruction as mostly negative compared to Dunning's more "judiciously" reasoned conclusions.[39]

Even white historians joining the growing chorus against the scientific racism in Reconstruction studies singled out Burgess. As early as 1913 Burgess's student Charles A. Beard criticized the racist notions of Teutonic civilization and government found throughout Burgess's scholarship. Francis B. Simkins argued in 1939 that the alleged innate inferiority of black Southerners was a fundamental flaw in many historians' interpretations of Reconstruction, and he held Burgess's writings to be "more prejudiced" than even those of Rhodes. "The impartial historian," Simkins declared, could not accept Burgess's claim, given recent anthropological studies. In the same year, Edward Norman Saveth evaluated Burgess's place in "the reign of the Teutonophiles," labeling the theories as outmoded and overreaching.[40]

By the 1940s Burgess's star had begun to dim noticeably. Howard K. Beale reviewed the Dunning School in 1940 without a nod to Burgess. In his 1951 classic, *Origins of the New South, 1877–1913,* C. Vann Woodward noted Dunning's important contributions—but not those of Burgess—in establishing Columbia as the new center of scholarship on the Reconstruction South. Four years later Woodward placed Dunning in a more important light, as one of the "authorities" whom Southerners cited to justify the establishment of Jim Crow laws. In 1959 Bernard A. Weisberger gave equal billing to, and found equal fault with, Burgess and Dunning, but Wendell Holmes Stephenson in 1964 devoted a chapter to Dunning and overlooked Burgess when assessing the pioneers of southern history. For Kenneth Stampp in 1965, it was Rhodes, not Burgess, who was the primary force behind the Dunning School's racism. In David Donald's more thorough revisionism of the same year, Burgess completely disappeared, and Dunning and his students were the only representatives of the former interpretation. Among political scientists, Burgess's legacy faded even more quickly. Bernard Brown noted in his 1951 retrospective that Burgess "found it easier to impress than to convince the political scientists of his era." Woodrow Wilson remained unconvinced, and, aside from legal scholars, Nicholas Murray Butler was perhaps Burgess's "only major convert."[41]

Burgess's slide from relevancy continued into the modern era. In his 1980 survey of Reconstruction historiography, John Hope Franklin ignored Burgess while analyzing Dunning, his school, and their significance. Joe Gray Taylor, LaWanda Cox, and Harold D. Woodman followed Franklin's lead seven years later. Even Peter Novick, in an extended study of racism in American historians during the era, portrayed Burgess as only one of many who supported "Dunning's picture" of Reconstruction. In his 1988 masterpiece on Reconstruction, Eric Foner equally acknowledged Burgess and Dunning as the racist "mentors" to a generation of influential historians, but he adopted the "Dunning School" moniker and failed to distinguish Burgess's racist theories from Dunning's.[42] The trend among historians and political scientists continued into the 1990s and 2000s, as Burgess was either subsumed under the Dunning label or ignored entirely.[43]

Some scholars still find relevance in Burgess, correctly placing him in the pantheon of greats in founding modern scholarship. Political scientists such as Somit and Tanenhaus rightfully recalled Burgess's place in the founding of their discipline, and Belz noted Burgess's importance in pioneering "realistic" constitutional history. Larry Kincaid lumped Burgess and Dunning together as part of the "nationalist" school that vastly improved the writing of Reconstruction history by overturning the interpretations of the "Republican apologists." And more recently, the legal scholar Angela P. Harris, the legal historian R. Volney Riser, and the political scientist Michael J. Shapiro have recognized Burgess's leadership in linking whiteness and citizenship within various turn-of-the-century issues. Writing in the *PSQ*, Michael H. Frisch correctly surmised that John W. Burgess "was to political science what Herbert Baxter Adams . . . was to history—the virtual creator in the American university of the research-oriented, graduate seminar–focused, professional discipline."[44]

But Burgess was a key figure in the writing of American history as well. His importance to the Dunning School lay not in the originality of his ideas about race and professionalism but in the force with which he pursued them, the science with which he defended them, and the proximity with which his door lay to Dunning's. Burgess was the godfather behind the Dunning School's racism. He did not invent that racism—it was pervasive in the intellectual environment—but he certainly gave it a seemingly logical explanation, one derived from "science." Dunning borrowed from it, and his students applied it to their state studies.

Notes

1. John W. Burgess, *Reminiscences of an American Scholar: The Beginnings of Columbia University* (New York: Columbia University Press, 1934), 3–9, 13–18, 22–29, 31–36, 75; Eric Cyril Bellquist, "Personal and Miscellaneous," *American Political Science Review* 25 (February 1931): 163.

2. Burgess, *Reminiscences*, 47, 51–52, 54–57, 75.

3. Ibid., 66, 71–72, 77, 85–86.

4. Albert Somit and Joseph Tanenhaus, *The Development of American Political Science: From Burgess to Behavioralism* (Boston: Allyn & Bacon, 1967), 8, 15–16, 19–20, 37–38; Burgess, *Reminiscences*, 64, 85–86, 96–97, 105, 107, 110, 120–25, 132–35, 137.

5. Burgess, *Reminiscences*, 142, 146–48, 150–51, 161, 187–89, 194–95, 198–204, 211–16, 230; Somit and Tanenhaus, *Development*, 11, 21, 46–48. Burgess taught Theodore Roosevelt during 1880–82.

6. Somit and Tanenhaus, *Development*, 17n13, 51–52, 52n2, 61, 69, 202; Bur-

gess, *Reminiscences*, 322–28, 331–32, 334–37, 342–45, 369–79, 397–401; Bellquist, "Personal and Miscellaneous," 163.

7. John W. Burgess, *Political Science and Comparative Constitutional Law*, vol. 1, *Sovereignty and Liberty* (Boston: Ginn, 1890), vi, xvii–ix, xv, 228–29, 264. Though the Fourteenth Amendment (1868) granted federal citizenship and protections to freedpeople, the Supreme Court began to undermine its intent with the Slaughterhouse Cases (1873) by ruling that states, not the federal government, controlled most citizenship rights.

8. Burgess, *Reminiscences*, 289–91; John W. Burgess, *The Middle Period, 1817–1858* (New York: Charles Scribner's Sons, 1897), ii–xii, xiii–xv; John W. Burgess, *The Civil War and the Constitution, 1859–1865*, 2 vols. (New York: Charles Scribner's Sons, 1901), 1:viii, 23–25, 43–44; 2:vii; John W. Burgess, *Reconstruction and the Constitution, 1866–1876* (New York: Charles Scribner's Sons, 1902), vii–ix, xii.

9. Burgess, *Reminiscences*, 342–45; John W. Burgess, *The Administration of President Hayes* (New York: Charles Scribner's Sons, 1916), vi, vii, xi, 3; John W. Burgess, *The Reconciliation of Government with Liberty* (New York: Charles Scribner's Sons, 1915), vi–xix; John W. Burgess, *Recent Changes in American Constitutional Theory* (New York: Columbia University Press, 1923), ix.

10. John W. Burgess, review of J. I. Clark Hare, *American Constitutional Law*, in *Political Science Quarterly* 4 (June 1889): 350–52; John W. Burgess, "Political Science and History," *American Historical Review* 2 (April 1897): 401–8.

11. Bernard Edward Brown, *American Conservatives: The Political Thought of Francis Lieber and John W. Burgess* (New York: Columbia University Press, 1951), 116.

12. Philip Stokes, *Philosophy: The Great Thinkers* (London: Arcturus Publishing, 2007), 118–20; Brown, *American Conservatives*, 116–18, 175; Bert James Loewenberg, "John William Burgess, the Scientific Method, and the Hegelian Philosophy of History," *Mississippi Valley Historical Review* 42 (December 1955): 496–98, 505–9. Burgess acknowledged that wars could be necessary evils contributing to greater universal reason.

13. Loewenberg, "John William Burgess," 492–93, 494–98, 508–9; Peter Novick, *That Noble Dream: The "Objectivity Question" and the American Historical Profession* (Cambridge: Cambridge University Press, 1988), 21, 24–28, 30–31; Georg G. Iggers, "The Image of Ranke in American and German Historical Thought," *History and Theory* 2, no. 1 (1962): 18, 19–21, 23–25, 27, 34–36.

14. Novick, *That Noble Dream*, 31, 33, 40, 45, 47, 51–52, 84, 87–88; Loewenberg, "John William Burgess," 491–94, 506–8.

15. Reginald Horsman, "Origins of Racial Anglo-Saxonism in Great Britain before 1850," *Journal of the History of Ideas* 37 (July–September 1976): 387–91; Benjamin Isaac, "Proto-Racism in Graeco-Roman Antiquity," *World Archaeology* 38 (March 2006): 40, 44–45; Paul A. Fortier, "Gobineau and German Racism," *Comparative Literature* 19 (Autumn 1967): 342–45; Stephen T. Asma, "Metaphors of Race: Theoretical Presuppositions behind Racism," *American Philosophical Quarterly* 32 (January 1995): 24; Alan Davies, "Racism and German Protestant

Theology: A Prelude to the Holocaust," *Annals of the American Academy of Political and Social Science* 450 (July 1980): 29; Dante A. Puzzo, "Racism and the Western Tradition," *Journal of the History of Ideas* 25 (October–December 1964): 580–81; Novick, *That Noble Dream*, 61, 68–70, 72–78; Somit and Tanenhaus, *Development*, 44. This idealization of ancient Germans found its way into the twentieth century and eventually Nazi thought. For more on Tacitus and race theory, see Nell Irvin Painter, *The History of White People* (New York: W. W. Norton, 2010). Painter (245–48) argues that Burgess's Teutonist teachings had a significant influence on Theodore Roosevelt.

16. Somit and Tanenhaus, *Development*, 24–26, 28, 30–31, 63–64; Brown, *American Conservatives*, 113.

17. Burgess, *Reminiscences*, 245–50, 254–55; Brown, *American Conservatives*, 125.

18. Burgess, *Reminiscences*, 254–55; John W. Burgess, *The Foundations of Political Science* (New York: Columbia University Press, 1933), 5–6, 20–22, 29–30, 36–41, 43–48; Donald L. Grant and Mildred Bricker Grant, "Some Notes on the Capital 'N,'" *Phylon* 36, no. 4 (1975): 435. Burgess used the word *negro* uncapitalized, despite the fact that W. E. B. Du Bois and others had, from the 1890s on, actively campaigned for capitalization.

19. E.J.J., review of John W. Burgess, *Political Science and Comparative Constitutional Law*, in *Annals of the American Academy of Political and Social Science* 1 (April 1891): 681–82, 684–85; Thomas Thornely, review of John W. Burgess, *Political Science and Comparative Constitutional Law*, in *English Historical Review* 7 (April 1892): 388–92; Woodrow Wilson, "A System of Political Science and Constitutional Law," *Atlantic Monthly*, May 1891, 694–99; "Books Received," *Harvard Law Review* 47 (December 1933): 387; "Book Reviews and Notices," *American Political Science Review* 27 (December 1933): 1023; Brown, *American Conservatives*, 113, 131–32; Somit and Tanenhaus, *Development*, 28, 30–31.

20. Burgess, *Civil War*, vol. 1, advertisements.

21. Burgess, *Middle Period*, vii–xii; Burgess, *Civil War*, vol. 1, advertisements; Charles H. Levermore, review of John W. Burgess, *The Middle Period, 1817–1858*, in *American Historical Review* 2 (July 1897): 746–48; John L. Stewart, review of John W. Burgess, *The Middle Period, 1817–1858*, in *Annals of the American Academy of Political and Social Science* 11 (January 1898): 89–92; W. H. McKellar, review of John W. Burgess, *The Middle Period, 1817–1858*, in *Sewanee Review* 5 (July 1897): 349–66.

22. Burgess, *Middle Period*, 40–42, 53–54, 248–50, 366, 473; Levermore, review of *Middle Period*, 746–48.

23. Burgess, *Civil War*, vol. 1, advertisements; B.J.R. [Burr J. Ramage], review of John W. Burgess, *The Civil War and the Constitution, 1859–1865*, in *Sewanee Review* 10 (April 1902): 238–39; W. G. Brown, review of John W. Burgess, *The Civil War and the Constitution, 1859–1865*, in *American Historical Review* 8 (January 1903): 368–70.

24. Burgess, *Civil War,* 1:1–6, 17, 312; 2:117.

25. W. G. Brown, review of John W. Burgess, *Reconstruction and the Constitution, 1866–1876,* in *American Historical Review* 8 (October 1902): 150–52; Burgess, *Reconstruction,* 43; Benjamin F. Shambaugh, review of John W. Burgess, *Reconstruction and the Constitution, 1866–1876,* in *Annals of the American Academy of Political and Social Science* 20 (September 1902): 127–30; State Historical Society of Iowa, "The Benjamin F. Shambaugh Award," www.iowahistory.org/about/assets/shambaugh-awards.pdf (accessed February 2, 2011); Benjamin W. Wells, review of John W. Burgess, *Reconstruction and the Constitution, 1866–1876,* in *Sewanee Review* 10 (April 1902): 239–43.

26. Burgess, *Reconstruction,* vii–ix, xi–xii.

27. Ibid., 1–7, 17, 32, 43–45, 52–53, 55, 69–70, 73–79, 111, 215.

28. Ibid., 133–35, 148, 150, 245.

29. Ibid., 244–49, 251–52, 255–59, 275.

30. Ibid., 263–64, 272, 279, 296–98.

31. Somit and Tanenhaus, *Development,* 3, 3n2. They cited Brown's *American Conservatives* as the "one recent study in which Burgess is taken at all seriously."

32. Robert A. McCaughey, *Stand, Columbia: A History of Columbia University in the City of New York, 1754–2004* (New York: Columbia University Press, 2003), 202–5; *Political Science Quarterly,* 1886–1922; Philip R. Muller, "Look Back without Anger: A Reappraisal of William A. Dunning," *Journal of American History* 61 (September 1974): 328; Vernon L. Wharton, "Reconstruction," in *Writing Southern History: Essays in Historiography in Honor of Fletcher M. Green,* ed. Arthur S. Link and Rembert W. Patrick (Baton Rouge: Louisiana State University Press, 1965), 306; William Archibald Dunning, *Essays on the Civil War and Reconstruction and Related Topics* (1898; reprint, New York: Macmillan, 1931), vii, ix; William Archibald Dunning, *Reconstruction, Political and Economic, 1865–1877* (New York: Harper and Brothers, 1907). Four of Dunning's chapters in *Essays* had previously appeared in *Political Science Quarterly.*

33. Burgess, *Reconstruction,* title page; Dunning, *Reconstruction, Political and Economic,* front matter, title page, 342–43; McCaughey, *Stand, Columbia,* 200, 203–4; Somit and Tanenhaus, *Development,* 17n13, 51–52, 52n2, 69; Burgess, *Reminiscences,* 226.

34. David W. Southern, *The Progressive Era and Race: Reaction and Reform, 1900–1917* (Wheeling, Ill.: Harlan Davidson, 2005), 70–71; DocSouth staff, "Controversial History: Thomas Dixon and the Klan Trilogy," *Documenting the American South,* http://docsouth.unc.edu/highlights/dixon.html (accessed May 24, 2011). Burgess and Dunning were also competing for general readers with Thomas Dixon Jr. and his highly successful, melodramatic, and fictional Ku Klux Klan trilogy published between 1902 and 1907.

35. Wharton, "Reconstruction," 298, 304–6, 305n29.

36. Muller, "Look Back without Anger," 328–38. Muller perceived an "intellectual divergence" of Dunning from Burgess developing shortly after the lat-

ter signed the former's dissertation, but he noted that this did not involve racial matters.

37. Mark M. Krug, "On Rewriting of the Story of Reconstruction in the U.S. History Textbooks," *Journal of Negro History* 46 (April 1961): 135; Herman Belz, "The Constitution and Reconstruction," in *The Facts of Reconstruction: Essays in Honor of John Hope Franklin,* ed. Eric Anderson and Alfred A. Moss Jr. (Baton Rouge: Louisiana State University Press, 1991), 194–96, 205, 211; Joe W. Trotter, "W. E. B. Du Bois: Ambiguous Journey to the Black Working Class," in *Reading Southern History: Essays on Interpreters and Interpretations,* ed. Glen Feldman (Tuscaloosa: University of Alabama Press, 2001), 73–74.

38. Charles M. Andrews, "These Forty Years," *American Historical Review* 30 (January 1925): 225, 235; Bellquist, "Personal and Miscellaneous," 163–64; Charles W. Ramsdell, "The Changing Interpretation of the Civil War," *Journal of Southern History* 3 (February 1937): 10–11; E. Merton Coulter, *The South during Reconstruction, 1865–1877* (Baton Rouge: Louisiana State University Press, 1947), 47, 139–42; Avery Craven, *Reconstruction: The Ending of the Civil War* (New York: Holt, Rinehart and Winston, 1969), 244–45nn10–11, 308–9.

39. Norman P. Andrews, "The Negro in Politics," *Journal of Negro History* 5 (October 1920): 421–22; W. E. B. Du Bois, *Black Reconstruction in America, 1860–1880* (1935; reprint, New York: Atheneum, 1992), 718–20, 726, 731; A. A. Taylor, "Historians of the Reconstruction," *Journal of Negro History* 23 (January 1938): 16–18, 20–24.

40. Max Lerner, "The Political Theory of Charles A. Beard," *American Quarterly* 2 (Winter 1950): 306–8; Charles A. Beard, *An Economic Interpretation of the Constitution,* (1913; reprint, New York: Macmillan, 1921), 2–3; Francis B. Simkins, "New Viewpoints of Southern Reconstruction," *Journal of Southern History* 5 (February 1939): 50–51, 58–59; Edward Norman Saveth, "Race and Nationalism in American Historiography: The Late Nineteenth Century," *Political Science Quarterly* 54 (September 1939): 430–31, 434–36, 439–40.

41. Howard K. Beale, "On Rewriting Reconstruction History," *American Historical Review* 45 (July 1940): 807–9; C. Vann Woodward, *Origins of the New South, 1877–1913* (1951; reprint, Baton Rouge: Louisiana State University Press, 1993), 325, 442; C. Vann Woodward, *The Strange Career of Jim Crow* (1955; reprint, New York: Oxford University Press, 1974): 72–73, 105; Bernard A. Weisberger, "The Dark and Bloody Ground of Reconstruction Historiography," *Journal of Southern History* 25 (November 1959): 428, 436, 446; Wendell Holmes Stephenson, *Southern History in the Making: Pioneer Historians of the South* (Baton Rouge: Louisiana State University Press, 1964), ix, 160, 186; Wendell Holmes Stephenson, *The South Lives in History: Southern Historians and Their Legacy* (Baton Rouge: Louisiana State University Press, 1955), 5–6, 64, 99, 117, 153; Wharton, "Reconstruction," 304; Kenneth M. Stampp, *The Era of Reconstruction, 1865–1877* (1965; reprint, New York: Vintage Books: 1967), 5–7, 9, 11–13, 20–23; David Donald, *The Politics of Reconstruction, 1863–1867* (1965; reprint, Cam-

bridge: Harvard University Press, 1984), xiii; Brown, *American Conservatives*, 177; Wilson, "A System," 694–99.

42. John Hope Franklin, "Mirror for Americans: A Century of Reconstruction History," *American Historical Review* 85 (February 1980): 3–4, 6; Joe Gray Taylor, "The White South from Secession to Redemption," in *Interpreting Southern History: Historiographical Essays in Honor of Sanford W. Higginbotham,* ed. John B. Boles and Evelyn Thomas Nolen (Baton Rouge: Louisiana State University Press, 1987), 182–84; LaWanda Cox, "From Emancipation to Segregation: National Policy and Southern Blacks," in Boles and Nolen, *Interpreting Southern History,* 199–200; Harold D. Woodman, "Economic Reconstruction and the Rise of the New South, 1865–1900," in Boles and Nolen, *Interpreting Southern History,* 258; Novick, *That Noble Dream,* 74–80, 230; Eric Foner, *Reconstruction: America's Unfinished Revolution, 1863–1877* (1988; reprint, New York: First Perennial Classics, 2002), xvii–xviii, 609–10.

43. Edward L. Ayers, *The Promise of the New South: Life after Reconstruction* (New York: Oxford University Press, 1992), 422–23; Robert C. Lieberman, "The Freedmen's Bureau and the Politics of Institutional Structure," *Social Science History* 18 (Autumn 1994): 407–9; Dewey W. Grantham, *The South in Modern America: A Region at Odds* (1994; reprint, New York: HarperPerennial, 1995), 27, 34–35; Hugh Tulloch, *The Debate on the American Civil War Era* (Manchester, U.K.: Manchester University Press, 1999), 212–18; Michael Perman, *Struggle for Mastery: Disfranchisement in the South, 1888–1908* (Chapel Hill: University of North Carolina Press, 2001), 11–12; Laura F. Edwards, "Southern History as U.S. History," *Journal of Southern History* 75 (August 2009): 547; Caroline E. Janney, "War over a Shrine of Peace: The Appomattox Peace Monument and Retreat from Reconciliation," *Journal of Southern History* 77 (February 2011): 99.

44. Somit and Tanenhaus, *Development,* 3; Herman Belz, "The Constitution in the Gilded Age: The Beginnings of Constitutional Realism in American Scholarship," *American Journal of Legal History* 13 (April 1969): 110, 112–13, 119; Larry Kincaid, "Victims of Circumstance: An Interpretation of Changing Attitudes toward Republican Policy Makers and Reconstruction," *Journal of American History* 57 (June 1970): 49–51; Angela P. Harris, "Equality Trouble: Sameness and Difference in Twentieth-Century Race Law," *California Law Review* 88 (December 2000): 1940–41; R. Volney Riser, "Disfranchisement, the U.S. Constitution, and the Federal Courts: Alabama's 1901 Constitutional Convention Debates the Grandfather Clause," *American Journal of Legal History* 48 (July 2006): 239–41; Michael J. Shapiro, "Social Science, Geophilosophy and Inequality," *International Studies Review* 4 (Summer 2002): 26–28; Michael H. Frisch, "Urban Theorists, Urban Reform, and American Political Culture in the Progressive Period," *Political Science Quarterly* 97 (Summer 1982): 298.

2

William Archibald Dunning

Flawed Colossus of American Letters

James S. Humphreys

The influence of the American historian William Archibald Dunning hovers over the study of United States history and political science like a ghostly apparition, one that modern scholars have found impossible to avoid. Dunning arguably contributed more than any other scholar to those two fields, when both were in their nascent stages in the late nineteenth and early twentieth centuries. His scholarly corpus of writing included forty-three articles on history and political science topics, two books on the Reconstruction era, and three works on Western political theory.[1] Dunning also played a major role in the development of the American Historical Association (AHA) and the American Political Science Association (APSA) and served as mentor to a legion of history and political science graduate students at Columbia University. Many of his students went on to outstanding careers in their fields after leaving Columbia. Although his arduous scholarly activities and teaching responsibilities often drained his energy, Dunning reveled in his work, approaching it with a zeal uncommon even for historians. Yet present-day scholars remember Dunning primarily as the founder of the school of Reconstruction thought that bears his name: the Dunning School. This approach stands out as the first coherent, overarching theory of the study of Reconstruction, a theory that shaped both scholarly and popular attitudes toward the subject for half a century and one that, though misguided, remains influential.

The Dunning School portrayed Radical Reconstruction as an abject failure, cast blacks as ill-equipped for the responsibilities of freedom, and described southern whites as hapless victims of the Reconstruction policies of the federal government. Few challenges to the Dunning view, from either scholars or nonspecialists, arose during Dunning's lifetime, as the pervasive racism in American society and the widespread desire to promote sectional reconciliation created a congenial environment for the acceptance of a prowhite southern view of Reconstruction.[2] Later, however, twentieth-century scholars eviscerated Dunning's work for its racial biases and other excesses, dismantling his reputation as an outstanding scholar that he had worked assiduously to gain.

Dunning's anti-Radical view of Reconstruction developed in spite of his northern birth. That is not to say he was unique; many Americans in the North in the nineteenth century held a jaundiced view toward Radical Reconstruction and toward blacks. John H. Dunning and Catherine D. Trelease were married in 1849. In 1855 their two-year-old son, William Archibald, died of an illness, and on May 12, 1857, the couple welcomed another son, whom they also named William Archibald. The child was born in the Dunning family's weathered but stately home in Plainfield, New Jersey.[3]

Dunning and his sister, Matilde, or "Willie and Tillie," as family members called them, grew up surrounded by stable, intelligent, and productive individuals. The scholar Anne W. Chapman described William Dunning's father as "a carriage manufacturer, amateur painter, and art critic." "John Dunning," she wrote "was a man of wide intellectual interests, which he passed on to his son." William's uncle Elijah Trelease died while serving in the Union Army during the Civil War. Typhoid took his life in 1862. Another uncle, William Trelease, an ardent opponent of slavery and a staunch supporter of the Union cause, served in a New Jersey regiment that fought in Virginia. "I think Willie does remarkably well at writing for one of his age," he explained in a letter to Catherine Dunning. "I hope both of your children will get a good education. I see the use of it. at my age." "Tillie," William Trelease wrote in a letter to Matilda Dunning, "do your best now while you have a chance and learn all that you can for you won['t] go to school always and I shall fell [sic] proud of you if you excel." William and Matilda Dunning surpassed their family's expectations. Matilda enrolled in the New Jersey State Normal School and in 1873 received a teacher's certificate qualifying her to work in the New Jersey public schools. William Dunning finished first in his high school class.[4]

The history of the Reconstruction era possibly began to interest Dunning as a young boy. He was eleven years old in 1868, the year Radical

Reconstruction reached its culmination with the impeachment of President Andrew Johnson. As he entered his teenage years, then, most of the burning political issues of the day stemmed from the debate over federal policy toward the South. Dunning's later statement that his father "first interested him in Reconstruction" suggests that his anti-Radical views may have been forming while he was still a boy through the influence of John Dunning.[5] The two probably discussed the Reconstruction of the southern states at length.

Dunning also grew up in the shadow of New York City, only thirty miles separating Plainfield from the United States' most exciting urban milieu. Dunning enrolled in New York City's Columbia College (later University), having been ordered to leave Dartmouth College after committing an indiscretion there, probably a youthful prank, given his mischievous and playful nature. Having lost his Dartmouth opportunity, he excelled academically at Columbia, finishing his undergraduate degree in 1881. During his early years of undergraduate school he took courses in mathematics, chemistry, history, English literature, and antiquities and later branched out to courses in political science, logic, philosophy, and physics. He enrolled in Greek and Latin classes every year of undergraduate school. He eventually completed a master's degree and then entered Columbia's Ph.D. program.[6]

Dunning followed the path of many young American scholars in the late nineteenth century when he enrolled at the University of Berlin to study for a year. German higher education enjoyed worldwide respect at this time and was also more affordable than university education at elite colleges in the United States. As Daniel T. Rodgers has pointed out, the Americans educated in Germany exerted a significant influence on progressive reform in the United States. Germany, and the rest of western Europe, tended to be ahead of the United States in the institution of progressive reform measures such as social security and workers' insurance. Germany's Chancellor Otto von Bismarck, for example, supported widespread social legislation as early as the 1880s. The comparative slowness with which progressive reform developed in the United States Rogers terms "American behindhandedness."[7]

The influence of German reform left a deep impression on American students. Though it caused some of the Americans to question the system of capitalism under which they had grown up, it also provoked them to consider the darker sides of activist government. For example, the same German political leaders who provided social insurance for their citizens also placed severe limitations on civil liberties. The Progressive movement in the United States usually received the support of the American students educated in Germany when the young scholars returned home. Dunning's twenty-five-dollar contribution to the 1920 presidential campaign of Democrats James M. Cox and Franklin D. Roosevelt sheds light on his political views.[8]

The emphasis on "scientific history" at Berlin, the university where the father of scientific history, Leopold von Ranke, had once taught, impressed Dunning. The scientific method was growing in importance to the study of the social sciences at the turn of the twentieth century. This approach stressed the importance of research and objectivity as the basis of reliable scholarship. The writing of history, according to the Rankean model, included little room for speculation, legend, or prolixity. Ranke knew, however, that scientific history would not be completely unbiased. The historian would be influenced by his environment. The historian's duty was to cull from his arrangement of facts an overarching meaning of the past, thereby probing the mind of God. Emphasizing both the role of a Supreme Being in the unfolding of history and the primacy of political events to the study of the past infused Rankean historical writing with a mystical, nationalistic ethos.[9]

Peter Novick, in his magisterial work, *That Noble Dream: The "Objectivity Question" and the American Historical Profession,* argued that American students who studied in Germany in the nineteenth century perverted Ranke's idea of scientific history as an inexact and spiritual discipline designed to exalt the state to one of a detached and exacting search for historical truth. The Americans applied the principles of scientific history to their work in a literal fashion, dispensing with mysticism in favor of empiricism. To them, researching and collecting the facts of history mattered more than attempting to divine the meaning of the past; questing for historical accuracy, not God's intentions, stood out as their ultimate aim. The scientific method, as defined by American scholars, dovetailed with the goals of late nineteenth-century progressive thinkers, who sought to cure political and social ills through the application of reform measures. The introduction of the historical seminar in American universities, the growing professionalization of the historical guild in the United States, and the adoption of the scientific method as interpreted by American scholars—all reflected the influence of German scholarship and the international Progressive movement. American historians, and scholars in other fields as well, moved in these two powerful currents of thought, both of which stressed the equipping of elites through professional training to solve society's most vexing social ills.[10]

Dunning attempted to inculcate the scientific method in his students when he began teaching in Columbia's Political Science Department after finishing his Ph.D. in 1885. His dissertation addressed the effect of the Civil War and Reconstruction on the U.S. Constitution.[11] John W. Burgess, a mentor of Dunning's, continued to serve on the faculty. Dunning's hiring at his alma mater enabled him to remain in New York City and determined the later course of his personal and professional life.

In the early decades of the twentieth century, William Dunning emerged as the most influential historian of the post–Civil War period. In 1898, two years after Dunning noted in the pages of the *American Historical Review* (*AHR*) "the real need . . . of a clear-cut unbiased narrative of the facts of reconstruction history," officials of the Macmillan Company published his *Essays on the Civil War and Reconstruction and Related Topics*. Dunning's goal in the essays was to shed light on "the constitutional and political history" of the Civil War and Reconstruction era for "the younger generation of reading men." Dunning declared in the preface that "Reconstruction . . . is to most people merely a synonym for bad government, and conveys no idea of the profound problems of statecraft that had to be solved between 1865 and 1870." In the volume of essays, then, he sought to illuminate the complexity of the legal and political challenges faced by federal and state officials during the Civil War and Reconstruction.[12]

Dunning pointed out in chapter 1, "The Constitution of the United States in Civil War," that the events of the war clearly established the supremacy of the national government within the country's system of federalism. Before 1861 governments on both levels, state and federal, exercised sovereign powers over their jurisdictions. The exigencies of the Civil War, however, allowed Union officials to expand the powers of the U.S. government, which resulted in the diminution of state power in the North. The development of a national banking system and the vigorous exercise of war powers by President Lincoln stood out as examples of federal amalgamation of power during the war years. Dunning viewed these trends as constitutionally justifiable, given the Confederacy's threat to dissolve the United States. The triumph of the Union destroyed state sovereignty by discrediting secession while establishing the national government as supreme.[13]

After demonstrating that Union victory "removed one pregnant source of confusion at the very basis of our system" involving the dual and competing nature of sovereignty within a federal structure, Dunning explored the stages through which Reconstruction policy passed. He pointed out that during the period of Presidential Reconstruction, federal officials placed mild readmission requirements on the ex-Confederate states. As members of Congress began to assert authority over Reconstruction, however, they came to favor "the theory of forfeited rights." According to this theory, the states had temporarily lost the rights associated with state power before the Civil War. The states would have their rights restored when they met stipulations outlined by Congress.[14]

Members of Congress shifted from the forfeited-rights notion after the ranks of the Radical Republicans grew as a result of the fall elections of 1866. The failure of southern state legislatures to ratify the Fourteenth Amendment angered Radical Republicans, who employed their newly gained power in Congress to pass the Military Reconstruction Act of 1867, which placed the southern states under the supervision of the U.S. military. The act, Dunning asserted, invested inordinate power in Union commanders, who used their authority to undermine civilian rule in the South. Dunning lamented that "the orders of the commanders reached the commonest concerns of every-day life, and created the impression of a very real tyranny." Union officers, for instance, sometimes removed civil officials from office and oversaw the allocation of public money. The definition of loyalty to the United States became increasingly strict as Radical Reconstruction progressed, leaving many white Southerners unable to participate in public life. Federal officials forced state lawmakers to write new constitutions and demanded the ratification of the Fourteenth Amendment, which made blacks citizens, and later the Fifteenth Amendment, which enfranchised black males. Dunning argued that the "theory of state suicide," the notion that the southern states, by seceding, had given up all power and were no longer states, was now clearly driving federal policy toward the South. The theory reflected the draconian nature of Radical Reconstruction.[15]

Dunning regarded both the rule of U.S. military forces in the South and the "theory of state suicide" as the backbone of Radical Reconstruction. Through the intimidating presence of Union troops and with the once formidable powers of the states diminished, the Radicals could achieve their cherished goal of enfranchising black Southerners. Dunning argued that black suffrage hindered the process of Reconstruction, making it impossible for southern whites to view fairly the Radical plan for restoration of the ex-Confederate states. Radical Reconstruction, he asserted, stood a greater chance of success had black voting rights not been inextricably linked to it. He also saw the potential for success in Presidential Reconstruction had that plan been allowed to come to fruition. Instead, he declared, "there was only disaster in the application of first the one and then the other."[16]

Dunning added to a later edition of *Essays* a chapter in which he surveyed the myriad ways in which white Southerners undermined and eventually dismantled federal Reconstruction policies. Based on a 1901 article written by Dunning for the *Atlantic Monthly,* the chapter was titled "The Undoing of Reconstruction." In it Dunning identified three eras during which white Southerners employed different methods of combating federal Reconstruction policies. White opponents of Reconstruction, he explained, resorted to intimidation and violence against blacks during the first era, which lasted from 1870 to 1877. Their efforts reduced black voting so drastically that the southern Democratic Party arose from its postwar doldrums. The Republican Party, however, remained intact in the South, as did the legal basis of black political power, so white Southerners destroyed both of them during the era from 1877 to 1890. Dunning declared, "Exploitation of the poverty, ignorance, credulity, and general childishness of the blacks was supplemented, on occasion, by deliberate and high-handed fraud." The use of poll taxes, rampant bribery, and other dishonest tactics virtually ended black voting and, consequently, vitiated the political strength of the southern Republicans. Democratic lawmakers in the South were then free to write new state constitutions disfranchising blacks. They achieved their goals concerning the freedmen with methodical and ruthless efficiency. According to Dunning, "The political equality of the negro is becoming as extinct in law as it has long been in fact, and the undoing of reconstruction is nearing completion."[17]

Dunning viewed Reconstruction's demise as a predictable development necessary to maintain white supremacy in the South. He claimed that even "Jefferson and Clay and Lincoln" regarded black subordination as the only workable arrangement for "two races so distinct in characteristics as to render coalescence impossible." The failure of Radical Reconstruction, therefore, validated the racial thinking of the country's greatest solons, while it revealed the speciousness of the racial philosophy of the abolitionists who proclaimed that "abolition and negro suffrage would remove the last drag on our national progress." Abolitionist pieties, wrote Dunning, had failed, and in the wake of their collapse white Southerners designed a social and economic system similar to slavery. Dunning declared "that slavery had been a *modus vivendi* through which social life was possible; and that, after its disappearance, its place must be taken by some set of conditions which, if more humane and beneficent in accidents, must in essence express the same fact of racial inequality." White dominance, he also suggested, might turn out to be a permanent state of civil society.[18]

Dunning's *Essays* received positive scholarly reviews. In the *Annals of the American Academy of Political and Social Science,* University of Pennsylvania Professor L. S. Rowe offered Dunning's book "a warm welcome as an important contribution to American constitutional history." Rowe praised the author for discarding "traditional constitutional formulae when they do not harmonize with facts" and applauded his "ability to weigh the merits and defects of political measures which few modern writers have equaled, and none excelled." "The story which Professor Dunning tells," he explained, "is one long conflict between the spirit of legality and the uncompromising necessities of military rule."[19]

Rowe interpreted Dunning's volume as justification for the successful attempts of members of Congress and the president to amass enormous power in their hands in order to defeat the Confederates and to reconstruct a fractured nation. The challenge to preserve the Union in the face of a massive rebellion rendered obsolete antebellum interpretations of the Constitution and American federalism. But, in Dunning's opinion, explained Rowe, "adaptation" was necessary because "the interests of the country were best served by the assumption of authority by the executive and legislative."[20]

Frederick W. Moore, writing in the *AHR,* pointed out that Dunning was able to craft out of his meticulous research a volume accessible to scholars and general readers alike. "His results," according to Moore, "are succinctly stated. The temper in which he writes is wholesome." Dunning had clearly not allowed his faith in scientific history to become a pedantic pursuit.[21]

Essays may not have been pedantic, but it was, in places, turgid and prolix. In *Reconstruction, Political and Economic, 1865—1877,* a 1907 work published by Harper and Brothers, Dunning displayed his ability as a stylist, producing a far more lively work than his *Essays. Reconstruction* appeared as volume 22 in The American Nation series, edited by the Harvard University historian Albert Bushnell Hart. Among the other scholars who had published works in the series were Edward Channing, John Spencer Bassett, and Frederick Jackson Turner. Dunning dedicated his volume "To the Memory of My Father by Whom I Was First Inspired with Interest in the Problems of Reconstruction."[22]

Among the sources Dunning used to write *Reconstruction* were his students' works. Dunning described Walter Lynwood Fleming's *Civil War and Reconstruction in Alabama* (1905) as "a great mass of social and economic as well as political facts, with a marked southern bias in their interpretation," and he found Fleming's two-volume *Documentary History of Reconstruction* (1906–7) "very valuable for this period." In addition to Fleming's works, the state studies of Reconstruction by Joseph Grégoire de Roulhac Hamilton, James Wilford Garner, and Edwin Campbell Woolley provided Dunning with research material. Dunning also cited Paul Leland Haworth's book on the disputed election of 1876. By using his students' books in his own writing, Dunning revealed the respect he held for his young charges, whose work he had guided at Columbia University. Consulting their state studies of Reconstruction, as the historian Philip R. Muller has pointed out, also allowed him to complete his book quickly and may have made him more partisan against Radical Reconstruction.[23]

Another work, which Dunning held in great esteem, also appeared in the footnotes to *Reconstruction*. That was James Ford Rhodes's *History of the United States from the Compromise of 1850* (nine volumes, 1892–1922). A businessman from Boston, Rhodes was representative of the amateur historians who both dominated the writing of American history and provided leadership in historical organizations in the late nineteenth century. These amateur historians would be eclipsed by professionally trained scholars, like Dunning, as the study of history became more professionalized in the twentieth century. Because Rhodes was an amateur did not mean his work was poor—far from it. Dunning viewed volumes 5, 6, and 7 of *History of the United States* as "the only comprehensive narrative covering the years of reconstruction in a scientific spirit." He often consulted Rhodes's *History* in his own work and assigned it to his graduate students at Columbia University.[24]

Dunning wrote that his primary aim in *Reconstruction* was to illuminate the effect of Reconstruction on the North, not the South, in order to portray the era as "a step in the progress of the American nation." According to him, "The social, economic, and political forces that wrought positively for progress are to be found in the record, not of the vanquished, but of the victorious section." Reconstruction, Dunning declared, "transformed the nation," prompting a sea change seen "chiefly in the politics of the North and West."[25]

Few major events of the era eluded Dunning's attention in *Reconstruction*. Presidential Reconstruction, Radical Reconstruction, Andrew Johnson's impeachment, Ulysses S. Grant's administration, the 1873 depression, and the 1876 presidential election—all these happenings Dunning explored and analyzed, in crisp, fast-paced prose.

Dunning portrayed Radical Reconstruction as an overreaction to events transpiring in the South. He heaped scorn on Radical Republican leaders, who capitalized on the unwillingness of members of Congress to reach reasonable compromises dealing with the restoration of the southern states. These divisions allowed the Radical Republicans to seize control of Reconstruction. The Radicals, speculated Dunning, used the southern states' rejection of the proposed Fourteenth Amendment as a pretext for punishing the white South. Had the proposal been accepted by southern lawmakers, Dunning believed, the Radicals would have still gone forward with their "revolutionary" policies.[26]

The leaders of the Radical Republicans in Congress, in Dunning's opinion, lacked both emotional balance and political moderation. Dunning excoriated the "truculent, vindictive, and cynical" manner of Congressman Thaddeus Stevens, whose domineering political power sprang from "a total lack of scruples as to the means in the pursuit of a legislative end." Dunning accused Massachusetts Senator Charles Sumner of harboring "narrow fanaticism." "He would shed tears at the bare thought of refusing to freedmen rights of which they had no compulsion," Dunning wrote, "but would filibuster to the end of the session to prevent the restoration to the southern whites of rights which were essential to their whole concept of life." The author railed against Secretary of War Edwin M. Stanton, "this strange personage," for supposedly fomenting rebellion in Congress against President Johnson. Stanton's "amazing record of duplicity strongly suggests the vagaries of an opium-eater." Dunning's colorful, overwrought portrayals of Radical leaders prompted a confused James Ford Rhodes to ask Dunning, "Does 'suggests the vagaries of an opium-eater' intimate that Stanton was a victim to opium?"[27] Dunning had clearly abandoned his pursuit of writing scientific history in his harsh evaluation of Radical Republican politicians.

Dunning conceded that southern whites mistreated blacks and violated their political and civil rights, but he saw the policies of the Radical Republicans, not white racism, as the main reason for whites' anger toward the freedmen. Had the Radicals been less vindictive, he asserted, southern whites would have been more cooperative. In his opinion, "Southern whites, subjugated by adversaries of their own race, thwarted the scheme which threatened permanent subjection to another race." Radical Reconstruction, Dunning declared, exacerbated rather than lessened racial and sectional strife in the South after the Civil War. The turmoil did not yield to normalcy until Radical Reconstruction collapsed in 1876.[28]

Scholarly praise for *Reconstruction* surpassed that given Dunning's *Essays.* "Hart ought to be proud of such a contribution to his series," explained James Ford Rhodes, who regarded *Reconstruction* as "a credit to American historical scholarship." "Mr. Dunning's book is of extraordinary excellence," gushed E. Benjamin Andrews, a Union Army veteran, a University of Nebraska–trained Ph.D., and that university's chancellor. Writing in the *AHR,* Andrews saw "great and lasting" importance in *Reconstruction.* He lauded Dunning's "eminent fairness and justice" and described his "'nutshell' explanations of imbroglios and knotty points [as] being his forte." Although, like Dunning, Andrews denounced what he considered to be the extremism of Radical Reconstruction and while he praised the author for highlighting "the patience, patriotism and, in the main, wisdom shown by the Southern people proper in the terrible and to a great extent, needless sufferings through which they were made to pass," Andrews detected a "somewhat onesided and 'northern'" approach to Reconstruction in Dunning's work. According to Andrews, Dunning had underestimated "the menace of black rule" to white control and had neglected "the 'underground work' of all sorts that must have been performed in homes, shops, stores, lodges, clubs and other private circles to have led Southern Saxondom to its victorious rally against threatening barbarism." The failure to explore the overthrow of Radical Reconstruction in the South stood out, in Andrews's mind, as the author's "worse fault," although Dunning had written in the preface to *Reconstruction* that he did not intend to delve deeply into that subject.[29]

The history of Reconstruction was not the only field to which Dunning made major contributions. Dunning's *History of Political Theories,* a three-volume work, absorbed much of his scholarly efforts during the last two decades of his career. Philip Muller believed that Dunning developed an interest in the subject during a sabbatical in Europe. Dunning, undoubtedly detecting gaps in the subject, such as the lack of a volume in English dealing with classical and medieval thought, set out to remedy these omissions. The first volume of his trilogy, focusing on ancient and medieval political theory, was published by the Macmillan Company in 1902. The second volume, published in 1905, focuses on the political thought of the Protestant Reformation, the Puritan Revolution, and the Enlightenment. The third volume, beginning with the political thought of the Age of Revolution and ending with the rise of socialism, anarchism, and communism, came out in 1920. Although reviewers lauded these works as pathbreaking, Dunning's contributions to the history of political thought have been largely forgotten.[30]

Any scholar who produces five monographs has done plenty to advance his fields of expertise. Dunning, however, also served in professional organizations and promoted scholarly journals founded in the late nineteenth century to advance the study of history and political science. Dunning, for instance, penned numerous articles and book reviews for the *Political Science Quarterly* (*PSQ*). As managing editor of the *PSQ* for nearly ten years, he worked assiduously to produce a first-rate journal. Charles E. Merriam applauded "his discriminating judgment and his editorial care and skill." Dunning, Merriam explained, deserved credit for "maintaining the high standards of a periodical notable in the field of political science." Dunning was also a member of the APSA, serving as its president in 1922. He contributed articles to the *AHR* and in 1913 served as president of the AHA. As president, he filled a post once held by Henry Adams, James Ford Rhodes, Theodore Roosevelt, and other notable figures. Dunning significantly aided the development of the APSA and the AHA.[31]

As Dunning wrote, taught, and participated in professional organizations, Columbia University's academic reputation, like Dunning's, continued to soar. Columbia emerged as the best university in the country for the study of southern history in the early twentieth century. That distinction had earlier belonged to John Hopkins University in Baltimore, where Herbert Baxter Adams oversaw the Department of History, Politics, and Economics until his death in 1901. Although Adams was neither a Southerner nor a historian of the South, he promoted the study of the region at Johns Hopkins. Students from colleges in Maryland, Virginia, and North Carolina competed for scholarships reserved for them at Hopkins, and by 1896 the curriculum included southern history courses. Five years earlier, university officials had accepted two collections of documents, one of them dealing with slavery. Like Dunning's students, many of the historians who studied under Adams ended up in the South as editors, teachers, and scholars.[32]

Johns Hopkins officials offered Dunning an opportunity to teach at their university when Adams died in 1901, but he decided to remain in New York City. Consequently, Columbia University surpassed Johns Hopkins in the field of southern studies. By this time Columbia's History Department had few equals. Columbia officials awarded Dunning the Lieber Professorship of History and Political Science in 1904.[33]

Dunning's scholarly success, combined with his upper-middle-class breeding and attractive personality, brought him academic accolades and social prominence enjoyed by those who are exceptionally gifted or exceptionally lucky or both. Dunning was both. The typical image of the university professor as an absent-minded, socially inept figure, leading a cloistered existence among his dusty book-lined shelves, never applied to him. Few individuals were as well connected socially as Dunning, who frequented exclusive social clubs in Washington and New York City, where he moved in circles that included the country's most famous politicians, academics, and businessmen.[34]

Dunning worked hard at completing his professional duties, but he often found time for fun. After a two-hour golf game with a friend Dunning referred to as "Ford," probably Worthington Chauncey Ford, the Library of Congress's chief archivist, at Chevy Chase, Maryland, Dunning told his wife, Charlotte, "He beat me, but not very badly." Then, after "lunch in the cozy club house," he and Ford conducted research for almost four hours "in the library, all by ourselves." There Dunning discovered what he considered to be convincing evidence that the historian George Bancroft had penned Andrew Johnson's December 1865 statement concerning Reconstruction. The origins of the proclamation, which Johnson's contemporaries viewed "as a statesmanlike and altogether admirable paper," had been kept secret for decades. "I don't believe you can form any idea of the pleasure it gives me to have discovered this little fact," he wrote to Charlotte, adding, "It's the pleasure the gold hunter has in striking a good nugget after grubbing around in rubbish for a week." Dunning declared his golfing and researching excursion "one of the most delightful days of my life"; "tomorrow I shall put in a long and solid day's work, then dine with [Frederic] Bancroft & then take the train for N.Y."[35]

When Dunning found time to teach and to write is difficult to determine, so busy was his social schedule. Invitations to social occasions poured in from such notable figures as Senator Marcus Alonzo Hanna, manager of William McKinley's 1896 presidential campaign, and Lord James Bryce,

British ambassador to the United States in the early twentieth century. Three days after the signing of the armistice ending World War I, Dunning received an invitation to dine with the president-elect of Czecho-Slovakia, T. G. Masaryk, the Polish National Committee's president and world-renowned pianist, Ignacy Jan Paderewski, and the head of the Senate Foreign Relations Committee, Gilbert M. Hitchcock. "Dr. Masaryk," R. J. Caldwell wrote to Dunning, "is the spokesman of all these allied peoples numbering sixty millions."[36] The restless boy once expelled from college now moved among the world's great leaders.

Dunning experienced both professional success and personal happiness. Few individuals have been as psychologically and emotionally well-balanced as the Columbia professor, whose personality sparkled with joie de vivre. The mischievous side of his nature remained with him as he aged. As Philip Muller has observed, "At Columbia, he seems to have channeled his more spirited element into private correspondence and concentrated on moving up the academic ladder." Dunning, for example, once sent this poem, written in both English and Latin, to a friend:

Take me to a tavern when my time has come for dying;
Put a bottle to my lips when I all stark am lying,
So that when the angels for my spirit come a-flying,
God be good to this old drunkard, they will all be crying.[37]

Considering the elitist environment in academe, it was probably best that such playfulness remained private.

A source of great happiness for Dunning was his marriage to Charlotte Loomis. The two were wed in 1888. Dunning dubbed Charlotte "sweetheart" and "my darling abandoned wifey" in his letter describing his day playing golf and researching. The time had been enjoyable for him, he explained, "but don't fancy that I shan't be glad to get back to you. And I'[m] going to treat you werry [sic] beautiful to make up for my neglect." After his wife developed a chronic illness, Dunning sometimes fretted over her condition and his difficulty in paying her medical bills. He and Charlotte nevertheless remained deeply devoted to each other.[38]

The Dunnings often vacationed at Lake Sunapee in New Hampshire. They took numerous pictures during these outings, snapshots of themselves boating on the lake or relaxing on the deck of their cottage, Dreamland. With a happy marriage, a satisfying job, a busy social schedule, and a delightful city all around him, Dunning led a fulfilling existence.[39]

Dunning seemed constantly to be on a stage, playing a role he cultivated to near perfection in a production he directed. Even his premature balding contributed to his scholarly mien. His thick beard, contrasted with the balding, his wide mustache, his tiny eyeglasses, his hat and cane, and his expensive suits gave him a stately, dignified appearance. Dressed in this way, he seemed a paragon of intellectual talent, the epitome of a Columbia don. Plenty of substance, however, lurked behind this carefully cultivated image of sophistication.[40]

While many students relished the opportunity to study under Dunning and were often mesmerized by their charismatic mentor, not all of them were so admiring. Dunning exerted limited influence over his most famous pupil, the Georgian Ulrich Bonnell Phillips, whose primary field of study was slavery and plantation life, not Reconstruction. Phillips was influenced more by University of Wisconsin professor Frederick Jackson Turner and Turner's "frontier thesis." Phillips said that he benefited academically from contact with Dunning. "But," as Phillips's biographer Merton Dillon has written, "Dunning lit no fires for Phillips. He was no Turner." Phillips earned a reputation as the leading authority in his field after leaving Columbia University.[41]

Many other Dunning students from the South chose the Reconstruction era as their main area of study. The historian Wendell H. Stephenson contended that although Dunning and his students enjoyed "a wholesome, constructive relationship," the neophytes disagreed with their mentor on the best point of view from which to study Reconstruction. Dunning wrote about the period from a national perspective, whereas his students emphasized Reconstruction on the state and local levels. Dunning's writings also probably revealed less bias than those of his southern students, who often nursed deep-seated racial and sectional prejudices that were reflected in their approach to Reconstruction. Among the monographs written under Dunning's guidance were James Wilford Garner's *Reconstruction in Mississippi*, published in 1901; Walter Lynwood Fleming's *Civil War and Reconstruction in Alabama*, 1905; Joseph Grégoire de Roulhac Hamilton's 1914 study, *Reconstruction in North Carolina;* and Clara Mildred Thompson's 1915 work, *Reconstruction in Georgia: Economic, Social, Political, 1865–1872.*[42]

Vernon L. Wharton, in a 1965 essay, explained that not all the monographs written by Dunning's students came from the same mold. Some revealed greater quality and objectivity than others. He cited the works of C. Mildred Thompson and Joseph G. de Roulhac Hamilton as examples of reliable and partisan studies. Thompson, he argued, strove for balance in dealing with postbellum issues in *Reconstruction in Georgia.* Her writing revealed little antiblack bias, and she noted positive developments that occurred under Georgia's Radical government. Thompson argued, for instance, that Georgia society became more democratic during the Reconstruction era. The views expressed in her book hardly coincided with the harsh conception of Reconstruction later ascribed to Dunning's students.[43]

Joseph G. de Roulhac Hamilton produced a more biased account of the era in *Reconstruction in North Carolina.* He expressed strong disapproval of Congressional Reconstruction and anyone associated with it, whether black or white, scalawag or carpetbagger. Wharton wrote that *"Reconstruction in North Carolina* had the tone of a white Democratic broadside." That a staunchly Democratic newspaper, the *Raleigh Sentinel,* served as one of Hamilton's main sources gave credence to Wharton's claim that the author's work lacked objectivity. The works of Thompson and Hamilton, as well as the books on Reconstruction by the other students of Dunning, demonstrated that the young scholars sometimes differed on significant points. Their views did not always coincide with Dunning's.[44]

Like all great teachers, Dunning engaged in a symbiotic relationship with his students. He helped make their reputations, and they promoted his. Refusing to act dictatorially toward the young scholars under his tutelage, he encouraged them to engage in creative and independent thought and to draw their own conclusions from their research. After reading Hamilton's thesis on North Carolina during Reconstruction, he wrote to Hamilton, "Don't take my suggestions too seriously. It is your production & you are wholly at liberty to disregard any that you don't like." Dunning then told Hamilton that he had produced "good stuff" and declared, "You have the satisfaction of knowing that you are enabling lots of people to get such a knowledge of N.C. as they can get nowhere else in the world."[45]

The efforts of Dunning's students did not always meet Dunning's approval. Dunning once admonished Hamilton for writing especially harshly about North Carolina governor William Woods Holden's aggressive efforts to suppress Ku Klux Klan terror in the state. Hamilton, he pointed out, had underestimated the threat posed by the Klan and had not "given his [Holden's] side of the matter enough show." Dunning saw good reasons for Holden's actions and encouraged Hamilton to "give to Holden a little more justification" for attempting to bring peace to North Carolina, albeit through forceful tactics.[46]

The avuncular Dunning usually showered his students with unrestrained praise tinged with false modesty. Dunning ruminated over his relationship with them in a congratulatory letter to Hamilton after the completion of Hamilton's book on Reconstruction in North Carolina: "You must remember that we ancients who are getting into the sere and yellow have really no function left to us but that of being useful to the kids who are doing the real work." If Dunning was solicitous of his students, most of his students greatly admired him. Frank Porter Graham informed Hamilton: "I have just come out off my first seminar and now I know the Dunning that you have often told me about, genial, lovable, droll, and critical. I think I am going to like him fine." C. Mildred Thompson, in a letter inviting Dunning to speak at a Phi Beta Kappa meeting at Vassar College, where she was teaching in the History Department, told him, "There is no one who can better represent to us both the charm and the wisdom of the scholar's learning." Dunning's students may have also realized that their mentor's charming and wise exterior masked an intense desire for worldly success and a penchant for self-promotion.[47]

The Dunning scholars announced at a December 1913 meeting of the AHA in Charleston, South Carolina, that they were preparing a Festschrift for their mentor. Dunning at that time was completing his term as president of the AHA. James Garner, professor of political science at the University of Illinois, edited the Festschrift, titled *Studies in Southern History and Politics*. Among the fifteen chapters Dunning's students contributed to the volume were Garner's "Southern Politics since the Civil War," U. B. Phillips's "The Literary Movement for Secession," and Hamilton's "Southern Legislation in Respect to Freedmen, 1865–1866." *Studies in Southern History and Politics* brought together under one cover writings of outstanding scholars of the American South, and Dunning had exerted a profound influence on many of these intellectuals.[48]

James Garner, in the preface to the Festschrift, praised Dunning's "numerous and substantial" books on "later American history and the history of political theory." He noted his mentor's "preeminent position" among the scholars whose work had recently "awakened interest in historical research and in the study of the social sciences." Garner also lauded

Dunning's election to the presidency of the AHA as "the goal which awaits the most eminent historical scholars of the country." Few men of letters could claim such a record of accomplishment.[49]

Dunning's stellar contributions as a teacher and mentor also received Garner's attention in the preface. "For more than twenty-five years," Garner explained, "he has been a distinguished member of a distinguished faculty and during this period hundreds of toilers for the doctorate have sat at his feet and received inspiration and wisdom from his teaching." *Studies in Southern History and Politics* represented a "modest contribution to the historical literature of a period in the study of which he has done so much to stimulate interest among investigators, and it is their [Dunning students'] hope that it may not prove unworthy of him whom they all honor and hold in such high esteem." Garner had eloquently captured the intense devotion most of Dunning's students felt toward their mentor.[50]

Dunning reacted to news of the Festschrift as if it was the highlight of his career. "The look on Dunning's face when you made your announcement was itself worth going to Charleston to see," Charles W. Ramsdell told Hamilton one month after the AHA meeting. Dunning's feeling of surprise soon yielded to a spirit of gratitude. In an eloquently written letter to the students who had participated in producing the Festschrift, he explained that "from the point of view of scientific history and politics, . . . the contents of the book have amazed and delighted me." Over time, he predicted, the volume would come to be regarded as "a definitive interpretation of the Old South and its extinction, as they appeared to your generation," meaning that "you have the satisfaction of knowing that your volume will stand through the ages . . . as the dominant judgment of American historical scholarship in the first quarter of the twentieth century."[51]

That his students had mastered the craft of scientific history, as evidenced by their excellent essays, clearly gratified their professor, but Dunning admitted to them that "a detached and objective evaluation of your work" was "preposterous." The presentation of the "beautiful" Festschrift represented "the supreme honor that a teacher can receive from his students." The students' praise recorded in the outset of the book caused "dimness in the eyes and grippings in the throat." Dunning then characteristically declared himself unworthy of such an honor.[52]

The appreciation and respect Dunning held for his students, who had brought him "pedagogic joy," permeated his letter to them. The success the young scholars had experienced since leaving Columbia was for Dunning a source of "the keenest pleasure."[53] He continued:

> You are all teachers now, and you will hand on the torch to a generation that I shall not know. It is unlikely that any of you, however much more deserving of it, will be favored with so exceptional a body of students as it has been my fortune to teach. That occurs, in the nature of things, but once in many generations. Yet I can find nothing more devoutly to pray for than that this unlikely thing may happen, and moreover that each of you may in the fullness to time receive from those whom you have served such recognition as you have been kind enough to give to me.[54]

The presentation of the Festschrift stood out for Dunning as another significant accolade in a career studded by numerous honors. Dunning's life, however, was in decline. A sense of his own physical and intellectual deterioration began overtaking him when he was in his mid-fifties. Contributing to his strain was the death of his beloved wife in 1917 after a lengthy illness. Not surprisingly, Dunning found completing the final book in his political theory trilogy especially arduous. Weary and frustrated, he expressed relief when the project was completed with the publication of the last volume in 1920. Members of the APSA elected him president for 1922, but he never finished his term of office. Dunning died on August 25 of that year. Matilde Dunning later scrawled the words "Will's last letter to me— M.M.D." on the outside of an envelope holding a letter from her brother dated March 12, 1922.[55]

The anti-Radical view of the Dunningites constituted "the orthodox story of southern Reconstruction," to use Vernon Wharton's phrase, within a decade after Dunning's death. The 1915 film *Birth of a Nation*, which glorified the white South's defeat of Radical Reconstruction through Klan violence, and Claude Bowers's 1929 *The Tragic Era*, which also denounced the Radicals, played major roles in popularizing the anti-Radical view. The Dunning school endured, permeating Reconstruction studies until the mid-twentieth century. Many nonacademics embraced it as an accurate portrayal of the history of the United States after the Civil War. Reconstruction scholars found themselves confronted with the Dunning School whether they agreed with or opposed its tenets.[56]

Few historians in the early twentieth century heeded the reservations of scholars who dissented from the Dunning view of Reconstruction. The dissenters nevertheless raised important questions about what they regarded as inaccuracies and biases in the Dunning approach. A bold challenge to the Dunning school ironically came from one of Dunning's students, a South Carolinian, Francis Butler Simkins, who completed a doctoral degree at Columbia University in 1926. Simkins was enrolled in Dunning's Reconstruction seminar in the spring of 1922, when Dunning became seriously ill and never recovered.[57]

Dunning influenced Simkins, an eccentric and independent-minded scholar, far less than he did his earlier students. In 1932 the University of North Carolina Press published Simkins's first major work, *South Carolina during Reconstruction*. Simkins coauthored the book with Duke University professor Robert Hilliard Woody, a North Carolinian. In it the two scholars argued that Reconstruction was not simply a record of bad government and Negro rule, but also one of "constructive" developments. "For this reason," the authors wrote, "we forgo the temptation of following in the footsteps of historians who have interpreted the period as only a glamorous but tragic melodrama of political intrigue." This objective attitude represented an important step forward in the study of Reconstruction.[58]

Simkins and Woody, while admitting that Radical Reconstruction in South Carolina was not a complete success, identified numerous achievements registered by the Radicals after the Civil War. One accomplishment, for example, was the writing of the 1868 state constitution, which mandated universal education and other progressive measures. The institution of sharecropping and the development of all black churches, both of which offered the freedmen a degree of independence from whites, stood out as other achievements. Simkins also explored the collapse of Radical Reconstruction and the rise of Bourbon rule in South Carolina, citing violence against black and white Republicans as a main reason the Democrats triumphed in the 1876 elections.[59]

South Carolina during Reconstruction presented the Reconstruction period in a more nuanced and progressive light than did earlier versions of the era, but an even bolder challenge to the Dunning orthodoxy came in 1935 with the publication of W. E. B. Du Bois's *Black Reconstruction*. Du Bois applied Marxist theory to the history of Reconstruction, an approach that in one way made him similar to Dunning. Both men attempted to explain the era through a metahistorical mechanism, that is, an overarching theory that subjected complex events to simple explanations.[60]

Du Bois's version of Reconstruction, by investing blacks with a degree of agency no other thinker had accorded them and by relying on Marxist theory to explain the relationship among poor whites, ex-slaves, and wealthy elites, stands out as the most radical scholarly interpretation of the era ever written. Du Bois termed the slow erosion of slavery during the Civil War as a "general strike" on the part of the slaves against southern planters. He credited blacks with playing a major role in the Union war effort. After the war, the efforts of poor whites and blacks to gain voting and property rights galvanized the white upper classes in a struggle to block Radical Reconstruction. Powerful whites, by resorting to racist demagoguery, also drove a wedge between poor whites and ex-slaves, whose alliance could not be allowed to endure because it threatened the economic hegemony of the upper classes. Their ploy to rob the poor of any opportunity at advancement, Du Bois asserted, obviously worked. Reconstruction's collapse, engineered by a union of powerful northern and southern financial interests, gave rise to a racial and economic system that constituted "a new and vaster slavery." The failure of the proletarian revolution in the South may have once again left blacks at the mercy of the master class, Du Bois wrote, but it failed to crush the desire of blacks to break the shackles of a bourgeoisie-dominated society.[61]

Du Bois, in *Black Reconstruction*, decried the prowhite southern biases that characterized Reconstruction studies in the late nineteenth and early twentieth centuries. He asserted that many historians of Reconstruction had done a disservice to the study of scientific history by eschewing their responsibility to be objective. He credited Dunning's writing, which, he thought, was not without racial slurs against blacks, as being more balanced than his students' "one sided and partisan" approach. Du Bois labeled much of the students' work "thoroughly bad, giving no complete picture of what happened during Reconstruction, written for the most part by men and women without broad historical or social background, and all designed not to seek the truth but to prove a thesis." Even worse, Dunning and many of his young charges—Ramsdell, Woolley, Fleming, Thompson, Hamilton, and others—"believe the Negro to be sub-human and congenitally unfitted for citizenship and the suffrage." Du Bois accused the Dunningites of promoting "a nation wide university attitude . . . by which propaganda against the Negro has been carried on unquestioned." The Dunning School of Reconstruction, in Du Bois's mind, reeked of racism against blacks and violated basic standards of scientific history.[62]

The revisionist studies of Simkins and Du Bois may have undermined the legitimacy of the Dunning school, but the more powerful forces unleashed by the Second World War destroyed it. The period from 1939 to 1949 was arguably the most transformative era in modern history. World War II resulted in a myriad of profound changes, such as the defeat of European fascism, the collapse of Western colonialism, and the rise to global supremacy of the United States. Vast intellectual changes, related especially to race, also descended on the Western world as a result of the Second World War. White Americans, having entered the war to defeat enemies whose racist ideology drove them to maniacal extremes, found the basis of their own racism toward minorities called into question. As Merton Dillon has pointed out, the slavery practiced in the Americas in the nineteenth century appeared even more horrible in light of the holocaust against the Jews and other peoples considered undesirable by the Nazis. No longer could racism against blacks and other minorities be justified on the basis of science, when the term "scientific racism" now conjured images of Josef Mengele and other Nazi "doctors."[63]

The Second World War also provided the impetus for the civil rights movement in the United States. Many American scholars who entered the historical profession shortly before World War II supported and participated in the struggle for black rights after the war and sought ways to advance the movement through their historical writing. After the war the historical guild increasingly welcomed minority scholars into its ranks and became more open to the influence of Marxist thought on the writing of history. Little wonder, then, that the work of Dunning and his students became primary targets of many Reconstruction scholars in the second half of the twentieth century.[64]

William Dunning and the school of Reconstruction bearing his name await a biographer who will treat them fairly, eschewing the polemical tone that has too often characterized historians' analyses of his and his students' scholarship. A biography of Dunning would have to illuminate not only his contributions to Reconstruction, but also his achievements in other areas related to the early development of history and political science as academic disciplines. Dunning's work with the AHA and the APSA helped establish two professional organizations that continue to thrive today. His books on political theory added depth and analysis to neglected aspects of that field of study. His influence on a generation of graduate students enabled the scholars who studied under him to dominate their disciplines and to carry on his legacy after his death. These accomplishments merit greater attention from today's scholars. Dunning was a prominent member of the small vanguard of professionally trained academics who constructed the intellectual and organizational foundation of their fields of study in the late nineteenth century. Modern-day scholars, whether they realize it or not, continually confront Dunning's influence on American letters. William Dunning was a flawed colossus, but a colossus nonetheless.

Notes

1. John Harelson Hosmer, "William A. Dunning: The Greatest Historian," *Mid-America: An Historical Review* 68 (April–June 1986): 58.

2. For an analysis of the attitudes toward race that promoted the Dunning view of Reconstruction in the late nineteenth and early twentieth centuries, see Kenneth M. Stampp, "The Tragic Legend of Reconstruction," in Stampp, *The Era of Reconstruction 1865–1877* (New York: Alfred A. Knopf, 1965), 3–23.

3. Marriage certificate for John H. Dunning and Catherine Trelease, William A. Dunning (hereinafter cited as WAD) Collection, box 4, "Dunning, William A.: Family Documents 1849" file, Rare Book and Manuscript Library, Columbia University, New York. For the death of the two-year-old boy, see the small folder containing a lock of blond hair titled "William Archibald Dunning—died Sept. 1—1855 aged about 2 years—Hair," William A. Dunning Collection, box 6. In a letter probably to John and Catherine Dunning, Frank A. Trelease mentioned "the death of your little boy" from a "sickness." See Frank A. Trelease to "Dear Friends," October 28, 1855, William A. Dunning Collection, box 2. For photographs of the home in which WAD was born, see photograph marked "My birthplace," July 28, 1917, William A. Dunning Collection, box 7; see also photographs marked "Birthplace of William A. Dunning," n.d., and "Birthplace of W. A. Dunning—Many years later—Conditions changed," n.d., "Photographs" Album, William A. Dunning Collection, box 7. For verification of WAD's birth on May 12, 1857, see Clyde Furst to WAD, October 19, 1920, William A. Dunning Collection, box 1.

4. For the use of "Willie and Tillie" as a reference to WAD and his sister, see William Trelease to Catherine Trelease Dunning, April 2, 1864, William A. Dunning Collection, box 2; Anne W. Chapman, "William A. Dunning," in *Dictionary of Literary Biography: Twentieth-Century American Historians,* ed. Clyde Wilson, vol. 17 (Detroit: Gale Research, 1983), 148. For information on Elijah Trelease's death, see the grave inscription for Elijah S. Trelease under "Trelease," "Vail Cemetery Inscriptions," www.findagrave.com/cgi-bin/fg.cgi?page=pv&GRid=61644 66&PIpi=191507; see also "#39 Elijah S. Trelease," "Burial Record of New Jersey Soldiers: Philadelphia, Pennsylvania," in "N.J. Civil War Record: Page 1736," http://slic.njstatelib.org/slic_files/searchable_publications/civil war/NJCWn1736.

html; William Trelease to Catherine Trelease Dunning, May 20, 1863, August 31, 1863, November 30, 1863, and March 20, 1864, William A. Dunning Collection, box 2; William Trelease to Matilda M. Dunning, August 31, 1863[?], William A. Dunning Collection, box 2; photocopies of receipts for Matilda Dunning's payment to the New Jersey State Normal School, January 31, 1871, September 5, 1872, October 30, 1872, Ellis A. (?) Apgar (?), Lewis M. Johnson, "State Of New Jersey. Department of Public Instruction, Superintendent's Office. Third Grade State Certificate," awarded to Matilda Dunning, June 26, 1873, William A. Dunning Collection, box 4, folder 17; Philip R. Muller, "Look Back without Anger: A Reappraisal of William A. Dunning," *Journal of American History* 61, no. 2 (September 1974): 326.

5. For the influence of WAD's father on WAD's interest in Reconstruction, see commemoration page in WAD, *Reconstruction, Political and Economic, 1865–1877* (New York: Harper and Brothers, 1907).

6. Muller, "Look Back without Anger," 326–27; F. A. P. Barnard to John H. Dunning, photocopies of WAD's undergraduate Columbia College transcripts, November 14, 1878, December 16, 1878, January 20, 1879, February 26, 1879, March 12, 1879, April 11, 1879, May 19, 1879, June 24, 1879, July 6, 1880, March 12, 1881, William A. Dunning Collection, box 7, folder "Dunning—Biographical Columbia College—ca. 1878–1881."

7. Chapman, "William A. Dunning," 148–54; Daniel T. Rodgers, *Atlantic Crossings: Social Politics in a Progressive Age* (Cambridge: Harvard University Press, 1998), 71–72, 85–111, 368, 71.

8. Rodgers, *Atlantic Crossings*, 85–111; Democratic National Committee to WAD, September 24, 1920, William A. Dunning Collection, box 1.

9. James S. Humphreys, *Francis Butler Simkins: A Life* (Gainesville: University Press of Florida, 2008), 36; Georg G. Iggers, *Historiography in the Twentieth Century: From Scientific Objectivity to the Postmodern Challenge* (Hanover, N.H.: University Press of New England, 1997), 1–35; Peter Novick, *That Noble Dream: The "Objectivity Question" and the American Historical Profession* (Cambridge: Cambridge University Press, 1988), 21–31.

10. Novick, *That Noble Dream*, 28–60.

11. Charles E. Merriam, "William Archibald Dunning," *American Political Science Review* 16, no. 4 (November 1922): 692–94; WAD, *The Constitution of the United States in Civil War and Reconstruction, 1860–1867* (New York: J. F. Pearson, 1885).

12. WAD, review of Eben Greenough Scott, *Reconstruction during the Civil War in the United States of America*, in *American Historical Review* 1 (July 1896): 750–52; WAD, *Essays on the Civil War and Reconstruction and Related Topics* (1898; reprint, New York: Peter Smith, 1931), vii–viii. Citations are to the Peter Smith edition.

13. WAD, "The Constitution of the United States in Civil War," in *Essays on the Civil War and Reconstruction*, 1–62.

14. WAD, "The Constitution of the United States in Reconstruction," ibid., 63–135; "Military Government during Reconstruction," ibid, 136–75; "The Process of Reconstruction," ibid., 176–252; "The Impeachment and Trial of President Johnson," ibid., 253–303; "The Constitution of the United States in Civil War," ibid., 62; "The Constitution of the United States in Reconstruction," ibid., 109.

15. WAD, "The Constitution of the United States in Reconstruction," ibid., 63–135; "Military Government during Reconstruction," ibid, 136–75; "The Process of Reconstruction," ibid., 176–252; "The Impeachment and Trial of President Johnson," ibid., 253–303; "Military Government during Reconstruction," ibid., 146; "The Constitution of the United States in Reconstruction," ibid., 105.

16. WAD, "The Constitution of the United States in Reconstruction," ibid., 105, 122–23; "Military Government during Reconstruction," ibid., 138–43, 174–75.

17. WAD, "The Undoing of Reconstruction," ibid., 353–85, 372, 383.

18. Ibid., 383–85.

19. L. S. Rowe, review of WAD, *Essays on the Civil War and Reconstruction*, in *Annals of the American Academy of Political and Social Science* 12 (November 1898): 93–95.

20. Ibid.

21. Frederick W. Moore, review of WAD, *Essays on the Civil War and Reconstruction and Related Topics*, in *American Historical Review* 3 (July 1898): 761–63.

22. WAD, *Reconstruction, Political and Economic;* for "List of Authors and Titles" in The American Nation: A History series, see ibid., front matter; for WAD's dedication to his father, see ibid., dedication page.

23. Muller, "Look Back without Anger," 331–32; for WAD's opinion of the sources he consulted, see "Critical Essay on Authorities," in WAD, *Reconstruction, Political and Economic*, 342–57, 353, 344.

24. James Ford Rhodes, *History of the United States from the Compromise of 1850 to the End of the Roosevelt Administration*, 9 vols., new ed. (New York: Macmillan, 1928); John David Smith, *An Old Creed for the New South: Proslavery Ideology and Historiography, 1865–1918* (1985; reprint, Athens: University of Georgia Press, 1991), 113–14; Novick, "The Professionalization Project," in Novick, *That Noble Dream*, 47–60; WAD, "Critical Essay on Authorities," in WAD, *Reconstruction, Political and Economic*, 342; For WAD's use of Rhodes's work in his classes, see *Columbia University Bulletin of Information*, 21st ser., no. 19 (New York: Columbia University, 1921), 18.

25. WAD, "Problems of the Restored Union (1865)," in WAD, *Reconstruction, Political and Economic*, 3–17; WAD, "The Electoral Commission (1877)," ibid., 323–41; WAD, preface, ibid., xv–xvi.

26. WAD, "Radical Reconstruction at Washington (1866–1868)," ibid., 85–92, 86.

27. Ibid., 86–92, 86, 87, 91; James Ford Rhodes to WAD, August 26, 1907, William A. Dunning Collection, box 2.

28. WAD, preface to *Reconstruction, Political and Economic,* xv; WAD, "The Election of Grant (1868)," ibid.; 135; WAD, "The Movement towards White Supremacy in the South (1874–1875)," ibid., 266–80; WAD, "The Electoral Commission," ibid., 341.

29. James Ford Rhodes to WAD, August 25, 1907, William A. Dunning Collection, box 2; E. Benjamin Andrews, review of WAD, *Reconstruction, Political and Economic, 1865–1877,* in *American Historical Review* 13, no. 2 (January 1908): 371–73. For another positive review of WAD's book, see L. S. Rowe, review of WAD, *Reconstruction, Political and Economic, 1865–1877,* in *Annals of the American Academy of Political and Social Science* 32 (September 1908): 189–90.

30. Muller, "Look Back without Anger," 327–28; James Sullivan, review of WAD, *A History of Political Theories, Ancient and Mediaeval,* in *American Historical Review* 7, no. 4 (July 1902): 747; C. E. Merriam, review of WAD, *A History of Political Theories, Ancient and Mediaeval,* in *American Journal of Sociology* 7, no. 6 (May 1902): 851–53; WAD, *A History of Political Theories, Ancient and Mediaeval* (New York: Macmillan, 1902); WAD, *A History of Political Theories, from Luther to Montesquieu* (New York: Macmillan, 1905); WAD, *A History of Political Theories, from Rousseau to Spencer* (New York: Macmillan, 1920); for reviews of two of these works, see C. E. Merriam, review of WAD, *A History of Political Theories, Ancient and Mediaeval,* in *American Journal of Sociology* 7, no. 6 (May 1902): 851–53; James Sullivan, review of WAD, *A History of Political Theories, Ancient and Mediaeval,* in *American Historical Review* 7, no. 4 (July 1902): 747–49; William A. Hammond, review of WAD, *A History of Political Theories, Ancient and Mediaeval,* in *Philosophical Review* 12, no. 2 (March 1903): 199–207; Ernest Baker, review of WAD, *A History of Political Theories, from Rousseau to Spencer,* in *American Historical Review* 26, no. 4 (July 1921): 772–73.

31. For examples of WAD's book reviews in *PSQ,* see WAD, review of William Ernest Montgomery, *The History of Land Tenure in Ireland,* in *Political Science Quarterly* 4, no. 4 (December 1889): 673–75, and WAD, review of Bernard Bosanquet, *The Philosophical Theory of the State,* in *Political Science Quarterly* 14, no. 3 (September 1889): 530–33. For examples of WAD's articles in *PSQ,* see WAD, "The Constitution of the United States in Civil War," *Political Science Quarterly* 1, no. 2 (June 1886): 163–98, and WAD, "Paying for Alaska," *Political Science Quarterly* 27, no. 3 (September 1912): 385–98. Merriam's praise for Dunning is in Merriam, "William Archibald Dunning," 692–94. For examples of WAD's articles in the *American Historical Review,* see WAD, "More Light on Andrew Johnson," *American Historical Review* 11, no. 3 (April 1906): 574–94, and WAD, "The Second Birth of the Republican Party," *American Historical Review* 16, no. 1 (October 1910): 56–63. See the list titled "Ex-Presidents of the Association" on letterhead in Charles Homer Haskins to WAD, January 10, 1914, William A. Dunning Collection, box 1.

32. Raymond J. Cunningham, "Herbert Baxter Adams," in *Dictionary of Literary Biography,* vol. 47, *American Historians, 1866–1912,* ed. Clyde N. Wilson

(Detroit: Gale Research, 1983), 30; Chapman, "William A. Dunning," 151; Wendell H. Stephenson, "A Half Century of Southern Historical Scholarship," *Journal of Southern History* 11 (February 1945): 4–8.

33. Chapman, "William A. Dunning," 151; Muller, "Look Back without Anger," 326–27.

34. William T. Caldwell, general manager of Cosmos Club, e-mail message to author, June 1, 2009; photocopy of WAD's Cosmos Club membership card, October 6, 1919, in Joanne M. Pierre, manager of Membership and Administrative Affairs of Cosmos Club, e-mail message to author, June 1, 2009; A. W. Noyes to WAD, March 12, 1920, and Charles Homer Haskins to WAD, January 10, 1914, both in William A. Dunning Collection, box 1.

35. WAD to Charlotte Dunning, April 24, 1905, photocopy, Joseph Grégoire de Roulhac Hamilton Papers, #1743, folder 1, Southern Historical Collection, Louis Round Wilson Special Collections Library, University of North Carolina at Chapel Hill.

36. Marcus Alonzo Hanna to WAD, n.d., and R. J. Caldwell to WAD, November 14, 1918, both in William A. Dunning Collection, box 1.

37. Muller, "Look Back without Anger," 326; WAD to "Dr. Dana," n.d., Hamilton Papers, folder 1.

38. Chapman, "William A. Dunning," 149; WAD to Charlotte Dunning, April 24, 1905.

39. Frederic Bancroft to Joseph Grégoire de Roulhac Hamilton, August 10, 1914, Hamilton Papers, folder 8; Gary Knapp to WAD, June 13, 1916, William A. Dunning Collection, box 1. For a photo of Lake Sunapee, see the picture with the caption "Lake Sunapee from 'Dreamland,' the summer residence of Prof. Wm A. Dunning, of Columbia University," n.d., William A. Dunning Collection, box 7, "Photographs" album; for pictures of Dreamland, see the photograph marked "Dreamland: L. Sunapee, N.H.," n.d., and other photographs marked "Dreamland," William A. Dunning Collection, box 7, "Photographs" album; for a photograph of WAD in the Adirondack Mountains, see photograph marked "W. A. Dunning Adirondacks" showing WAD leaning against a tree with a hammock in the background, n.d., William A. Dunning Collection, box 7.

40. For photographs revealing WAD's premature loss of hair and showing his professorial image, see the photo marked "W. A. Dunning" picturing WAD in a suit and holding a top hat, n.d.; the photo by Herman Wunder marked "W. A. Dunning" showing WAD in bow tie and what appears to be an academic gown, n.d.; the photo marked "W. A. Dunning" showing him in suit with hat, cane, and overcoat, n.d.; the photos of WAD seated taken by Pach Bros, n.d.; and numerous pictures of WAD taken throughout his lifetime, all in William A. Dunning Collection, box 7.

41. Stephenson, "A Half Century of Southern Historical Scholarship," 18–19; Merton L. Dillon, *Ulrich Bonnell Phillips: Historian of the Old South* (Baton Rouge: Louisiana State University Press, 1985), 17, 20–25.

42. Stephenson, "A Half Century of Southern Historical Scholarship," 19–22; Vernon L. Wharton, "Reconstruction," in *Writing Southern History: Essays in Honor of Fletcher M. Green,* ed. Arthur S. Link and Rembert W. Patrick (Baton Rouge: Louisiana State University Press, 1967), 304–5; James Wilford Garner, *Reconstruction in Mississippi* (New York: Macmillan, 1901); Walter Lynwood Fleming, *Civil War and Reconstruction in Alabama* (New York: Columbia University Press, 1905); Joseph Grégoire de Roulhac Hamilton, *Reconstruction in North Carolina* (New York: Columbia University Press, 1914); Clara Mildred Thompson, *Reconstruction in Georgia: Economic, Social, Political, 1865–1872* (New York: Columbia University Press, 1915).

43. Wharton, "Reconstruction," 298–304.

44. Ibid., 302–5; Stephenson, "A Half Century of Southern Historical Scholarship," 19–22.

45. Muller, "Look Back without Anger," 334–36; WAD to Joseph Grégoire de Roulhac Hamilton, April 11, 1906, Hamilton Papers, folder 1.

46. WAD to Joseph Grégoire de Roulhac Hamilton, March 18, 1911, Hamilton Papers, folder 3.

47. WAD to Joseph Grégoire de Roulhac Hamilton, August 12, 1912, Hamilton Papers, folder 4; Frank Porter Graham to Joseph Grégoire de Roulhac Hamilton, October 7, 1915, Hamilton Papers, folder 13; C. Mildred Thompson to "My dear Dr. Dunning," December 2, 1915, William A. Dunning Collection, box 2.

48. Charles W. Ramsdell to Joseph Grégoire de Roulhac Hamilton, January 5, 1914, Hamilton Papers, folder 7; WAD to Joseph Grégoire de Roulhac Hamilton, October 19, 1914, Hamilton Papers, folder 8; Merriam, "William Archibald Dunning," 692; James W. Garner, "Southern Politics since the Civil War," in James W. Garner et al., *Studies in Southern History and Politics* (New York: Columbia University Press, 1914), 367–87; Ulrich B. Phillips, "The Literary Movement for Secession," in Garner et al., *Studies in Southern History and Politics,* 33–60; J. G. de Roulhac Hamilton, "Southern Legislation in Respect to Freedmen, 1865–1866," in Garner et al., *Studies in Southern History and Politics,* 137–58.

49. James Wilford Garner, preface to Garner et al., *Studies in Southern History and Politics,* v.

50. Ibid.

51. Charles W. Ramsdell to Hamilton, January 5, 1914, Hamilton Papers, folder 7; WAD, "To the Authors, all and singular, of Studies in Southern History and Politics, heartfelt greeting," in James W. Garner Papers, box 2: 1908–1929, folder 1911–1915, University Archives, University of Illinois–Champaign-Urbana.

52. WAD, "To the Authors."

53. Ibid.

54. Ibid.

55. Muller, "Look Back without Anger," 327–28; Chapman, "William A. Dunning," 149; Merriam, "William Archibald Dunning," 692, 694; Thomas

S. Barclay to WAD, February 20, 1922, Dunning Collection, box 1; WAD to Matilda Dunning, March 12, 1922, Dunning Collection, box 4, folder 17.

56. Wharton, "Reconstruction," 296–97, 307; John Hope Franklin, "Silent Cinema as Historical Mythmaker," in *Myth America: A Historical Anthology,* ed. Patrick Gerster and Nicholas Cords, 2 vols. (St. James, N.Y.: Brandywine Press, 1997), 2:110–17; Claude G. Bowers, *The Tragic Era: The Revolution after Lincoln* (Cambridge, Mass.: Houghton Mifflin, 1929); Chapman, "William A. Dunning," 152.

57. Humphreys, *Francis Butler Simkins,* 62, 66.

58. Ibid., 66–67; Francis Butler Simkins and Robert Hilliard Woody, *South Carolina during Reconstruction* (Chapel Hill: University of North Carolina Press, 1932), vii–ix.

59. Simkins and Woody, *South Carolina during Reconstruction,* 101–2, 434–43, 381–85, 406–34. For the 1876 election and the rise of the Bourbons, see Simkins and Woody, "The Campaign of 1876" and "The Dual Government," ibid., 474–513, 514–41.

60. W. E. Burghardt Du Bois, *Black Reconstruction: An Essay toward a History of the Part Which Black Folk Played in the Attempt to Reconstruct Democracy in America, 1860–1880* (New York: Harcourt, Brace, 1935).

61. Ibid., 381–430, 55, 17.

62. Ibid., 711–14, 717–25, 710, 720, 731, 719.

63. Dillon, *Ulrich Bonnell Phillips,* 141.

64. Novick, *That Noble Dream,* 48–60.

3

James Wilford Garner and the Dream of a Two-Party South

W. Bland Whitley

James W. Garner has long been characterized as the most balanced and least strident of William A. Dunning's students. Although in its general outlines Garner's view of Reconstruction differed little from most of his Dunningite peers', his tone, approach, and in some cases findings were strikingly discordant. In private Garner even went so far as to praise James L. Alcorn, Mississippi's first elected Republican governor under Reconstruction, who had embraced the political conditions of Reconstruction in the hopes of taking charge of a biracial political coalition. In a letter to Alcorn's widow, Garner admitted that Alcorn had "pursued the wise course" and regretted "that his white fellow citizens did not follow his leadership." Garner may not have been completely sincere on this point. He was no doubt ingratiating himself to an elderly woman, and his statement certainly did not point toward a favorable judgment of the congressional policy that had resulted in Alcorn's election. Indeed, Garner's treatment of Alcorn's tenure as Mississippi governor was brief and relatively uncomplimentary, his portrait of Alcorn himself dismissive and even sarcastic. Still, his willingness to contact would-be ideological adversaries bespoke his tendency to negate political passions in favor of a detached and cooperative research mentality. Comfortable in the North and among Northerners, Garner spent much of his career rejecting parochial concerns for a political perspective that seemed to owe more to Mugwumpish liberalism than to neo-Confederate partisanship.[1]

A sketch of Garner's career underscores his journey from local to international concerns. He was born on November 22, 1871, in Pike County, which borders Louisiana in southwestern Mississippi. Garner's family had deep roots in the area, his great-grandfather James Garner having settled there in 1811. Although the Garners were not wealthy, several members of the family had filled positions in local government. Garner's father was a farmer, and Garner's early exposure to farm life probably informed his determination to become something other than, in his words, "a knot on a log." Much of Pike County consisted of poor pine land, but some of it was better suited to plantation agriculture. Before the Civil War close to half of the population had been enslaved, and throughout the postbellum era racial percentages remained consistent; whites held a slight majority over African Americans. Such a ratio made for a volatile political dynamic. Garner would have undoubtedly grown up hearing stories about the turmoil that pervaded the Louisiana-Mississippi border region, where armed gangs conducted a violent challenge to the Reconstruction regime. Pike was controlled by Republicans for much of the period, and although political differences were handled more calmly than elsewhere, it did experience a good deal of violence spilling over from neighboring Amite, an extraordinarily disorderly county. One of Garner's uncles was elected, as a Democrat-Conservative, mayor of the town of Summit during the Redemption campaign of 1875.[2]

In addition to political conflict, Pike was the scene of a notable attempt at economic modernization when the president of the New Orleans, Jackson, and Great Northern Railroad (later the Illinois Central) decided in 1872 to relocate the line's train maintenance yards from New Orleans to the county, where he incorporated McComb. The town attracted skilled workers from the North and also became a center for the region's nascent timber industry. Although it never became the industrial powerhouse that its founder envisioned, McComb offered a different vista for an area still defined largely by a hardscrabble, rural economic and social structure.[3]

Garner worked his way through Mississippi Agricultural and Mechanical College (now Mississippi State University), graduating in 1892, and taught high school for a few years. On December 24, 1895, he married Therese Leggett, daughter of a Pike County planter. The following fall he entered the graduate school at the University of Chicago, from which he received a master's degree in political science in 1900. His instructors included Henry Pratt Judson and Hermann E. von Holst, who chaired the History Department. Von Holst taught the American history seminar that Garner took in 1898 and was an interesting mentor for a young scholar from Mississippi interested in Reconstruction. The first fully trained academic historian to make the United States his main field of inquiry, von Holst offered, in his eight-volume *Constitutional and Political History of the United States* (1876–92), a highly nationalistic, antislavery, and pro-Republican interpretation of the sectional crisis. Here, then, is the first evidence of Garner's willingness to seek out points of view different from those to which he had previously been exposed. During the summer of 1900, after working as an instructor of history at Bradley Polytechnic Institute (now Bradley University) in Peoria during the previous academic year, Garner finished his thesis, "The Administration of Governor Ames in Mississippi." Unfortunately, no copies of the thesis have survived.[4]

In the spring of 1900 Garner was awarded a fellowship to pursue a Ph.D. in political science at Columbia. There he worked closely with William A. Dunning, John W. Burgess, and John Bassett Moore and established himself as, in Dunning's phrase, "one of the coming men." Dunning described Garner's "ability to turn off work" as "a constant source of amazement to me" and exclaimed that "no man has ever come under my observation here that has impressed me as more scholarly in instinct." Garner published *Reconstruction in Mississippi* in 1901 and earned his doctorate the following year. After a year teaching at Columbia and another at the University of Pennsylvania, Garner took charge of the Political Science Department at the University of Illinois, where he remained for the rest of his career.[5]

With the exception of a four-volume popular history of America that Garner cowrote with the former Massachusetts congressman Henry Cabot Lodge, *Reconstruction in Mississippi* remained his sole historical work. Instead, he threw himself into research in political science. Maintaining the productivity that had so impressed Dunning, Garner published over the course of his career scores of articles and reviews for academic journals, political science textbooks for college and high school students, and two major works on legal issues raised by World War I. He also weighed in on issues of the day in a variety of newspapers and magazines, such as the *New York Times,* the *Dial,* and the *North American Review.* An early emphasis on criminal justice (he served for a time as editor of the *Journal of Criminal Law and Criminology*) yielded eventually to the field that would largely define Garner's career: international law. He became a well-known champion of internationalist policies and delivered lectures in France (including a stint as a lecturer for Allied troops during World War I), the Hague, and

Calcutta. He was a member of the advisory committee for the first conference on the codification of international law, and his work informed a draft
convention on the law of treaties, which was presented in 1935. Garner
planned to retire to a home he had purchased in Magnolia, Mississippi, but
shortly before he was to finish his career at Illinois, he was stricken with
meningitis and died in 1938.[6]

Politically and intellectually, Garner might best be considered a conservative adherent of the Progressive movement. Distrustful of democracy,
he embraced governmental reforms that promoted efficiency and facilitated
the work of disinterested experts. He considered himself a scientist and
strongly defended the scientific study of government, by which he meant
a coordinated and systematic classification of facts gleaned from reason,
observation, and experience. This dispassionate approach informed his
scholarly work, as well as his support for good government reforms. At one
time a member of the Urbana City Council, in which capacity he had supported a commission form of governance, he became the first head of the
Illinois Bureau of Municipal Statistics, which catalogued information on
demographic and economic trends. Garner's local advocacy drew fire on at
least one occasion from a democratic-minded critic in a Champaign, Illinois, newspaper. Under the headline "Aristocratic Viewpoint," an account
of a Garner presentation in favor of the commission form of government
referred to the "shower of criticism which his talk has called forth among
the rank and file of the people." Garner, the editorial continued, "is by
nature and association an aristocrat. He is one of those Southerners who
believes that 'niggers' and 'poor white trash' have no rights which his swell
elegant ones are bound to respect."[7]

Whether or not the criticism accurately reflected something about Garner, it was certainly the kind of heated comment that he avoided in his own
work and that probably confirmed his distrust of intense partisanship. His
own political stances indicated his preference for focusing on issues, not
parties. He criticized both the "dollar diplomacy" of Grover Cleveland and
the bellicose posture of Theodore Roosevelt and became a strong supporter
of Wilsonian internationalism. Encouraged perhaps by Herbert Hoover's
work overseas, he voted for the Republican in 1928 and again in 1932. His
work with the archnationalist von Holst and with Lodge testified to Garner's capacity for sublimating his personal views to a larger goal. Cooperating with Lodge was particularly striking, given Garner's research interests.
As a Massachusetts congressman, Lodge had repeatedly pushed for adop-

tion of federal enforcement of election laws in the South, and in 1890 his Elections Bill, criticized by white Southerners as the "Force Bill," called for federal supervision of all congressional elections.[8]

In longer works Garner tended to present his opinions not through explicit editorializing, but more obliquely by leading readers through a careful survey of the evidence. His widely used college textbook *Introduction to Political Science* (1910, updated in 1928 as *Political Science and Government*), for example, weighed without opinion the purported strengths and weaknesses of different government forms, while directing readers to a conclusion that the best governments were those best adapted to their populations, keeping in mind such cultural elements as "the intelligence and political capacity of the people, their history and traditions, [and] their race characteristics." Ultimately, this view allowed Garner to praise the Anglo-American "disposition to judge the value of government by the degree to which it awakens and stimulates the interest of the citizens in public affairs, inculcates habits of loyalty and patriotism in the people, and promotes civic virtues generally." Such a disposition, however, need not include "extreme" forms of democracy, such as the enfranchisement of unqualified voters or the influence of voters over matters that few people were competent to assess. Similarly, Garner's two major works on international law, the two-volume *International Law and the World War* (1920) and *Prize Law during the World War* (1927), illuminated the efforts of the Allied and Central powers to defend, circumvent, and recast international legal standards that the war had disrupted or rendered moot. Implicitly arguing against those who claimed that such a massive war had nullified the concept of international law, Garner effectively compiled a "digest of the laws of war" that developed during the conflict. Presenting all sides' positions with respect, he ultimately vouched for those developed in British courts. Reviewers, while occasionally chiding him for being too measured, agreed that he had judiciously compiled and presented reams of evidence that could inform the development of new international legal standards on warfare.[9]

In shorter works, Garner deployed his arguments more forcefully. The early portion of his career as a political scientist was driven largely by his disgust at the inefficiency of the American criminal justice system, which he targeted in a series of articles in both popular and academic journals. He scorned what he considered the excessive concern for procedure and the rights of defendants, which distinguished the American legal system from more efficient European models, going so far as to challenge the reasonable-doubt standard and the need for unanimity in jury decisions. He favored measures that would augment the decency and honor incumbent on jury duty and speed up trials by curbing peremptory challenges. Citing the sharp increase in homicides and violent crimes and the failure of convictions to keep pace, he argued that lynch law had become a horrifying result of the courts' failure to provide legal justice. In his views of criminal procedure, then, Garner combined a desire for scientific efficiency, disgust with the anarchy of the mob, and an implicit defense of elite governance. In the later phase of his career, Garner's ardent defense of internationalism led him to criticize American isolationism and to defend the League of Nations and World Court in several articles and addresses in the 1920s and 1930s. Constraints on the sovereignty exercised by states were necessary to prevent an international Hobbesian order. Progress, "whether it be local, national, or international," depended on some sacrifice of liberty. Indeed, although not bound by international codes, states should, Garner argued, strive to bring their statutes in accordance with developing international norms. This was not, to say the least, a point of view advanced by many white Southerners during the first decades of the twentieth century.[10]

Many of the themes, approaches, and views that guided Garner's political science work were apparent in his first and only major history, *Reconstruction in Mississippi*. There too presided Garner's measured tone, willingness to present different sides of particular issues, defense of American constitutional forms, distrust of thoughtless partisanship, and abhorrence of mob violence. Although working in a different discipline from the one he would make his specialty, Garner approached Reconstruction as he did the subjects of all his other major works. His preference was for governmental reform enacted by a conservative elite, a preference that harmonized quite well with the approach and philosophy of his Columbia mentors.

Of those mentors, William Dunning certainly exerted the greatest influence over Garner's first work. Like other examples of the Dunning School, Garner's account strayed from a narrow discussion of politics to encompass social and economic aspects of the period. It employed a wide range of source material, including military and congressional reports, legislation and court decisions, personal testimony, correspondence, and newspaper accounts. Still, Dunning's actual input is hard to discern. In his preface to *Reconstruction in Mississippi*, dated March 25, 1901, Garner identified Dunning as his instructor and thanked him for reviewing and correcting the manuscript but was silent on the question of Dunning's influence over his research. He did take detailed, albeit often illegible, notes on Dunning's lectures on Reconstruction. The only potential direct connection between the lectures and Garner's finished work is an anecdote about the Union military's meddling with a Vicksburg Episcopal church, whose members objected to the minister's willingness to say a prayer for the president (that is, Lincoln). Dunning certainly influenced Garner's history, but some of Garner's more striking research strategies predated his arrival at Columbia. Most notably, Garner began reaching out to former members of Mississippi's Republican regime and incorporating their perspectives before he had become Dunning's student. In acclaiming his fellowship award, the campus newspaper at Bradley Polytechnic, where Garner was then teaching, reported in its April 1900 issue Garner's intent to publish his manuscript "A History of Secession, Reconstruction, and Revolution in Mississippi." Given these details, it seems possible that Garner arrived in New York with a full manuscript, which would explain why he was able to publish *Reconstruction* during his first year at Columbia, before finishing his degree.[11]

Whatever Dunning's influence on Garner's work had been, there is little question that Garner retained respect and affection for the "Old Chief" long after he left Columbia. He took charge of coordinating and editing the testimonial volume published in Dunning's honor in 1914 as *Studies in Southern History and Politics*. Originally conceived by Joseph G. de Roulhac Hamilton, who wrote to Garner about it sometime in 1911 or 1912, the project ended up under Garner's direction after a series of miscommunications between the two. In a letter to Hamilton, Garner hoped that "some one else can be prevailed upon" to edit the volume, but he stated that he was willing to do so if his "colleagues will promise their best cooperation." So that "the work will be an honor to Dunning and a credit to the scholarship of those who are responsible for it," Garner insisted that he expected "to be given the full power of an editor, including the right to refuse to publish any paper that in my judgment ought not to go into the book."[12]

Garner took his role seriously, assigning topics and trying to ensure that contributions were original and not just a retread of previously published material. In three cases he appears to have enacted his prerogative to reject essays—a preliminary list he circulated to Hamilton included essays by Paul Haworth (on elections in the South during Reconstruction), George H. Porter (on the Democratic Party), and Francis W. Coker (on the Confederate government), none of which appeared in the book. Instead, Garner substituted contributions from Ulrich Phillips ("The Literary Movement for Secession") and C. Mildred Thompson ("Carpet-baggers in the United States Senate"). He also insisted on changes: for example, he advised Hamilton against use of the term *black codes* in the title of Hamilton's contribution, as the term "seems to me to be a little lacking in dignity" and "does not give any clue to the content of the paper." After Dunning thanked Garner for the Festschrift, Garner exclaimed that he "never did anything that has given [him] more pleasure." Dunning, whatever his influence on Garner's first published work, remained a touchstone for Garner well after his time at Columbia.[13]

Reconstruction in Mississippi followed a largely chronological approach, from secession and war to the departure of Republican Governor Adelbert Ames in 1876. Garner interspersed the central political narrative with topical sections on subjects such as economic devastation, postal and train service disruption and revivification, the changing status of African Americans, education, and white vigilantism and terrorism. Garner told his story through the presentation of documents, not through a strong authorial voice. Adopting the pose of a balanced, though not neutral, observer, he tried to guide readers to particular conclusions about the events and outcomes of Reconstruction through his own presentation of the historical evidence, rarely stating his opinions explicitly. Although he drew from a wide range of sources, Garner relied heavily on the testimony that filled federal reports. That many of these reports included majority and minority summaries made them ideal for Garner's practice of weighing opposing points of view. They also protected him from accusations that his southern background unduly influenced his account. He was not, as had some of his predecessors and contemporaries, rendering a brief on behalf of Mississippi whites opposed to Reconstruction. He was instead taking contemporaneous testimony of all parties, generated by federal authorities, to weave a different analysis, neither wholly condemnatory nor celebratory of federal policy. His correspondence with former members of the Republican regime served a similar purpose and allowed Garner to impart fair motives on figures with whose policies he disagreed. This was doubly the case when those figures themselves had come to decry congressional Reconstruction, as did Henry R. Pease, who had been superintendent of education and a U.S. senator, and Ridgley C. Powers, a former governor. Garner hewed closely to a scholarly approach that rejected popular historical narratives in favor of historical evidence.[14]

This is not to say that Garner melted completely into the background. Indeed, he identified his white southern point of view as an inescapable and salutary facet of the work. In his preface he discussed his belief that he could write unabashedly as a Southerner without narrowing the scope of the study so that it reflected only the southern perspective. He took it for granted that his own background would inform the study, but, contrary to some of the warnings he had received that his attempt to historicize Reconstruction might be premature, he believed that a dispassionate analysis was then possible. Furthermore, such an attempt was best left to someone from the South because "it is the Southerners who best understand the problems which the reconstructionists undertook to solve and the conditions under which the solution was worked out." Like almost all commentators of his era as well as many extending to the present, Southerners were assumed to be white, a rhetorical exclusion that consigned African American Southerners to secondary roles in the dramatic transformations of the Reconstruction era. Read together with his matter-of-fact assertion regarding the superiority of the local knowledge that white Southerners brought to bear on the situation, Garner's perspective echoed those of other conservative white Southerners who assumed that they were uniquely qualified to manage the region's race relations.[15]

Garner's commitment to this perspective, both personally and as a historical posture, was a central element of *Reconstruction in Mississippi*. Conservative whites, whether former Redeemers or Republicans, were his most favored informants. Indeed, in his view it was "their opinions only that possess[ed] any historical value." If there were heroes in his account, they were clear-eyed conservatives who neither clung to the past and to the chimera of southern independence nor capitulated to the radical Republican effort to restructure southern society. In short, his heroes tended to be Whigs, either lukewarm supporters or outright opponents of Confederate independence, and committed to rebuilding Mississippi within the Union. With regard to the freedmen, neither the proscriptive strategy favored by bitter-enders nor political equality factored much into this vision; rather, practicality was to govern political decision making. Efforts to render the status of freedpeople little better than it had been under slavery were impractical and unwise. Equally unwise, however, was the radical plan of granting them political privileges on a par with whites. Both derived from popular prejudices: on the one hand, race hatred and a commitment to the Lost Cause, and on the other, resentment of southern whites. Popular prejudices, and one might add popular historical narratives, only hindered the goal of good analysis, as necessary to governance as it was to scholarly work.[16]

Take, for example, the short shrift Garner granted to defenses of the Confederate cause, which defined the worldviews of many white Southerners of his era. Contrary to the many white southern analyses that have privileged states' rights, he bluntly declared that the "real cause of the Civil War" was the "perpetuation and extension of the system of negro slavery." He made a point of indicating that the state Democratic Convention of 1834 had explicitly disavowed the concept of secession and that even as sentiment in the state shifted on this question during the 1840s and 1850s, significant Unionist influence persisted. As were other members of the Dunning School, Garner was attuned to the lack of unity that increasingly hindered the Confederate war effort. Rather than universal and sustained white resistance to Union troops during the war, Garner found a rapid collapse of Confederate morale, as state authorities turned increasingly to unpopular conscription efforts and as the Union capitalized on Ulysses S. Grant's victory at Vicksburg to assume control of more and more Mississippi territory. Even his criticism of William T. Sherman's "peculiar theory of war" and "wanton" destruction of civilian property was restrained by his reliance on Sherman's own wartime reports.[17]

Garner's emphasis on the divisions that plagued the Confederate war effort in Mississippi, as well as the attention he paid to antebellum Unionist dissent, served to raise the possibility of intrawhite political competition in the postbellum era. He never made such an argument explicit. Rather, he repeatedly highlighted those whites who in his rendering appeared to offer a path out of the interlocking dilemmas that plagued postwar Mississippi. He found wisdom primarily among those who now accepted, even embraced, defeat and reunion with the northern states. William L. Sharkey, who served as provisional governor of the state after its surrender, emerged as Garner's ideal leader in many respects—pragmatic in his acceptance of the totality of the Confederacy's defeat and of emancipation, economic in his administration, and obedient to federal authority without sacrificing the state's legal independence, when such independence was at all feasible. Garner's respect for this approach extended to his discussion of the convention called in 1865 to ratify emancipation, not only as a de facto result of the war but as a policy embraced by the authority of the state.[18]

Portrayed by Garner under the rubric of "ableness," the stars of his account advocated unconditional acceptance of the abolition of slavery in the state and the granting of limited citizenship rights to African Americans. Rash and quixotic, by contrast, were those who clung to some notion that Mississippi retained any capacity to resist the mandates of Presidential Reconstruction. Garner seems to have adopted the concept of ableness from contemporary accounts and used it to denote a kind of sober eloquence and the combination of intelligence, experience, and restraint that he perceived in leaders like Sharkey, William L. Yerger, and Amos R. Johnston, all prewar Whigs. Such leaders displayed in Garner's account a commitment to governing based on actual economic and political conditions, rather than on adherence to a hardened political ideology. Those secessionists who likewise accepted the political necessity of surrendering to the logic of Presidential Reconstruction also earned Garner's respectful attention. In these conservatives Garner recognized a leadership cadre capable of restraining both the popular racism of many Mississippi whites and the unrealistic expectations of freedmen.[19]

There were, of course, three major impediments to the full flowering of this political leadership, one of which Garner hardly seems to have recognized, and another to which he paid little attention. First and foremost, Garner's sympathies for elite conservatives led him to exaggerate how divergent their views were from those of the mass of Mississippi whites. He failed to acknowledge the temporary Whig ascendance that characterized the state's politics immediately following the war. Both the Convention of 1865 and the legislature of the same year, which passed the notorious Black Codes, were populated largely by former Whigs. The first elected governor, Benjamin L. Humphreys, had likewise been a Whig. Far from politically astute, these leaders displayed a resolve to fix African Americans in a degraded status, between enslavement and actual citizenship. In that sense their conservatism differed little from the more stringent policy supported by the smaller Democratic camp in the legislature. Although Garner was mildly critical of the Black Codes, he mostly vouched for the need for legislation that would settle the state's labor problems and "force [the Negro] to cease his roving and become a producer." Garner's failure to address the interests of freedpeople in the postwar settlement of labor issues should not surprise anyone, but it does point to his blinkered faith in the political wisdom of the Whiggish camp. He assumed that African Americans should have accepted whatever settlement conservative whites devised, rather than seek political allies offering more liberal terms.[20]

Garner emphasized the northern Republican response to the Black Codes and other aspects of the intransigence of Mississippi whites as the primary impediment to the full emergence of the sober leadership he preferred. Departing from his usual policy of muting his editorial remarks, he reserved his sharpest critiques for the development of the congressional policy, which he viewed as inherently unconstitutional. It is worth noting that, so far as they were reflected in Garner's notes, Dunning's lectures withheld judgment on the congressional plan, merely introducing the political theories that informed them and discussing the mechanisms by which they were passed and implemented. Garner's assessment was far sharper in its condemnation of the underlying constitutional logic, although he resorted to his typically dull, understated fashion in characterizing the policy as of "doubtful validity."[21]

Likewise, in a section he labeled "National Inquest," he dismissed the validity of the congressional report of 1866 that, in describing the rising refusal of southern whites to acknowledge the rights of freedpeople, had informed Radical Reconstruction. Differentiating the Radicals' report from an earlier report commissioned by Johnson and written with the participation of Ulysses S. Grant, Garner stressed how haphazardly the committee had recruited testimony and the low bar it had set for assessing the relative loyalty of white Southerners, who could hardly have been expected to embrace federal authority and forsake allegiance to their Confederate chiefs so soon after the war. This seemingly reasonable critique was more than a little disingenuous. Grant had not even reported on Mississippi; rather, Carl Schurz had handled that part of Johnson's commission. Garner did not ignore Schurz's report entirely, but he failed to comment on Schurz's finding that many, if not most, Mississippi whites refused to acknowledge that a free labor system required a philosophy different from that required by a slave system. Schurz's analysis varied little in that sense from that of the report commissioned by Radicals in Congress. The overall effect of Garner's distortion of the contrasting reports was to delegitimize the assumptions underlying the congressional plan.[22]

This overt, if often understated and obscured, hostility to Radical Reconstruction informed Garner's analysis of Mississippi's 1868 Constitutional Convention, which descended at times to the rank stereotyping that many associate with the Dunning School and seems one instance in which Garner allowed popular narratives to overwhelm his scholarly approach. Stressing the length of time that the convention met and the relatively high per diem, he portrayed the convention as little more than a vehicle for Radical Republican peculation. Although citing only the convention journal with an occasional reference to a federal report, Garner's account was just slightly less negative than those that circulated in the Democratic press of the time: "Never had a legislative body or a state convention in Mississippi placed so high an estimate upon the value of its services. And what seems almost incomprehensible, there was a feeling that they had a legitimate right to exploit the taxpayers to any extent they pleased." Garner actually paid little attention to the drafted constitution itself, instead focusing on a slew of relief measures that the convention had felt bound to tackle, being the only elected body in the state. These became further evidence of extravagance.[23]

Such a departure from the book's dispassionate tone and approach served a critical role in Garner's overall interpretation. For Garner, the ascendance of radical Republicans and the universal backing they received from Mississippi blacks made it impossible for most Mississippi whites to split into political factions on the basis of issues unrelated to the forces unleashed by Reconstruction. It left little room for elite conservative leadership to exercise more than rhetorical guidance. Garner could ultimately blame congressional policy on the ugly bitterness that consumed most Mississippi whites. Of the political empowerment of freedmen Garner wrote, "That such a policy could have been carried through, unattended by social and political disorders . . . no intelligent man will for a moment expect." It was "one of the most dangerous experiments ever undertaken by the lawmakers of any country."[24]

Having established his negative assessment of the congressional plan, Garner returned to a more dispassionate approach. He did not withhold his views, but, in contrast to his analysis of the Reconstruction committee's report and the 1868 Convention, he ceded space to perspectives more sympathetic to Reconstruction. Even on the issue of military government, he established an even-keeled tone. Although often highly critical of certain policies, his account was largely descriptive, providing useful information such as the number and type of military commissions, which he viewed as unconstitutional, that were convened to prosecute crimes. He criticized the policy of removing civil officers in favor of military and convention appointees as a violation of the "Anglo-Saxon instinct for home rule," but he acknowledged that it was necessary for the fulfillment of the congressional policy. Garner had included some negative asides to the Freedmen's

Bureau in a few spots, but his chapter devoted to that organization was neutral and detached. Based largely on military and congressional reports, his account was framed by the perspective of bureau officials themselves. The complaints of Mississippi whites served as ballast, not to define the overall account.[25]

Perhaps the most puzzling aspect of *Reconstruction* is the relative lack of attention it pays to the period between passage of the 1868 constitution and the election of Adelbert Ames as governor in 1873. The Republican administration elected in 1869 and led first by the native Republican and "persistent Whig" James L. Alcorn and then by the conservative Northerner Ridgley C. Powers, both of whom might have appealed to Garner's own perspective, inspired little commentary. Alcorn, the first governor elected under the new constitution, received slightly more attention, much of it unsympathetic. Garner deprecated Alcorn's management of government finance, questioned his sincerity, and allowed the sarcastic characterizations of the contemporary press to undercut his coverage of Alcorn's speeches. Given the different assessment he delivered to Alcorn's widow, his easy dismissal of Alcorn is surprising and difficult to explain. Having focused on the Ames administration in his master's thesis and worked extensively on the formative earlier period of Reconstruction, Garner may simply have lacked the time and energy for a full examination of the period that was neither formative to congressional policy nor critical to Reconstruction's dismantling. Another possible explanation for Garner's treatment of Alcorn's "wise course" is the distinction Garner probably drew between locally and federally devised racial settlements. Although Alcorn's accommodation of black political aspirations, which he outlined in speeches and pamphlets during the Presidential and early in the Congressional Reconstruction periods, may have struck Garner as the right policy, his embrace of the Republican Party during the time of congressional ascendance took things too far. Rather than devising a viable racial settlement that might have attracted significant white support, he had achieved power through his acceptance of the Radicals' more egalitarian approach.[26]

It is his treatment of the Radicals, nevertheless, on which Garner's reputation for fair-mindedness has been rooted. The book's portrait of Adelbert Ames, a former Union general who had been one of the military governors of the state preceding its readmission, was a key facet of Garner's overall treatment of the state's radicals. Ames had shared his papers from the period with Garner and had patiently answered the young scholar's queries, thus earning some goodwill. Ames appears in the work as an honorable man of high character, misguided idealism, and conservative governing instincts. Garner debunked claims that Ames had acted corruptly or out of vindictiveness and praised Ames's commitment to economical government (always a key criterion for Garner). Debunking most of the impeachment charges that Mississippi Democrats had brought against Ames in 1876, Garner argued that though Ames had been unwise in waging intraparty and interparty battles, he had never been corrupt. Moreover, his management of state finances had been sound. Indeed, Garner largely exonerated Radical Republicans from the widespread assumptions regarding their peculation and mismanagement. He made some effort to catalogue corruption among Republican local officials, using for his evidence almost exclusively testimony from congressional reports, but he did not come up with a long list of miscreants. His analysis of Republican tax policy reached similarly muted conclusions. Garner found the situation far from dire, and a table listing taxation levels of Democratic and Republican counties left readers with the impression that on average Republican tax collectors were only slightly more aggressive than their Democratic counterparts.[27]

Garner also did not shy away from frank assessments of the political violence that white opponents of Reconstruction had launched against Republicans. Basing his account largely on congressional reports, which had been full of horrifying testimony about physical attacks and murder, Garner occasionally rationalized the violence but never dismissed it as a figment of Republican propaganda. He did, however, discount racial motivations as a primary factor in the violence, comparing vigilante groups like the Klan to those in Europe such as the Carbonari and Illuminés. This denial of race as a factor somewhat contradicted Garner's analysis of violent white campaigns against black education. Although never saying so, Garner presented evidence that pointed to almost universal white opposition to education for blacks, an opposition that mellowed only toward the end of Reconstruction. Garner ultimately blamed political violence on the "dangerous experiments" at the heart of the congressional policy, but he never dismissed the violence that had been critical to the Redemption campaign of 1875 as unimportant to that campaign or a trumped-up Republican fiction.[28]

Reconstruction in Mississippi has received consistently positive appraisals since its publication. In reviews and historiographical retrospectives Garner has repeatedly appeared as the sage moderate who forged a dispassionate yet critical history of Reconstruction, rarely, if ever, allowing his prejudices as a white Southerner to overwhelm his analysis. Praising his voluminous research, scholarly presentation of facts, willingness to set aside personal feelings, and fair-minded appraisals of the key actors, both southern and northern, reviewers such as W. G. Brown in the *American Historical Review* were quick to declare it "the best account we have of Reconstruction anywhere." In *Political Science Quarterly*, Theodore Clark Smith proclaimed that "in thoroughness of research and scientific accuracy of treatment it is not likely to be surpassed." An anonymous reviewer in the *New York Times* argued that though other works on the topic would appear, none could "take clearer ground."[29]

Part of the reason for this reception was the overwhelming hostility toward Reconstruction that had taken root throughout the country. Expecting lurid tales of corruption and fierce denunciations of unscrupulous agents of Reconstruction policy, reviewers marveled at Garner's willingness to impart fair motives to his subjects. His appraisal of "carpet-baggers," wrote the anonymous reviewer in the *Chicago Tribune*, was "nothing less than magnanimous." Those who had grown up regarding Reconstruction as a shameful exercise of federal power would now gain understanding of "the extraordinary difficulties under which this government labored." Brown ended his appraisal by stringing together examples of incompetent local government from Garner's account, as if to underscore that Garner's fair-mindedness might have obscured some aspects of the "upside-down arrangement" under the Reconstruction regime. The facts were there, just not the aggressive tone that would have brought them to life for readers. In this sense, Garner's reputation derives in part from his divergence from what educated people of his era expected from a history of Reconstruction, particularly one written by a white Southerner.[30]

Garner has retained this reputation as the most balanced and fair-minded of the Dunning School. W. E. B. Du Bois, for example, singled out Garner's as perhaps the only work that displayed "scientific poise" in its discussion of African Americans. Garner conceived "the Negro as an integral part of the scene and treat[ed] him as a human being." It was not so much that Garner's interpretation differed from that of his peers but that it did not become a vehicle for racial prejudice. African Americans may not have drawn much praise from Garner, but neither did they draw the kind of contempt appearing in some of the other state histories. (In this regard Du Bois elevated J. G. de Roulhac Hamilton as the most extreme.)[31]

As Reconstruction historiography increasingly adopted Du Bois's perspective, views on Garner's contribution remained fairly consistent. Vernon L. Wharton, whose work *The Negro in Mississippi* (1947) displaced aspects of Garner's account while retaining others, noted Garner's hostility to Radical Reconstruction and sympathy for the policy's opponents but also declared that "little that has been learned in the succeeding sixty years would serve greatly to alter or even to add to Garner's story." In his introduction to a 1968 edition of *Reconstruction in Mississippi*, Richard N. Current was more critical, accurately noting Garner's adherence to a conservative perspective that had fostered and remained tethered to stereotypes of the different actors on the radical side of Reconstruction. Although Garner had presented a mostly fair-minded account of Radical motives and even "anticipated Revisionist views on certain topics," his dismissal of the legitimacy of the freedmen's political aims had placed him squarely in the same camp as his more virulent peers.[32]

This sample of reflections on Garner and his contribution to Reconstruction historiography offers a good window into the work's place in studies of Mississippi and the broader region. When viewed through the prism of the white actors it discussed, *Reconstruction in Mississippi* hinted at the revisionist perspective that displaced that of the Dunning School. Sympathetic, though not uncritical, portraits of leading northern-born Republicans such as Ames and Henry R. Pease, critiques of shortsighted attempts by white leaders to reject all efforts to adjust to the new order of things, and relatively frank accounts of white intimidation and violence combined to create a history of the period that operated as far more than the brief for white Southerners that characterized other histories of Garner's era (and many that appeared afterward). Some portions, such as his dismissal of charges of corruption against the Republican regime, would not have appeared completely out of place in a revisionist history. As Current noted, it is telling that Garner's fiercest critic over the years was his fellow Mississippian John S. McNeily, who blasted the soft treatment that Garner delivered to Radical governance. Garner's detached, scholarly approach contrasted sharply with most of the articles contributed by white Mississippian students, professional historians, and gentlemen lawyers to *Publications of the Mississippi Historical Society,* which had been inaugurated at the end of the nineteenth century and to which Garner also contributed.[33]

When, however, attention is redirected to the efforts of freedmen to secure a place for themselves far removed from the enslavement of the antebellum era, Garner's account tended to operate from far more retrograde assumptions. His criticism of the Black Codes was tempered by his view that some such legislation was entirely necessary, given the extent to which freedmen had been "demoralized" by "unscrupulous" agents of the Freedmen's Bureau. He attributed the failures of the plantation system during the period immediately following the war (a period when the state experienced an infestation of army worms) to the "unreliable character of negro labor." He was quick to indicate, often with the sketchiest of information, the unfitness for office of many of the African Americans who served the state and local governments, although he was willing to acknowledge those individuals who acquitted themselves well. In sum, his perspective was grounded in assumptions that traced most of the problems associated with the postbellum adjustment to the political elevation of freedmen and to the unrealistic expectations they developed (owing to the encouragement of northern whites). Nowhere does he probe the attitudes of the freedpeople themselves or attempt to analyze events from their perspective.[34]

It is of course no great accomplishment to hammer Garner for his short-sightedness on these racial issues. His portrait of Reconstruction, although highly critical of congressional policy and its implementation in Mississippi, avoided much of the rank stereotyping and demonization that marred many other accounts. In discussing the overthrow of Reconstruction, it lacked the triumphant tone that characterized popular narratives and many of the histories that filled the pages of the organ of the Mississippi Historical Society. Although Garner certainly shared the widespread faith that Mississippi was in better hands after Redemption than during Reconstruction, he was by no means satisfied with developments in the state. Two years after the publication of his history, he shuddered at the rise of James K. Vardaman, who translated white supremacist fervor into a program for dominating the state's politics and marginalizing nonpopulist perspectives. Vardaman's rhetoric, Garner wrote, "for low-down vulgarity and indecency exceeds anything that ever fell from the lips of a public man." Such rhetoric had deformed politics in Mississippi and made it unresponsive to the kind of good government reforms and sober reflection of national affairs that Garner preferred. Focused so exclusively on dismantling the influence of African Americans and resisting federal power, southern whites had marginalized themselves from the main political currents of American society. The dismantling of black suffrage and the acquiescence of Northerners to this development, however, had rendered such intense unity unnecessary.

There was no reason, Garner wrote in 1910, that white Southerners could not "be divided on economic issues as the fingers of the hand, to use a figure employed by Booker Washington, and yet remain united as the hand itself on the question of white supremacy." Two-party competition was not only possible at the time but essential to the proper development of the South's economy and society. Garner wished for the resurgence of a white-led Republican Party in the South, which would help white Southerners regain influence over national affairs and improve chances for reform in the region.[35]

Garner's distrust of white solidarity had roots in his views of Reconstruction and was shared by other commentators who hoped that Mississippi whites might shed their exclusively parochial perspective. It reflected an elitist perspective that scorned both the racial egalitarianism of Congressional Reconstruction and the *Herrenvolk* democracy that had become the rhetorical foundation for the Democratic Party's grip on power in the South. Unlimited black manhood suffrage, the original sin, had spawned the white-line strategy that had come to dominate the Democratic Party's efforts. Garner borrowed from the views of William Sharkey and other leading conservatives in leveling his most pointed criticism against congressional policy and characterizing it and the Freedmen's Bureau as the "chief obstacle to good feeling between" whites and blacks. Modern views regarding race and democratic governance make it difficult to engage Garner and his Dunning School collaborators without condemning them as beyond the pale. But it is certainly worth asking what good came out of congressional strategy. Recently, in fact, the civil rights historian Adam Fairclough has argued that Dunning and his students were essentially correct in condemning the precipitous decision to grant unlimited suffrage to freedmen, which, like them, he considers the principal irritant between whites and blacks in the postbellum South. He adds to their critique an argument in favor of extended federal control of the region through a form of territorial governance (one borrowed from Dunning's Columbia mentor and associate, John W. Burgess).[36]

Garner's own counterfactual vision rested not on extended federal influence, to which he largely objected, but on a return of two-party competition, much as had existed in the South before the Civil War. It is important to note that Garner did not pull this vision out of thin air. It reflected to a large degree a real impulse among the politicians and commentators whom he praised in his account. Although never denying what they viewed as the horrible consequences of congressional policy, many influential whites targeted white intransigence against expanded rights for freedmen as equally deserving of scorn. They used their substantial leverage to gain a platform in the state press, most notably in the *Clarion,* the principal organ of the Democratic-Conservative movement. The racial division that had come to define postbellum politics, the paper argued in one editorial, resulted from white resistance and anger. A system less structured by racial division would have been healthier: "Disembarrassed of the negro question by a full recognition of the equal rights of all men before the law, the Conservatives will be free to address themselves to the main, practical issues of the canvass." Frank Johnston, a prominent attorney and the son of one of Garner's favorites, Amos R. Johnston, argued in one article that speedy acquiescence to the Fourteenth Amendment would have guaranteed racial harmony and encouraged the acceptance by Mississippi blacks of a subordinate political status. Such views lent themselves to a far less celebratory view of the violent Redemption campaign of 1875 and of the political dynamic that it continued to enforce. Whereas Dunbar Rowland, state archivist and president of the Mississippi Historical Society, rhapsodized that Redemption had ensured a "time when peace and good-will will reign supreme," Garner recognized that however necessary, the overthrow of Republican power and influence had resulted in the "political effacement of the South and the loss of its leadership in national affairs." White supremacy, in short, was not sufficient.[37]

Garner's counterfactual, Burkean vision retains appeal. It holds out the tantalizing hope that one hundred years of bitter racism and counterproductive governance might have been avoided. It is worth questioning, nevertheless, the sincerity of the elite moderates that Garner preferred. Individuals arguing for fair treatment of freedpeople and robust debate among whites did exist, and many were sincere. It is impossible to separate their stance, however, from the supplicant rhetorical posture mandated by federal intervention. Calls for moderation existed in direct proportion to the level of interest in southern affairs existing in the North. When northern authorities took a more hands-off approach, the views of many would-be moderates in Mississippi differed little from those of white-line absolutists. It is also doubtful that freedmen would have accepted whatever racial settlement a Whiggish-oriented leadership devised. To be sure, had leading blacks foreseen the nadir that succeeded their all-too-brief experience with political equality, they might have chosen a more gradualist path. Lacking that foresight, freedmen displayed nothing but a fierce commitment to achieving autonomy and political influence. Although they were certainly not advocating political supremacy or proscriptive measures against whites, they showed no inclination to accept the subaltern role that commentators such as Garner envisioned. Even had they been, most whites were far from willing to cede any political space.[38]

Ultimately, these kinds of counterfactual questions may boil down to how one views the relative centrality of rhetorical tone to the operation of postbellum southern politics. Did the sober detachment of Garner and other moderate observers and participants promise a better political road? Was that moderation irrevocably marginalized by federal policy? Or did the racist appeals of the Democratic Party, which by Garner's time had emerged in their most baroque and pathological formulations, speak to something deeper within the white population, something that transcended whites' resentment of Congressional Reconstruction? Elite-driven moderation may or may not have been something of a chimera. All scholars should appreciate, nonetheless, the relative fair-mindedness and rigor Garner brought to bear in researching and writing about a subject to which he was personally connected and from which he was removed by a mere twenty-five years.[39]

Notes

1. James Garner to Amelia Alcorn, October 26, 1901, James Lusk Alcorn and Family Papers, Mississippi Department of Archives and History (hereinafter cited as MDAH); for responses from former Republican officials, see James W. Garner Papers, MDAH; for Garner's assessment of the Alcorn administration, see James W. Garner, *Reconstruction in Mississippi* (1901; reprint, Baton Rouge: Louisiana State University Press, 1968), 277–89; on Garner's preference for a two-party system, see his articles "New Politics for the South," *Annals of the American Academy of Political and Social Science* 35 (1910): 172–83, and "Southern Politics since the Civil War," in Garner, ed., *Studies in Southern History and Politics* (New York: Columbia University Press, 1914), 367–87.

2. For details of Garner's life, see John A. Fairlie, "Biography of James Wilford Garner," in Garner, *Studies in Government and International Law* (Urbana: University of Illinois Press, 1943), 1–9, and *National Cyclopaedia of American Biography*, 31:225–26; on the Louisiana-Mississippi border region, see Samuel C. Hyde, *Pistols and Politics: The Dilemma of Democracy in Louisiana's Florida Parishes, 1810–1899* (Baton Rouge: Louisiana State University Press, 1996), and William Bland Whitley, "Precious Memories: Narratives of the Democracy in Mississippi, 1865–1915" (Ph.D. diss., University of Florida, 2003), 92–94; *Mis-*

sissippi in 1875. Report of the Select Committee to Inquire into the Election of 1875 (Washington, D.C., 1876), 73–105, 1209–15; *Mississippi. Testimony as to Denial of Elective Franchise in Mississippi at the Elections of 1875 and 1876* (Washington, D.C., 1877), 476–89.

3. On McComb, see William C. Harris, *Day of the Carpetbagger: Republican Reconstruction in Mississippi* (Baton Rouge: Louisiana State University Press, 1979), 524–25.

4. Other courses that Garner took at Chicago included constitutional history of the United States, financial history of the United States, modern European history, diplomatic history, and Roman history; Garner Papers, University of Illinois Archives (hereinafter cited as UI), Urbana, box 1. On von Holst, see Clyde N. Wilson, ed., *Dictionary of Literary Biography*, vol. 47, *American Historians, 1866–1912* (Detroit: Gale Research, 1986), 145–47; thesis title is from communication with University of Chicago archivists, October 11, 2010.

5. William A. Dunning to Professor Rowe, March 21, 1903, Garner Papers, UI, box 1.

6. For a complete bibliography of Garner's works, see Garner, *Studies in Government and International Law,* 39–50; see also, Fairlie, "Biography," 9, 14–20, 25–26.

7. Clipping from unidentified newspaper, January 7, 1911, in Garner Papers, UI, box 1.

8. *Dial: a Semi-Monthly Journal of Literary Criticism, Discussion, and Information* 47 (December 16, 1909), 503–4; Fairlie, "Biography," 26–27.

9. James Garner, *Introduction to Political Science: A Treatise on the Origin, Nature, Functions, and Organization of the State* (New York: American Book Company, 1910), 17–18; Garner, *Political Science and Government* (New York: American Book Company, 1928), 407–11, 440; for Garner's revulsion at the results of Mississippi's new primary elections law, see his letter to the editor in the *Outlook* 75 (September 12, 1903): 139–40; Henry F. Munro, review of Garner, *International Law and the World War,* in *Political Science Quarterly* 36 (1921): 511–15; Amos S. Hershey, review of same, in *Journal of International Relations* 12 (1921): 110–12; C. John Colombos, review of Garner, *Prize Law during the World War,* in *Journal of the Royal Institute of International Affairs* 6 (1927): 330–31; Philip C. Jessup, review of same, in *Political Science Quarterly* 43 (1928): 450–52.

10. James Garner, "Criminal Procedure in the United States," *North American Review* 191 (January 1910): 49–63; Garner, "American versus English Courts," *North American Review* 192 (August 1910): 250–57; Garner, "Crime and Judicial Inefficiency" and "The Reform of Criminal Procedure in the United States," in Garner, *Studies in Government and International Law,* 92–127; Garner, "Lynching and Criminal Law," *South Atlantic Quarterly* 5 (October 1906): 333–41; Garner, *American Foreign Policies: An Examination and Evaluation of Certain Traditional and Recent International Policies of the United States* (New York: New York University Press, 1928); Garner, "Limitations on National Sovereignty in International

Relations," in Garner, *Studies in Government and International Law,* 357; Garner, "Responsibility of States for Injuries Suffered by Foreigners within Their Territories on Account of Mob Violence, Riots, and Insurrection," in Garner, *Studies in Government and International Law,* 390–91.

11. *Peoria Tech,* April 1900, news clipping in Garner Papers, UI, box 1; for correspondence with Mississippi Republicans, see James W. Garner Papers, MDAH; see also Garner, *Reconstruction in Mississippi,* viii, 281, 290, 293; for the anecdote, see Garner's course notebook, "Lectures of Reconstruction," Garner Papers, UI, box 1, and Garner, *Reconstruction in Mississippi,* 35–36; on Dunning, see Philip R. Muller, "Look Back without Anger: A Reappraisal of William A. Dunning," *Journal of American History* 61 (1974): 325–38.

12. For the miscommunication between Garner and Hamilton, see Garner to J. G. D. Hamilton, February 27, 1913, in Joseph G. de Roulhac Hamilton Papers, ser. 1, folder 1743, Southern Historical Collection, Chapel Hill, N.C.; Garner to Hamilton, March 1, 1913, ibid.; Garner to Hamilton, March 25, 1914, ibid.

13. For the preliminary list of essays, see Garner to Hamilton, September 27, 1913, Hamilton Papers; Garner to William A. Dunning, February 26, 1915, William A. Dunning Papers, box 1, Columbia University Archives, New York.

14. For the less "scientific" accounts of Mississippi Reconstruction, against which Garner can be positioned, see many of the histories published in the Mississippi Historical Society's house journal, *Publications* (or *PMHS*), many of which were written by former Redeemers; Ethelbert Barksdale's contribution to Hilary A. Herbert, *Why the Solid South? or, Reconstruction and Its Results* (Baltimore: R. H. Woodward, 1890), 321–48; see also Whitley, "Precious Memories," chap. 5.

15. Garner, *Reconstruction in Mississippi,* viii.

16. Ibid., 153.

17. Ibid., 1, 12, 16. For the significance and pervasiveness of Lost Cause mythology, see Charles Reagan Wilson, *Baptized in Blood: The Religion of the Lost Cause* (Athens: University of Georgia Press, 1980); Gaines Foster, *Ghosts of the Confederacy: Defeat, the Lost Cause and the Emergence of the New South* (New York: Oxford University Press, 1987); David W. Blight, *Race and Reunion: The Civil War in American Memory* (Cambridge: Harvard University Press, 2001), and W. Fitzhugh Brundage, *The Southern Past: A Clash of Race and Memory* (Cambridge: Harvard University Press, 2005). For another example of southern white disunity, see Walter L. Fleming, *Civil War and Reconstruction in Alabama* (New York: Columbia University Press, 1905), 127–43.

18. On Sharkey, see Garner, *Reconstruction in Mississippi,* 75; and his entry in *American National Biography,* ed. John A. Garraty and Mark C. Carnes (New York: Oxford University Press, 1999) (hereinafter cited as *ANB*).

19. Garner, *Reconstruction in Mississippi,* 81–94.

20. Ibid., 118. For the composition of the 1865 Convention, see William C. Harris, *Day of the Carpetbagger,* 50–51.

21. Garner, *Reconstruction in Mississippi,* 158; for Dunning's views, see Dun-

ning, *Reconstruction, Political and Economic, 1865–1877* (New York: Harper and Brothers, 1907), 88–90, 93–95; for his lectures, see Garner's lecture notes, pp. 7–12, Garner Papers, UI.

22. Senate Executive Document 2, 39th Cong., 1st sess., esp. 19–20, 106; House Report no. 30, 39th Cong., 1st sess.

23. Garner, *Reconstruction in Mississippi*, 189.

24. Ibid., 353. For a very different take on the convention that highlights divisions among the Republican members, Conservative obstructionism, and the rabid hostility of the Democratic press, see Harris, *Day of the Carpetbagger*, chap. 4.

25. Garner, *Reconstruction in Mississippi*, 169, 184, 232.

26. On Alcorn, see Lillian A. Pereyra, *James Lusk Alcorn: Persistent Whig* (Baton Rouge: Louisiana State University Press, 1966); Harris, *Day of the Carpetbagger*, 246–48, 290; and his entry in *ANB*.

27. On Ames, see his entry in *ANB;* and Blanche Ames, *Adelbert Ames, 1835–1933; General, Senator, Governor . . .* (New York: Argosy-Antiquarian, 1964). For the tax tables, see Garner, *Reconstruction in Mississippi*, 312–13.

28. For an analysis of Democratic-Conservative efforts to depict political violence against Republicans as exaggerated or fictional, see Whitley, "Precious Memories," chap. 2.

29. W. G. Brown, review of Garner, *Reconstruction in Mississippi*, and Edwin C. Woolley, *The Reconstruction of Georgia*, in *American Historical Review* 7 (April 1902): 582–84; Theodore Clarke Smith, review of Garner, *Reconstruction in Mississippi*, in *Political Science Quarterly* 16 (December 1901): 719–21; review of same in *New York Times*, October 12, 1901, 13.

30. Review of Garner, *Reconstruction in Mississippi*, in *Chicago Tribune*, July 13, 1901; Brown, review of Garner, *Reconstruction in Mississippi*, and Edwin C. Woolley, *The Reconstruction of Georgia*.

31. W. E. Burghardt Du Bois, *Black Reconstruction: An Essay toward a History of the Part Which Black Folk Played in the Attempt to Reconstruct Democracy in America, 1860–1880* (New York: Harcourt, Brace, 1935), 720.

32. Vernon L. Wharton, "Reconstruction," in *Writing Southern History: Essays in Historiography in Honor of Fletcher M. Green*, ed. Arthur S. Link and Rembert W. Patrick (Baton Rouge: Louisiana State University Press, 1965), 300; Richard N. Current, introduction to Garner, *Reconstruction in Mississippi* (Baton Rouge: Louisiana State University Press, 1968), xxix.

33. Current, introduction, xxvi–xxvii; for McNeily's thorough yet virulent histories, see his "Climax and Collapse of Reconstruction in Mississippi, 1874–1876," *PMHS* 12 (1912): 283–474, and "War and Reconstruction in Mississippi, 1863–1890," *PMHS*, 2nd ser., 2 (1918): 165–535; for the perspective on Reconstruction that emerged in the *PMHS*, see Whitley, "Precious Memories," chap. 5.

34. Garner, *Reconstruction in Mississippi*, 118, 136.

35. For triumphal narratives, see Dunbar Rowland, "The Rise and Fall of Negro Rule in Mississippi," *PMHS* 2 (1899): 189–200; Charles Hillman Brough,

"The Clinton Riot," *PMHS* 6 (1902): 53–63; for Garner's objection to Vardaman-ism, see his "A Mississippian on Vardaman," *Outlook* 75 (September 12, 1903): 139–40; on the need for a two-party system, see Garner, "New Politics for the South," *Annals of the American Academy of Political and Social Science* 35 (January 1910): 177.

36. Garner, *Reconstruction in Mississippi,* 153; Adam Fairclough, "Was the Grant of Black Suffrage a Political Error? Reconsidering the Views of John W. Burgess, William A. Dunning, and Eric Foner on Congressional Reconstruction," *Journal of the Historical Society* 12 (June 2012): 155–88; Fairclough, "Congressio-nal Reconstruction: A Catastrophic Failure," *Journal of the Historical Society* 12 (September 2012): 271–82.

37. *Jackson (Miss.) Weekly Clarion,* June 6, 1874, and June 10, 1873; Frank Johnston, "Suffrage and Reconstruction in Mississippi," *PMHS* 6 (1902): 147, 177; Rowland, "The Rise and Fall of Negro Rule," 200; Garner, "Southern Politics since the Civil War," 370.

38. For works on Mississippi Reconstruction that recognize a split between some whites' moderation and the more racist orientation of the mass of white vot-ers, see Wharton, *The Negro in Mississippi,* 89–96; William C. Harris, *Presiden-tial Reconstruction in Mississippi* (Baton Rouge: Louisiana State University Press, 1967), 243–47; Harris, *Day of the Carpetbagger,* 674–77; for skeptical views, see Michael Fitzgerald, *The Union League Movement in the Deep South: Politics and Agricultural Change after Reconstruction* (Baton Rouge: Louisiana State University Press, 1989), esp. 246–48; Chris Waldrep, "Black Political Leadership: Warren County, Mississippi," in *Local Matters: Race, Crime, and Justice in the Nineteenth-Century South,* ed. Christopher Waldrep and Donald G. Nieman (Athens: Uni-versity of Georgia Press, 2001), 225–50; Nancy Bercaw, *Gendered Freedoms: Race, Rights, and the Politics of Household in the Delta, 1861–1875* (Gainesville: Univer-sity Press of Florida, 2003); Whitley, "Precious Memories," 37–44, 111–12.

39. For a sharp analysis of recent trends in accounts of the political history of Reconstruction, see Michael W. Fitzgerald, "Reconstruction Politics and the Politics of Reconstruction," in *Reconstructions: New Perspectives on the Postbellum United States,* ed. Thomas J. Brown (New York: Oxford University Press, 2006), 91–117.

4

Ulrich B. Phillips

Dunningite or Phillipsian Sui Generis?

John David Smith

The Georgia native Ulrich Bonnell Phillips (1877–1934), along with his Columbia University mentor, William A. Dunning, set the standard for early twentieth-century scholarship on plantation slavery and the Civil War and Reconstruction, respectively. Contextualizing the work of Phillips, Dunning, and others of their era, the historian Steven Hahn notes that such "early scholars saw the dynamics of national development in the transmission of Anglo-Saxon ideals and institutions, in the conflicts between different white interest groups and classes, and in the Anglo conquest of the frontier." Southern historians of Phillips and Dunning's time in particular maintained "that the regional struggle for white supremacy over what they regarded as a backward and inferior race ultimately became the foundation upon which a bitterly divided nation could reconcile."[1]

In 1907 Phillips framed the Civil War era in terms of what he later would call the "central theme" of southern history: Southerners' recurring preoccupation with maintaining white supremacy. Secession signified their response to "the world's problem of equity in human relationships," he said. White Southerners' commitment to slave labor "clashed with the predominant idea of the period"—free labor. Though defeated in civil war, whites never surrendered their commitment to racial hegemony over blacks. "Facts of human nature and the law of civilized social welfare are too stubborn for the theories of negrophiles as well as of negrophobes," Phillips added. "The slave labor problem has disappeared, but the negro problem remains."[2]

Phillips espoused these ideas and, because of the lasting importance of his two landmark books, *American Negro Slavery* (1918) and *Life and Labor in the Old South* (1929), he became the preeminent historian of slavery and the Old South until the late 1950s.[3] Despite efforts by revisionists to contextualize and explain the importance of Phillips's writings, his reputation as a historian nonetheless declined expeditiously in the post–civil rights decades. In a typical dismissive reference to Phillips, in 2011 a historian referred to him as "the father of the proslavery school of Southern history," who, "at Columbia, professionalized the study of the South in the 1920s by defending slavery, calling it a system of 'gentleness, kind-hearted friendship and mutual loyalty,' concepts which guided several generations of historians."[4] Years before, writing in the *New York Times,* the esteemed African American literary critic and historian Saunders Redding blasted "the notoriously biased Columbia school of historians, led by Ulrich B. Phillips."[5]

Despite these and numerous other negative evaluations of Phillips's significance, he nevertheless ranked as the foremost southern historian of his day and had a distinguished career during the first three decades of the twentieth century, including professorships at Wisconsin, Tulane, Michigan, and Yale. In 1928 Phillips received Little, Brown and Company's $2,500 prize for the best unpublished manuscript in American history for that year. The following year an Albert Kahn Traveling Fellowship enabled Phillips to study plantations comparatively worldwide. Writing in 1925, the University of Chicago historian William E. Dodd described Phillips as "one of the best scholars in the country." He added, however, "But, like nearly all historians of our day, I think he has a strong tendency [to] plead a cause—in his case that of the old South."[6]

Phillips was one of only a handful of Dunning's students who did not focus his research on constitutional, institutional, or political history, especially the history of Reconstruction. That is not to say, however, that Phillips lacked interest in, knowledge of, and strong passions about what white Southerners of his day considered the most tumultuous period in American history. Though like other contemporary white Southerners Phillips identified with the New South's Confederate forebears, he never glorified the war, referring to it instead as a "cataclysm." In 1925 he wrote that "many folk of the old regime were destroyed by the war—not merely soldiers on the battlefield, but civilians white and black, driven or lured from shelter, sustenance, and sanitation." He recounted how slaves by the thousands died during the war and how the conflict left many slave owners "utterly broken." Those who survived the war had to begin their lives anew "under conditions of general derangement and almost universal poverty. The landholders possessed land and managerial experience—and worthless Confederate currency. The freedmen had liberty, and little else but a residual acquiescence in the necessity of working for a living."[7] Phillips ended *Life and Labor in the Old South* with an eloquent but stern warning about the pathos of war generally and the War between the States in particular.[8] By the early 1930s Phillips had joined the revisionists, concluding that the Civil War was avoidable, the result of folly, in his words, "a calamity of misguided zeal and blundering."[9]

Yet Phillips retained the Dunningites' disdain for Reconstruction. In 1909 he decried what he termed "the domination of carpet-baggers and scalawags, when radicalism became rampant" after 1868. Determined to rebuild their economies during Reconstruction, many southern states began to bolster their infrastructure and transportation networks. Phillips, however, considered such projects only venues for "recklessness and corruption." In his opinion, "The favorite practice was for carpetbaggers like [Daniel H.] Chamberlain in South Carolina and the Stantons in Alabama, financed by Wall Street brokers like Henry Clews, to buy up the members of the legislatures and the stocks of the corporations simultaneously. The legislatures would then vote millions of dollars in bonds or endorsements to the corporations, whose carpetbag officials would put most of the proceeds into their own or their confederates' pockets." Such characterizations of the alleged waste, corruption, and thievery of Radical governments were standard fare in the so-called Dunning School of Reconstruction studies. Phillips suggested that although the "Reconstruction thieves" did lay two or three thousand miles of roads across the South, the heavy debts their corruption caused by 1873 continued to have an adverse effect on southern economic recovery at century's end.[10]

As for political Reconstruction per se, in 1928 Phillips explained that white Southerners welcomed President Andrew Johnson's restoration program, believing that it put into place Abraham Lincoln's "back to normalcy" plan. Southern hearts sank, however, when congressional Republicans "overslaughed the presidential programme and set events in train which seemed to make 'the Africanization of the South' inescapable." According to Phillips, "To most of the whites, doubtless, the prospect showed no gleam of hope." Phillips agreed with the Confederate critic Edward A. Pollard, who argued in *The Lost Cause Regained* (1868) that white Southerners went to war in 1861 not over constitutional rights, but to protect slavery and to prevent race war. They had no reason to expect generosity in the wake of Confederate collapse. "Virtually all respectable whites had entered the Democratic ranks in the late sixties to combat à outrance the Republican programme of negro incitement. A dozen years sufficed to restore white control, whereupon they began to differ among themselves upon various issues."[11]

In 1904 Phillips blamed white Southerners' continuing overdependence on cotton production as the indirect result of "the radicalism of the republican majority at Washington and the carpet-baggers in the field in the South." By excluding moderate Southerners from Reconstruction state governments, Phillips maintained, Republicans left the door open "to the domination of the extremists of the Tillman type when the reconstruction governments were overthrown. Out of the ashes of war and reconstruction there arose the 'Solid South.'"[12] Later that year Phillips held emancipation and Republicans of the Reconstruction period responsible for undoing the civilizing qualities of slavery and for encouraging segregation of and by whites and blacks. Blacks' "concentration in city slums is vicious; their isolation from white neighbors in the black belt of the seacoast cannot cease to mean stagnation, if not retrogression, for them; the race prejudice taught them by the carpetbaggers was and is a positive injury; their general aloofness upon small farms must insulate them in large measure from the best influences for progress in the South of today."[13]

In 1910 Phillips blamed the "cataclysm of war" and what he termed the "false reconstruction" for stifling the positive qualities of the plantation system. Continuation of the plantations of the antebellum South, Phillips supposed, "would have required some provision whereby such laborers as the system had schooled into superior efficiency might easily withdraw from the gangs and set themselves up as independent artisans, merchants, or farmers." Though he criticized slavery and the plantation system for capitalizing labor and rendering the southern economy static and inelastic, Phillips nevertheless considered the plantation necessary for most of the region's slaves. Under Reconstruction planters had little stimulus to "graduate at least the ablest of their laborers into the industrial democracy" where they could crop small farms, work in factories, and live in cities adjacent to plantations. "The remodeling and partial replacement" of the antebellum plantation "was necessary in the progress of [the South's] industrial society."[14]

In 1907 Columbia University Press refused to print Phillips's reference to Reconstruction as the "Hell that is called reconstruction" in the dedication for a book of his that the press had accepted for publication. Though

William H. Carpenter, secretary of the press, agreed with Phillips's sentiments toward Reconstruction, he informed Phillips that his polemical language signified "an appeal to sectional feeling which the University and the
Press which represents it can not stand for, since . . . it must occupy broadly
a judicial position without prejudice in any direction." Phillips acquiesced,
emending his reference to Reconstruction as "the troublous upheaval and
readjustment which followed" the war.[15]

Years before, while still a graduate student at Columbia, Phillips published two book reviews of Edwin C. Woolley's *The Reconstruction of Georgia:* one in the *Atlanta Constitution* and the other in the *Publications of the
Southern History Association*. Woolley was a contemporary of Phillips's at
Columbia, completing his dissertation in 1901, presumably under Dunning's supervision, and his thesis appeared in the university's prestigious
Studies in History, Economics and Public Law series.[16]

In his *Atlanta Constitution* review, Phillips remarked approvingly
that the time finally had arrived when historians could adopt a "magisterial attitude" toward the post–Civil War era. He praised Woolley as a
Northerner with "a cosmopolitan frame of mind" who wrote a fair and balanced account, avoiding the "luridness" characteristic of earlier accounts
of Reconstruction. Previous histories of the period, according to Phillips,
emphasized either "tyranny and corruption" on the one side, or "sedition
and outrage" on the other. Phillips added, "Our individual point of view
exaggerates the tyranny or the sedition as the case may be."[17]

Phillips agreed with both Woolley's commendation of President Andrew
Johnson's restoration of Georgia in December 1865 and his condemnation
of the Radical Republicans' Reconstruction program that ensued in March
1867. Phillips complimented the author for avoiding partisanship, instead
explaining motives, discrediting traditions, "and here and there assigning
a modicum of praise or censure to the chief actors in the drama." Though
he welcomed Woolley's book, Phillips nevertheless faulted his emphasizing
political science and his paying short shrift to local history. The book was
Georgia history written through the lens of Washington, not Atlanta, Phillips complained, a weakness perhaps not surprising "from one not a native
of Georgia." Phillips also mentioned that Woolley paid insufficient attention to "conditions in Georgia just before the war."[18] That would become
the subject of Phillips's own dissertation. Phillips concluded that despite
Woolley's good work, "the field is still open for a history of the people of
Georgia under the reconstruction régime."[19]

Whereas his fellow graduate students at Columbia conducted research on state histories of the post–Civil War South, Phillips focused on pre–Civil War history. In his 1902 dissertation, "Georgia and State Rights," Phillips tracked the development of political sectionalism in antebellum Georgia. This was one of the historian's few works in political history; most of his writings treated southern economic and social history.

Unquestionably, Columbia broadened Phillips's intellectual horizons, providing him exposure to John W. Burgess's neo-Hegelianism and James Harvey Robinson's "New History." Columbia's graduate training incorporated the broad scope of the human past, not just military and political events. But Phillips seems to have benefited little from Dunning's influence and, significantly, unlike other Dunning students, retained little affection for his *Doktorvater* or his Columbia years. Dunning's legion of former graduate students, most notably Joseph Grégoire de Roulhac Hamilton of the University of North Carolina, heaped praise on and expressed affection for their beloved "Old Chief." Phillips, however, conspicuously omitted his doctoral mentor from among those who influenced his research and writing. In 1909, in a rare instance, Phillips quoted Dunning's assessment of John C. Calhoun's *Disquisition on Government* (1851) as "in some respects the most original and the most profound political essay in American literature."[20]

The historian David Donald explains that Dunning subscribed to the "'sink or swim' school of graduate instruction," rarely engaging with students' doctoral dissertations until they were virtually complete and submitted for his approval. "A broadly tolerant man, Dunning allowed his students to pursue their own paths."[21] In contrast to historians' general assumptions about Dunning, he in fact was less concerned with encouraging a "school" per se than allowing considerable diversity in the dissertation topics his students selected.

For whatever reason, Dunning and Phillips never became close personally or professionally. Instead, Phillips revered Frederick Jackson Turner, considering him his foremost teacher, and all but ignored Dunning's influence. Though Phillips had many close friends in the historians' guild and socialized often with historians at meetings and at his home, he rarely communicated, mentioned, or met with his mentor. Ironically, though Phillips ranks as the best-known and perhaps most accomplished of the Dunning School, his focus on the economic and social history of the antebellum South, not the political history of Reconstruction, and his decision to distance himself from Dunning personally and socially have resulted in historians rarely identifying him with the Dunning School.[22]

That said, in 1904 Phillips recalled that his student days at Columbia furnished him with "a number of very pleasant memories," but he warned a prospective graduate student there to avoid working with the colonialist Herbert L. Osgood, whom Phillips considered "so fearfully dry and uninteresting—the sort of uninteresting plodder that no man ought to be." Phillips recommended instead that the potential Columbia student enroll in one of Dunning's classes—"for the sake of getting his method." Dunning would prove "to be the most cordial and suggestive man there," Phillips said, adding that "[William Milligan] Sloane would be if he could." Phillips noted that Dunning gladly gave advice to students. He and Professor James Harvey Robinson "consider that they are there to be used."[23] Years later, in 1911, Phillips married the daughter of Columbia's renowned economist Richmond Mayo-Smith.

Phillips had less pleasant memories of Burgess. Writing in 1905, he recalled that "Burgess is certainly exasperating and it was probably only a sense of humor (on my part, certainly not on his!) which prevented a challenge from me similar to that of the Southerner of last year who asked him if he really *believed* what he said. But an appreciation of the ridiculousness of things enables one to find frequent sources of joy even in Gotham." So unimpressed was Phillips with Burgess that he recommended that a Columbia student drop Burgess's lecture course because in it he "will do nothing but recite his 'Middle Period.'" Still, Phillips admitted that he was "too radical to judge Burgess fairly," and that he was "too conservative to do [Franklin Henry] Giddings justice."[24]

Though Phillips found his Columbia professors wanting, Dunning at least held him in high regard. Writing to Turner just weeks before the young Georgian defended his doctoral thesis, Dunning ranked Phillips as among Columbia's best graduate students. Whereas most Columbia doctoral students received fellowships for only one year, in a highly unusual move the School of Political Science awarded Phillips support for a second year. "His work has been admirable," Dunning informed Turner, "and I should think that he would make a first class teacher & lecturer." Dunning praised Phillips's research and writing in "Georgia and State Rights" as "thoroughly good." Dunning also complimented Phillips's personality and presence, explaining that "Phillips has the self-possession and physical presentableness that will carry him through agreeably & successfully before a class or an audience." Having written this, Dunning nevertheless observed one weakness in Phillips, "his tendency to slight work that is not just to his taste. He is most indefatigable in the field that attracts him, & this carries him so far as to hurt him sometimes in other fields." Dunning did not consider this a serious deficiency, however. "Altogether," he informed Turner, "I am ready to [recommend] him as strongly as any man whom we have ever had at Columbia in History."[25]

A year later, recommending Phillips for a fellowship from the newly established Carnegie Institution of Washington, Dunning described his former graduate student "as a man of extraordinary endowment and capacity." Phillips's recently completed dissertation "was a very high grade piece of work on several obscure phases of political development in Georgia," Dunning wrote. He noted that Phillips had numerous contacts in the South who would facilitate his unearthing primary sources in the region. "I know of no man who would give better promise of important contributions to our knowledge in this field" than Phillips, Dunning added.[26]

Dunning's encomiums about his former student appear all the more surprising given Phillips's lukewarm, if not outright negative, response to an invitation to contribute an essay to a Festschrift for Dunning upon his assuming the presidency of the American Historical Association (AHA). Communication between Phillips and Dunning's other former graduate students suggests a possible strained relationship between Phillips and Dunning—at least on Phillips's part. In April 1911 Phillips responded coolly to an invitation to contribute to a volume to honor Dunning. Writing to Hamilton, Phillips insisted that he did not mean to show disrespect to Dunning, but he simply felt obliged to raise questions about such a project's appropriateness, its viability, and his possible role therein.

First, Phillips feared that publication of such a tribute could establish a bad precedent "upon the younger generation" of scholars who might feel compelled to produce similar volumes. Phillips next warned Hamilton that it probably would be difficult to find a publisher interested in such a project; most presses required a guaranteed number of sales before taking on similar works. Third, Phillips reminded Hamilton that unlike the other Dunning students, who had written about Reconstruction, he worked primarily in the antebellum period. Phillips then informed Hamilton that collected essays succeeded best when organized around a central topic, not disparate themes and chronological periods. "I have no equipment and no material for writing on Reconstruction," Phillips explained. Finally, he told

Hamilton that he had "resolved months ago to leave off the product of isolated essays and stick to some larger projects." In closing, Phillips told Hamilton that though "I feel regret in saying it, . . . you had better leave me out of your plans."[27]

Phillips's disinclination to participate in the Dunning Festschrift elicited critical comments from Dunning's other students who, like Hamilton and Charles W. Ramsdell of the University of Texas, relished the opportunity to honor Dunning with an essay collection. Ramsdell "greatly marveled" at Phillips's "lukewarmness" and doubted the validity of his argument that publishing a volume to honor Dunning would establish a bad precedent. On two occasions the University of Illinois historian James W. Garner, who organized and edited the collection, informed Hamilton that Phillips was not interested in participating in the project, remarking, "I don't think we shall be able to count on Phillips. . . . But there are enough others without him if he does not care to join us." Another contributor, Walter Lynwood Fleming of Louisiana State University, told Hamilton: "I do not think that Phillips's opinion about this matter is worth anything at all. Leave him out." He took another jab at Phillips, informing Hamilton, "I do not think that Phillips has any patent on the plan because it is nothing new. You can look at the shelves in your library and find plenty of such volumes." Though as late as September 1913 Phillips remained both uncommitted to and unlisted by the editor as contributing to the Festschrift, he did attend a dinner to honor Dunning's AHA presidency in December of that year.[28]

Despite his reservations about contributing to the commemorative volume, in February 1914 Phillips informed the historian Claude H. Van Tyne that he had written a 10,000-word essay to honor Dunning.[29] In "The Literary Movement for Secession" Phillips surveyed what he termed "pamphleteering in the fifties"—the creative and intellectual justifications for southern national independence. It appeared in *Studies in Southern History and Politics, Inscribed to William Archibald Dunning . . . by His Former Pupils the Authors,* published by Columbia University Press in 1914. In addition to essays by Fleming, Phillips, Ramsdell, Hamilton, and Garner, the book included contributions by Milledge L. Bonham Jr., Sidney D. Brummer, C. Mildred Thompson, Edwin C. Woolley, William Watson Davis, W. Roy Smith, William K. Boyd, Holland Thompson, Charles Edward Merriam, and David Y. Thomas.

Though Dunning directed Phillips's doctoral work, he always acknowledged the mentorship of, inspiration from, friendship with, and affection for Turner. This may explain Phillips's less than warm relationship with Dunning. Phillips's widow recalled, "His friendship with Prof. Turner was one of the high lights of his life."[30] Phillips, while studying at the University of Georgia, had fortuitously attended the 1898 summer term at the University of Chicago, where he took classes with Turner. Then researching political parties in antebellum Georgia, Phillips embraced Turner's economic determinism and regionalism, his vision of the frontier as a democratizing "process," and the western historian's insights into American sectionalism. In 1902 Turner hired Phillips at Wisconsin, the young scholar's first job and the stimulus for both his Progressive Weltanschauung and much of his early published work.[31] According to the historian John Herbert Roper, Turner encouraged Phillips to venture to New York to study in 1900. "Together the two made the choice that most Southern boys made then: Phillips would study with William Archibald Dunning at Columbia University. That remarkable teacher, whose great powers exerted such a profound influence on a coterie of Southern academics, could only modify the direction already set by Turner's protégé."[32]

Phillips's selection of "Georgia and State Rights" as his dissertation topic reflected Turner's influence, not Dunning's. Phillips, who had begun working on the history of antebellum Georgia politics as a master's student at Georgia under the historian John H. T. McPherson, credited Turner with emphasizing the importance of the nullification movement in the evolution of the state's complex antebellum political system as Georgians moved from being firm nationalists to advocates of states' rights. Largely a work of political economy and historical geography, Phillips's doctoral thesis traced the development of factions and political groups across Georgia from the American Revolution onward, assessing politicians' debates and shifting allegiances on state, regional, and federal questions, including Indian removal, the tariff and nullification, the U.S. Bank, and the protection of slavery.[33]

Phillips made clear that not only did Georgia politicians differ with federal officials over what they deemed to be their state prerogatives, but they also fought pitched internecine battles over statewide power and place. Phillips rejected class as an explanation for intrastate political factionalism, arguing that "the contrast between the extremes of wealth and poverty in the South has been exaggerated," that "the line of separation between the classes was itself vague and varying," and that "thrift and improvidence caused elevation and retrogression in the scale of wealth in many individual cases." Their varying responses to the federal government's alleged usurpations of state privilege, according to Phillips, shaped antebellum Georgians' political allegiances. Ultimately Abraham Lincoln's election in 1860, and their fear for the protection of slavery, convinced white Georgians to embrace secession in order to defend their state's sovereignty. Following Lincoln's election, Phillips explained, "Georgians of every faction had the fellow feeling of a common defeat, and they determined to waste their strength no more in fruitless dissensions, but to work, and if need be to fight, together in the patriotic cause." Even so, he remained undecided about secession's ideological meaning. "It is not easy to determine whether the policy of secession was radical or conservative," Phillips concluded. "Its advocates as well as its opponents claimed the quality of conservatism for their respective causes, and each party had some ground for their contention."[34]

Though Turnerian in inspiration, Phillips's Dunning-directed dissertation was a model "scientific" thesis for its day, narrating and presenting new factual information more than outlining a clear and definitive argument. He informed readers that his method was "that of the investigator rather than the literary historian. The work is intended to be a thorough scientific treatment of its subject." To that end Phillips conducted extensive research in local court records and obscure Georgia newspapers. More than one-third of Phillips's footnotes cite newspapers, most often Milledgeville's *Federal Union*.[35] As a measure of its quality, in 1901 "Georgia and State Rights" won the AHA's Justin Winsor Prize for the best unpublished work by a promising scholar in the history of the Western Hemisphere. The cash award included publication of the dissertation by the AHA under the auspices of the Smithsonian Institution.[36] The book appeared in 1902. The Indiana University historian James A. Woodburn remarked that despite its many strengths, "a spirit of sympathy with the Southern point of view pervades the volume."[37]

In contemporary parlance, Woodburn's reference to "the Southern point of view" meant that Phillips sympathized with states' rights and the maintenance of white supremacy. For example, Phillips noted that "slavery was distinctly a patriarchal institution," that the bondsmen and bondswomen only rarely "were governed by harsh overseers," and that white Georgians had grown increasingly antislavery in sentiment "until [William Lloyd] Garrison began his raging." Phillips insisted that "a softer side to the slave system" existed "than that which such prejudiced observers as [Frederick Law] Olmsted and Frances Kemble have described." The young historian insisted that his comments were intended not to defend slavery, but rather "to show why the Southern people, who were intimately acquainted with negro character and with the mild nature of his servitude, were less prone to condemn the system than were those who stood afar off and ostentatiously washed their hands of the whole foul business."[38] Phillips suggested that their pragmatic determination to maintain racial control, not party affiliation, motivated white Georgians to leave the Union. To a degree this argument foreshadowed Phillips's point, published years later in a Festschrift dedicated to Turner, that "if we are to interpret correctly the character and career of any political party we must beware of expecting too complete a consonance between their logical interests as we look back upon them and their actions, allegiances, and war-cries."[39]

Phillips's *Georgia and State Rights,* now more than a century old, unequivocally passed the historiographic test of time, having appeared in two reprint editions.[40] It remains a staple in antebellum Georgia historiography. In his revisionist *Cultivating Race: The Expansion of Slavery in Georgia, 1750–1860* (2012), the historian Watson W. Jennison credits Phillips with establishing the thesis that "white Georgians uniformly embraced Indian removal as the only solution to the seemingly intractable dilemma over the state's western lands. Moreover, he noted, the 'Indian question,' never produced any substantive political divisions because all white men could agree on the necessity of expelling the Indians to the lands west of the Mississippi." Since the publication of Phillips's monograph, Jennison maintains, "historians have largely hewed to this argument."[41] Another modern scholar, Anthony Gene Carey, the most recent student of Georgia's secession, finds Phillips's 1902 study "surprisingly useful considering that it is nearly a century old. Phillips concentrates on the period before 1840, is strong on details, and emphasizes . . . the importance of national issues in shaping Georgia party alignments."[42]

Whereas Dunning's other students embedded race, and the alleged inferiority of blacks and the retrogression of the freedpeople, at the center of their interpretations of the postbellum South, Phillips identified slavery as an evolving economic, social, and political force that shaped life and labor in the emerging antebellum South. To a certain degree he both subscribed to and challenged Turner's famous 1893 "frontier thesis." In lectures, for example, before the University of Tennessee's Summer School of the South in 1903, Phillips described Southerners on the move—from

Virginia to Maryland, from Virginia across the trans-Appalachian frontier to Kentucky and Tennessee, from the Carolinas south to Georgia and
then westward across Alabama to the emerging cotton kingdom of the old
Southwest. In every case white Southerners took their institutions, most
notably the plantation system, with them. "They moved into the West after
roads were built, carrying their families, their property, and their slaves.
They also carried their aristocratic ideals and proved a leaven among the
backwoods people."[43]

In his Knoxville lectures Phillips waxed poetic on the virtues of what he
affectionately termed the "plantation régime." Plantation owners ruled and
set the tone for southern life generally. "It was not until within ten or fifteen
years of our own day," he said, "that the democratic element in South Carolina has been able to throw off the control of the aristocratic families." Phillips credited plantation culture with spawning "an unusual class of men and
that planters, notwithstanding their fewness, were the controlling element
in the whole South and indeed of the whole United States for many years."
Phillips lauded the Old South as a "unique civilization" with standards of
behavior and character set by Virginia's first settlers, the Cavaliers. Theirs
were "the high ideals of a country gentleman, individuality and distinction. Their birth and the institution of slavery made them natural leaders
of men," Phillips said. "There was a great tendency to individual independence and a repugnancy toward any use of force."[44]

Many of Phillips's pathbreaking interpretations of slavery and plantation life already were in place by 1909, when he published several seminal
articles in the first multivolume history of the South, the landmark *South
in the Building of the Nation.* Slavery operated less formally, less autocrati-
cally than its critics had assumed, Phillips explained. It was an institution
characterized by "variety" and "considerable elasticity." "The actual régime
was one of government not by laws but by men. In fact each slave was under
a paternalistic despotism, a despotism in the majority of cases benevolent
but in some cases harsh and oppressive, a despotism resented and resisted by
some upon whom it was imposed but borne with light heartedness, submis-
sion and affection by a huge number of the blacks."[45]

Phillips argued that the character of master-slave relations depended
less on laws than on two human factors: "the master's interest, comfort,
principles, and desire for good repute" and "the slave's own character and
attitude." Most interactions between the two, Phillips argued, "were largely
informal, extralegal, and varied widely. The master's interest, however, and

generally his inclination, lay in cultivating the goodwill and affection as well as in preserving the good health of his slaves; for even a slave could be counted upon to do better work from loyalty and in the hope of rewards than from the fear of punishment." No matter what slave laws decreed, Phillips averred, masters lived and worked with their bondsmen and "had to make shift to get along with their slaves. An unfruitful servant could not be discharged."[46] Therein lay Phillips's interpretation of plantation paternalism and the key to his understanding of African American slavery.

In the half dozen years after leaving Columbia in 1902, Phillips published widely, including the pathbreaking *History of Transportation in the Eastern Cotton Belt to 1860* (1908) and fifteen articles. Praising Phillips's book in the *Annals of the American Academy of Political and Social Science,* the University of Pennsylvania's G. G. Huebner commented that the author, "having been a native of the Eastern Cotton Belt, has drawn upon his personal knowledge of the agricultural and geographical conditions which his subject involves, and has been in a position to gather much local information."[47] In these years Phillips also began studying and compiling data on the economic history of slavery. In a draft proposal for a projected three-volume "Economic History of Negro Slavery in North America" (to be coauthored with the Wisconsin political scientist Charles McCarthy), Phillips sketched out the topics that preoccupied him and dominated his research for the next decade and a half.

Phillips found intriguing slavery's protean qualities, the diversity of slave workers, and the essential economic weakness of capitalizing labor. "The South," he explained, "never grew out of the colonial stage of industry in the ante-bellum period." His preliminary research suggested that "slavery was maintained, and slave prices were high, merely because in the lower South the prevailing system promised a greater margin of profit for the time being than any other one easily feasible. It could not last." Phillips observed that slaves consumed too much of the South's wealth. "The competition of planters tended to raise the price of slaves and lower the price of the staples, thereby reducing the margin of profit." In their prospectus Phillips and McCarthy emphasized the importance of defining the economics of slavery broadly and comparatively, thereby showing how slavery influenced all human institutions in the South. "To be of value," they wrote, "the study must be evolutionary and dynamic." Despite their ambitious prospectus, Phillips and McCarthy never published their book.[48]

In 1908 Phillips moved to Tulane, where he excelled in locating and researching plantation documents, census data, and other primary sources. These formed the basis of his monumental documentary edition *Plantation and Frontier Documents: 1649–1863* (two volumes, 1909), a rich compendium of excerpts from planters' diaries, travelers' journals, and merchants' account books. Phillips's friend Alfred Holt Stone, an influential Mississippi planter and economist, praised *Plantation and Frontier* in the *American Historical Review* as "an event of first importance to students of American history and economics." He commended the collection for pinpointing "the economic inertia of the plantation system," in both Old and New Souths, and for providing a "corrective" to false representations of the Old South by chauvinists on both sides of the Mason-Dixon Line.[49] Decades later the historian Fletcher Green considered Phillips's documentary edition "the most important single collection of published source documents on the plantation regime of the pre–Civil War South."[50] In 1911 the University of Michigan, noticing Phillips's rising star, hired him away from New Orleans. He taught in Ann Arbor for eighteen years. In terms of scholarship, these were his most productive years.

In 1913 Phillips published one book and edited another—*The Life of Robert Toombs* and *The Correspondence of Robert Toombs, Alexander H. Stephens, and Howell Cobb.* In a review essay Benjamin B. Kendrick of Columbia University complimented Phillips's biography of Toombs for the distance that the author had established between himself and the famous Georgia fire-eater. According to Kendrick, Phillips "gives without indication of his own feeling the point of view of Toombs in regard to the political issues of his time, and devotes a considerable portion of his attention to setting forth the underlying conditions which caused Toombs and other Southerners to defend slavery and secession."[51]

While at Michigan, Phillips also contributed important articles on comparative slave systems, slave economics, and slave crime. In 1915, for example, he wrote "that in spite of the diminished efficiency of the general run of the negroes, the labor cost per pound of cotton is not so great [today] as it was in 1860, and that there is no tendency toward the unremitting enhancement of the labor-cost ratio such as there was in the slaveholding régime."[52] In his most significant essay in these years, "The Central Theme of Southern History," which appeared in 1928 in the *American Historical Review,* Phillips argued that throughout southern history one theme— southern whites' determination to control blacks—solidified whites of all classes. "Whether expressed with the frenzy of a demagogue or maintained with a patrician's quietude," the core value of white Southerners was "a common resolve, indomitably maintained," that the South "shall be and remain a white man's country."[53]

Phillips took a leave of absence from Michigan during World War I and tested his theories about race relations while volunteering as an educational secretary and superintendent with the Young Men's Christian Association at the U.S. Army's cantonment at Camp Gordon, Georgia, a training facility for black and white troops near Atlanta. In this capacity, what Phillips termed "a roving commission," he worked largely as a cultural affairs officer, supervising the teaching of illiterate soldiers to read and write and of foreign troops to speak English and, to those who expressed interest, elementary French. Phillips joked that his responsibilities consisted mostly of "et ceteras," which afforded him opportunities to engage with black and white recruits in varied settings.[54] Phillips's observations of the men of the two races interacting socially (though "of course quartered separately"), he recalled, "reënforced my earlier conviction that Southern racial asperities are mainly superficial, and that the two great elements are fundamentally in accord. That the harmony is not a new thing is evinced by the very tone of the camp."[55]

That Phillips compared chattel slavery with life in the rigidly segregated U.S. Army suggests that he believed, even a half century after emancipation, that African Americans continued to work best under white control. Like slaves, the black soldiers reportedly excelled at performing rote tasks such as military drill under the discipline of white officers and black non-commissioned officers. According to Phillips, the black men exhibited

the same easy-going, amiable, serio-comic obedience and the same personal attachments to white men, as well as the same sturdy light-heartedness and the same love of laughter and of rhythm, which distinguished their forbears. The non-commissioned officers . . . show a punctilious pride of place which matches that of the plantation foremen of old; and the white officers who succeed best in the command of these companies reflect the planter's admixture of tact with firmness of control, the planter's patience of instruction, and his crisp though cordial reciprocation of sentiment. The negroes are not enslaved but drafted; they dwell not in cabins but in barracks; they shoulder the rifle, not the hoe; but the visitor to their company streets in evening hours enters nevertheless a plantation atmosphere.[56]

Phillips noted approvingly that when relaxing in their barracks (he termed it "the quarter"), the black troops sang "Down by the Riverside." This "old-time unmartial" spiritual contained the refrain "I ain' go' study war no mo' / I ain' go' study war no mo' / Study war no mo'!" Not only did the black solders sing but, according to Phillips, they also gambled mindlessly. "The grim realities of war, though a constant theme in the inculcation of discipline, is as remote in the thought of these men as is the planet Mars," he observed. In Phillips's opinion, "It may be that the change of African nature by plantation slavery has been exaggerated. At any rate a generation of freedom has wrought less transformation in the bulk of the blacks than might casually be supposed."[57] Reviewing Phillips's *American Negro Slavery* (1918), W. E. B. Du Bois was astounded that Phillips saw the black troops at Camp Gordon as radiating the "same easy-going amiable serio-comic obedience" of antebellum slaves. For Phillips the mass of African Americans remained fixed and unchanged from the fourteenth to the twentieth century, Du Bois complained. When Phillips listened to the African American soldiers at Camp Gordon, all he heard was "the throwing of dice."[58]

Like Du Bois, the historian Adriane Lentz-Smith recently has charged that Phillips's observations at Camp Gordon underscore the degree to which racism both blinded him to the progress by African Americans since emancipation and deafened him to the cries of Jim Crow–era blacks for true freedom and justice. As Lentz-Smith observes correctly, "Phillips heard the singing" at Camp Gordon, "but he did not actually listen." He was unattuned both to *why* the men sang—the burdens their people had experienced before, during, and after emancipation—and to *what* they sang. "To truly hear African Americans," she explains, "Phillips would have had to listen past his prejudices, to understand black people as fully human, and to see black troops as men, not children." Ignoring their struggles and accomplishments since emancipation, Phillips overlooked how African Americans had grown and changed. "The system of Jim Crow that Phillips had helped to construct had waged war on black citizenship since the late nineteenth century," Lentz-Smith maintains. To the soldiers "Down by the Riverside" may have signified a range of emotions, from defiance to despair, but, Lentz-Smith adds, "it was never the unthinking, unchanging 'old-time' song that Phillips imagined."[59] According to the historian Sterling Stuckey, both in his observations of blacks at Gordon Camp and in his scholarship, Phillips misinterpreted African Americans as "Sambos." He missed the irony of the singing of the troops he observed just as his myopia blinded him to the barbarities of slavery and Jim Crow–era racism.[60]

Several years after Phillips returned to teach at Michigan, in 1921, reports surfaced that students and faculty at the university had joined the Ku Klux Klan. Phillips responded by denouncing the antiblack, anti-Catholic, anti-Jewish, and anti-immigrant order then making inroads in the Midwest. "An organization which deems it necessary to exist in secret as the K.K.K. order appears to do," he explained in an interview, "in my opinion, has no reason for existing except in extraordinary times. At present there is absolutely no need for such an order."[61] When and which "extraordinary" events would in Phillips's judgment have warranted the Klan's existence?

Years before, Dunning's disciples who studied Reconstruction had explained away the Klan as an unfortunate extralegal force necessary to maintain racial and social control following emancipation. Phillips viewed slavery through a similar lens, interpreting the "peculiar institution" as indispensable to maintain racial order in the Old South. "Plantation slavery," he explained in 1918 in *American Negro Slavery*, "had in strictly business aspects at least as many drawbacks as it had attractions. But in the large it was less a business than a life; it made fewer fortunes than it made men."[62] In 1929, perhaps recalling his observations of black enlistees at Camp Gordon, Phillips likened the corps of slave laborers to "a conscript army, living in barracks and on constant 'fatigue.' Husbands and wives were comrades in service under an authority as complete as the commanding personnel could wish." Though slavery regimented the black workforce, the plantation, in Phillips's opinion, served as "a homestead, isolated, permanent and peopled by a social group with a common interest in achieving and maintaining social order. Its régime was shaped by the customary human forces, interchange of ideas and coadaptation of conduct."[63]

Phillips, as John Herbert Roper and Daniel Joseph Singal have explained, underscored the continuity, based on white supremacy, that connected the Old and New South and southern Progressivism.[64] According to Roper, the Georgia historian's "research was so thorough, his writing so felicitous, and his students so numerous and influential that while he died in 1934, his depiction of a continuous South remained in the 1950s almost an academic commonplace." Roper further notes that as Phillips matured as a historian, he "discarded many of the Progressive assumptions of his training to focus instead on social motivation, that is, genteel racism; and this made Phillips's story of continuity appealing to the consensus era which preferred social to economic analysis, even as it made him repellant to the rapidly growing civil rights movement."[65]

Whereas Dunning, according to David Donald, considered white Southerners' unwillingness to live as political and social equals with blacks "a central theme of Reconstruction history," Phillips applied this thesis to the antebellum South and then to the first New South.[66] The historian Glenda Gilmore recently argued that "Phillips mounted an enormous effort to provide an intellectual justification for the successful white southern political revolution of the 1890s that stripped African Americans of the right to vote, segregated them, and relegated them to the lowest rungs of the economic order."[67] Cognizant of growth and change on the part of black and white Southerners across the emancipation divide, he nonetheless adhered to the Progressive-era ideal of Reconstruction as a tragic mistake and the Old South as a kinder and gentler time of racial adjustment, not conflict—an ideal, according to the historian Margaret Abruzzo, "of mild-mannered masters, happy slaves, and mutual affection."[68] For Phillips the masters' "despotism, so far as it might properly be so called, was benevolent in intent and on the whole beneficial in effect."[69] This was the "cause" that Dodd had observed was so central to Phillips's creed.

Educated in the Dunning School, Phillips in turn spawned the so-called Phillips School of slavery studies that "diffused itself throughout Southern thought" and dominated slavery scholarship until Kenneth M. Stampp published *The Peculiar Institution* in 1956.[70] Both schools came under heavy fire by World War II–era revisionists whose writings overturned historical interpretations of Reconstruction and slavery, respectively. The revisionists' writings, of course, reflected the biases and social agendas of their day, much as the Dunning School historians had in theirs.

Notes

I wish to thank Amanda Binder, Ann Davis, and Lois Stickell, librarians at Atkins Library, University of North Carolina at Charlotte, for obtaining research materials for my use. J. Vincent Lowery generously shared essential items with me. James J. Harris served as my research assistant.

1. Steven Hahn, "African-American Life in the Nineteenth-Century South: "A Review Essay," *Arkansas Historical Quarterly* 50 (Winter 1991): 353.

2. Ulrich Bonnell Phillips, "The Slave Labor Problem in the Charleston District," *Political Science Quarterly* 22 (September 1907): 439.

3. There are two excellent biographies of Phillips: John Herbert Roper, *U. B.*

Phillips: A Southern Mind (Macon, Ga.: Mercer University Press, 1984), and Merton L. Dillon, *Ulrich Bonnell Phillips: Historian of the Old South* (Baton Rouge: Louisiana State University Press, 1985). For an anthology of critical essays on Phillips, see *Ulrich Bonnell Phillips: A Southern Historian and His Critics,* ed. John David Smith and John C. Inscoe (1990; reprint, Athens: University of Georgia Press, 1993).

4. R. Blakeslee Gilpin, *John Brown Still Lives! America's Long Reckoning with Violence, Equality, and Change* (Chapel Hill: University of North Carolina Press, 2011), 229–30n64. Phillips in fact never held a regular teaching appointment at Columbia. He taught summer school there in 1916 and 1928. See Ulrich B. Phillips to Yates Snowden, July 23, 1916, and May 28, 1928, Yates Snowden Papers, South Caroliniana Library, University of South Carolina, Columbia.

5. Saunders Redding to the Editor, *New York Times,* June 28, 1964, BR 24.

6. William E. Dodd to Mr. Chapin, November 17, 1925, William E. Dodd Papers, Manuscript Division, Library of Congress, Washington, D.C.

7. Ulrich B. Phillips, "Plantations with Slave Labor and Free," *American Historical Review* 30 (July 1925): 748–49.

8. Ulrich Bonnell Phillips, *Life and Labor in the Old South* (Boston: Little, Brown, 1929), 366.

9. Ulrich B. Phillips, "Memorial Day Address," *Yale Alumni Weekly,* June 5, 1931, 968. For context, see John David Smith, "U. B. Phillips, the North Carolina Literary and Historical Association, and the Course of the South to Secession," *North Carolina Historical Review* 87 (July 2010): 253–82.

10. Ulrich B. Phillips, "Railway Transportation in the South" in *The South in the Building of the Nation: A History of the Southern States Designed to Record the South's Part in the Making of the American Nation; to Portray the Character and Genius, to Chronicle the Achievements and Progress and to Illustrate the Life and Traditions of the Southern People,* ed. Julian A. C. Chandler et al., 12 vols. (Richmond: Southern Historical Publication Society, 1909), 6:307. Phillips referred to John C. and D. N. Stanton, Boston capitalists who, with state funding, built the Alabama and Chattanooga Railroad Company. It later defaulted on its state-funded bonds.

11. Ulrich B. Phillips, "The Central Theme of Southern History," *American Historical Review* 24 (October 1928): 40–42.

12. Ulrich B. Phillips, "Conservatism and Progress in the Cotton Belt," *South Atlantic Quarterly* 3 (January 1904): 4.

13. Ulrich B. Phillips, "The Plantation as a Civilizing Factor," *Sewanee Review* 12 (July 1904): 266.

14. Ulrich B. Phillips, "The Decadence of the Plantation System," *Annals of the American Academy of Political and Social Science* 35 (January 1910): 40.

15. William H. Carpenter to Ulrich B. Phillips, October 16, 1907, Ulrich B. Phillips Papers, Southern Historical Collection, University of North Carolina at Chapel Hill; Ulrich Bonnell Phillips, *A History of Transportation in the Eastern Cotton Belt to 1860* (New York: Columbia University Press, 1908), dedication.

16. Edwin C. Woolley, *The Reconstruction of Georgia* (New York: Columbia University Press, 1901).

17. Ulrich B. Phillips, review of Edwin C. Woolley, *The Reconstruction of Georgia*, in *Atlanta Constitution*, June 30, 1901, 11.

18. Ibid.

19. Ulrich B. Phillips, review of Edwin C. Woolley, *The Reconstruction of Georgia*, in *Publications of the Southern History Association* 6 (January 1902): 176.

20. Ulrich B. Phillips, "Economic and Political Essays in the Antebellum South," in Chandler et al., *The South in the Building of the Nation*, 7:190.

21. David Donald, "Introduction to the Torchbook Edition," in William A. Dunning, *Essays on the Civil War and Reconstruction* (1898; reprint, New York: Harper & Row, 1965), xi.

22. In a 1964 book review Saunders Redding charged Charles E. Silberman, editor of *Fortune* magazine and author of *Crisis in Black and White*, with confining his historical research to works by what he termed "the notoriously biased Columbia school of historians, led by Ulrich B. Phillips." Saunders Redding, "A Reply," *New York Times*, June 28, 1964, BR 24. See Redding's review of Silberman's book, "Some Facts of the Matter," ibid., May 31, 1964, BR 7, 20.

23. Ulrich B. Phillips to Yates Snowden, October 15 and September 20, 1904, Snowden Papers. Sloane (1850–1928), a distinguished French historian, held the Seth Low Professorship in History, founded the U.S. Olympic Committee, and served as president of the American Historical Association in 1911. See "Columbia's New Professor: William M. Sloane of Princeton to Take the Chair of History," *New York Times*, November 17, 1896, 9.

24. Phillips to Snowden, January 13, 1905, Snowden Papers. Phillips referred to Burgess's *The Middle Period, 1817–1858* (1897). Giddings (1855–1931) was a renowned sociologist who joined the Columbia faculty in 1894. He served as president of the American Sociological Association, 1910–11.

25. William A. Dunning to Frederick Jackson Turner, April 20, 1902, Frederick Jackson Turner Correspondence, University of Wisconsin Archives.

26. William A. Dunning to Gentlemen, April 17, 1903, Ulrich B. Phillips folder, Carnegie Institution of Washington Archives, Washington, D.C. On Phillips and primary sources for the study of southern history, see John David Smith, "'Keep 'em in a fire-proof vault'—Pioneer Southern Historians Discover Plantation Records," *South Atlantic Quarterly* 78 (Summer 1979): 376–91; John David Smith, "The Historian as Archival Advocate: Ulrich Bonnell Phillips and the Records of Georgia and the South," *American Archivist* 52 (Summer 1989): 320–31; and John David Smith, "Ulrich Bonnell Phillips's *Plantation and Frontier:* The Historian as Documentary Editor," *Georgia Historical Quarterly* 77 (Spring 1993): 123–43.

27. Ulrich B. Phillips to J. G. de Roulhac Hamilton, April 25, 1911, J. G. de Roulhac Hamilton Papers, Southern Historical Collection, Louis Round Wilson Special Collections Library, University of North Carolina at Chapel Hill.

28. Charles W. Ramsdell to J. G. de Roulhac Hamilton, April 20, 1911, and March 4, 1913; James W. Garner to Hamilton, February 27 and March 1, 1913; Walter Lynwood Fleming to Hamilton, March 1, 1913; Garner to Hamilton, September 23 and 27, 1913; and Ramsdell to Hamilton, December 3, 1913, all in Hamilton Papers.

29. Ulrich B. Phillips to Claude H. Van Tyne, February 15, 1914, Claude H. Van Tyne Papers, Bentley Historical Library, Michigan Historical Collections, University of Michigan.

30. Ulrich Bonnell Phillips, "The Traits and Contributions of Frederick Jackson Turner," *Agricultural History* 19 (January 1945): 21. Mrs. Phillips's quote derives from a headnote appended by Everett E. Edwards to Phillips's posthumous publication.

31. See Phillips's telling anecdote about Turner in Avery O. Craven, "Some Historians I Have Known," *Maryland Historian* 1 (Spring 1970): 11.

32. John Herbert Roper, "Introduction to the ROSE Edition," in Ulrich B. Phillips, *Georgia and State Rights* (1902; reprint, Macon, Ga.: Mercer University Press, 1984), xvii.

33. Ulrich Bonnell Phillips, *Georgia and State Rights: A Study of the Political History of Georgia from the Revolution to the Civil War, with Particular Regard to Federal Relations* (Washington, D.C.: Government Printing Office, 1902), 5. No copies of Phillips's master's thesis, "Georgia and State Rights" (University of Georgia, 1899), exist. But Roper maintains that it appeared as chapters 4 and 5 in *Georgia and State Rights*. See Roper, "Ulrich Bonnell Phillips: His Life and Thought" (Ph.D. diss., University of North Carolina at Chapel Hill, 1977), 224, and Roper, "Introduction to the ROSE Edition," xvi.

34. Phillips, *Georgia and State Rights*, 107, 192, 207.

35. Ibid., 6. Sixty-nine, or almost 47 percent of Phillips's 148 newspaper citations in the book, derived from the *Federal Union*.

36. "A LaGrange Boy Wins Great Honors in Windsor [sic] Prize," *La Grange (Ga.) Reporter*, January 3, 1902, 1.

37. James A. Woodburn, review of Ulrich Bonnell Phillips, *Georgia and State Rights*, in *American Historical Review* 8 (July 1903): 786.

38. Phillips, *Georgia and State Rights*, 154, 158, 154–55.

39. Ulrich Bonnell Phillips, "The Southern Whigs, 1834–1854," in *Essays in American History Dedicated to Frederick Jackson Turner*, ed. Guy Stanton Ford (New York: Henry Holt, 1910), 203.

40. In addition to the Mercer University Press edition (with an introduction by John Herbert Roper) cited above, see Ulrich B. Phillips, *Georgia and State Rights* (Antioch, Ohio: Antioch Press, 1968). This edition includes Louis Filler's introduction, "Ulrich B. Phillips: A Question of History and Reality," v–xiv.

41. Watson W. Jennison, *Cultivating Race: The Expansion of Slavery in Georgia, 1750–1860* (Lexington: University Press of Kentucky, 2012), 370n1. Contrary to Phillips and later scholars, Jennison argues that white Georgians "were divided

along class and regional lines and over their thoughts concerning the proper treatment of the Indians, their abilities to assimilate into American culture, the modes of their removal, and their place in society" (189).

42. Anthony Gene Carey, *Parties, Slavery, and the Union in Antebellum Georgia* (Athens: University of Georgia Press, 1997), xvii.

43. Ulrich B. Phillips lecture transcriptions, 1903, Philander P. Claxton Papers, Special Collections Library, University of Tennessee, Knoxville. They contain variant titles and nonconsecutive pagination. On Phillips's teaching at the Summer School of the South, see Dillon, *Ulrich Bonnell Phillips*, 48–49.

44. Phillips lecture transcriptions, 1903, Claxton Papers.

45. Ulrich Bonnell Phillips, "Racial Problems, Adjustments and Disturbances," in Chandler et al., *The South in the Building of the Nation*, 4:226, 200.

46. Ibid., 201, 202, 206.

47. G. G. Huebner, review of Ulrich B. Phillips, *History of Transportation in the Eastern Cotton Belt to 1860*, in *Annals of the American Academy of Political and Social Science* 33 (March 1909): 252.

48. Charles McCarthy and Ulrich B. Phillips, "The Economic History of Negro Slavery in North America," unpublished manuscript, n.d., Ulrich B. Phillips Papers, Sterling Memorial Library, Yale University.

49. Alfred Holt Stone, review of Ulrich B. Phillips, ed., *Plantation and Frontier Documents: 1649–1863*, in *American Historical Review* 16 (October 1910): 138, 139.

50. Fletcher M. Green, ed., *Ferry Hill Plantation Journal, January 4, 1838–January 15, 1839* (Chapel Hill: University of North Carolina Press, 1961), vii.

51. Benjamin B. Kendrick, "Toombs and Stevens," *Political Science Quarterly* 29 (September 1914): 491.

52. Ulrich B. Phillips, "Black-Belt Labor Slave and Free," in *Lectures and Addresses on the Negro in the South* (Charlottesville: Michie, 1915), 35.

53. Phillips, "The Central Theme of Southern History," 30–43.

54. "Letters from the Front," *Michigan Alumnus* 24 (December 1917): 151–52; (February 1918): 283–84.

55. Ulrich Bonnell Phillips, *American Negro Slavery: A Survey of the Supply, Employment and Control of Negro Labor as Determined by the Plantation Régime* (New York: D. Appleton, 1918), [ii].

56. Ibid.

57. Ibid., [ii–iii].

58. W. E. B. Du Bois, review of Ulrich B. Phillips, *American Negro Slavery: A Survey of the Supply, Employment and Control of Negro Labor as Determined by the Plantation Régime*, in *American Political Science Review* 12 (November 1918): 723.

59. Adriane Lentz-Smith, *Freedom Struggles: African Americans and World War I* (Cambridge: Harvard University Press, 2009), 2.

60. Sterling Stuckey, "From the Bottom Up: Herbert Aptheker's *American Negro Slave Revolts* and *A Documentary History of the Negro People in the United*

States," in *African American History and Radical Historiography: Essays in Honor of Herbert Aptheker,* ed. Herbert Shapiro (Minneapolis: MEP Publications, 1998), 41–43.

61. "The Ku Klux Klan at U. of M.," *Michigan Daily Sunday Magazine,* October 2, 1921, 1; "Ku Klux Klan of 50 Said to Exist in College Faculty," *New York World,* October 2, 1921, clippings in Tuskegee Institute News File, 1899–1988 (reel 13, 1921), Tuskegee University Archives.

62. Phillips, *American Negro Slavery,* 401.

63. Phillips, *Life and Labor in the Old South,* 196.

64. John Herbert Roper, "A Case of Forgotten Identity: Ulrich B. Phillips as a Young Progressive," *Georgia Historical Quarterly* 60 (Summer 1976): 165–75, and Daniel Joseph Singal, "Ulrich B. Phillips: The Old South as the New," *Journal of American History* 63 (March 1977): 871–91.

65. John Herbert Roper, *C. Vann Woodward, Southerner* (Athens: University of Georgia Press, 1987), 144.

66. Donald, "Introduction to the Torchbook Edition," xii.

67. Glenda Gilmore, "Which Southerners? Which Southern Historians? A Century of Southern History at Yale," *Yale Review* 99 (January 2011): 57.

68. Margaret Abruzzo, *Polemical Pain: Slavery, Cruelty, and the Rise of Humanitarianism* (Baltimore: Johns Hopkins University Press, 2011), 236.

69. Phillips, *American Negro Slavery,* 328.

70. Stanley M. Elkins, *Slavery: A Problem in American Institutional and Intellectual Life* (1959; reprint, New York: Universal Library, 1963), 13–16. The historian E. Merton Coulter identified a cadre of scholars who followed Phillips's lead as early as 1934. See Coulter's review of Ralph B. Flanders, *Plantation Slavery in Georgia,* in *Mississippi Valley Historical Review* 21 (June 1934): 95–96. The fullest analysis of the extent and influence of the so-called Phillips School appears in Robert William Fogel and Stanley L. Engerman, *Time on the Cross: Evidence and Methods* (Boston: Little, Brown, 1974), 178–247.

5

The Steel Frame of Walter Lynwood Fleming

Michael W. Fitzgerald

It was a professional experience with which present-day authors might feel an uneasy sympathy. Walter Fleming, at age thirty-one, had just published his first and most significant work, *Civil War and Reconstruction in Alabama* (1905). The liberal journal of opinion the *Nation* found the book worthy of an extended review, which would have seemed promising news save that the editor was Oswald Garrison Villard. The grandson of the abolitionist William Lloyd Garrison and himself a future founder of the NAACP, Villard branded the work a piece of southern propaganda. Proslavery assumptions and regional defensiveness provided "the steel frame" of Fleming's analysis. The editor termed the approach incredible because it assumed that only conservative white Southerners could understand black people, slave or free. Villard conceded Fleming's industriousness, but in barbed fashion: "No possible field of information which he has desired to acquire seems to have been left unexplored." Villard even likened Fleming's biased practice of history to an efficient guillotine. All northern testimony was disregarded, unless it backed the southern version of events, in which case it was summarily accepted. After all this, Villard scornfully concluded, "And yet there are people who deny that history is a science!"[1]

Faced with a damaging critique, the fledgling historian apparently tried to cushion the blow. Fleming had written to Villard, assuring him of his relative political moderation, but the editor's response suggested that contemporary developments would fuel his irate commentary. "I wish the Southern people could awake to a realization of the injury being done them by the abuse of the Negro by conscienceless politicians of the Tillman and Vardaman stripe," Villard wrote.[2] In view of what was happening in turn-of-the-century Alabama, when disfranchisement and even peonage were in the news, Fleming needn't have bothered with denials, because the work had obvious contemporary overtones. Disfranchisement was the "long-finished work of necessity," the culmination of white resistance to Reconstruction, and Fleming ended the book with an appendix demonstrating its effect. Fleming expressed no misgivings, save that he doubted that the new 1901 disfranchisement constitution had permanently eliminated all black influence.[3] Small wonder that the author Myrta Lockett Avery counseled a nervous Fleming, "Of course the 'Nation' will roast you! There will not be a cinder left."[4]

Though Villard's critique was unusually pointed, it was not the only muted commentary Fleming's work received. In 1905 the Dunning School's scholarly predominance was not that pervasive in public discourse, at least not in its more uninhibited formulations. One academic reviewer scorned the personal tone of Fleming's book: Reconstruction had not been "fully completed in his own case."[5] The *New York Times* review, by the historian William E. Dodd, agreed with the emerging Dunning School's approach, and he was impressed with the industrious research of Fleming's eight-hundred-page work. Still, Fleming was "not unpartisan in his judgments, however accurate his statement of fact." The *Times* headlined the review "An Alabamian's View of the Contest," an observation that reflected an undertone of much of the commentary.[6] William A. Dunning privately wrote that Fleming had gone a bit far, and he commented in print on Fleming's masses of evidence as having a "marked southern bias in their interpretation," surely not the kind of statement one desires from a mentor.[7] The public commentary was so sharp that Fleming received sympathy letters from white Southerners with similar views. Lockett helpfully suggested that the hostile reviews would help gain attention for the book and increase its sales.[8] Another correspondent added that anything about African Americans was a red flag to Villard and his associates. Still, he concluded, "That fellow Dodd's article in the N.Y. Times is more reprehensible for he is a Southerner!"[9]

The bruising reception of Fleming's first book initiated the pattern of a lifetime. Given northern predominance in the national press, regional tensions remained professionally salient, which encouraged the defensive tone of his writing. And as critics frequently suggested, his own personal background fueled his historical scholarship, though in more subtle ways than generally depicted. Walter L. Fleming was born in Brundidge, in Pike County, in April 1874, the very year of Reconstruction's overthrow in Alabama. He was the grandson of a middling landowner who held two slaves in 1860.[10] Fleming thus was not of a planter background, as the historian Sarah Wiggins points out, and he lived in the poorer southeastern region of the state, just beyond the wealthy plantation belt. This liminal social position perhaps influenced his scholarship, encouraging reflection on white Alabama's interconnected class and geographic divisions. Regardless, Fleming fell heir to strong Confederate loyalties; his youthful father had served briefly in the cavalry, and his family was prosperous enough to have both black and white tenants after the war. Fleming came of age in the midst of the agrarian revolt of the 1890s, and he worked the fields himself until age twenty.[11] Fleming's personal response to Populism is unclear, but he apparently imbibed some of the grievances of his insurgent region; his work emphasized Alabama's underlying tension between the rich plantation belt areas and the poorer, white-dominated counties. His Reconstruction book concluded that the black belt had long had "an undue and disturbing influence in white politics" because the Fifteenth Amendment had given that section enhanced representation, along with black votes that could be counted however the planters chose. Fleming recurrently depicted the racial politics of Reconstruction as superimposed on this long-standing regional conflict.[12]

Fleming attended college at Alabama Polytechnic Institute (later Auburn University), becoming a star student at a then nonelite institution; he taught in the public schools before serving in the Spanish-American War.[13] Promoted by faculty mentors, Fleming was admitted in 1900 to the graduate program at Columbia University, under William A. Dunning, the era's premier scholar of Reconstruction. He completed his studies with dispatch; Fleming was hired at West Virginia University in 1903, finishing his dissertation in 1904 and his book the following year. Despite this objective success, he experienced considerable discomfort during his sojourn in New York. A colleague recalled the older Fleming as inarticulate in extemporized public speech, no matter how brief, and as having a tendency toward blunt expression; these traits may have made the young Southerner's classroom experience difficult, and sectional tensions certainly contributed to his unease. Seminar discussions with Northerners were heated to the point of potential fisticuffs, and Dunning too noted that his student wasn't "any too much reconstructed himself."[14] In 1902 Fleming wrote to Alabama's governor for copies of the new state constitution, observing, "I have some rather rampant Republican acquaintances to whom I want to show it. The most of them seem to think that it disfranchises at once & forever all negroes whether educated, or property holders, or not."[15] Fleming sought to defend the disfranchisement constitution of 1901 against the charge of improperly restricting the suffrage. Technically, he was right: all of 2 percent of the state's black male population could register to vote, as his book would demonstrate. Skeptics could hardly be pacified by actual inspection of the document, which suggests a certain intellectual isolation on Fleming's part.[16]

Despite the overall prosouthern interpretation of the work of Dunning and his students, Fleming seemingly had something more to prove, for a mixture of personal and intellectual reasons. He did not confidently assert an ideological position, the merit of which ought to be apparent to all; he was only half expecting external readers to be persuaded, and he wasn't going to coddle them. Northern criticism contributed to Fleming's association of his southern identity with an unyielding defense of white supremacy. Strong rhetoric thus peppered his published work from the beginning. For instance, in 1905 an essay appeared in *Political Science Quarterly* that encouraged immigration to the southern states. Fleming's piece won editorial notice in the South, in part because it boldly proclaimed free labor a failure: "The negro cannot furnish either in quality or in quantity the labor necessary to develop the South. By its lack of initiative and inventive genius the black race has acted as a hindrance to progress." Whatever the merits of this viewpoint as agricultural history, the tone reflects his mindset as he approached his study of Reconstruction. "Agricultural development in the black belt is at a standstill because of the worthlessness of the black and the difficulty of getting more white labor," he crisply concluded.[17]

This, then, is the intellectual grounding of Fleming's major work, *Civil War and Reconstruction in Alabama*. Modern readers generally bridle at both the tone and substance. Physical inspection of aging copies at university libraries will probably reveal a century's aggregation of underlined passages, occasionally studded with exclamation marks. The book provided negative inspiration to generations of revisionists. Still, Fleming's congruence of personal and scholarly viewpoint explains its peculiar usefulness. His forthright hostility to Reconstruction facilitated the recovery of white oral testimony and written sources. Letters to him were often reproduced, accurately and at length. His certainty that the evidence bore his position out to all unprejudiced (southern, white) observers made him present material that more judicious advocates might have obscured. Fleming's work also furnishes modern readers with a bracing immersion in a different array of racial presuppositions, often fruitful in its own right. Finally, Sarah Wiggins still spoke for the profession in her 1978 comment that "Fleming had the courage to tackle a survey of the entire Civil War and Reconstruction period in Alabama, a feat none of the rest of us have had the nerve to attempt."[18] The book improbably remains the only substantial political survey of the Reconstruction era in Alabama, and so it is the obvious starting point for scholars. Because it is the basis of Fleming's scholarship and reputation, it requires extended discussion here.

Despite the speed with which it was produced, less than five years, the work was considered well executed by the standards of the time. More recent historians echo this perception, perhaps in deference to the work's bricklike heft. By modern scholarly standards, however, there are issues. Fleming provides no bibliography, but it appears that he examined primarily newspapers and other published sources available to him in New York City. I have been unable to find a single manuscript source cited in the book.[19] He did not consult the unusually complete Alabama governors' correspondence, laden with evidence of violence. Nor does the huge Freedmen's Bureau correspondence appear, even though other scholars were using it. To be fair, archival collection of manuscripts was just beginning at this time, and Fleming himself took an active interest in furthering that cause, in Alabama and elsewhere.[20] His lack of manuscript sources is not exceptional by comparison to other Dunning students, but it bears interpretive significance. The book's research may not be thin, but it is narrow, because it relies heavily on the press. Fleming omitted the manuscript sources replete with Republican victims' testimony, which might have moderated his findings.

Fleming faithfully articulated the viewpoint of the sources he most trusted, ex-Confederates and states' rights Democrats. He took evident pains with his manuscript, printing several sections in regional publications such as the *Gulf States Historical Magazine*. For the book these portions were stylistically altered but not interpretively changed, which suggests they expressed his considered reflection. Publishing in such journals credentialed him with a southern constituency, and he solicited assistance from readers for his "elaborate History of Reconstruction in Alabama," noting that he had spared neither time nor expense in gathering material.[21] Fleming did occasionally seek the insight of former Republican leaders, in one case negotiating with an aging carpetbagger over the cost of the ex-politician's sending the historian his reflections on the era. He also interviewed the

Freedmen's Bureau head in Alabama, General Wager Swayne, in 1901.[22] Fleming conceded that he was "an intelligent, educated man" despite his lack of sympathy for southern principles. Fleming's surprisingly favorable impression of Swayne probably tainted him in the eyes of later historians, who have been critical of the patrician general for excessive moderation. Fleming's willingness to hear conflicting interpretations, however, was limited to those of white Republicans. He referred repeatedly to conversations with aging freedmen, but there is no evidence he sought the viewpoint of African American political leaders.

The book's unusual length reflects its intellectual ambition: he called it "a general history with especial reference to local conditions in Alabama." His mentor, Dunning, emphasized constitutional issues, but Fleming had a different perspective. His animating conviction was that Reconstruction politics was really about the preservation of the prevailing racial order. Here, perhaps, he benefited from firsthand testimony; at the level of individual white recollections, face-to-face interaction with the freedmen loomed large. Thus, he interlaced his political narrative with separate chapters on the economic, social, and even religious history of the state to an extent that reviewers found repetitive. Today's readers will probably be more impressed with his depiction of a global challenge to established racial mores. In his introduction he anticipated criticism for paying so much attention to race, preemptively responding that "after all the negro, whether passive or active, was the central figure of the period."[23]

Emancipation is the core issue of the book, but the influence of slavery on the development of Alabama is another central theme. Despite the importance of this work in the historiography of Reconstruction, well over the first third is about the prewar and wartime period, and in general the work tilts toward the early years of the era. As Fleming explained, "It seemed to me that an account of ante-bellum conditions, social, economic, and political, . . . would be indispensable to any just and comprehensive treatment of the later period."[24] This reflects Fleming's conviction that the Reconstruction issues grew out of overlapping regional and class divisions in the state, between the Whiggish planters of the south-central black belt and the more egalitarian Jacksonian small farmers of northern Alabama. He saw the latter section as more prone to antisecession views, disaffection with the Confederacy, and, after the war, quasi-Unionist ambivalence toward Reconstruction; south Alabama, by contrast, less touched by battle and occupation, remained identified with the Confederacy and its legacy. He generally avoided choosing sides in this geographic dispute, but he approved of those who subordinated narrow self-interest to the wider goal of racial unity under the umbrella of the Democratic Party.

Stripped of their turn-of-the-century intellectual baggage, these emphases deserve serious consideration. Unfortunately for Fleming's reputation, the tenor of his expression obscures the merit of his arguments for modern readers. For example, his awareness of class divisions manifests itself in a harsh tone toward wartime and postwar white dissidents. "Tories," or Unionists, were "an unpleasant and violent part of the population." During the Civil War Fleming's southeastern wiregrass region of the state experienced considerable draft resistance, and the local memories may have sharpened his rhetoric. He noted that the "social contempt" against wartime Unionists extended even to their grandchildren.[25] Draft resisters in the mountains were "shut off from the world, a century behind the times," and their alienation and general depravity moved them to support Reconstruction. "To-day," he concluded, "those people are represented by the makers of 'moonshine' whiskey and those who shoot revenue officers."[26] Confederate conscription meant that the best men went into the army, never to return, whereas "a class of people the country could well have spared survived to assist a second time in the ruin of their country in the darker days of Reconstruction."[27] For Fleming, it would seem, the very existence of Unionists and scalawags might have been dispensed with altogether.

Similar authorial statements mark the text, especially in the footnotes. "Any stick is good enough to beat slavery with," he observed in a historiographic aside.[28] Carpetbaggers come in for particular attention, and one suspects that his sojourn in New York City colored his rhetoric and his perception that outsiders were incapable of grasping southern realities. Fleming began his discussion of federal occupation with a long discussion of postwar frauds in captured cotton undertaken by soldiers, treasury agents, and others. This characterization has considerable merit, but other Northerners come in for substantial criticism with less justification. Most of those who testified before Congress in 1866 were "ignorant, prejudiced officers of volunteers from the West." The chapter on the Freedmen's Bureau starts off by placing it among the causes of disorder, while minimizing the wave of violence the agency attempted to repress. Fleming saw no beneficial effect for the agency, rather the contrary.[29]

As for the freedpeople, Fleming's satiric bent interacted unfortunately with his racial views. The emancipated slave "did not feel that he was really free" until he sued someone, Fleming averred, and numbers of such statements enliven the text. Fleming contended that slaves were about as faithful to the Confederacy as their masters were. During Presidential Reconstruction, legislation to regulate the freedpeople's labor was essential, because they insisted on living without work. Though the resulting Black Codes were ill-timed politically, "it would have been well for the negro if they had been passed into law and enforced."[30] Often Fleming's statements reflect the imprint of the concerns of his own time. "The negro was as wax in the hands of a stronger race," he observed. This makes little sense in view of his emphasis on malign black agency during Reconstruction, but the more recent fraudulent manipulation of black votes to beat back the Populist revolt in Alabama probably explains his emphasis.[31]

Now, it is the nature of such a distillation of quotations to sharpen an author's viewpoint, perhaps unfairly. Still, arresting statements abound, and perhaps his middling-class background made it difficult to assume a consistent paternalistic tone that might have served him better professionally. Strong expressions abound in his writing, which contributed to his reception as an unreconstructed Southerner. His observations touching on gender are difficult to read today. As freedwomen moved to the cities, he wrote, "immorality was general among them." Furthermore, "Upon the negro woman fell the burden of supporting the children. Her husband or husbands had other duties." This plural usage is open to a variety of readings, mostly unedifying, but Fleming concluded with an unambiguous observation: "Children then began to be unwelcome and foeticide and child murder were common crimes."[32] No footnote burdens this passage.

With reference to black suffrage, Fleming burlesqued the idea of intentional political participation. He spent a chapter on the Union League, the Republican organization that epitomized the points Fleming chose to stress. The secret leagues facilitated "absolute control" of the freedman by alien adventurers from the North. Fleming emphasized the "weird initiation ceremony" that made the freedman "feel fearfully good from his head to his heels."[33] He explained that alcohol on salt burns with a peculiar flame that made the faces of the freedmen appear ghostly, a key to the effect. The point is that the new voters had no idea what they were doing. Freedmen were told "that if they did not vote they would be reenslaved and their wives made to work the roads and quit wearing hoopskirts." Despite his statement that most freedmen behaved remarkably well under these teachings,

Fleming concluded that the league prompted terrorism because some of the methods of the Loyal League were similar to those of the Ku Klux Klan.[34] The statement is literally true, in that they both were oath-bound groups, but it equates a boisterous electoral organization with a terrorist movement.

The narrative of Reconstruction politics occupies much of the book, and Fleming generally followed the Dunning School outline. Reconstruction broadly was an era of corruption and government extravagance, fueled by the demands of the newly enfranchised freedmen and their preference for northern-origin leadership. He emphasized Alabama's conflict within the Republican Party between the moderate "scalawag" faction of Governor William H. Smith and his northern-origin and African American "Radical" opposition, led by U.S. Senator George E. Spencer. Fleming viewed Spencer with evident distaste, seeing him as the stereotypic carpetbagger, with some justification. Fleming's preference for Governor Smith, however, appears premised largely on the notion that despite his Unionism, Smith "shared the dislike of his class for negroes."[35] Governor Smith was perhaps the most conservative of the Republican Reconstruction governors, and his social acceptability to white Democrats credentialed him in Fleming's eyes. He used Smith's opportunism to illustrate the southern racial consensus: no native white could legitimately feel that the Democrats were intransigent on racial or sectional issues, and the Unionist governor's evident hypocrisy demonstrated it.

Fleming placed interpretive stress on the financial ruin Reconstruction brought, emphasizing carpetbagger profligacy and irresponsible Republican legislators, white and black. During the Reconstruction era, state and local taxes skyrocketed, and Alabama's debt went from about $7 million to $30 million during Governor Smith's administration. The bulk of the money went to endorsement of railroad projects, whose eventual failure indeed bankrupted the state. Fleming's assessment of the fiscal record of Republican rule is broadly accurate, and legislative corruption indeed seems to have been common; overenthusiastic modern revisionists find tough going in defending Alabama's railroad Reconstruction. The problem for Fleming was that his leading carpetbagger, Senator Spencer, had little direct involvement in the administration of the railroad policies. Nor did the freedmen or their leaders. Governor Smith and his favored moderate faction did, along with numerous bipartisan collaborators. Fleming did conclude that Smith was a poor financial administrator, "criminally careless" in his implementation of the railroad law.[36] Still, Fleming emphasized Radical fiscal irresponsibility and Governor Smith's relative budgetary restraint. Fleming also termed Smith personally honest, dubiously. Nothing contradicts his narrative of black and carpetbagger irresponsibility, even the evident malfeasance of a racially conservative scalawag governor.

The more sensitive interpretive point raised by *Civil War and Reconstruction in Alabama* is the depiction of the Ku Klux Klan, the White Leagues, and racist violence. Most Reconstruction scholars, writing in the midst of an era of lynching and race riots, shied away from outright celebration of terrorists. However much they sympathized with the grievances that inspired violence, the emphasis was more on political and legal means of resistance. Edwin C. Woolley's 1901 study of Georgia concedes that attacks on freedmen were numerous, contradicting Democratic denials. James Garner's study of Mississippi, that same year, refrains from positive endorsement of the Klan at least. Fleming responded very differently. As J. Vincent Lowery recently noted, Fleming was the Dunning student most inclined to espouse the Klan with vigor and to celebrate its accomplishments.[37]

Morality aside, there are instructive aspects to Fleming's treatment of terrorists' "counter-revolution." For one thing, Fleming took few pains to minimize the extent: "In one sense practically all able-bodied native white men belonged to the order, and if social and business ostracism can be considered as a manifestation of the Ku Klux spirit, then the women and children were also Ku Klux." Fleming's treatment of terrorism is so discursive that themes rather than outright argumentation emerge, but several points stand out. Fleming sharply distinguished between the early Klan, in which the best men were members, and the later spurious Klan, which often undertook undisciplined violence to gratify private ends, or enlisted poorer men motivated by economic rivalry and crude racism. The class animus evident elsewhere in his writing is apparent here; Fleming even claimed that in the hills the spurious Klan bands were "largely composed" of Radicals and former Union men, though the evidence is thin. Fleming contended that Nathan Bedford Forrest officially disbanded the formal Klan around early 1869, and that the more respectable planter elements left it about then. Fleming largely acquitted the political elite of direct control of the terrorist movement, though in the case of the Knights of the White Camelia (which Fleming spells Camilia), strongest in the black belt, he was not so sure. Fleming depicted two terrorist movements, an uninhibited one in the up-country and a more restrained one in the plantation belt. Still, overall, "it was the middle classes, so to speak, and later the lower classes, who felt more severely the tyranny of carpet-bag rule, who formed and led the Klan."[38]

Fleming had much more to say about the goals and composition of the Klan than most of his scholarly contemporaries, and Lowery recently concluded that he was the most significant turn-of-the-century interpreter. If modern readers can disentangle Fleming's racial views from what he had to say, there are a number of instructive elements. He corresponded with several former Klan leaders, among them the homicidal Ryland Randolph, editor, state representative, and head of the Tuscaloosa Klan. Fleming's approach facilitated candid admissions of the activities of such former Klansmen, letters that were quoted at length in his footnotes and remain accessible in his papers.[39] Fleming described a multifaceted terrorist movement, political, social, and economic, that was responding to the profound challenge of emancipation. As he concluded, "It was not so much a revolution as a conquest of revolution. Society was bent back into the old historic grooves from which war and Reconstruction had jarred it."[40] Revisionists like Eric Foner could hardly have stated the case better themselves.

Fleming's reading of the evidence, though, has less to commend it. He drew on three dense volumes of congressional Klan testimony, but he generally accepted the Democratic version and the few Republicans who minimized the terror. Democrats tended to talk about social grievances, Republicans about Klansmen's actions, and he was more interested in the former. Fleming subsumed misdeeds under an occasional reference to excesses, undertaken mostly by spurious Klansmen. Only native Southerners, it seems, could understand the evidence: "The negro testimony, however worthless it may appear at first sight, becomes clear to any one who, knowing the negro mind, remembers the influences then operating upon it."[41] Fleming dismissed freedmen as congenitally untruthful, even when describing widely acknowledged killings. Furthermore, Fleming was harsh on the congressional inquisitors of the Klan and their testimony. He assailed the "delightfully partisan" index, which is admittedly more focused on violence than Democratic explanations. Congressmen summoned poor witnesses, especially "ignorant negroes who could only tell what they had heard or had feared." Scholars need to mine the dense testimony themselves, because Fleming scanted evidence that contradicts his central themes.

These are among the major points of Fleming's most important work, though, given its length, there are certainly others. For instance, the chapter on postwar denominational rivalries is still valuable for his description of a religious Reconstruction that largely paralleled the political struggle. His chapter on the postwar plantation reflects on decades of rural change, informed by his own experience growing up on the farm. On the other hand, the politics of the 1870s receives short shrift, and one suspects that Fleming concluded that the book was long enough. He dispatched the Greeley campaign of 1872 in a few sentences, and the Democratic statewide defeat of the same year in a paragraph or two, despite the unique nature of the Republican comeback of that year. The interpretive significance is that it shortchanges Democratic disunity, the tendency toward racial moderation of some of the black-belt planters. Here, too, the narrative instead emphasizes the inevitability of racial extremism, violence, and states' rights Democratic fundamentalism as the route to Redemption.

As Fleming completed the book, he entered a period of substantial productivity. None of his subsequent works have the intellectual importance of *Civil War and Reconstruction in Alabama,* but they deserve some discussion in that they extended its themes. He edited a two-volume documentary history of Reconstruction, which for many decades served as a standard. The subtitle describes the topic as Reconstruction, "Political, Military, Social, Religious, Educational and Industrial, 1865 to 1906." This litany reflects the interconnected emphases of his Alabama book, and the terminal date emphasized the contemporary relevance. He concluded with highlights of the disfranchisement constitutions, which brought the Reconstruction disputes to a final culmination. Fleming wrote privately that he wanted to preempt any "New Englander or Wild Westerner" from undertaking such an anthology, a strategy that was successful in that the book long remained influential. In 1966 it appeared in a reprint edition, to which David Donald contributed a new introduction. Donald observed that it was accurate in its transcriptions, and it remained "the broadest and best-balanced collection of original sources on the Reconstruction era."[42] Fleming was notably sparing in his marginal comments, which served the longevity of that work well. The folly of Reconstruction seemed so apparent that he let documents mostly speak for themselves.

Whatever the intellectual merit of Fleming's work, he clearly intended to justify southern racial practices in an era of disfranchisement and Jim Crow. Even his position on lynching is unsettling to modern sensibilities. His entry in the 1911 edition of the *Encyclopaedia Britannica* on lynch law observes: "With the increase of negro crimes came an increase of lynchings, due to prejudice, to the fact that for some time after Reconstruction the governments were relatively weak . . . to the fact that negroes nearly always shield criminals of their own race against the whites, and to the frequent occurrence of the crime of rape by negro men upon white women."[43] Fleming didn't endorse the practice here, but his wording comes suggestively close, and he articulated similar ideas elsewhere. His writing on the Ku Klux Klan is premised on the concept that extralegal and even violent means were necessary to turn back the challenge of Reconstruction and, thus, morally justified.

One particular work highlights this emphasis. In 1905, the same year his Alabama book was published, Fleming reprinted a new edition of D. L. Wilson and John C. Lester's obscure 1884 memoir of the creation of the Klan, augmented by internal documents provided largely from his own sources. In the original pamphlet the authors had expressed mild misgivings for excessive violence that had occurred under the name and method of their organization. In his extensive introduction, Fleming explained that they "went too far in the direction of apologetic explanation" in hope of general acceptability, especially in the North. Fleming termed superficial their implication that the Klan methods were unnecessary, because in much of the South black majorities could not have been overcome without force. In Fleming's words, "The remnants of such a secret, illegal order were certain to degenerate finally into violence, but before it reached this stage it had accomplished much good in reducing to order the social chaos." Fleming thus took founding members of the Ku Klux Klan to task for racial backsliding.[44]

Fleming's position owed much to his concerns at the time. "In a wider and truer sense the phrase 'Ku Klux Movement' means the attitude of southern whites toward the various measures of the Reconstruction lasting from 1865 to 1876, and to some extent, almost to the present day," he concluded. With this endorsement of the movement's continuing relevance, small wonder that he began accumulating materials for a full-scale history of the Ku Klux Klan.[45] To an unusual extent for a professional historian, he worked with groups like the United Daughters of the Confederacy, promoting their rehabilitation of the Klan. He corresponded extensively with such groups, occasionally appearing at meetings. In 1914, the year before the film *The Birth of a Nation* was released, he even provided documents and illustrations for a laudatory history targeted at young people under the organization's auspices, for which he was duly acknowledged.[46]

Viewed in a certain light, Fleming displayed a certain integrity; he resisted muting his tone to suit the sensibilities of polite opinion. In a review of a work by W. E. B. Du Bois, no less, he observed that "there was no family life worthy of the name in Africa, and that the negro family, such as it is, was forcibly created by slavery."[47] His racial views remained fairly constant, and his promotion of southern values remained consistent as well. For the series *The South in the Building of the Nation* (1909) he edited two volumes of biographical essays. Fleming noted, "Hitherto the biographical estimates of Southerners have been, in general, rather unfriendly, contemptuous, or inadequate." Fleming would show instead the "best products of the South, the rich fruitage of Southern civilization." The volume includes an appreciative essay on Booker T. Washington, though somehow Frederick Douglass escaped notice despite his southern birth. Another essay is more unsettling. Nathan Bedford Forrest was a born genius, and his military career was one of the most brilliant in history. Unremarked is his leadership in the Ku Klux Klan, which Fleming had recently demonstrated in other publications.[48]

Perhaps the culmination of Fleming's scholarship on Reconstruction was his popular history of the entire era, *The Sequel of Appomattox* (1919). Though it examines the southern states and the nation as a whole, interpretively it is *Civil War and Reconstruction in Alabama* writ large. Much of the evidence and some of the text directly derive from that work. But he clearly took previous stylistic and organizational criticisms seriously; it is a short, readable, unfootnoted version of his previous findings, well received by critics. Here, too, Fleming drew contemporary points freely. The class tensions within white society received substantial attention, especially the outsize influence of black-belt planters. After Redemption, he observed, "the Democratic dictators of the negro vote ruled fairly but not always acceptably to the white counties which are now the source of their political power." The Populist revolt clearly remained in the back of his mind as he outlined the results of Reconstruction. He thus depicted disfranchisement as "a demand from the people of the white counties that the negro be put entirely out of politics."[49]

The timing of the book, in the midst of the mass rebirth of the Ku Klux Klan, offers a test of Fleming's commitments. By this point, some scholars writing in the Dunning framework evidenced second thoughts; for example, in 1915 C. Mildred Thompson in her Georgia study wrote of the Klan's legacy with misgivings.[50] Fleming did concede that the Klan's "methods frequently became unnecessarily violent and did great harm to

Southern society." Still, he placed this chapter after his discussion of Reconstruction's fiscal woes and corruption, despite the fact that the Klan's origin mostly antedated these issues. And his fundamental viewpoint changed little: "When a people find themselves persecuted by aliens under legal forms, they will invent some means outside the law for protecting themselves; and such experience will inevitably result in a weakening of respect for law and in a return to more primitive methods of justice."[51] This concluded his chapter on the Klan, and it is striking that he remained so resolute, though he eventually shelved his long-planned history of the Klan, perhaps in deference to a changed climate of opinion.

One can discern some variation in the tone of his writing. His Alabama book contains a vaguely favorable reference to the Tuskegee Institute and similar industrial schools. He published an extended article in 1906 in the *Yale Review,* expanded into a book in 1927, on the Freedman's Savings and Trust Company. Fleming characterized the failed bank as one of the few sensible attempts to aid the ex-slaves. Emphasis is on the victimization of the freedmen that was due to irresponsible behavior by northern philanthropists and Republican politicians. The bank also fell victim to the corrupt climate in Washington: "Most of the incompetent officers, it seems, were black; most of the corrupt ones were white."[52] He moderated his treatment of racial matters, and because this sorry episode supports several of his other favored themes, it seems better scholarship than most of his work. Fleming even defended the bank managers from some of the charges of outright theft made by Democrats at the time, and he exculpated the bank's short-term head Frederick Douglass from responsibility. Modern studies of the topic are within hailing distance of his conclusions.[53] In a broader sense, Fleming's focus on the freedmen sometimes propelled him toward interesting topics. One piece is a broadly sympathetic study of Pap Singleton, the Kansas Exoduster leader; Singleton's self-help and separatist inclinations struck Fleming favorably. Another article examines a grassroots predecessor of the modern reparations movement, turn-of-the-century efforts to win recompense for slavery. Fleming emphasized that the elderly ex-slaves were fleeced by fly-by-night operators, but the evidence is susceptible to various interpretations. In his Alabama book he added that few of the ex-slaves would talk to whites about the topic, an insight that might have moved him to reflection on the limitations of his evidence elsewhere.[54]

With Fleming's initial publications came professional success; he was hired at Louisiana State University in 1907 and stayed a decade before moving on to Vanderbilt. Fleming continued to publish as he moved into administration, some five thousand pages' worth, much repeatedly adapted from previous publications. As time went on, his scholarship became less focused on Reconstruction and thus of less importance in assessing him as a Dunning student. He did write a history of Louisiana State University, much of it published posthumously, and a 1912 study of William T. Sherman as college president there, which was surprisingly appreciative of the future general's conservative politics.[55] Fleming became dean at Vanderbilt, which enabled him to shape a young generation of white Southerners, always a goal close to his heart. The 1930 agrarian manifesto *I'll Take My Stand* is dedicated to Fleming, to which "some of the contributors owe doctrine and example," the equivocal phrasing possibly suggesting some indecision on this point.[56] Poor health forced retirement and he died in 1932, at the age of fifty-eight. His early death prompted an outpouring of favorable commentary by former students and colleagues, and he inspired two substantial profiles in the *Journal of Southern History*. Fletcher M. Green called him *the* historian of Reconstruction, seemingly surpassing his mentor, Dunning. Fleming was prominent enough to have had a liberty ship named after him during World War II.[57]

Despite these eulogies, Fleming's scholarly reputation did not long survive him. His recycled material, and posthumous publication of other writing, quickly gave his work an old-fashioned reputation. He became an obvious target as racial norms changed. In the radical 1930s leftists and African American scholars led the charge. In 1935 W. E. B. Du Bois's *Black Reconstruction* referred to Fleming as "anti-Negro" but having a certain fairness and scientific bent. Still, Du Bois characterized the documentary history as thesis-driven, and he termed the Alabama book "pure propaganda."[58] Horace Mann Bond likewise observed an emphasis on the "brutish ignorance" of the freedmen, and he suggested as well that Fleming's personal origins reveal a "typical class attitude" of hostility toward highland Tories.[59] In a 1950 review essay in the *Journal of Negro History*, Robert D. Reid offered an effective, brief rejoinder to Fleming. He just quoted choice passages from the Alabama book, concluding that "it is high time for some industrious historian" to correct the "misconceptions and mistakes of Fleming."[60]

To date, no one has taken up that challenge fully, but scholars touching on Alabama have distanced themselves progressively from his work.

In 1955 Wendell Holmes Stephenson named Fleming as one of the three leading southern historians he profiled, calling him a "Historian of Conservatism."[61] Stephenson offered something of a rear-guard defense of Fleming's work, dated as he conceded it was. Since that time, as the revisionists have swept the field, scholarly references to Fleming have grown frosty. John Hope Franklin took him to task for his elastic use of the term *carpetbagger* for individuals long resident in Alabama. In a 1978 reprint edition of Fleming's Reconstruction book, Sarah Wiggins asserted its continuing importance as the only work of its kind. Still, she called Fleming a white supremacist, "a child of his own age," who depicted the Ku Klux Klan as "a noble group" and the Democrats as "white knights of virtue." Other scholars are curtly dismissive. In 1989 my own first book, on the Union League, characterized Fleming as a "pro-Klan historian." Fleming served as a touchstone for the most extreme position possible against Reconstruction; any concessions he made to the opposite view simply had to be correct, because they came from Fleming.[62]

Though predictable in context, this dismissal is, in a sense, too bad. His deteriorating reputation made it too easy to reject what he had to say about how the Reconstruction government functioned. As should be evident, Fleming's racial and class biases are so dated that one cannot now accept any of his characterizations unexamined. White supremacy remained the steel frame of his analysis. But Fleming had reflected on the long arc of southern history, and how Reconstruction segued into the Jim Crow and disfranchisement era. His emphasis on the long-standing class and regional divisions within white society remains important as a theme in the field. And who better to turn for the violence that overthrew Reconstruction than one who celebrated that triumph and who cultivated the participants? He accumulated, preserved, and published materials that later scholars could put to different use.

Notes

    1. Review of Fleming, *Civil War and Reconstruction in Alabama*, in *Nation*, April 26, 1906, 348–50.
    2. Villard to Fleming, November 21, 1905, Walter L. Fleming Papers, New York Public Library.
    3. Walter L. Fleming, *Civil War and Reconstruction in Alabama* (New York: Columbia University Press, 1905), 801.
    4. Myrta Lockett Avery to Fleming, February 24, 1906, Fleming Papers.

5. Charles C. Pickett, review of Fleming, *Civil War and Reconstruction in Alabama,* in *Annals of the Academy of Political and Social Science* 27 (March 1906): 174.

6. William E. Dodd, "More New Books on Our Civil War: An Alabamian's View of the Contest," *New York Times,* January 20, 1906, BR 34.

7. William A. Dunning, *Reconstruction, Political and Economic, 1865–1877* (New York: Harper and Brothers, 1907), 353.

8. M. L. Avery to Fleming, May 10, 1906, Fleming Papers.

9. Yates Snowden to Fleming, May 7, 1906, Fleming Papers.

10. Sarah Woolfolk Wiggins, introduction to Walter Lynwood Fleming, *Civil War and Reconstruction in Alabama* (1905; reprint, Spartanburg, S.C.: Reprint Co., 1978), v, vii. Fleming's grandfather's name is misspelled in the slave and population schedules as "John A. Flemming." On the family's class origins, Fletcher M. Green's biographic piece on Fleming characterizes his father as a "well-to-do planter," an impression that may have been gathered from Fleming himself; see Fletcher M. Green, "Walter Lynwood Fleming: Historian of Reconstruction," *Journal of Southern History* 2, no. 4 (November 1936): 498.

11. Fleming, *Civil War and Reconstruction in Alabama,* 724; Green, "Walter Lynwood Fleming," 497–521; Thomas McAdory Owen, *History of Alabama and Dictionary of Alabama Biography,* 4 vols. (Chicago, 1921), 3:587.

12. Fleming, *Civil War and Reconstruction in Alabama,* 800, 802.

13. *The South in the Building of the Nation,* 13 vols. (Richmond: Southern Historical Publication Society, 1909–13), 11:349. Fleming was profiled as a promising undergraduate in the *Atlanta Constitution,* January 26, 1896.

14. William C. Binkley, "The Contribution of Walter Lynwood Fleming to Southern Scholarship," *Journal of Southern History* 5, no. 2 (May 1939): 144; Philip R. Muller, "Look Back without Anger: A Reappraisal of William A Dunning," *Journal of American History* 61, no. 2 (September 1974): 336.

15. Fleming to Gov. William Jelks, November 16, 1901, Governor's Papers, ent. SG23643, folder 7, Alabama Department of Archives and History. For a discussion of Fleming's letter, see R. Volney Riser, *Defying Disfranchisement: Black Voting Rights Activism in the Jim Crow South, 1890–1908* (Baton Rouge: Louisiana State University Press, 2010), 138, 248, 291. My thanks to Professor Riser, University of West Alabama, for bringing this to my attention. See Green, "Walter Lynwood Fleming," 501–2.

16. Fleming, *Civil War and Reconstruction in Alabama,* 806–7.

17. Walter L. Fleming, "Immigration to the Southern States," *Political Science Quarterly* 20, no. 2 (June 1905): 279. This piece won favorable editorial notice in the *Atlanta Constitution,* July 9, 1905.

18. Wiggins, introduction to Fleming, *Civil War and Reconstruction in Alabama,* 1978 ed., viii.

19. One hesitates to make negative categorical statements about the contents of an eight-hundred-page book, but a reasonably careful search of the footnotes revealed none.

20. Access to the governors' papers may have been limited, because the Alabama

Department of Archives and History was just being established at this time. His local connections and positive relationship with the director, Thomas McAdory Owen, however, make it seem probable that he could have examined them had he sought access. On Fleming's interest in intellectual freedom in examining archival sources without preconditions, see Wendell Holmes Stephenson, *The South Lives in History: Southern Historians and their Legacy* (Baton Rouge: Louisiana State University Press, 1955), 101.

21. *Gulf States Historical Magazine* 1 (November 1902): 221.

22. Fleming, *Civil War and Reconstruction in Alabama*, 380, 315, 429–30.

23. Ibid., vii.

24. Ibid.

25. Ibid., 316, 321.

26. Ibid., 114.

27. Ibid., 102.

28. Ibid., 726.

29. Ibid., 315, 421.

30. Ibid., 317, 378.

31. Ibid., 437, 210.

32. Ibid., 763.

33. Ibid., 553, 559, 560.

34. Ibid., 514.

35. Ibid., 683.

36. Ibid., 591.

37. Edwin C. Woolley, *The Reconstruction of Georgia* (New York: Columbia University Press, 1901), 61–62; James Wilford Garner, *Reconstruction in Mississippi* (New York: Macmillan, 1901), 338–53. On the outlier status of Fleming with respect to the Klan, see James Vincent Lowery, "Reconstructing the Reign of Terror: Popular Memories of the Ku Klux Klan, 1877–1921" (Ph.D. diss., University of Mississippi, 2008), 155–75, esp. 163.

38. Lowery, "Reconstructing the Reign of Terror," 155; Fleming, *Civil War and Reconstruction in Alabama*, 661, 667–68, 688–89.

39. Fleming, *Civil War and Reconstruction in Alabama*, esp. 677–78.

40. Ibid., 689–90.

41. Ibid., 702–3.

42. Walter L. Fleming, ed., *Documentary History of Reconstruction: Political, Military, Social, Religious, Educational and Industrial, 1865 to 1906*, 2 vols. (1906; reprint, New York: McGraw-Hill, 1966), vi; Lowery, "Reconstructing the Reign of Terror," 158–59.

43. Walter L. Fleming, "Lynch Law," *Encyclopaedia Britannica* (1911), 17:170.

44. J. C. Lester and D. L. Wilson, *Ku Klux Klan: Its Origin, Growth and Disbandment*, ed. Walter L. Fleming (New York: Neale, 1905), 18–19.

45. Ibid., 35–36. Lester was one of the six original founders of the Pulaski Klan, Wilson an early recruit.

46. Lowery, "Reconstructing the Reign of Terror," 161; S. E. F. Rose, *The Ku Klux Klan or Invisible Empire* (New Orleans: L. Graham, 1914), 9.

47. Walter L. Fleming, review of W. E. B. Du Bois, *The Negro Church*, in *Political Science Quarterly* 19, no. 4 (December 1904): 702–3.

48. *The South in the Building of the Nation*, 11:vii, viii, 232; 12:513. Fleming was the editor, rather than the author, of these entries.

49. Walter L. Fleming, *The Sequel of Appomattox: A Chronicle of the Reunion of the States* (New Haven: Yale University Press, 1919), 304. He had made similar observations in his book on Alabama. This line of argument, however, is dubious. In Alabama disfranchisement passed with overwhelming (and fraudulent) reported totals from the black-belt counties; it was narrowly defeated in the predominantly white counties. See Glenn Feldman, *The Disfranchisement Myth: Poor Whites and Suffrage Restriction in Alabama* (Athens: University of Georgia Press, 2004), 178–81.

50. C. Mildred Thompson, *Reconstruction in Georgia* (New York: Columbia University Press, 1915), 401, chap. 14.

51. Fleming, *The Sequel of Appomattox*, 264.

52. Fleming, *Civil War and Reconstruction in Alabama*, 733–34; Fleming, *The Freedmen's Savings Bank: A Chapter in the Economic History of the Negro Race* (Chapel Hill: University of North Carolina Press, 1927), 41, 56, 61.

53. Carl R. Osthaus, *Freedmen, Philanthropy, and Fraud: A History of the Freedman's Saving Bank* (Urbana: University of Illinois Press, 1976), is the modern revisionist study of the bank that nonetheless came to somewhat similar conclusions. Osthaus did not explicitly engage Fleming's arguments, which I interpret as tacit admission of the point. I should concede that the anonymous reviewer for the *Journal of Negro History*, most probably Carter G. Woodson, would not agree with my characterization of Fleming's work. He described it as awash in misinformation. See *Journal of Negro History* 13, no. 1 (January 1928): 106–8.

54. Walter L. Fleming, *Ex-Slave Pension Frauds* (Baton Rouge: Ortlieb's Printing House, 1910); Fleming, *Civil War and Reconstruction in Alabama*, 447.

55. Walter L. Fleming, *Louisiana State University, 1860–1896* (Baton Rouge: Louisiana State University Press, 1936); Fleming, *General William T. Sherman as College President: A Collection of Letters, Documents, and Other Material* (Cleveland: Arthur H. Clark, 1912).

56. Twelve Southerners, *I'll Take My Stand: The South and the Agrarian Tradition* (New York: Harper and Brothers, 1930), 5.

57. For fulsome praise by former students and colleagues, see Fletcher M. Green, "Walter Lynwood Fleming," 501–2, 521; William C. Binkley, "The Contribution of Walter Lynwood Fleming to Southern Scholarship," *Journal of Southern History* 5, no. 2 (May 1939): 143–54; "Names Chosen for Three Liberty Ships," *New York Times*, November 7, 1943, 44.

58. W. E. B. Du Bois, *Black Reconstruction: An Essay toward a History of the*

Part Which Black Folk Played in the Attempt to Reconstruct Democracy in America, 1860–1880 (New York: Harcourt, Brace, 1935), 721, 731.

59. Horace Mann Bond, *Negro Education in Alabama: A Study in Cotton and Steel* (Washington, D.C.: Associated Publishers, 1939), 28, 8.

60. Robert D. Reid, review of Fleming, *Civil War and Reconstruction in Alabama*, in *Journal of Negro History* 35, no. 4 (October 1950): 453–56.

61. Stephenson, *The South Lives in History*, 95–120.

62. John Hope Franklin, *Race and History: Selected Essays, 1938–1988* (Baton Rouge: Louisiana State University Press, 1989), 391–92; Wiggins, introduction to Fleming, *Civil War and Reconstruction in Alabama*, 1978 ed., iv; Michael W. Fitzgerald, *The Union League Movement in the Deep South: Politics and Agricultural Change during Reconstruction* (Baton Rouge: Louisiana State University Press, 1989), 216, 38, 68, 127.

6

Ransack Roulhac
and Racism

Joseph Grégoire de Roulhac Hamilton and Dunning's Questions of Institution Building and Jim Crow

John Herbert Roper Sr.

Joseph Grégoire de Roulhac Hamilton (1878–1961). Saying the name slowly produces a humor not inappropriate, almost like the old W. C. Fields routine in which the comedian with orotund vowels recited pretentious names of pretentious people. He liked to be called Roulhac, and the sycophantic intoned the maternal name with awe, the many critics with contempt. Too, photographs of Hamilton reveal a feminist's nightmare of Patriarch, an African American's nightmare of The Man, a Sixties Radical's nightmare of Authority. In his essay in this book, J. Vincent Lowery offers a seriocomic image of Hamilton so enraged over an issue of southern honor—that is to say, racist pride and prejudice—that he lost all control and threw a silly fit unworthy of the gentleman-scholar he usually modeled for others. Easily caricatured, self-documented as a white supremacist and a male chauvinist, in print in favor of many wrong causes, Hamilton has stood there prominently in his photographs, in his portraits, even with his name on a building housing the Departments of History, Political Science, and Sociology at the University of North Carolina.

Those who studied in Chapel Hill in the 1960s and 1970s, many of them members of and scholars in the civil rights movement, found Hamilton to be everywhere in signs and symbols—and generally there in a bad

179

way. Yet Paul Green and C. Vann Woodward and J. Carlyle Sitterson and George Brown Tindall spoke of their admiration, respect, and personal fondness for Hamilton. In a similar vein Joel Williamson, beloved mentor of many revisionist and activist historians, knew Hamilton through the correspondence and the publications that he left.[1]

What to make of a racist character who may be the most problematical of all the students of William Archibald Dunning? In his proclamations and practices, he was in all ordinary senses and in any historical sense racist. In his institution building, especially of the magnificent archival depositories of the University of North Carolina, he was also racist, the effects of which lasted much longer than anything he ever said or wrote. Initially, and thereafter for long decades, the facilities he built were off-limits to African American scholars and researchers. Yet, in building his archival depository so well and in staffing it so intelligently, he—certainly without meaning to do so—established the very means—serious primary research work—that permitted later generations of more liberal, indeed plainly better, scholars to countermand his own worst offenses. Once Jim Crow was dismantled—and, in fact, before it was dismantled, thanks to some clever procedures of his staff—African American scholars could use the full fruits of his labors. Much of the best consciously revisionist work about slavery, Reconstruction, civil rights, race relations, and all aspects of southern social structures and functions is possible exactly because Hamilton established the Southern Historical Collection and filled it with dense and richly textured primary sources from all regions of the South.

To start with, Hamilton is inexplicable—and useless to scholars of another era—without understanding the sprawling and oddly interlocked family in which he lived. Then, too, Hamilton is inexplicable—and useless to scholars of another era—without understanding his Old North State when the twentieth century was new. For still another, Hamilton is inexplicable—and even more useless to latter-day scholars—without understanding his University of North Carolina (UNC), especially in the days of presidents Edward Kidder Graham, Harry Woodburn Chase, and Frank Porter Graham. Finally, Hamilton is inexplicable—and even more useless to us—without understanding the pursuit of the muse Clio in his day. Especially for his interaction with family members and friends throughout the Carolinas and Alabama, there are "deep reciprocities" between what Hamilton actually lived and what he wrote about, between the personal biography and the professional history, and these deep reciprocities must be plumbed.[2]

The first two considerations, the family and North Carolina, are very much intertwined and must be taken up together. Hamilton's family was noted for its size and scope, so different from today's families, yet it was very much a type for a class of landowning extended families in the decades before the Civil War. He was born on August 6, 1878, in the onetime state capital of Hillsborough in the red-clay piedmont, whose gentle slopes gave gradually to the long and old Appalachian mountains in the west. Yet Hillsborough is also close to the broad inner-coastal plain with its black, waxy soil in the east. He was then, fittingly, born near all things that made up North Carolina. Too, his father, Daniel Heyward Hamilton, and his mother, Frances Gray de Roulhac Hamilton, bore in their very names the stamp of old, old families that interconnected and interacted across state lines, much as did the Lees and the Hamptons and the Prestons. Looking at all the Hamiltons and the Heywards and the de Roulhacs, one recalls the exasperated words of Joel Williamson, usually precise with such definitions, who said that Hamilton "was mostly from South Carolina." Perhaps more useful is the model proffered by another historian, Orville Vernon Burton: it is an Abramic family in which a sprawling household contains many mansions and many shacks, and where a ruling landowning father has extended his personal power into every room, mansion or shack, and this Abramic figure has locked arms with similar landowning fathers without regard to state boundary lines.[3]

Those interlocking arms very much took account of color and class, locking some in and locking some out. The historian William L. Barney in his researches noted that the Hamiltons crossed state lines with ease, that their slave-based enterprises were globalized in a self-conscious way, that they operated in "rutted tributaries" on behalf of creditors in Providence and Boston and Manhattan and London, but they did so as those who benefited handsomely and not as the victims who did the actual stoop labor. Barney also observed that the Hamiltons and their relations and their friends understood that their far-flung lands were investment capital and not something sentimental and that their numbers of slaves were human capital, also an investment; and he noted that the Hamiltons in particular were adept at borrowing for further investment by leveraging the value of their human and land possessions. From his family, then, Hamilton defined place more in terms of social positioning than in terms of geographical sit-ing, and he could and did wax eloquent about Blue Ridge as well as Atalaya Cove, Alabama black belt as much as piedmont red clay, sand-hills bays as much as Winyah Bay. From old-time family investments and investitures, Hamilton the historian and the man claimed all of the South, and he claimed it with a proprietary arrogance at once stunning and yet unremarkable, at once preposterous in the land of Thomas Jefferson and yet commonplace in the land of landowning patriarchs who claimed Abram's tribal authority over all the children of all the colors and castes. And of course one has to remember that Jefferson's stirring writings about physiocratic landholding and localistic power and shared neighborliness had little to do with his actual operations at Monticello or his conduct as the president who gave slavery a base in the fertile delta of the Mississippi River Valley by paying on executive authority and without congressional discussion a king's ransom, to gain the empire beyond the Appalachian chain, and did so in a personal deal cut with Bonaparte the emperor.[4]

Inheriting this much from sprawling and interconnected and fully globalized families, Hamilton in writing about the antebellum South and the wartime South and the Reconstruction South and the self-proclaimed New South was often writing about people from whom he descended. Columbia University had cachet, and William Archibald Dunning, with his endowed chair named for Francis Lieber, and with his membership in the Cosmos Club, and with his connections to university press editors and to trade press agents, had his own long arm and his own *gloire,* and all these things were useful to the aspiring young scholar "on the make." To be sure, the operating model for Hamilton in conducting professional business was always at Morningside Heights (where Columbia University had moved from Madison Avenue in 1896), and it was Dunning; but for conducting personal affairs and for taking the measure of society and societal problems, the examples came always from old friends and family whose arms were not so much long as locked, and all those examples hailed from points well south of the East River and, indeed, well south of the Potomac.

Ironies of all kinds abounded for Hamilton the man and the scholar, and it certainly can be said that he sought Hamiltonian ends with Jeffersonian means, and that when he did so as a publicist or as a scholar, he was chronicling his own family and his own ancestors' friends, who could remember when Federalists were important in their South Carolina lowcountry and when Whigs were important in all regions of the Old North State. And the Hamilton in this important label was not a relative but rather

Alexander Hamilton, who proffered the teleological goal of a fully indus-trialized, globally financed, and commercially rationalized United States. Hamilton the historian saw nothing contradictory in adapting an industrial and global-commercial model to slavery, and he saw much that was attrac-tive in adapting such a model to the postbellum, post-slavery New South he wanted to see. Ever anxious that the patrician, patriarchal, Abramic fathers—Big Daddies, if you will—maintain social control over the plain-folk white people as well as over the black people, Hamilton knew from his own family the way an elite could use Jeffersonian language of plainness and physiocracy and brotherhood to vouchsafe privileges for bankers and mill owners and railroad financiers, and he was pleased as a historian to see the Democratic Party manipulate language of Jefferson and for that matter language of the Lost Cause of the Confederacy as well as the rawest lan-guage of racism, all such manipulations intended to ensure that black and white labor could not unite to take political action against their common economic grievances.

Nor was Hamilton a mere detached observer in these processes, for he wrote editorials and gave speeches tirelessly in such a cause. And again, in this scholar-activism on behalf of New South business expansion, he was following examples provided for generations by his own family. Paul Gas-ton, in the marvelous *The New South Creed* (1970), in which he portrayed a bourgeois managerial elite manipulating agrarian folklore and mytholo-gies in behalf of new structures of industrial and commercial enterprise, described men he saw in action—and one of the most visible of those men was Hamilton, as the historian and archivist presented himself to Gas-ton the graduate student and the young researcher. Like those other men limned in *The New South Creed,* Hamilton of UNC was acting as his fam-ily had taught him to, teachings reinforced by lessons he could document as he gathered their papers and those of other planters.[5]

Born four years after Reconstruction had ended in the Old North State, Hamilton was raised by a father and a mother who clearly recalled times of regional opulence and familial authority as well as a recent time of regional defeat and familial problems with credit. Episcopalian in a land of Methodists and Baptists, Hamilton knew ritual and rubrics and the psalm-ody, whereas his neighbors knew piety and emotionalism and personalism and Wesleyan hymns. Hamilton's primary education came largely at home at the feet of Daniel and Frances Hamilton, and then he was sent off to the Sewanee Academy, where he could be prepared for scholarship and lead-

ership in the post-Reconstruction New South that was building railroads
and insurance and realty firms and establishing textile mills and mining
operations, but all underneath the umbrella of Old South values—and all
those agrarian values were filtered through the carefully ground lenses of
apologists for the Lost Cause. This sectarian training was theologically lati-
tudinarian, but it was class specific in terms of teaching young men how
to work with and lead a very non-Episcopalian working class of small-time
farmers and mill workers who were Southern Baptists—or often pietists in
freestanding and unaffiliated Protestant churches.[6]

This academy prepared him for the University of the South on the
same campus, and its deliberately gothic architecture and Germanic organ-
icism gave outward and visible signs of the noblesse oblige taught there,
especially by the theologian William Porcher DuBose. The emphasis on
German Romanticism and the discussions of duty and order and societal
place reinforced a certain racism known to the practitioners in Sewanee as
Volksgeistian, and explored at some length by Joel Williamson under his
modified label of *Volksgeistian* conservative racism. Many scholars have
insisted that any sort of racism has always existed along a spectrum. The
idea of such a spectrum of racism was noted memorably by Arnold Marshall Rose in his studies alongside Gunnar Myrdal, it was described by C.
Vann Woodward, and it was demonstrated quantitatively by the Nobel lau-
reate economist Gary Stanley Becker. The turn-of-the-century spectrum
included at its left end a very few liberals who considered a possibility of
racial equality but who grew increasingly quiet as the twentieth century
unfurled. The spectrum included a broad middle of conservatives who
snidely treated black people as infantile and who understood the need for
black labor and felt a need for control over this valued labor. At its right-
most extreme was a murderous Negrophobic faction that not only talked
the language of racial genocide, but on occasion practiced it, as seen in
country lynch mobs and urban race riots that slaughtered some four thousand black men and women in the period 1889–1920. Hamilton absorbed
this conservative racism, with its celebration of segregation and its talk of
directing and controlling black people and poor whites; he did so in formal
academic processes but he probably was only finding professorial words to
confirm familial prejudices formed in the crib and preached at the hearth.[7]

Otherwise, the teachers at the University of the South emphasized
German language, German philosophy, German high arts, and German
history as well as German historiography as preached and practiced by Leo-

pold von Ranke. That German system of analysis, primarily associated with the University of Berlin, styled itself scientific and considered that history was indeed a science with a scientific method of patiently building an argument inductively—apparently never deductively—from the primary sources. Rankean scientism replaced the older system of great man history practiced by gentleman historians who had leisure rather than a profession and who seldom provided documentation for what they wrote concerning generals and kings and other great men, sometimes writing as if those great men acted virtually alone on the historical stage. And those primary sources had to be above all focused on institutions and on political matters involving institutions. From E. A. Freeman they took a restatement of Rankean science: "History is past politics, and politics present history."[8]

Earning the baccalaureate and the master's degrees in history from the University of the South, Hamilton went off to Columbia University to study alongside other conservative racist Southerners under William Archibald Dunning. Note, however, the historiographic patterns—so-styled scientific history heavily inductive and focused, if not fixated, on political institutions—he had developed before he sat in a seminar with Dunning and the Dunningite School. If Dunning can be excused for not creating racial prejudice among his graduate charges, he must also be excused—at least in the case of Hamilton—from developing Rankean scientific historiography, since it was already there when those scholars, and others, enrolled for their doctoral studies.[9]

Before studying with Dunning, Hamilton had taught briefly at a military academy in Oxford, North Carolina, among the gently sloping tobacco farms of the upper-eastern piedmont, and this foray in 1901 put him in the middle of North Carolina New South politics at a particularly bloody and racially conscious time: his own Democrats and the rival Republicans struggled not only with each other but also with the agrarian reform represented by Marion Butler's Populists. The latter agrarians were quite the white supremacists, but they could and did cooperate or, as they phrased it, "fuse" with black voters who otherwise voted Republican. The results in the period of the late 1880s to 1898, the period memorably styled "fluid" in race relations by George Brown Tindall, have interested historians ever since, especially C. Vann Woodward, who spoke of the period as a time of "forgotten alternatives" concerning all aspects of race relations and economic policy. For Hamilton, however, especially in that year in

Oxford, Fusion politics, black voting, agrarian reform, and the like were a nightmare. In several places he said, and in print he pronounced, that black people simply lacked the intellect to enter into contracts, serve on juries, and conduct complex business, and they were much more disastrous if involved meaningfully in politics. Fusion attempted all of that to some degree, and, what was worse for Hamilton, the Populists opposed efforts to develop a manufacturing base and the corresponding financial apparatus to fund it and the corresponding commercial apparatus to buy and sell the inputs and outputs of the New South industry he saw developing farther west and south in the cities and mill villages of the piedmont. He was active in Democratic politics, then generally called Conservative, in this frenetic year during which the last of the Fusionists were put out of effective commission, most blacks were disfranchised politically and otherwise Jim Crowed commercially, and the state's Republicans were gradually converting themselves to a business party with a base in the western mountains and commitments to "lily-white" racism.[10]

In Morningside Heights, Hamilton the student flourished, being personally drawn to Dunning and delighted with the energy and resources of "the million footed city" that has ever drawn and repulsed North Carolinians. His dissertation he had in his head upon his arrival, and what he needed in the city were the marvelous libraries of secondary sources and the carefully archived manuscripts and contemporaneous newspapers of primary source collections. Among other things, as is noted almost as a commonplace nowadays, Reconstruction historiography as practiced by Dunning students served to reunite business elites of the New South and New York; both groups knew how to manipulate racist language among the unhappy white farmers of the declining, almost déclassé middle class of plain folk, and how to manipulate such racist language among the still hopeful but desperately struggling mill hands of the piedmont textile centers. As Philip Muller has insisted, little of this was created by Dunning—although he benefited from it much more than Muller may have let on—and in any case Hamilton for his part arrived largely formed in his opinions and even his research techniques and needed mostly time and encouragement, both of which the suave and attractive Dunning provided at Columbia.[11]

Always a facile writer who could overwhelm readers with the force and volume of his prose, Hamilton became a writing machine while at Columbia, and much of that must be properly ascribed to the coaching and the warm encouragement given him by Dunning. Much of the undeniable charm that is remembered of Hamilton, especially by those who disagreed with him, is southern by style and comes from his family; but in substance it comes from the past master Dunning, whose professional behavior and influences—not his historiographical slant—were everything for the student Hamilton.[12]

Under Dunning, Hamilton assayed a history of Reconstruction in North Carolina. He could do the secondary reading and he could learn how to do the primary archival work, that is, the research techniques of the properly scientific historian. He did so. Much actual research and much of the finished writing he had to do back in North Carolina, especially since many sources were not then housed properly in an archival setting for scholars. This acute want never left Hamilton, and it was always remembered as he labored over the decades to establish the Southern Historical Collection (SHC) at the main university library in Chapel Hill as a place where scholars could gain ready access to contemporaneous newspapers, newsletters, diaries, and correspondence. Successfully completing his course work and with the kindest of biblical patriarchal blessings from Dunning, Hamilton returned to the Old North State to find his raw data and arrange them into the story he already had laid out in his head.

From 1904 to 1906, two full academic years, he served as principal at Wilmington High School on the ancient shoreline. In Wilmington, once rice country and as such affined with some of his lowcountry South Carolina family members, Hamilton lived within very recent memory of the bloody racist campaign of 1898. On November 10, 1898, a white mob terrorized black people in town and overthrew the city's interracial Fusion government. In the aftermath of the riot, African Americans lost much of their economic standing and their political voice as the city's new white government acted on the mob's "White Declaration of Independence" and state Democrats introduced Jim Crow measures to the Tarheel State.[13]

Hamilton defended this terrorist campaign in his writing and in his publicizing. For him, the affairs of that year answered what was left ambiguous by the Redeemers in the period 1875–77—it definitively removed black people from power, at least in Wilmington, and created a state Republican Party that could exist only by proclaiming itself "lily white." Thus, he was living in the city where both of his goals were met: probusiness politics was represented in both the Republican and the Democratic parties; Populists were politically dead and gone; and black people were removed from the political calculus. Hamilton collected a lengthy firsthand account by

Wilmington's George Rountree in which Rountree described the violent racist actions in 1898 as a noble mission, a verdict affirmed by Hamilton. In defending that terrorist campaign in his writing and his publicizing, Hamilton often relied on Rountree's account—which is often quite candid about the violence and fraud—and he retained the manuscript, placing it in a safe place in his own growing collection of primary sources. Whatever else, Hamilton, through his own collection of primary documents and accounts of this grisly incident of extreme racism, understood full well just how violent and fraudulent were the events and actions of 1898—and he celebrated the results in full knowledge of that Negrophobic violence.

In that conjunction of time and space, Hamilton focused Reconstruction in North Carolina on the ironies inherent in the continuing struggles between the antebellum figures William Woods Holden and William Alexander Graham. He was quite partisan toward Graham both before the war and afterward, but he did carefully note the twists and turns in political allegiances and the resulting changes in programs. As he chronicled it, there was an east-west struggle between Holden and Graham. Holden operated a Raleigh newspaper, but he was working in behalf of western interests who had abandoned the Whig Party and become free-trade and antitariff and antibank Democrats. On the other side was Graham, a Whig who attempted to develop businesses but became an antisecession Democrat who warned presciently what a large-scale civil war could do to the Old North State. Graham's fears were realized by the result of the war, although he had worked so hard in behalf of the Confederacy that he was banned from postbellum officeholding for the effective remainder of his lengthy political career. Furthermore, Graham was compelled to work with his old rival Holden, who became governor in 1868.[14]

Interestingly, Hamilton was careful to note several false starts at Reconstruction, in 1862, not only before Andrew Johnson's presidential phase of Reconstruction, but even before Lincoln had established much of a cohesive executive- and commander-in-chief plan. Graham was unable to gain clearance to reenter politics officially and thus worked behind the scenes in behalf of Democrats who sought to build business, but also with those who resisted the participation by former slaves in politics. Hamilton noted that of fifty members of the 1868 state senate, twelve were Democrats generally styled Conservatives; three were blacks who called themselves Republicans; seven were Northerners transplanted and styled by the historian as Carpetbagger Republicans; and the remaining twenty-eight were Tarheel born and bred and thus styled scalawags by Hamilton because they were Republicans who supported at least a modicum of rights for the former slaves. Hamilton himself could not abide the idea of black people voting or holding office, and thus he was most sympathetic to the editor and backstage political manipulator Graham, who said that black suffrage was unwarranted because he considered that "native" and "inherent racial characteristics" made Negroes unfit to perform complicated tasks of public service, especially voting and officeholding.[15]

He did note good humanitarian work by the occupying army in 1865 and 1866, especially as led by General Daniel Sickles, and good work by the small and newly created Freedmen's Bureau; he considered that the ravages of the Civil War were responsible for the initially poor harvest and for subsequent malnourishment, but he saluted federal agencies for preventing the lack of crops from becoming full-scale starvation. In keeping with his old-style Whig and new-style Progressive interests, he celebrated the building of railroads and the efforts to construct schools and was pleased to see postbellum commitments to roads and schools. The dissertation was concluded with the inauguration of Governor Holden, who was described as addressing an "enormous audience, composed, for the most part, of negroes." Holden's speech was summarized to show a hope that black suffrage would become acceptable to North Carolinians once white people saw good conduct by black officeholders and black voters; and the governor spoke firmly against racial integration of schools and generally against social integration of any public activities. The dissertation writer summed up, "As a whole, the address gave a better promise for the future than was expected, and far better than was fulfilled." In other words, this particular study ended before the most explosive issues of Reconstruction were brought to the stage.[16]

He taught and wrote and spoke at some length about the Union League of black Republicans; about the Ku Klux Klan and its leader, Josiah Turner of Raleigh, editor of the *Raleigh Sentinel;* about the paramilitary fighting between Governor Holden's agent General George W. Kirk (known for Civil War butchery of civilians and wounded soldiers that was uncharacteristic for that war) and Conservative Democrat armed forces; about the eventually successful efforts to impeach, convict, and remove Governor Holden; about the violent and fraud-ridden successful replacement of a Republican majority in the General Assembly by Conservative Democrats often in league with Klan forces. In terms of carefully annotated, focused narrative, however, there are only a few chapters on Reconstruction in his *History of North Carolina* (1919). Despite his training as a Reconstruction specialist, the great bulk of his work concerned other things, and his two Reconstruction monographs stop this side of a full treatment of the actual working out of constitutional Amendments Thirteen, Fourteen, and Fifteen, to say nothing of the complexities in executing the rights and prerogatives stated in the Civil Rights Act of 1875. Apparently his racist disdain for the very idea of black people voting and holding office and managing public affairs convinced him that no in-depth study was needed of the several years— decades in fact in the heavily black eastern Carolina—when black politicians actually held office and executed public operations. Far more deeply did he work with the party politics between 1835 and 1860 and from the end of Reconstruction until the end of World War I.[17]

One aspect of North Carolina Reconstruction that he did write about at length was the so-styled Holden-Kirk war. As a *Volksgeistian* conservative, Hamilton opposed the Ku Klux Klan in its later phases in the 1920s, and he celebrated those like Zebulon Vance and Charles Brantley Aycock, who as governors eschewed violent approaches to politics and who protected the personhood of black citizens from lynchings and race riots. Yet for the Holden-Kirk war, as for the Wilmington Race Riot of 1898, when Conservative Democrats in fact did use fraud and violence to extremes, Hamilton noted the instances of abuse and accepted all of it as necessary. Thus, Hamilton violated some of his own preferred principles, which were noblesse oblige and conservative-mandated order and stability. He criticized Governor Holden for seeking federal money and federal troops to protect black citizens terrorized by the Reconstruction-era Klan. He was correct in noting that the former terrorist Kirk was improperly employed to help defend black persons, but he failed to note the serious dangers black people faced. Furthermore, he lionized Josiah Turner, the self-styled "King of the Ku Klux Klan," in these disputes, and he showed no sympathy at all for black persons and their white Republican allies threatened not only in their political rights but in their basic civil rights to personhood as we understand such rights today. Nor could he muster the kind of limited sympathy for black suffering that most *Volksgeistian* conservative racists of his own day could express. In history, and certainly in historiography, context is everything, but on these points of Klan violence in the Reconstruction era, Hamilton was simply wrong in all contexts.[18]

In his monographs and in his many public addresses, classroom lectures, and seminar discussions, Hamilton plainly delighted in the impeachment trial and subsequent conviction of Governor Holden, proceedings in which Graham served as plaintiff's counsel; and he expressed his pleasure that Conservative Democrats, or Redeemers, returned to power through efforts of Turner and his fellow Klansman the lower-house assemblyman Frederick W. Strudwick. He described the Redeemers, not inaccurately, as probusiness commercialists who were removing black people from power and who were removing white agriculturists from the stage. The close attention to class conflict and class identity, the emphasis on economic plans in competition, and the focus on economic development all smack of Progressive historiography, practiced in the era by Frederick Jackson Turner and Charles Austin Beard. Only the white supremacy sounded like the scientific historiography practiced in a seminar for Dunning—and we know from Muller and from our own studies that Hamilton did not learn racism from Dunning any more than he learned economic determinism or class analysis from him.[19]

Ever mindful of the need to display his wares as publicly as possible, Hamilton contracted in 1906 with distinguished local printer, the Presses of Edwards & Broughton in Raleigh, to publish his book. And the interpretation spread rapidly. He expanded the original 264-page monograph into a hefty 683-page volume, brought out in 1914 by Columbia University. In the intervening eight years *Reconstruction in North Carolina* was expanded in sheer size, in documentation, and above all in prestige, as it then had nothing less than the kingly imprimatur of an Ivy League university.

It was thus early reviewed, and favorably, in the right professional journals, even before Dunning could arrange to publish the monograph in his own university's publication series. The interpretations that economic development had to proceed after the ruinous war and that the black former slaves needed to be controlled in some status less than truly free were popular among academics and among those business leaders who were readers in the day. And the interpretations, in their Edwards & Broughton incarnation throughout North Carolina and in their Columbia University imprint in academic libraries, spread rapidly. The book provided a heavily documented narrative that pleased most white Southerners and was hardly displeasing to most white Northerners—especially those who in the emerging Progressive era hoped to make common cause with New South business interests to develop truly integrated commerce and finance for the entire nation.[20]

The awarding of his Ph.D., the signature of Dunning on his doctoral thesis, the publication of a heavily documented monograph, and an appointment as associate professor of history at the state university in Chapel Hill all came at once in 1906. No starry-eyed idealist, Hamilton bargained to be an associate professor on the basis of his Columbia degree, his personal recommendation by Dunning, and his record of service and rank as principal of a major public school in an important port city. Not long thereafter, he met Mary Cornelia Thompson of Raleigh, whom he married in 1908, and she became his full scholar-partner in two monograph biographies, his publicist-partner in hundreds of pamphlets and newsletters, and his institutionalist-partner as he worked with newly emerging academics and builders to make the University of North Carolina a significant research university in his New South. By the accounts of those who worked with him and by the correspondence record, Mary Cornelia Thompson Hamilton was equal partner in the personal and the professional realms, if otherwise the compleat Southern Lady in manner and deportment.[21]

From 1908 onward Hamilton was in the middle of, and sometimes the leader of, the social sciences at UNC, especially as those studies and their practitioners were committed to interdisciplinary cooperation between and among sociologists, economists, geographers, political scientists, and historians. All this started in the Progressive era, and it was to some degree a studied copy of the University of Wisconsin and its institutionalized Laboratory of Democracy. This dramatic change in the university could be traced not only to the famous "little black notebook" of President Edward Kidder Graham, but also to Hamilton. Indeed, UNC's favorable reputation from the days of the New Deal onward has as much to do with activist scholarship among social scientists as with scholarship in any other field of study. Many of those scholar-activists worked on the side of the angels: for example, William Terry Couch, the courageous director of the university's press; Howard Washington Odum, creator and sustainer of the Institute for Research in the Social Sciences (IRSS); Guy and Guion Johnson, crusading scholars of social history; and Fletcher M. Green and Howard Kennedy Beale, departmental colleagues (and all their distinguished doctoral students). With them all was the Pulitzer Prize–winning playwright Paul Green, who worked with the social scientists while teaching philosophy. Yet very much a part of all this, friend of all, coworker with all, frequently the mastermind of all, was Joseph Grégoire de Roulhac Hamilton—one who could never be called an angel.[22]

Besides the scholarly monographs, he wrote hundreds of newsletters and newspaper articles, such as his stirring calls in the *Charlotte Observer* and the *Raleigh News and Observer* to "wake up Rip Van Winkle" in the Old North State. He cooperated with, and in some cases led, Odum and Rupert Bayless Vance and the researchers and fellows of IRSS as they campaigned for the moral application of scientific research to problems of society and the environment. By voting record and by the parlance of the day, he was a Progressive who believed in and applied the moral triptych of morality, order, and progress to make aspects of society better—usually such things were called New, as in New Lands, New Law, New Roads, New Freedom, New Nationalism, and above all a New South—but for whites only.[23]

Nothing was new about racism, however, although specific programs to enforce white superiority were in some cases new. The historians Tindall and Woodward noted ruefully that it was North Carolina Progressives who instituted legal Jim Crow in the state. This Jim Crow aspect of the North Carolina Progressives, including the UNC Progressives, was one of the many galling ironies that exercised a later generation of UNC graduate students such as C. Vann Woodward, Bennett Harrison Wall, George Brown Tindall, Joseph Carlyle Sitterson, Paul Gaston, and many others as they contemplated their Progressive mentors. One of this group, Weldon A. Brown, even produced an unpublished novel, "Upward," in which the graduate students emerge from their hypocritical training to bring meaningful reform all over the South and thus undo what their intellectual fathers should not have done and do instead what their intellectual fathers ought to have done. Brown, a student of Reconstruction under Hamilton, shared his typescript with Woodward, Sitterson, and others, and he left it there in Hamilton's archives, where it can be read today.[24]

Above all else Hamilton from 1908 onward focused his attentions on gathering data and collecting primary sources for the study of North Carolina. He established personal and professional friendships with important regional figures, notably Robert Digges Wimberly Connor, who was building archival collections in Raleigh and who would become the first archivist of the United States in 1934. In his quest to build archival holdings, Hamilton traveled far afield, including trips to university centers in France and Germany. As he worked to professionalize the study of history at UNC and throughout North Carolina, he was awarded the chair of Alumni Professor of History in 1908; this emphasis on professionalization was one of the markers for Progressive politics but also for Progressive historians and demonstrated how completely the research university itself was Progressive. When World War I erupted, he became institutionally involved in several government-sponsored educational programs of the Woodrow Wilson wartime administration: director of War Department education programs in North Carolina; director of the War Issues courses for the Fourth District of the Student Army Training Corps; lecturer in the citizenship unit, Army Educational Corps; and education consultant to the general staff of the War Department.[25]

In this transition from peacetime Progressivism to wartime Progressivism, about 1911, Hamilton cooperated with James W. Garner and Walter Lynwood Fleming and others to develop a Festschrift in honor of Dunning. Largely the work of Garner and Fleming, this collection, *Studies in Southern History and Politics,* was published by Columbia University Press. Hamilton's contribution, "Southern Legislation in Respect to Freedmen, 1865–1866," dealt with the infamous Black Codes, and the work showed the historian at his best and at his worst. At his worst, he declared as a stated fact rather than as an opinion that there were innate limits for black people, and therefore, he said, there was an obvious need to impose societal controls. At his best, he was accurate in describing the economic needs for an agricultural people who were trying rather ham-handedly to start industrializing; and at least for North Carolina, he was again fair in his treatment of army officials and the Freedmen's Bureau. Also at his best, he demonstrated the great range of legislation concerning freedmen, and he noted that North Carolina's early Reconstruction leaders wisely eschewed the Black Codes and instead wrote legislation that provided meaningful freedom with regard to property ownership, jury service, business transactions of all sorts, voting rights for the men who had been slaves, and even provisions for officeholding. Too, he marked precisely the draconian and above all "impolitic" features of the more well-known Mississippi and South Carolina Black Codes. He usefully remarked that those two extreme cases were quite different in kind and in degree from the legislation produced in other regions of the South. Most important, he was meticulous in gathering and presenting the data, and anyone can use the research piece today, regardless of political perspective, with the confidence that he was accurate in his statements and citations. Indeed, many of those documented citations in proof made by latter-day revisionist critics were possible largely because of Hamilton's own efforts to gather and archive and catalogue the primary sources—a point noted pointedly by Woodward, Williamson, Tindall, and the former SHC directors J. Isaac Copeland and Carolyn Wallace.[26]

In 1920, after the war's end, Hamilton was awarded one of the first Kenan professorships when the university established some chairs for its favored research scholars, chairs at the time richly endowed. Those professorships remain important, and it was Hamilton who showed all of them how to be professional scholars on the national as well as the regional scenes. He worked to build a graduate center, cooperating with Odum and the regionalists. Like his fellow Progressive historians of a more national scope—Parrington, Beard, and Turner—Hamilton was sometimes as much economist or geographer as historian. He cooperated with James Sprunt to develop a series of published historical monographs for the UNC Historical Society, and in the 1920s Hamilton cooperated with William Terry Couch to develop the UNC Press into a premier academic publisher. Perhaps most interesting, when the crusading pacifist and civil rights activist Howard Kennedy Beale arrived on campus, Hamilton befriended him and was quite pleased with Beale's analysis of economic determinism and class conflict during Reconstruction. He was also supportive of Beale's sympathetic treatment of black aspirations in Reconstruction, however, despite Hamilton's own racist politics and racial assumptions.[27]

As the decades ran on, and as more activist-scholars came to use his archives, Hamilton was ever the Rankean professional, eager that all types of scholars actively use the primary sources he was making available. He did not change his mind about race and society, however, but continued to speak and to behave as a *Volksgeistian* conservative racist. Although Hamilton died in 1961, before the full-fledged development of revisionist studies of Reconstruction, he unwittingly contributed to its coming by establishing the SHC. In fact, the historian personally assisted the great John Hope Franklin to do research in the SHC in defiance of state Jim Crow laws forbidding such aid. Nevertheless, Hamilton continued to express disdain for the intellectual powers of black scholars. The mind runs to Thomas Jefferson engaging warmly with Benjamin Bannecker in discussions about higher mathematics but simultaneously insisting that black people could not do higher mathematics. Hamilton was in no other sense at the level of Jefferson, but the damnable qualities of racist assumptions ran through and subsumed the better natures in both intellectuals.[28]

He attained the nickname Ransack (a play on his ancestral maternal name, de Roulhac) during his drives throughout the South gathering primary sources. Although UNC provided him almost no money to buy such resources, he and his "constant companion," Mary Cornelia Hamilton, relied on their own personal charm (and some legend has it a certain disingenuousness) to remove valuable papers from people's attics and basements and closets. Those attempting to build archives in other states, especially in the Deep South, often complained that he all but robbed South Carolina, Alabama, and Mississippi of important primary sources. Joel Williamson has defended Hamilton from the Ransack charge by noting that somebody had to do this work for himself; and Williamson, Woodward, Tindall, Copeland, Wallace, and Franklin more than once noted the dint of considerable personal and professional effort from Hamilton and his fellows at the SHC.[29]

In 1930 Hamilton resigned from the History Department to run the SHC full time, although he continued to offer some graduate courses and an occasional undergraduate course a couple of times per year on the old academic quarter system. Only a few years later, in 1934, when his old friend R. D. W. Connor officially became the first archivist of the United States, Hamilton and Connor worked with the UNC historians and the UNC library school to establish useful professional relationships for aspirant archivists in the nation's capital as well as in North Carolina. Hamilton continued to run the SHC for long years, still being heavily involved even in the late 1950s, when Mary Cornelia Hamilton began to suffer ill health; she died in 1959. His strong comrade and constant companion removed from his side, Hamilton himself began to slow down and to disengage from the university and the community. He died in 1961.[30]

In assessing any historian, one important question is always: Did he or she leave works in which the facts are generally correct and in which the sources of the facts are quite obvious and are based on primary research that can be revisited by those of us who may disagree? For Hamilton, the answer is resoundingly affirmative. Furthermore, the sources that need to be reviewed, especially for Reconstruction, were themselves largely gathered and then arranged by Hamilton, who took an additional step in making the foundation of his written history very accessible to other scholars. Too, he was helpful to those like Beale and Woodward and the many graduate students and visitors who took opposing ideological views of the facts and pattern of Reconstruction. No serious researcher complains of Hamilton as director of the SHC, and of the black scholars of the Jim Crow era, at least Franklin was able to work with the old racist—and with more tolerant members of his staff—to do useful research in primary sources as a young scholar.

Hamilton, then, represented the racism of an era and a place, and there is no question that his regional and personal racism got in the way of his attempts at fair historical assessment of certain events, such as the Holden-Kirk war and the Wilmington Race Riot and the Ku Klux Klan as it really was, 1868–72. On the other hand, his personal ideas about race and politics never got in the way of establishing a place where scholars could use primary sources for their own interpretations, and his personal prejudices never got in the way of his generous help to those with whom he disagreed. On balance, he seems a good historian flawed by racism in his interpretation and a great institutionalist unflawed by that selfsame racism in his building and running the SHC and various publishing outlets. With regard to the subject of this book, Hamilton does not fit easily into some kind of Dunning School, unless the term means only *racist* and tells us nothing about operating assumptions about class conflict, economic structures, and regional rivalries. And this paper only reinforces Phil Muller's original contention that Hamilton learned nothing of racism from Dunning, but came to Columbia University with such prejudices already fully formed. On the other hand, Hamilton's most enduring personal characteristics appear to be a uniquely southern expression of the man William Archibald Dunning and the way that august figure showed scholars how to be professionals in the service of Clio regardless of personal history or historiography.

Notes

1. John Herbert Roper, "Confessions of a Chapel Hill Liberal," *Southern Cultures* 6, no. 3 (Fall 2000): 112–18; author interviews of J. Isaac Copeland (November 19–20, 1979, and October 11, 1982), William Terry Couch (January 10–11, 1980), Guy Johnson (January 11, 1980), Guion Johnson (January 11, 1980), Frank Weir Klingberg (November 10, 1978), Joseph Carlyle Sitterson (November 10, 1978), Comer Vann Woodward (July 18, 1978); and personal correspondence with George Brown Tindall and Joel Williamson, 1987, John Herbert Roper Papers

(hereinafter cited as JHR), Southern Historical Collection of the Library of the University of North Carolina at Chapel Hill (hereinafter cited as SHC).

2. For the "deep reciprocities" concept, see David Minter, *William Faulkner: His Life and Thought* (Baltimore: Johns Hopkins University Press, 1980); James L. Roark of Emory University showed me Minter's work and concepts.

3. Joel Roudolph Williamson, "C. Vann Woodward and a New Humanism," in *C. Vann Woodward: A Southern Historian and His Critics,* ed. John Herbert Roper (1997; reprint, Athens: University of Georgia Press, 2012); Orville Vernon Burton, *In My Father's House Are Many Mansions* (Chapel Hill: University of North Carolina Press, 1985). Joseph Grégoire de Roulhac Hamilton Papers, esp. field guide to collection, SHC, hereinafter cited as JGdeRHP, SHC; there are also notes in Joseph Grégoire de Roulhac Hamilton Papers, University Archives of the University of North Carolina, hereinafter cited as UA/UNC.

4. William L. Barney, *Nineteenth Century Southern Political Leaders* (New York: University Publishers of America, 1978); Barney, *The Secessionist Impulse: Alabama and Mississippi in 1860* (1975; reprint, Tuscaloosa: University of Alabama Press, 1990). I also benefited from conversations with Barney in 1987 and with UNC English Professor Lee Green in 1989.

5. Apologies to Joseph Hamilton Basso, a *New Yorker* editor and novelist who seems to have been the first to describe Theodore Roosevelt the way New Deal scholars describe his cousin Franklin Delano Roosevelt, viz., as one seeking Jeffersonian ends by Hamiltonian means. Basso, "Apostle of the Obvious," in his *Mainstream* (New York: Ayer, 1943); Basso's point was presaged independently in Vernon Louis Parrington, *Main Currents in American Thought*, 3 vols. (New York: Harcourt Brace, 1927), and then parroted rather self-consciously in Henry Steele Commager, *The American Mind* (New Haven: Yale University Press, 1950). Paul Gaston, *The New South Creed: A Study in Southern Mythmaking* (New York: Knopf, 1970).

6. J[oseph] Carlyle Sitterson, "Joseph Grégoire de Roulhac Hamilton," *Dictionary of North Carolina Biography,* ed. William S. Powell (Chapel Hill: University of North Carolina Press, 1979–96), s.v.; Fletcher M. Green, "Joseph Grégoire Hamilton," 1962, Office, Secretary of the Faculty, UA/UNC; William Alexander Percy, *Lanterns on the Levee: Recollections of a Planter's Son* (1941; reprint, Baton Rouge: Louisiana State University Press, 1973).

7. Endnote matter, written largely by Arnold Marshall Rose, Gunnar Myrdal, et al., *An American Dilemma: The Negro Problem and Modern Democracy* (New York: Harper and Row, 1944), 1027–1100; Arnold M. Rose, *The Negro in America* (New York: Harper and Row, 1964); Gary Stanley Becker, *The Economics of Discrimination,* rev. ed. (Chicago: University of Chicago Press, 1971); C. Vann Woodward, *The Strange Career of Jim Crow* (1954; reprint, New York: Oxford University Press, 1989); Joel Williamson, *The Crucible of Race* (New York: Oxford University Press, 1984); Ralph Luker, "The Crucible of Civil War and Reconstruction in the Experience of William Porcher DuBose," *South Carolina Historical Magazine* 83

(1982): 50–78; and Luker, "William Porcher DuBose and Southern Theological Tradition, 1840–1922," in *Varieties of Southern Religious Experiences,* ed. Samuel J. Hill Jr. (Baton Rouge: Louisiana State University Press, 1988): 158–71; and DuBose, *Turning Points in My Life* (New York: Longmans, Green, 1912); lynching statistics, NAACP records gathered by Walter Francis White, *Rope and Faggot: A Biography of Judge Lynch* (New York: Arno, 1969).

8. John Higham, *History: Professional Scholarship in America* (Englewood Cliffs, N.J.: Prentice-Hall, 1965), 92–103; John Herbert Roper, *U. B. Phillips: A Southern Mind* (Macon, Ga.: Mercer University Press, 1984), 43, contrasts Frederick Jackson Turner with Ranke and Freeman.

9. On German scientism and Ranke, see Higham, *History,* 92–103; Roper, *U. B. Phillips,* 23–39; Sitterson, "Joseph Grégoire de Roulhac Hamilton"; Green, "Hamilton"; notes on Sewanee, correspondence, JGdeRHP, SHC.

10. On the era, see esp. James Logan Hunt, "The Making of a Populist: Marion Butler, 1863–1895," *North Carolina Historical Review* 62, nos. 1, 2, and 3 (1985 and 1986), and Hunt, *Marion Butler and American Populism* (Chapel Hill: University of North Carolina Press, 2003); also see Butler's newspaper, the *Caucasian,* North Carolina Historical Collection, Library of the University of North Carolina, and Butler Papers, SHC. Above all, see how Hamilton himself described events in his correspondence, JGdeRHP, SHC, and Hamilton with Robert Digges Wimberly Connor and William Kenneth Boyd, *History of North Carolina: North Carolina since 1860,* 6 vols. (Chicago: Lewis, 1919).

11. Nina Silber makes this point effectively in *The Romance of Reunion: Northerners and the South, 1865–1900* (Chapel Hill: University of North Carolina Press, 1993), and Joel Williamson, *The Crucible of Race,* has developed it in full. See also Philip R. Muller, "Look Back without Anger: A Reappraisal of William A Dunning," *Journal of American History* 61, no. 2 (September 1974): 325–38.

12. The tone emerges in correspondence; see Hamilton Papers, UA/UNC, and JGdeRHP, SHC. This tone is noted with admiration by J. Carlyle Sitterson and C. Vann Woodward and with resentment by Guy and Guion Johnson—who are especially sarcastic about the name Roulhac; see the interviews of Woodward, Sitterson, Guy Johnson, Guion Johnson, Copeland (November 19, 1979), and Couch, JHR, SHC.

13. H. Leon Prather Sr., *We Have Taken a City: Wilmington Racial Massacre and Coup of 1898* (Rutherford, N.J.: Fairleigh Dickinson University Press, 1984), and Williamson, *Crucible of Race.*

14. Hamilton, *Reconstruction in North Carolina* (Raleigh: Edwards & Broughton, 1906), 72–83; Hamilton, *Reconstruction in North Carolina* (New York: Columbia University Press, 1914).

15. Hamilton, *Reconstruction in North Carolina* (1906 ed.), 61–71.

16. Ibid., 152.

17. Hamilton, *Reconstruction in North Carolina* (1914 ed.); Hamilton, *Party*

Politics in North Carolina, 1835–1860 (Durham, N.C.: North Carolina Historical Society, 1916); and Hamilton et al., *History of North Carolina.*

18. Hamilton, *Reconstruction in North Carolina* (1914 ed.); Hamilton, *Party Politics in North Carolina;* and Hamilton et al., *History of North Carolina.* Cf. Allen W. Trelease, *White Terror: The Ku Klux Klan Conspiracy and Southern Reconstruction* (New York: Harper and Row, 1971).

19. Hamilton, *Reconstruction in North Carolina* (1914 ed.); Hamilton, *Party Politics in North Carolina;* and Hamilton et al., *History of North Carolina.* Cf. Trelease, *White Terror;* Muller, "Look Back without Anger."

20. Walter Lynwood Fleming, review of J. G. de Roulhac Hamilton, *Reconstruction in North Carolina,* in *American Historical Review* 12 (1907): 911–12; R. P. Brooks, review of Hamilton, *Reconstruction in North Carolina,* in *Mississippi Valley Historical Review* 2 (1915): 283–86. Gabriel Kolko gave fullest expression of this line of thinking, one in which extremely conservative scholars and New Left scholars came to agreement in terms of facts while disagreeing in terms of historical judgment about those facts. See Kolko, *The Triumph of Conservatism: A Re-interpretation of American History, 1900–1916* (New York: Free Press of Glencoe, 1963). More moderate expressions of the historical judgment about business leaders in the northern and southern regions are Silber, *The Romance of Reunion;* C. Vann Woodward, *Origins of the New South, 1877–1913,* rev. ed. (Baton Rouge: Louisiana State University Press, 1985), and Robert Green McCloskey, *American Conservatism in the Age of Enterprise, 1865–1910: A Study of William Graham Sumner, Stephen J. Field, and Andrew Carnegie* (1951; reprint, New York: Harper and Row, 1964).

21. See esp. Sitterson, "Joseph Grégoire de Roulhac Hamilton"; JGdeRHP, SHC; and Green, "Hamilton"; Sitterson's remarks were noted when I served as his grading assistant in 1972, in JHR, SHC.

22. In the rankings of major research universities by the Carnegie Foundation, 1929–60, UNC rated alongside the University of Virginia and the University of Texas despite the fact that material resources were and are greater—and even whole departments in humanities better—at the latter two schools than in Chapel Hill in the period. On UNC's national ratings and its slight monetary resources, see the correspondence among Edward Kidder Graham, Harry Woodburn Chase, and Frank Porter Graham in the Frank Porter Graham Papers, UA/ UNC; Howard Kennedy Beale's correspondence with Hamilton, JGdeRHP, UA/ UNC; and Paul Eliot Green Papers, SHC, UNC. Howard Kennedy Beale, "On Rewriting Reconstruction History," *American Historical Review* 45 (1940): 807–27; and Beale, *The Critical Year: A Study of Andrew Johnson and Reconstruction* (1930; reprint, New York: Frederick Ungar, 1958).

23. Hamilton, "A Plea for Constitutional Convention," *Raleigh News and Observer,* December 19, 1912–January 19, 1913, and newspaper clippings, esp. *Charlotte Observer,* 1912–60; James Sprunt Historical Publications, manuscripts and typescripts, 1908–24, JGdeRHP, UA/UNC, and James Sprunt Papers, SHC.

24. George Brown Tindall, *Emergence of the New South, 1913–1945* (Baton Rouge: Louisiana State University Press, 1967), and Woodward, *Origins of the New South;* Weldon Brown, "Upward," typescript, Weldon Brown Papers, SHC; interviews, JHR, SHC.

25. Sitterson, "Joseph Grégoire de Roulhac Hamilton"; Green, "Hamilton"; World War I folders, War Department folders, 1917–19, JGdeRHP, UA/UNC.

26. *Studies in Southern History and Politics, Inscribed to William Archibald Dunning . . . by His Former Pupils the Authors,* ed. James W. Garner (New York: Columbia University Press, 1914); Hamilton, "Southern Legislation in Regard to Freedmen, 1865–1866," ibid., 137–60; letters from Hamilton, Phillips, Garner, and Fleming about the project are in JGdeRHP, SHC; author's notes, JHR, SHC.

27. My interpretation of correspondence in JGdeRHP, UA/UNC, and JGdeRHP, SHC, and interviews, JHR, SHC. My interpretation was influenced by discussions with Sitterson, Joseph A. Herzenberg (who was a town councilman and local historian of UNC during the Frank Porter Graham years), and the SHC archivists Isaac Copeland and Carolyn Wallace; author's notes, JHR, SHC.

28. In regard to Franklin, Hamilton's personal role may have been fairly minimal, but Franklin does recall being able to use important documents in SHC in the period at end of World War II when Hamilton was in charge; apparently, Franklin was permitted to use the documents out of sight of white researchers, an ironical situation that put the late scholar in the middle of all the documents he needed and thus was more convenient than normal arrangements for the white scholars; see author interview of John Hope Franklin, November 10, 1978, JHR, SHC; on Jefferson and Banneker, see Winthrop D. Jordan, *White over Black: American Attitudes toward the Negro, 1550–1812* (Chapel Hill: University of North Carolina Press, 1968), 449–52, 454–55, 486.

29. Williamson, "C. Vann Woodward"; author interviews with Franklin, Woodward, and Sitterson, JHR, SHC; on Williamson, Tindall, Copeland, and Wallace, see author interviews with Copeland, JHR, SHC.

30. Correspondence of Sprunt, Couch, Wilson, and Frank Porter Graham, JGdeRHP, UA/UNC; author interviews with Franklin, Woodward, and Sitterson, JHR, SHC; Sitterson, "Joseph Grégoire de Roulhac Hamilton"; Green, "Hamilton"; Hamilton's obituary appeared in the *Chapel Hill Weekly,* November 16, 1961.

7

Paul Leland Haworth

The "Black Republican" in the Old Chief's Court

J. Vincent Lowery

Scholars have rarely mentioned Indiana-born Paul Leland Haworth in connection with the group of historians referred to as the Dunning School even though Haworth completed his dissertation under Columbia University professor William Archibald Dunning's direction in 1906. Scholars' omission of Haworth from their assessments of Dunning and his students has possibly resulted from Haworth's lack of professional accomplishments compared to his more well-known southern classmates, but also because Haworth clashed with them on interpretations of Reconstruction and what was then termed the Negro Problem. These disagreements were not lost on W. E. B. Du Bois, who organized the bibliography of *Black Reconstruction* (1935) on the basis of the racial attitudes of the authors of the works cited. Du Bois characterized the writings of Dunning and most of his students as "Standard—Anti-Negro." In contrast, Du Bois described Haworth's *Reconstruction and Union, 1865–1912* (1912) as "Fair to Indifferent on the Negro," even calling his work "invaluable."[1] Du Bois's assessment calls attention to an important discrepancy between the work of Haworth and that of those scholars traditionally associated with the Dunning School that modern scholars have overlooked. A careful study of Haworth and his work thus challenges their assumptions about the members of the Old Chief's court.

Haworth's work at Columbia and his subsequent publications suggest that Columbia's History Department was not a factory merely producing racist historians and histories. Instead, the program attracted aspiring historians interested in the highly politicized subject of Reconstruction. Haworth's Indiana Quaker roots and his Progressive philosophy influenced his study of Reconstruction and the Negro Problem. While most of his southern-born comrades sought to defend the emerging Jim Crow order through their study of Reconstruction, Haworth attempted to undermine that order by proving that southern whites, not southern blacks, were the true cause of the Negro Problem. Although Haworth, like others of his day, believed that African Americans were inferior to whites, he attributed blacks' condition to their oppressive treatment by southern whites. His racial philosophy thus distinguishes him from the better-known Dunningites.

The North Carolinian Joseph Grégoire de Roulhac Hamilton recalled the contentious relationship between Haworth and the southern members of the Dunning School in an interview with the historian Wendell Holmes Stephenson. According to Stephenson, Hamilton "delighted to tell stories of sectional rivalry in Dunning's seminar," in which the "damnyankee" Haworth clashed with his southern-born classmates. Hamilton remembered one particular altercation he had with Haworth in the seminar room during a study session. Stephenson recorded Hamilton's recollection: "Tiring of northern jibes, Hamilton hurdled the seminar table to have at him [Haworth], but other members intervened to prevent a renewal of clash and conflict a generation after Appomattox." Hamilton's memories of this incident illustrate the degree to which Haworth was an outsider during his days at Columbia and within the phase of Reconstruction historiography known as the Dunning School.[2]

Haworth studied the past to understand better the contemporary Negro Problem. His presentist philosophical approach to history warrants placing him in the same category as scholars such as Frederick Jackson Turner, James Harvey Robinson, and Charles Beard, the foremost Progressive historians of the early twentieth century. These historians imagined the social applications of their studies, believing that the historical profession had to shed its political conservatism in favor of a more critical, Progressive mentality. Haworth's scholarship became increasingly focused on recent history, and he distinguished himself as a Progressive historian with the publication of *America in Ferment* (1915), a guide to the various problems plaguing the nation in the early twentieth century.[3]

Haworth's midwestern roots no doubt influenced his historical perspective. The historian David S. Brown observed the imprint of a unique regional mentality on midwestern scholars. According to Brown, "Unburdened by the quasi-aristocratic culture that stalked the southern imagination or the minority 'otherness' familiar to many in the ethnically tinged liberal intelligentsia, they were passionate about the possibilities of democracy and unafraid of popular protest, which both their scholarship and their teaching recognized as a vital part of the American political tradition."[4]

Haworth probably learned lessons in social justice during his childhood in the Quaker community of West Newton, and his upbringing would have affected his later views on race relations in the South. Indiana Quakers opposed the institution of slavery and, though the antebellum state legislature passed a series of measures that denied African Americans their rights, the state's Quaker communities often attracted blacks because of their willingness to support African Americans' freedom struggle. For example, George Julian, a leading Radical Republican from the Quaker region of Whitewater Valley, advocated "full legal equality for blacks" and "the granting of suffrage." Haworth's childhood in this environment no doubt caused him to view the past and present, particularly southern race relations, in a very different manner from that of his southern counterparts, most of whom received their early lessons from proponents of the cult of the Lost Cause.[5]

Haworth completed his bachelor's (1899) and master's (1901) degrees at Indiana University. He studied with the historians James Albert Woodburn and Ulysses Grant Weatherly, also a West Newton native. Woodburn wrote a number of books, including a biography of the Radical Republican Thaddeus Stevens. Acknowledging Stevens's many critics, Woodburn defended the Pennsylvania congressman's Reconstruction plan for attempting to extend the principles of the Constitution to protect freedpeople. Although Haworth questioned Stevens's motives, he agreed with Woodburn's assessment of the Radical Republican's postwar vision. Weatherly joined the Department of History at Indiana in 1895 and became chair of the Department of Economics and Social Science four years later. He cofounded the American Sociological Association in 1905. Weatherly studied a variety of subjects, including the race question in the Americas, and he struck a moderate tone.[6] Woodburn and Weatherly thus introduced Haworth to historical lessons that buttressed his Quaker beliefs.

After completing his studies at Indiana, Haworth traveled through the Deep South to study the Negro Problem. He then contributed "correspondence" reports for the *Indianapolis News* in 1901–2. These articles provide insight into Haworth's racial attitudes, and he continued to draw on his travels through the South in his dissertation and even repeated parts of these early writings in later publications. Haworth repeatedly challenged the ability of southern whites to solve the Negro Problem, rejecting their claims that they understood African Americans better than anyone else. Haworth dissented from the emerging belief, bolstered by scientific racism, that every race possessed natural characteristics that could not be altered. He asserted that African Americans would make significant advances if freed from white oppression and properly supported. Haworth concluded that any understanding of the Negro Problem could not be achieved "without a knowledge of this other problem. And this other problem, for lack of a better name, may be called, 'the problem of the white.'"[7]

Haworth reported his initial findings in an article titled "Of the Race Problem," published by the *Indianapolis News* in March 1901. This article reflected his belief that contemporary problems could best be understood by examining their historical roots. He declared that the contemporary struggles of African Americans resulted largely from "the wrong of slavery" and African Americans' "constant battle against white prejudice." According to Haworth, slavery caused "mental ossification for generations to come; it means moral degradation; it means loss of self-respect; it means, in fact, everything that is bad." Emancipation freed African Americans from the shackles of slavery, but southern whites took steps to reassert their authority over their former slaves. Southern whites justified their treatment of African Americans by citing the poor character of freedmen. Summarizing southern whites' racial attitudes, what others would brand their "Bourbon" mentality, Haworth concluded, "Having learned little and forgotten less, the majority of Southerners stubbornly refuse to recognize that blind adherence to this principle [that the subordinate position of African Americans is divinely sanctioned], with all that it has entailed, is responsible for the South being fifty years behind the North, and they still suicidally hold to the old theory."[8]

Haworth recognized that the white South endured hardships during Reconstruction that "she brought on herself, and for which the poor negro was not responsible. But the wrongs of reconstructed Southerners fade into nothingness when compared with the wrongs of negroes at the hands of Kukluxes and White Camelias." Haworth argued that the racial violence of Reconstruction inspired the "Civilized Barbarism" of lynching in the contemporary South. He shared with readers his encounter with a young white man who proudly retained a "souvenir" from the body of an African American lynching victim. Haworth concluded, "When such a state of affairs is possible, one wonders to himself whether it may not be possible that we are relapsing into barbarism." Seeking to sway his readers' opinions in favor of a more paternalistic attitude toward the African American, Haworth offered a final assessment of him: "The negro is neither an angel nor a brute. He is simply a man, who, because of misfortunes of environment extending back through hundreds of years, has been unable to cast off the 'brute inheritance' so successfully as his cousin of paler skin. Before condemning him, we should not forget the disadvantages under which he has struggled in the past nor should we forget the many, but less understood, disadvantages under which he struggles in the present."[9]

In a subsequent article in the *Indianapolis News* in December 1902, Haworth offered readers insight into southern whites' views on the education of African Americans. Haworth recognized that southern whites were unwilling to identify an African American "as anything other than a menial, with a menial's thoughts and a menial's morals. . . . They believe that all efforts to give him ideas out of keeping with his station in life are mistakes; hence they decry negro education and insist that it is a failure." Haworth observed that wise southern white men had begun to realize that they must abandon "the suicidal [racial] policy that has been the chief cause of that section's being at least a generation behind the North in mental, spiritual, and economic development." He argued that whites and blacks alike had to be educated in order to restore racial peace, to uplift both races, and to develop the economy of the region. Haworth acknowledged the value of industrial education but argued that African Americans must gain access to both industrial and classical education. He concluded, "Races are not civilized in a day. Ten centuries passed between the time when our Teutonic forefathers destroyed the Roman empire and the time when they had become sufficiently leavened by a Christian civilization to be ready for the Renaissance. And if our Teutonic forefathers were so long a time in bursting the bands of barbarism, we ought not to grow discouraged at the progress—small yet undoubted—that the negro race has made in less than forty years."[10] In both these articles Haworth struck a moderate chord when he advised readers to be patient with African Americans and recognize their progress despite being stifled by whites for generations.

Haworth was not content with simply uplifting African Americans to restore their rights as citizens eventually. In "Negro Disfranchisement in

Louisiana," which appeared in *Outlook* in May 1902, he argued that the southern white man "understands him [the Negro] too much as a mere animal rather than as a man with latent capabilities to be developed." Haworth argued that southern whites had to cease denying African Americans their constitutional rights. He noted that "the more intelligent" African Americans were willing to accept educational or property qualifications to vote if they were applied without racial distinction. Haworth concluded, "The negro problem is one which must be solved, and the only way to solve it is to make the negro—and also his white brother—a man. This can never be done by taking away his rights." Haworth's early publications thus illustrate that he had formed ideas about the antebellum and postbellum South very different from those of the southern-born students who flocked to Columbia to study with Dunning. Haworth was not immune to contemporary racism, but he assigned the greatest blame for the Negro Problem to white Southerners. His argument that they had to restore African Americans' rights as citizens distinguished Haworth as a racial progressive, especially within the context of the Dunning School historians.[11]

In spring 1901 Haworth applied for admission to Columbia's doctoral program in history. His mentors encouraged him to consider graduate programs in the East to further his professional development and increase his chances for future employment. They recommended that he apply for admission to the graduate programs at Harvard University, Yale University, the University of Pennsylvania, Johns Hopkins University, and Columbia. The death of Johns Hopkins's Herbert Baxter Adams in 1901 and the emergence of Dunning as the leading Reconstruction historian lured Haworth and his southern counterparts to Columbia. Dunning lamented that Haworth failed to submit his application before fellowship deadlines, explaining to one of Haworth's mentors, "It is too bad that he could not have known this for I am anxious to get in the track of men interested in Reconstruction." Unable to begin his work with Dunning, the following year Haworth instead taught at Michigan State Normal College (later Eastern Michigan University) and successfully reapplied for admission to Columbia's doctoral program in spring 1902. The school named him University Scholar in History, an award that provided the necessary financial resources for him to begin his doctoral studies.[12]

Haworth clashed with his southern classmates, as is reflected in Hamilton's recollection of his altercation with him. The correspondence between Hamilton and the Alabamian Walter Lynwood Fleming, two of Dunning's most unreconstructed students, reveals their contempt for Haworth. In one exchange Fleming ridiculed Haworth's belief in racial equality and his endorsement of Booker T. Washington's Tuskegee Institute as a model for African American education, writing, "If he wants to send his offspring to Booker T.'s school, it most probably suits them better than the Univ. of Va. or Wash. and Lee or Tulane." Fleming explained that he decided to publish a collection of Reconstruction-era documents (later issued as *Documentary History of Reconstruction,* two volumes, 1906–7) to "occupy the unworked field to the exclusion of such d—f—'s as Haworth. . . . I consider myself better qualified than a New Englander or a wild Westerner." Fleming's vitriolic assault on Haworth illustrates the degree to which the Alabama native believed that Haworth's midwestern roots and his racial views, seemingly intertwined, disqualified him as a historian. Fleming believed that southern whites alone possessed the necessary perspective and understanding of race to study Reconstruction.[13] Haworth dismissed the efforts of white Southerners to explain Reconstruction, writing in an unpublished version of his essay on black suffrage, "Some efforts have been made to defend the course of the South during this period [Reconstruction], but the arguments advanced are so utterly feeble and juvenile as to make refutation utterly unnecessary."[14] No historian thus more plainly questioned the attitudes of Dunning's southern-born students than Haworth. He apparently also took the fight to them directly in seminars too often imagined by historians as mere celebrations of the southern white point of view.

Haworth's life changed dramatically while he studied at Columbia. He married Martha Ackerman in 1903, and she gave birth to a son, Leland, in 1904 and to a daughter, Anna Ruth, one year later. Dissatisfied with his fellowships, Haworth pursued alternative means to provide for his family. After finishing his dissertation under Dunning's direction, Haworth hoped to aid Elroy McKendree Avery in the completion of *A History of the United States and Its People* (seven volumes, 1904–10) for the Burrows Brothers Publishing Company. In 1906 that publisher printed Haworth's dissertation on the election of 1876, and Haworth accepted an offer to assist Avery at the Cleveland, Ohio, publishing house.[15]

Haworth's *The Hayes-Tilden Disputed Election of 1876* (1906) challenged the contemporary understanding of that election and the accompanying Compromise of 1877, critically analyzing Democratic methods of Redemption and documenting the work of the Electoral Commission established by Congress in 1877 to settle the contested presidential election of 1876. The historian C. Vann Woodward later argued that Haworth was "blind to certain large aspects of the subject" of the compromise. In distinguishing the works of Haworth and Woodward, the historian Keith Ian Polakoff observed that the former lacked access to manuscript materials such as those that allowed Woodward to shed new light on the economic interests behind the compromise. Haworth credited the assistance he received from politicians and newspaper editors who played some part in the election and compromise, as well as the son of Rutherford B. Hayes, who granted him access to the president's personal papers. Haworth's footnotes, however, do not suggest that this material shaped his work to any significant degree, and the author acknowledged the limits of his research in the preface of the book. Haworth recognized that there were "matters which will, in all probability, always remain secrets, for the simple reason that those actors who could tell the truth concerning them will never do so."[16] Although Haworth failed to uncover any of these secrets, his study of the election and the compromise offered new insight into the subject while reflecting his desire to position the contemporary plight of African Americans within the historical context of the end of Reconstruction.

Unlike Woodward, Haworth devoted chapters to Republican rule during Reconstruction and the campaigns of 1876. Haworth neither overlooked Republican corruption nor concealed his belief that African Americans were ill prepared for the rights conferred to them during Congressional Reconstruction. He argued, however, that southern white intransigence on the race question was never justified. Haworth emphasized that violence and intimidation carried out on behalf of the Democratic Party in Florida, Louisiana, and South Carolina brought Reconstruction to an end.

Writing about Louisiana, for example, Haworth observed: "In perhaps no other state in the Union has there ever been such a disorderly condition of affairs as existed in Louisiana during the years from 1866 to 1877. Wholesale corruption, intimidation of negro voters by thousands and tens of thousands, political assassinations, riots, revolutions—all these were the order of the day in Louisiana politics." This bloody record began with the New Orleans Riot of 1866, an incident that Haworth characterized as "a most inhuman massacre," and was followed by the terrorist campaign of the Knights of the White Camelia in 1868. Like white Southerners, Haworth conceded that some attacks on African Americans were warranted. He also acknowledged the persistence of Republican corruption and political fraud cited by whites to justify their Redemptive campaign. Haworth, however, resisted any suggestion that such misrule justified the southern white conservative counterrevolution. About the 1876 campaign Haworth remarked: "Intimidation was, in truth, one of the central facts of the campaign. It was occasionally resorted to by Republicans, but it would be roughly correct to say that it was a weapon belonging to the Democrats." He argued that "in an absolutely fair and free election the state would have gone Republican by from five to fifteen thousand."[17]

In his treatment of South Carolina Haworth also emphasized Democratic misdeeds to explain the outcome of the election. Drawing on the works of the northern Republican journalist James S. Pike, South Carolina journalist and lawyer John S. Reynolds, and former carpetbagger governor Daniel H. Chamberlain, Haworth cited stories of greed and corruption within the state's Republican regime. Pike interviewed Democratic opponents of the state's Republican machine. Reynolds wrote *Reconstruction in South Carolina* (1905), a work that the historian Bruce E. Baker noted "straddled the divide between amateur and professional history, as did its author," and provided the most detailed account of Reconstruction in the Palmetto State to that date. Du Bois identified Pike and Reynolds as among those authors who "select and use facts and opinions in order to prove that the South was right in Reconstruction, the North vengeful or deceived and the Negro stupid." In 1901 Chamberlain contributed an essay to the *Atlantic Monthly* series on Reconstruction that, with the exception of the article by Du Bois, generally criticized the experiment of Reconstruction and defended the Redemption of the South. Chamberlain described Republican rule as corrupt and inept—the result of its dependence on ignorant freedmen. The former governor roundly denounced the methods of Redemption, but he sympathized with white Southerners' responses to Republican rule. Though Haworth relied heavily on sources to varying degrees critical of Republicans and the freedmen, he understood the plight of African Americans and criticized the methods white South Carolinians employed to redeem their state.[18]

Haworth accepted the probability that "in some cases no doubt the operations of the klans were to a certain extent justifiable, but in others the outrages committed not only were wholly without extenuation, but were brutal and fiendish beyond description."[19] He provided details of "riots" in Hamburg and Ellenton, South Carolina, in 1876 that reflected the brutal character of southern whites, many of whom believed that "the killing of a few negroes was not a matter of very great importance." Such attitudes crystalized into the spread of rifle clubs, or Red Shirts, during the election. Assessing the outcome of the election of 1876 in South Carolina, Haworth concluded, "If the election had been free and fair, the [Republican] majority would have been increased by many thousands."[20]

Haworth pinpointed the dangers of the national electoral crisis resulting from the disputed returns in Florida, Louisiana, and South Carolina. He observed that "at the time probably more people dreaded an armed conflict than had anticipated a like outcome to the secession movement of 1860–1861." Haworth found fault on both sides of the political divide as Congress attempted to sort out the election returns, but he asserted that the Democratic Party constituted the true threat to the Union. The Indiana Dunningite argued that the Electoral Commission prevented the resumption of war, asserting, "Without a shadow of a doubt the act creating that Commission was one of the wisest pieces of statecraft ever evolved by an American Congress."[21]

Woodward noted that the so-called bargain between southern whites and Hayes's supporters at the Wormley House Hotel on February 26, 1877, dominated popular perceptions of the compromise in the early twentieth century, but Haworth contributed little of substance to this interpretation. In his 1974 review of Polakoff's *The Politics of Inertia: The Election of 1876 and the End of Reconstruction* (1973), the historian Gerald W. McFarland observed, "Haworth implicitly played down a more dramatic interpretation of the compromise of 1877, one which identified it with the secret bargain made at the so-called Wormley Conference." To be sure, Haworth identified a "bargain" between "the friends of Hayes" and southern white politicians. Southern negotiators agreed that the region's Democrats would not filibuster to stall the congressional resolution of the election, and they guaranteed African Americans their civil rights. Although Haworth documented these details, he focused largely on the work of the Electoral Commission.[22]

In the end, Haworth did not entirely denounce the outcome of the election of 1876, which he credited with preserving the Union. On a mixed note, he remarked that "the Republican party practically disappeared in the South, and as a result the freedman in effect lost his political rights; but he preserved his civil rights, and he lived under a better government than when he himself had assisted in making and administering the laws." Even as Haworth identified what he perceived as the positive qualities of the outcome of the Compromise of 1877, he considered southern whites' resistance to the extension of rights to African Americans and the immorality and ignorance of Republican rule as its true lesson: "'He who is unwilling to concede liberty to others deserves it not for himself,' Haworth concluded, 'and under a just God cannot long retain it.'"[23]

Though contemporary historians regularly and widely reviewed the dissertations crafted in Dunning's famous seminar, they paid short shrift to *The Hayes-Tilden Disputed Presidential Election of 1876*. The *American Historical Review* (*AHR*) published the only scholarly review of Haworth's book. Its reviewer acknowledged the author's thorough research and arrangement of material, concluding that Haworth "has come as close to the truth of this exceedingly complicated affair as it is possible for one to attain by historical methods." The critic wrote that Haworth's work "possesses nearly every virtue desirable in a historical work, with one exception." The author, who may have even been one of Haworth's southern comrades at Columbia, asserted that "the monograph is thoroughly scientific in method and sound in its criticism of fact, but is equally unscientific in spirit and temper. The style occasionally descends perilously near flippancy and vulgarity at the expense of Southern Democrats." Most early Reconstruction historians dismissed Republican rule as a "tragic era" and accepted Democratic restoration of white home rule as a necessary outcome. As a result, contemporary historians generally ignored Haworth's critical analysis of the conduct of Democrats during the 1876 campaign. They presumed that such revisionism could be produced only by violating professional standards of objectivity.[24]

The influential editor Henry Watterson of the *Louisville Courier-Journal* also questioned Haworth's objectivity. Watterson accused Haworth of concealing his partisanship behind a thin veil of historical research. The Louisville editor's participation in the disputed election of 1876 certainly informed his criticism of the Columbia graduate's book. Watterson was Tilden's "most ardent southern supporter" and attended the Wormley Conference as the representative of the disputed state of South Carolina in February 1877. As Woodward observed, those Southerners involved in the Wormley Conference had a vested interest in the story of their arrangement with Hayes's representatives.[25] Watterson no doubt feared that Haworth's alternative account, enhanced by the work's academic and therefore seemingly authoritative nature, might challenge the accepted version of events.

Watterson denounced Haworth as "a very unfair critic and a crude thinker." He observed that Haworth relied heavily on such partisan publications as *Harper's Weekly* and the *Nation*. Watterson defended Democrats against Haworth's assertion that they surpassed the Republicans in intimidation and fraud. He also challenged Haworth's supposedly critical assessment of Tilden, whom Watterson described as "high-minded" and "courageous." The Kentuckian judged that Haworth's account of the election and the compromise was "worthless, containing nothing more than a half-statement of the Democratic case" and an unquestioning acceptance of Republican claims. Watterson went so far as to suggest that Columbia University should abandon its academic pursuits in favor of "shoemaking" if Haworth's book reflected the abilities of the school's faculty. The editor quipped that Haworth "would make an excellent cobbler in the department of scraps and mending."[26]

Undeterred by such criticism, Haworth in 1907 challenged the dominant prosouthern narrative of Reconstruction in a review of James Ford Rhodes's two-volume survey of the postwar years in *Political Science Quarterly*. Rhodes, a "gentleman historian," achieved renown and respect among professional historians despite his lack of academic training. His nine-volume *History of the United States from the Compromise of 1850* (1892–1922) reflected contemporary racial thought. In these volumes Rhodes described African Americans as inferior beings and rejected the idea of racial equality. He indicted Republican governments for corruption and misrule and characterized the Democratic counterrevolution as the restoration of good government.[27]

Haworth lashed out at Rhodes, possibly using him as a metaphorical surrogate for his Columbia classmates. Haworth advised historians to cease "apply[ing] principles and precepts which are admirable in times of peace" to their judgment of Reconstruction. Anticipating Charles and Mary Beard's assertion that the Civil War and Reconstruction represented a "Second American Revolution," Haworth declared, "The Civil War and the events that followed it assuredly constitute one of the greatest revolutions known to history." He argued that conditions compelled Congress to transform the South during Reconstruction. Haworth asserted that white Southerners would have resisted regardless of the path taken by the federal government: "Suppose the Johnson plan had been adopted by the Radicals. There would, from the very nature of the situation, have been great disorders in the South, that might well have surpassed those which actually did occur—and historians like Mr. Rhodes would now be chiding Charles Sumner and Thaddeus Stevens for their childlike faith in human nature."[28] Haworth thus challenged the Jim Crow–era interpretation of Reconstruction just as revisionist scholars later attacked the Dunning School. But contemporary scholars ignored his perspective.

Haworth's interpretation of Reconstruction and the Negro Problem kept him on the margins of the Dunning School. In 1911 J. G. de Roulhac Hamilton and another Dunning student, the Mississippian James Garner, began organizing a Festschrift in honor of the Old Chief. Hamilton planned to exclude Haworth from the project. Fleming apparently set aside his animosity for Haworth in the spirit of properly honoring Dunning and proposed that Hamilton invite Haworth to contribute an essay to the volume. After Hamilton rejected this suggestion, Fleming responded: "I think you are right about confining the work to Southern men for they will give a unity to the thing that will not exist if Haworth is put in." Two years later Garner sent Hamilton a list of scholars who had "definitely promised to contribute to the Dunning Testimonial," Haworth among them. Haworth's essay "Elections in the South during the Reconstruction Era," however, did not appear in the published volume. He explained to his former classmate Charles W. Ramsdell, then teaching at the University of Texas, "Owing to a combination of causes I did not contribute to the Dunning testimonial, but it has my best wishes."[29]

In 1914 Dunning's students scheduled a dinner to honor him at the American Historical Association meeting in Charleston, South Carolina, and Hamilton apparently continued to express antipathy toward Haworth. An exchange between Hamilton and the Floridian William Watson Davis about Haworth's possible presence at the dinner prompted Davis to respond, "I will not quote your hint as to that 'Black Republican,' P. L. Haworth. Haworth is a good fellow and I hope he comes." Though he favored Haworth's attendance at the dinner, Davis added, "I fear we are no nearer agreeing now on the election of 1876 than formerly."[30]

Haworth ultimately chose a career path beyond the historical profession that widened his distance from the other members of the Dunning School. He left the Burrows publishing house in 1910 after four years of service and taught for a year at Bryn Mawr College in Pennsylvania. At the age of thirty-five, Haworth "retired from teaching in order to have leisure for writing." He bought the West Newton, Indiana, farm that once belonged to his great-grandfather. The *Indianapolis Star* reported, "Although primarily interested in a crop that is sown with a fountain pen, reaped with a typewriter and thrashed with a printing press, he is also interested in farming, particularly fruit culture, but he admits that farming by proxy is the most satisfactory way of doing the work." Haworth continued to write, dabbling in historical fiction, completing a novel about the French and Indian War, *The Path of Glory*, in 1911. During this period the Indiana historian also began writing accounts of his travels in the Canadian Rockies, explaining to Hamilton his desire to travel in that region, hunt and fish, and write about his experiences. And he continued to write history.[31]

On Dunning's recommendation, Henry Holt and Company contracted with Haworth to write a book on late nineteenth-century U.S. history. *Reconstruction and Union, 1865–1912* appeared in 1912. Caught up in the Progressive movement, Haworth sought to understand the historical roots of contemporary problems, and he focused increasingly on recent American history. The Negro Problem remained important to him; the opening chapters of *Reconstruction and Union* examine the history of American race relations from the end of the Civil War to the rise of Jim Crow.[32]

Du Bois's characterization of *Reconstruction and Union* as "Fair to Indifferent on the Negro" is accurate.[33] Haworth's description of the freedmen at the moment of their liberation mirrored those of other members of the Dunning School. In his opinion, the freedmen were "intoxicated with the idea that they were their own masters." Haworth explained, "To many freedmen freedom meant primarily idleness, and some were sadly disillusioned when informed that they would still have to work for a living." Even as he offered this negative assessment, however, Haworth balanced it, observing that the ex-slave was "free from the individual master" but, in the words of Frederick Douglass, remained "the slave of society."[34] Haworth continued to argue that white Southerners held the key to the contemporary race problem. He asserted that they "failed to realize fully that they were a conquered people and that wisdom dictated that in all their acts they should be guided not only by ordinary rules but also by the prejudices of the conquerors." The Black Codes passed during Presidential Reconstruction made clear that "their framers did not yet realize that the old order had passed away."[35]

Though Haworth clearly sympathized with the freedpeople and their allies, he criticized the leading Radical Republicans, Charles Sumner and Thaddeus Stevens, the targets of some of the Dunningites' harshest attacks. Haworth described Sumner as "an idealist for human equality in theory but a snob in private practice." After Dunning read this assessment in the complimentary copy his former pupil sent him, the Old Chief remarked, "I've called that great statesman numerous things in my life, but I don't think I ever hit upon that epithet; yet it is so obviously accurate." Of Stevens, Haworth wrote: "Unlike Sumner, he hated Southerners personally." Despite his comments on Sumner and Stevens, Haworth nevertheless wrote that both statesmen labored to empower the freedmen and provide them with the necessary resources to sustain their freedom. Southern whites' actions compelled uncertain northern white voters to support a more forceful policy toward the South, even extending the right to vote to African Americans.[36]

Haworth echoed the sentiments of other Dunningites when he described Republican ineptitude and corruption during Reconstruction, but he broke ranks with them by objecting to the southern white response to Reconstruction. Haworth accepted the southern cry of Negro rule, arguing that "negroes were totally without political experience, and for the most part illiterate, ignorant, and unmoral." Aligned with northern whites, many of whom were interested only in "their own enrichment," African Americans participated in what Haworth described as "a carnival of misrule hitherto unapproached in American annals, though equaled in the same period in the metropolis of the country under Tweed." Presumably left with no other alternatives, southern whites resorted to forming secret orders to turn back Reconstruction and restore what they deemed the proper racial order. Haworth contended that "in many instances the orders ['the Ku Klux Klan, the Knights of the White Camelia, the Pale Faces, and the White Brotherhood'] did laudable work by helping to restrain lawlessness." Though Haworth repeated his earlier assertions that such groups initially served a reasonable purpose, he concluded, "Too often, however, the societies became the instruments of private vengeance and political proscription, and committed outrages as unjustifiable as they were cruel and fiendish."[37]

Upon reflecting on the immediate post–Civil War years, Haworth pondered: "It is easy now to point out the failures of Reconstruction. They are obvious. Probably military rule until the rights of freedmen had been established would have been better than negro suffrage, but it is certain that military rule or any other policy would have failed." He concluded that Reconstruction was doomed because of the determination of southern whites to resist any endeavors to reconstruct the former Confederate states in the interest of preserving some semblance of the old racial order. Despite the fact that southern whites effectively achieved this goal, Haworth observed, "economically and morally the negro has made commendable progress." He then repeated the comparison he had first made in the *Indianapolis News* in 1901–2, equating African Americans' development to European societies' slow, centuries-long progress toward the highest level of civilization.[38]

Haworth's bibliographical essay offers insights into his assessment of his fellow Dunningites' writings, while suggesting how he perceived the place of his own work in contemporary historiography. Haworth summarized John W. Burgess's *Reconstruction and the Constitution* (1902) as "somewhat dogmatic in conclusions." Haworth recognized "much illuminating material" in Fleming's *Documentary History of Reconstruction.* He noted that Fleming's *Civil War and Reconstruction in Alabama* (1905) was "excellent for the single state with which it deals," but he added that the work was "marked by a strong southern bias." In contrast, Haworth judged James W. Garner's *Reconstruction in Mississippi* (1901) to be "rigidly impartial."[39] Even as Haworth recognized the usefulness of other Dunning School works and shared some of their assessments of Republican rule during Reconstruction, he presented a very different interpretation of that era, one intent on placing African Americans' contemporary dilemmas in historical context and illustrating the extent to which whites were responsible for blacks' hardships. Haworth exposed the depths to which Democrats went to overturn Republican rule and strip blacks of their political rights, implicitly making the argument for the restoration of African Americans' freedoms as American citizens.

Haworth ended *Reconstruction and Union* with a chapter on the Roosevelt and Taft administrations that reveals his emerging Progressive spirit. Haworth became increasingly involved in the Progressive movement in 1912. When Indiana Republicans split over reform issues, he followed Senator Albert J. Beveridge and joined the Progressive Party, unsuccessfully running for a seat in the Indiana state legislature that year.[40] In 1915 Haworth published *America in Ferment,* which appeared in his own series titled Problems of the Nations, published by the Indianapolis-based Bobbs-Merrill Company.

In this work Haworth offered readers a Progressive diagnosis of the various problems plaguing the early twentieth-century United States. He devoted chapters to conservation, immigration, race relations, the labor movement, corporate greed, political corruption, the women's suffrage movement, and socialism, thereby reflecting his interest in a variety of Progressive causes. At times Haworth criticized the champions of reform and the entrenched establishment for adopting equally unreasonable agendas, but he repeatedly defended proposals designed to promote economic, polit-

ical, and social justice. Haworth noted, "A new battle is on in the age-
long struggle for human rights." He concluded: "We are in a transition
period and have not yet agreed on a new national purpose. . . . It is altogether probable that the next decade will determine the future of our Great
Experiment."[41]

Haworth's chapters "The Blood of the Nation" and "The Color
Line" explore the race problem. They reveal the extent to which Haworth
embraced contemporary racial thought, which relied increasingly on pseudoscientific methods to assess the natural qualities of the races of the world,
to rank them accordingly, and to legitimize the grand European imperial
march across the globe. In Haworth's discussion of the origins of the nation,
the Indiana Progressive stressed its Anglo-Saxon roots as holding the key
to the birth and development of American democracy, and, like many Progressives, he decried the influx of supposedly inferior peoples from eastern
Europe and Asia. Haworth advocated immigration restrictions to prevent
"race suicide" in the early twentieth century. He argued that assimilation-
ist efforts failed to transform the nation's immigrant population.[42] In words
indicative of contemporary racial categorization, Haworth described the
"problem" of the color line as composed of "four of the great branches of
the human race, the Amerind or Red Indian, the Malayan, the Mongo-
lian or Turanian and the Ethiopian." Haworth examined the conditions of
Asians and American Indians, but he devoted most of the chapter to the
plight of African Americans.[43]

Haworth consulted a variety of texts to supplement his own experiences
in the South and his historical research. Among those works were William
Hannibal Thomas's *The American Negro* (1901) and Thomas Nelson Page's
The Negro: The Southerner's Problem (1904), both reflecting the contemporary strains of Negrophobia and Haworth's own qualified acceptance
of some of their ideas. In contrast, he also relied on decidedly Progressive
works such as Ray Stannard Baker's *Following the Color Line* (1908), W.
E. B. Du Bois's *The Souls of Black Folk* (1903), and Booker T. Washington's *Up from Slavery* (1901). Haworth too reviewed collections of documents and articles compiled by the American Academy of Political and
Social Science and Tuskegee Institute to illustrate the advances made by
African Americans in freedom.[44] Like his earlier works, *America in Ferment*
reflects Haworth's moderate racial philosophy, as it balances a negative view
of African Americans with observations of their suffering at the hands of
southern whites and a defense of blacks' achievements since emancipation.

Haworth argued that African Americans had to receive the political rights and privileges conferred on them during Reconstruction and concentrated his attack on the Jim Crow laws and the failure of white Southerners to uphold the "separate but equal standard." Haworth acknowledged that conditions were improving in the South owing to the influence of liberal-minded whites such as Edwin A. Alderman, Walter Hines Page, and George Foster Peabody, who collaborated with leading African Americans such as Booker T. Washington. Despite such progress, Haworth lamented the continued suffering of African Americans and the hypocrisy of whites, concluding, "While we continue to burn men at the stake, sometimes on the mere suspicion of crime, and to beat to death wholly innocent black people in sudden up-flarings of racial hatred, it ill becomes us to protest against deeds done on the steppes of Russia or on the rubber plantations of Mexico."[45]

Before publishing the book, Haworth solicited Ramsdell's opinion on the chapter titled "The Color Line." Though the Texan confessed that he agreed with Haworth on "many points," he criticized him for continuing to adhere to the "old abolitionist ideas that the negro was the equal to the white man until degraded by slavery." Ramsdell acknowledged the depths of southern racism, but he faulted Haworth for not understanding the southern white mind as well as he thought he did.[46]

In his essay on Ramsdell in this volume, the historian Fred Arthur Bailey observes that Ramsdell's critique prompted Haworth to add a closing paragraph to that chapter in *America in Ferment,* in which he quoted Ramsdell's letter, thus giving his fellow Dunningite the final word on the subject. Haworth chose to quote only the portion of Ramsdell's letter with which he agreed. Like Haworth, Ramsdell endorsed Booker T. Washington's Tuskegee model as a means of solving the Negro Problem, which Ramsdell described as the "great black blight upon the industrial and social life of the South." Haworth blamed the race problem on southern whites, however, and advocated bestowing on African Americans political rights, thus violating the racial ethos southern Dunningites continued to espouse.[47]

Having apparently received a copy of *America in Ferment* from Haworth, Hamilton wrote to him to offer his own evaluation. Hamilton observed, "I was glad to see in your book that even your unreconstructed soul was seeing the light." The North Carolinian's assertion that Haworth's attitudes had changed dramatically missed the mark. Moreover, Hamilton's reversal of the labels "reconstructed" and "unreconstructed" identified Haworth as the unreformed belligerent, which underscored Hamilton's belief that his own ideas had become established orthodoxy.[48] Although modern scholars will identify shortcomings in Haworth's writings, his work nevertheless significantly challenged early Reconstruction historiography and the Jim Crow order in ways that troubled other members of the Dunning School. Haworth's scholarship foreshadowed arguments that overturned the Dunning School in the second half of the twentieth century.

In contrast to his study of the Compromise of 1877, *America in Ferment* received positive reviews from both academic and literary critics. In addition to the *American Journal of Sociology* and the *Mississippi Valley Historical Review,* newspapers in Baltimore, Boston, Chicago, Indianapolis, Los Angeles, Milwaukee, New York, and San Francisco printed summaries or reviews of Haworth's Progressive treatise. Reviewers compared *America in Ferment* to the works of such leading Progressive luminaries as Herbert Croly, Theodore Roosevelt, and Walter E. Weyl. The *Baltimore Sun* questioned Haworth's assessment of the color line, concluding, "His views of the 'Jim Crow' cars were possibly made by one not very widely experienced in travel through the country where the inconvenience of a large class of noisy, often ill kept, always pushing and seldom courteous travelers made the necessity of a journey anything but a delight to those who held higher standards." Yet the *Sun* nonetheless acknowledged Haworth's "keen understanding of conditions" plaguing the nation. The *New York Times* offered a more fatalistic account of the work and the Progressive movement in general, professing, "It is published a little late, for the fad is fading, but it may be recommended to the admirers of the Wisconsin idea."[49]

Two years after *America in Ferment* appeared, Haworth explained to readers why he eventually abandoned his study of the past in favor of documenting his wilderness experiences. In an autobiographical reflection that seemingly ridiculed the historians who disregarded his historical interpretations, Haworth mocked his earlier academic pursuits as a search for "vain degrees conferred by pompous pedagogues in parti-colored gowns." He reminisced, "I delved into dry subjects in musty libraries, wrote books that I hoped would seem learned, and came to have the pale face and stooping shoulders of the professional pundit." Echoing the rugged masculinity of Theodore Roosevelt, Haworth recalled "the primeval instinct" that awoke within him. He declared, "My youthful love of horses and guns, of clear water and the open country, surged once more hot and fierce; the thin veneer of supercivilization began to slough away." Those impulses compelled Haworth to return to the Canadian wilderness, and he continued to write about his experiences.[50]

After several years devoting himself to Progressive causes, the exploration of the Canadian wilderness, and his farm, Haworth returned to the classroom. He taught at Indiana University during the 1918–19 academic year. Haworth next served a term in the Indiana state legislature in 1921–22, before joining the Department of History and Political Science at Butler University, where he chaired that department until his death in 1938.[51] Haworth found frustrating the lack of financial reward in such endeavors, however. Years earlier he had admitted to Hamilton, "The simple truth is that a man is a fool to try to be a historian unless he has money." Haworth continued to publish historical works but never attained his former classmates' academic recognition or prestige.[52]

Haworth stood on the periphery of the Dunning School and the historical profession. His racial attitudes placed him at odds with his southern counterparts. Though he shared some of their negative views of African Americans, Haworth's Quaker upbringing and his Progressive impulses led him to criticize southern whites' intransigence on the Negro Problem and to advocate the extension of rights and privileges to African Americans, which in turn shaped his historical analysis of the postbellum South. As the "Black Republican" in the Old Chief's court, Haworth launched an early assault against his Dunning School comrades. In doing so, he anticipated the attacks by later revisionists who a half century later toppled their orthodox interpretation of Reconstruction.

Notes

This project was originally conceived in the office of John David Smith one afternoon during our brief time together at the University of North Carolina at Charlotte. John David took me under his wing and has fostered my development as a scholar even though I have since relocated to northeastern Wisconsin. My contribution to this collection is a testament to his support. Smith, Bruce E. Baker, Edward O. Frantz, and David Voelker graciously read early drafts of this essay and provided invaluable feedback. I also received essential research assistance from Kimberly Brown-Harden, Sally Childs-Helton and Marianne Eckhart, Allison DePrey, Suzanne Hahn, Carrie Schwier, Mitchell Scott, Sarah Traugott, and Matt Wilson.

1. W. E. B. Du Bois, *Black Reconstruction: An Essay toward a History of the Part Which Black Folk Played in the Attempt to Reconstruct Democracy in America, 1860–1880* (1935; reprint, New York: Atheneum, 1973), 724, 731, 732–33. Du

Bois did not include Haworth on the list of scholars who "studied the history of Negroes and write sympathetically about them." Du Bois listed Haworth's *The Hayes-Tilden Disputed Election of 1876*, along with several works by his fellow Dunningite Walter Lynwood Fleming, in the category of studies that "in most cases do not ignore the truth as to Negroes."

2. Wendell Holmes Stephenson, *Southern History in the Making: Pioneer Historians of the South* (Baton Rouge: Louisiana State University Press, 1964), 13. The historian Philip R. Muller identified this altercation as proof that many of Dunning's students "were both neophyte scholars and committed partisans." In his dissertation on the Dunning School, John H. Hosmer, one of the few scholars who identified Haworth's dissenting opinion, cited this incident as evidence that Dunning's southern students rejected their colleague from Indiana because of his critique of Jim Crow. Hosmer implied that Haworth's experiences at Columbia damaged the Indiana historian's academic career. See Philip R. Muller, "Look Back without Anger: A Reappraisal of William A. Dunning," *Journal of American History* 61 (September 1974): 335; Hosmer, "The Dunning School and Reconstruction according to Jim Crow" (Ph.D. diss., University of Arizona, 1983), 111–12.

3. Butler University, *The Drift* (Indianapolis: Butler University, 1926), http://digitalcommons.butler.edu/buyearbooks/13/ (accessed August 28, 2012); Peter Novick, *That Noble Dream: The "Objectivity Question" and the American Historical Profession* (Cambridge: Cambridge University Press, 1988), 86–108; Ellen Fitzpatrick, *History's Memory: Writing America's Past, 1880–1980* (Cambridge: Harvard University Press, 2002), 51–97; Paul Leland Haworth, *America in Ferment* (Indianapolis: Bobbs-Merrill, 1915). For a more in-depth study of the Progressive historians, see Richard Hofstadter, *The Progressive Historians: Turner, Beard, Parrington* (New York: Alfred A. Knopf, 1968). In a 1915 letter to Hamilton, Haworth expressed his admiration for Beard. He lamented that his fellow Hoosier Beard had not yet been named a full professor at Columbia because another faculty member believed he was "too much of a radical" for the title. See Paul Leland Haworth to J. G. de Roulhac Hamilton, March 7, 1915, Joseph G. de Roulhac Hamilton Papers, Southern Historical Collection, Manuscripts Department, Wilson Library, University of North Carolina at Chapel Hill (hereinafter cited as Hamilton Papers); Hosmer, "The Dunning School," 113.

4. David S. Brown, *Beyond the Frontier: The Midwestern Voice in American Historical Writing* (Chicago: University of Chicago Press, 2009), xvii.

5. Connie J. Zeigler, "West Newton," in *Encyclopedia of Indianapolis*, ed. David J. Bodenhamer and Robert G. Barrows (Bloomington: Indiana University Press, 1994), 1419; James H. Madison, *The Indiana Way: A State History* (Bloomington: Indiana University Press, 1986), 49, 99–100, 107–8, 195, 206; Jacquelyn S. Nelson, *Indiana Quakers Confront the Civil War* (Indianapolis: Indiana Historical Society, 1991), 4–6.

6. James Albert Woodburn, *The Life of Thaddeus Stevens: A Study in American Political History, Especially in the Period of the Civil War and Reconstruction*

(Indianapolis: Bobbs-Merrill, 1913), 486–90; Jesse J. Gant, "'Younger and More Irreconcilable': James Albert Woodburn's Undergraduate Orations at Indiana University, 1875–1876," *Indiana Magazine of History* 108 (June 2012): 146–85; Ulysses G. Weatherly to John W. Burgess, April 28, 1902, Paul Leland Haworth Family Papers, 1829–1957, Manuscript and Visual Collections Department, William Henry Smith Memorial Library, Indiana Historical Society, Indianapolis (hereinafter cited as Haworth Papers); "Ulysses Grant Weatherly, April 2, 1865–July 18, 1940," www.asanet.org/about/presidents/Ulysses_Weatherly.cfm (accessed September 26, 2012); James Albert Woodburn, *History of Indiana University*, vol. 1, *1820–1902* (Bloomington: Indiana University, 1940), 438; Ulysses G. Weatherly, "Racial Pessimism," *Proceedings of the Annual Meeting of the American Sociological Society* 14 (1923): 23–35.

7. For an analysis of northern white attitudes on the Negro Problem, see David W. Southern, *The Malignant Heritage: Yankee Progressives and the Negro Question, 1901–1914* (Chicago: Loyola University Press, 1968); George M. Fredrickson, *The Black Image in the White Mind: The Debate on Afro-American Character and Destiny, 1817–1914* (New York: Harper and Row, 1971), chap. 10; and Michael McGerr, *A Fierce Discontent: The Rise and Fall of the Progressive Movement in America* (New York: Oxford University Press, 2003), 182–202. Paul Leland Haworth, *The Hayes-Tilden Disputed Presidential Election of 1876* (1906; reprint, New York: Russell and Russell, 1966), x; Paul Leland Haworth, "Of the Race Problem," *Indianapolis News,* March 25, 1901, clippings file, Haworth Papers.

8. Haworth, "Of the Race Problem."

9. Ibid.

10. Paul Leland Haworth, "The Attitude of Southern Whites toward Negro Education," *Indianapolis News,* December 20, 1902, clippings file, Haworth Papers.

11. Paul Leland Haworth, "Negro Disfranchisement in Louisiana," *Outlook* 71 (May 17, 1902): 165–66. Hosmer suggested that this article was the cause of the altercation between Haworth and Hamilton. Haworth did not enroll at Columbia until several months after the article was published, but it reflects his outspoken opposition to the southern white solution to the Negro Problem, and he probably shared those sentiments with his classmates whenever the opportunity presented itself. See Hosmer, "The Dunning School," 111–12.

12. Paul Leland Haworth to John D. Haworth, n.d., William Archibald Dunning to James Albert Woodburn, March 8, 1901, Amos Hershey to Nicholas Butler, April 28, 1902, and Butler to Haworth, May 31, 1902, all in Haworth Papers; William A. Dunning, *Essays on the Civil War and Reconstruction and Related Topics* (New York: Macmillan, 1898). For the emergence of Columbia University as the premier graduate program in the nation, see Hosmer, "The Dunning School," 99–101.

13. Walter L. Fleming to Joseph G. de Roulhac Hamilton, March 3, 1904, Hamilton Papers; Hosmer, "The Dunning School," 112–13.

14. Paul Leland Haworth, "Negro Suffrage," ca. 1903, Haworth Papers.

15. Charles Burrows to Haworth, April 7, November 3, November 8, and November 24, 1906, Biographical Sketch, Haworth Papers.

16. C. Vann Woodward, *Reunion and Reaction: The Compromise of 1877 and the End of Reconstruction* (1951; reprint, Boston: Little, Brown, 1966), 252; Keith Ian Polakoff, *The Politics of Inertia: The Election of 1876 and the End of Reconstruction* (Baton Rouge: Louisiana State University Press, 1973), 332; Haworth, *Hayes-Tilden Disputed Election*, x; Gerald M. McFarland, "Another Perspective on the Compromise of 1877," *Reviews in American History* 2 (June 1974): 257–61. In addition to Polakoff's work, other criticisms of Woodward's revisionist account include Allen Peskin, "Was There a Compromise of 1877?" *Journal of American History* 60 (June 1973): 215–23, and Michael Les Benedict, "Southern Democrats and the Crisis of 1876–1877," *Journal of Southern History* 64 (November 1980): 489–524.

17. Haworth, *Hayes-Tilden Disputed Election*, 81, 84, 86–88, 92, 108, 118, 121.

18. James S. Pike, *The Prostrate State: South Carolina under Negro Government* (New York: D. Appleton, 1874); John S. Reynolds, *Reconstruction in South Carolina, 1865–1877* (Columbia, S.C.: The State Co., 1905); Daniel H. Chamberlain, "Reconstruction in South Carolina," *Atlantic Monthly*, April 1901, 473–84; Bruce E. Baker, *What Reconstruction Meant: Historical Memory in the American South* (Charlottesville: University of Virginia Press, 2007), 14–16, 32, 34, 36–38; Du Bois, *Black Reconstruction*, 732. For an analysis of the *Atlantic Monthly* series, see Richard N. Current, introduction to *Reconstruction in Retrospect: Views from the Turn of the Century*, ed. Richard N. Current (Baton Rouge: Louisiana State University Press, 1969), v–xxii.

19. Haworth, *Hayes-Tilden Disputed Election*, 125.

20. Ibid., 131–33, 156.

21. Ibid., 168–71, 333.

22. Woodward, *Reunion and Reaction*, 6–8, 11, 195–96, 204–5, 207; McFarland, "Another Perspective," 257–58; Haworth, *Hayes-Tilden Disputed Election*, 268–72.

23. Haworth, *Hayes-Tilden Disputed Election*, 304.

24. Review of Haworth, *The Hayes-Tilden Disputed Presidential Election of 1876*, in *American Historical Review* 12 (January 1907): 410–11. The Old Chief echoed the sentiments of this reviewer. In his "Critical Essays on Authorities" in *Reconstruction, Political and Economic, 1865–1877* (1907), Dunning acknowledged Haworth's thorough research and "impartiality," yet he also observed that Haworth's work was "perceptibly favoring the Republicans in interpretation." See Dunning, *Reconstruction, Political and Economic*, 354.

25. Charles Burrows to Paul Leland Haworth, November 3, 1906, Haworth Papers; Daniel S. Margolies, *Henry Watterson and the New South: The Politics of Empire, Free Trade, and Globalization* (Lexington: University Press of Kentucky, 2006), 40–43; Joseph Frazier Wall, *Henry Watterson: Reconstructed Rebel* (New York: Oxford University Press, 1956), 123–67; Haworth, *Hayes-Tilden Disputed*

Election, 268–70; Woodward, *Reunion and Reaction*, 11, 196–97; Polakoff, *The Politics of Inertia*, 310–11.

26. Charles Burrows to Paul Leland Haworth, November 3, 1906, Haworth Papers; "A Partisan Dissertation," *Louisville Courier-Journal*, August 9, 1906, 4. One newspaper detailing Watterson's criticism of Haworth's work attributed the Louisville editor's "attack" to Haworth's "playful remarks anent a certain fire-eating speech in which the colonel threatened to bring 100,000 Kentuckians to Washington and seat Tilden." According to this account, Watterson was so angered by Haworth's treatment of him in the book that Watterson sent copies of his editorial to Columbia University. School officials supposedly responded by suggesting Haworth "'raise 100,000 men and march for Louisville.'" See Indiana Scrap-Book Collection, vol. 3, Compiled and Presented to the Indiana State Library in Remembrance of Benefits Received by George S. Cottman, Indiana State Library, Indianapolis.

27. John David Smith, *An Old Creed for the New South: Proslavery Ideology and Historiography, 1865–1918* (1985; reprint, Athens: University of Georgia Press, 1991), 113–26; John David Smith, introduction to this volume; Robert Cruden, *James Ford Rhodes: The Man, the Historian, and His Work* (Cleveland: Press of Western Reserve University, 1961).

28. Haworth's only direct assault on Rhodes's work concentrated on factual errors in his treatment of the disputed election of 1876 and the Compromise of 1877. Haworth also repeated his own argument that had the election been conducted on fair terms, Republicans would have carried the disputed states. See his review of James Ford Rhodes, *The History of the United States from the Compromise of 1850 to the Final Restoration of Home Rule at the South in 1877,* in *Political Science Quarterly* 22 (September 1907): 513–18; Muller, "Look Back without Anger," 335n40; Charles A. Beard and Mary R. Beard, *The Rise of American Civilization* (1927; reprint, New York: Macmillan, 1954), chap. 18. Woodward acknowledged the inspiration the Beards' work had on his own study of the election and compromise. See Woodward, *Reunion and Reaction*, x.

29. W. L. Fleming to J. G. de Roulhac Hamilton, April 20, 1911, and May 4, 1911; James W. Garner to Hamilton, September 27, 1913, all in Hamilton Papers. [James W. Garner, ed.], *Studies in Southern History and Politics, Inscribed to William Archibald Dunning, Ph.D., LL.D., Lieber Professor of History and Political Philosophy in Columbia University, by His Former Pupils the Authors* (New York: Columbia University Press, 1914); Paul Leland Haworth to Charles Ramsdell, August 24, 1914, Charles W. Ramsdell Papers, Briscoe Center for American History, University of Texas, Austin (hereinafter cited as Ramsdell Papers); Haworth to Hamilton, March 7, 1915, Hamilton Papers. Hosmer proposed that Haworth sensed he had been shunned by his former comrades, although it is unclear why he was omitted, given Garner's intention to include him and Haworth's vague remark to Ramsdell. See Hosmer, "The Dunning School," 113nn42–43. I thank William Bland Whitley for sharing his own discoveries on the Dunningites' tribute to the

Old Chief. For more on the Festschrift, see Whitley, "James Wilford Garner and the Dream of a Two-Party South," in this volume.

30. Hosmer, "The Dunning School," 113; Paul Leland Haworth to J. G. de Roulhac Hamilton, March 7, 1915, and William Watson Davis to Hamilton, November 25, 1913, Hamilton Papers.

31. "Hoosier Contributes Book on Sociology and Politics," *Indianapolis Star,* March 3, 1915, clippings file, Haworth Papers; Haworth to Hamilton, March 7, 1915, Hamilton Papers; Paul Leland Haworth, "Lunge of French River," *Outing* 56 (April 1910): 18–27; Haworth, "Modern Viking," *Outing* 65 (December 1914): 265–74; Haworth, *The Path of Glory* (Boston: Little, Brown, 1911).

32. William T. Brewster to Paul Leland Haworth, May 11, 1911, Haworth Papers; Paul Leland Haworth, *Reconstruction and Union, 1865–1912* (New York: Henry Holt, 1912).

33. Du Bois, *Black Reconstruction,* 732.

34. Haworth, *Reconstruction and Union,* 8–9.

35. Ibid., 15–17.

36. Ibid., 19, 21–22, 27–31; William A. Dunning to Paul Leland Haworth, June 30, 1912, Haworth Papers.

37. Haworth, *Reconstruction and Union,* 43–45.

38. Ibid., 81, 84–85.

39. Ibid., 249.

40. Ibid., chap. 9; "Washington Briefs," *Indianapolis Star,* August 4, 1913; R. E. Banta, ed., *Indiana Authors and Their Books, 1816–1916: Biographical Sketches of Authors Who Published during the First Century of Indiana Statehood, with Lists of Their Books* (Crawfordsville, Ind.: Wabash College, 1949), 140; Madison, *The Indiana Way,* 218–21.

41. Haworth, *America in Ferment,* 6–7, 10.

42. Ibid., chap. 4. For a useful survey of racial thought in the early twentieth century, see Matthew Frye Jacobson, *Whiteness of a Different Color: European Immigrants and the Alchemy of Race* (Cambridge: Harvard University Press, 1998), chap. 2.

43. Haworth, *America in Ferment,* 113, 116–17.

44. Ibid., 460.

45. Ibid., 113, 146–50.

46. Charles W. Ramsdell to Paul Leland Haworth, September 5, 1914, Ramsdell Papers; Fred Arthur Bailey, "Charles W. Ramsdell: Reconstruction and the Affirmation of a Closed Society," in this volume. In his review of the book for *Southwestern Historical Quarterly,* Ramsdell noted, "Mr. Haworth makes no attempt to conceal his sympathy with reform," but he acknowledged that *America in Ferment* provided readers with "a clear statement of the social and industrial problems that beset the intelligent portion of our citizenship." After the publication of *America in Ferment,* Ramsdell informed Haworth that the book was the best survey of the relationship between past and present available for use in the

classroom. See Charles W. Ramsdell, review of Haworth, *America in Ferment,* in *Southwestern Historical Quarterly* 19 (October 1915): 207; Ramsdell to Haworth, September 17, 1915, Haworth Papers.

47. Bailey, "Charles W. Ramsdell"; Haworth, *America in Ferment,* 156.

48. J. G. de Roulhac Hamilton to Paul Leland Haworth, February 12, 1915, Haworth Papers; Haworth to Hamilton, March 7, 1915, Hamilton Papers; Hosmer, "The Dunning School," 113. The Bobbs-Merrill Company solicited the opinions of experts in those fields surveyed in *America in Ferment,* including the historian William E. Dodd, the Socialist Party leader Eugene V. Debs, and the African American novelist Charles W. Chesnutt. Chesnutt offered his own assessment of "The Color Line" to the book's publishers, writing, "In its treatment of the Color Line it is eminently just and fair in statement, and even when the reader may not agree with the views expressed, he has no doubt of the author's honesty and sincerity of opinion and love of the fiar [sic] play." See William E. Dodd to Paul Leland Haworth, May 9, 1914, Eugene V. Debs to Laurence Chambers, March 3, 1915, and Charles W. Chesnutt to the Bobbs-Merrill Company, April 23, 1915, Haworth Papers.

49. Review of Haworth, *America in Ferment,* in *American Journal of Sociology* 21 (July 1915): 108–9; review of Haworth, *America in Ferment,* in *Mississippi Valley Historical Review* 2 (December 1915): 425–26; reviews of Haworth, *America in Ferment,* in *Baltimore Sun,* March 3, 1915, *Boston Transcript,* March 6, 1915, *Chicago Public,* August 16, 1915, *Indianapolis Times,* April 23, 1915, *Los Angeles Tribune,* n.d., *Milwaukee Journal,* July 15, 1915, *New York Times,* July 4, 1915, *San Francisco Bulletin,* April 3, 1915, all in clippings file, Haworth Papers.

50. Paul Leland Haworth, *On the Headwaters of Peace River* (New York: Charles Scribner's Sons, 1917), vii. Haworth, *Trailmakers of the Northwest* (New York: Harcourt, Brace, 1921), also reflects Haworth's interest in the Canadian wilderness, as did his novel *Caverns of Sunset* (Indianapolis: Bobbs-Merrill, 1930). For an analysis of the standard of rugged masculinity popularized by Roosevelt, see Gail Bederman, *Manliness and Civilization: A Cultural History of Gender and Race in the United States, 1880–1917* (Chicago: University of Chicago Press, 1995), chap. 5.

51. "Dr. Haworth, Butler History Head, Is Dead," *Indianapolis News,* March 34, 1939, University Biography Files Collection, Special Collections, Rare Books, and University Archives of Irwin Library, Butler University, Indianapolis.

52. Haworth to Hamilton, March 7, 1915, Hamilton Papers. Among Haworth's history textbooks were *The United States in Our Own Times, 1865–1920* (New York: Scribner's, 1920), which was updated and reprinted several times, and, with Alfred W. Garner, *Our Country's History* (Indianapolis: Bobbs-Merrill, 1926).

8

Charles W. Ramsdell

Reconstruction and the Affirmation of a Closed Society

Fred Arthur Bailey

University of Texas Professor Charles W. Ramsdell stood to deliver his presidential address before the third annual convention of the Southern Historical Association on November 20, 1936. The scholars assembled before him in Nashville represented the history academy's dedication to strict professionalism in general and the specific application of its principles to southern chronicles in particular. Earlier generations of would-be historians fell short of a commitment to the absolute veracity of the past, Ramsdell explained to his audience. Their predecessors—some from the North, others from the South—looked on the southern region blinded by the trauma of the lamentable Civil War. "Since the conflict was primarily sectional," he observed, "mass opinion in each section, reinforced by common memories and prejudices, hardened into a tradition which was all but impervious to criticism." The professional historian's duty was to divorce himself from such intransigence, to rigorously investigate and judge primary documents, to embrace the intricate confluence of political, social, religious, and economic themes, and to produce an assessment of the past untainted by cultural biases. If the historian could attain that ideal, he concluded, then perhaps the same approach would enable contemporary scholars "to attack our present [social] problems with less of emotion and more of cool reason than we frequently display. That, at any rate, *should be* one of the lessons of History."[1]

The beneficiary of major renovations in the standards of historical

scholarship, Ramsdell set before his peers a historiographic rigor that neither he nor they could easily achieve. He fully appreciated that he was the
fortunate product of the dramatic intellectual innovations that late in the
nineteenth century shifted the domain of history writing from the amateur
and the antiquarian to the trained professional possessed of exacting skills
and high standards. By 1900, he reflected in his Nashville address, "the
growth of the great graduate schools had reached the point at which the
historical seminars were beginning to force the rewriting of American history." At such first-tier institutions as Harvard, Yale, Johns Hopkins, and
Columbia, dedicated instructors trained "young men and women . . . in
the techniques of historical investigation and writing and . . . introduced
[them] to profitable fields of research."[2]

Ramsdell happily counted himself among those who matriculated in
William Dunning's famed Columbia University seminars. There the young
Texan learned the new "techniques of historical investigation and writing,"
and from there he became one of those drawn to the call of "rewriting of
American history." His mentor thoroughly inculcated in him the ethics of
"scientific history," applying them especially to the study of the Civil War
and Reconstruction era. "Few episodes in recorded history more urgently
invite thorough analysis and extended reflection" than Reconstruction,
Dunning admonished his disciples. It was an epoch in which "southern
whites, subjugated by adversaries of their own race, thwarted the scheme
which threatened permanent subjection to another race."[3]

Ramsdell acknowledged the inevitability that many of those drawn to
Columbia were "Southerners [filled] with a consuming desire to study their
own section," eager to dig "out new materials in the fertile and unworked
field" of the Civil War and Reconstruction, and thrilled that their discoveries overturned the "theories and assumptions" of earlier northern-biased
historians. Having drunk deeply of the new standards of professionalism,
Ramsdell boasted that the Dunning-trained historians "searched through
dusty and forgotten official archives, examined old files of long neglected
newspapers, and unearthed hitherto unknown collections of private papers.
It is not surprising that they found many of the assumptions of the elder
historians defective through lack of accurate or sufficient information."[4]

Emboldened by his sense of superior training, Ramsdell marched
through his career supremely confident in his scholarly objectivity and
never questioned whether his own judgment might also be defective. He
spent his entire academic tenure at the University of Texas influencing gen-

erations of soon-to-be public school teachers and university professors and in them perpetuating ideas that had matured in the American South well before they were born. Ramsdell immersed himself in the political economy of southern historiography, in the polity of a closed society whose overlords rewarded conforming intellectuals who repeated the essential elements of a patrician-commanded southern history and severely punished other men of thought who refused to conform. He prospered in a world where regional power elites insisted on an interpretation of the past that justified their domination over society's political, cultural, and economic institutions, that protected them from the threatening ambitions of their lesser-status peers, and that supported their suppression of the civil rights of whites and blacks alike. Although the University of Texas professor occasionally objected to these restrictions on academic freedom, he shared with the South's ruling class the essence of its historical perspective and expressed in his scholarship concepts that endorsed its suzerainty over the southern domain.

Dunning and John Burgess at Columbia, along with Johns Hopkins's Herbert Baxter Adams, Harvard's Albert Bushnell Hart, and the *American Historical Review*'s J. Franklin Jameson, constituted the pioneering generation that professionalized the historical community, that campaigned for the designation of history as a unique college discipline, and that established the essential principles by which they instructed their proselytes to execute the craft. They were energized by the intellectual spirit sparked by Charles Darwin, and their call for "scientific history" demanded that historians purge themselves of personal inclinations; interpretation of the past should be in the mind of the reader unprompted by the historian's discourse. "The absorbing and relentless pursuit of the objective fact—of the thing that actually happened in exactly the form and manner of its happening," Dunning insisted, is "the typical function of the modern devotee of history." Ramsdell agreed. "Any historian who has both sense and honesty must see that a surprisingly large proportion of history . . . has been based upon the rankest sort of propaganda," he reflected in a letter. There "is perpetual warfare between investigation and tradition."[5]

As the nineteenth century merged into the twentieth, the scientific historian's disciples drifted into two distinct camps. Many remained faithful to their instructors' maxims, passing to their own students the insistence that the historian must remain true to facts untainted by personal, political, or social inclinations. Others drifted into apostasy, catching the spirit of the Progressive era and seeing in historical interpretation lessons useful to society's reform. Among them, Frederick Jackson Turner, Charles A. Beard, and William Edward Dodd forsook the dictums of their mentors, saw history as a social science generating practical lessons, and organized their historical materials into thesis-driven essays. To those who remained faithful to the scientific school—Ramsdell among them—their wayward peers had transgressed the crucial boundary separating the scholarly from the polemical. "I once heard our friend Beard, in a lecture here," wrote the University of Texas professor. He said "that it was the business of the historian to 'select the pertinent facts.' I wanted to stand up and shout the question, 'pertinent to what?' "[6] Neither Dunning nor Ramsdell nor any of the other advocates of the "scientific" approach fully appreciated the simple equation that no scholar can totally remove himself from his environment, that his own background along with contemporary cultural forces shape his approach to the past and influence the tenor of his writings.

Ramsdell was the product of a dichotomous society in which southern whites affixed to themselves the proud cognomen "Southerners" and at the same time relegated southern blacks to the status of aliens in their midst. Although he rarely broached the subject of race in his personal correspondence, in one notable missive Ramsdell articulated feelings as deep, as dark, and as passionate as those of any of his white peers.[7]

Paul Leland Haworth—an Indiana native and Ramsdell's friend and former compatriot in Columbia University seminars—provoked the outburst in late summer 1914. Both men had earned their doctorates in history, both returned to their native states in pursuit of scholarly endeavors, but though in Texas Ramsdell held firm to the creed of "scientific history," in Indiana Haworth quickly embraced the cause of Progressive reform. As Haworth neared completion of his manuscript *America in Ferment* (1915), a volume calling for cultural change across the broad social spectrum, he urged Ramsdell to read and critique his lengthy chapter labeled "The Color Line." Speculating that in "the South as a whole race relations [were] slowly improving," Haworth nonetheless preached that much more remained to be done. "It is the simple truth that the condition of the peon class in 'Barbarous Mexico' is hardly worse than that of many negroes in certain sections of certain southern states," he essayed, "while the persecution of Russian Jews by Russian Cossacks is rivaled by deeds done in brutal race riots." Appalled that in the contemporary South black men were burned at the stake "on the mere suspicion of crime," and "innocent black people" were often beaten to death "in sudden up-flarings of race hatred," he moralized that "it ill becomes us to protest against deeds done on the steppes of Russia or on the rubber plantations of Mexico."[8]

Ramsdell bristled at his friend's lamentable departure from the dispassionate standards of the historian even as he burned over what he considered the miscasting of the underlying causes of the South's racial tensions. To be sure, Ramsdell opened in his response, Haworth had been "careful to the facts," so that there was "little to dissent from that line." The problem, he emphasized to his northern friend, was his "interpretation of some of the facts . . . for it seems to me you have lost sight of a number of factors in the negro problem." Haworth had "not entirely broken" from the "old abolitionist ideas that the negro was the equal to the white man until degraded by slavery." To Ramsdell, peonage, racial violence, and disparagements of education characterized unfortunate elements of a conundrum that was hardly the fault of the white race and resulted largely from the immature character of the individual Negro. "It would be wrong to say that he is immoral; he is simply unmoral," the professor pontificated. "Everyone who knows much of negroes knows this to be true, yet I myself am often surprised by new and unexpected proofs of it." Peonage and violence were regretful but needful elements bringing order to a race that by its "own lack of character" and its "unreliability and brutality" struck fear into a white society anxious to protect its civilization. As for the disparity of education, Ramsdell knew from personal experience the problem's root. "Too often the negro teacher is a sorry leader of the flock—as also the negro preacher. It is notorious here in Texas . . . that negro teachers taking examinations for certification will most invariably cheat if there is the slightest opportunity."[9]

Prompted by Ramsdell's critique, Haworth amended his essay "The Color Line," composing a new concluding paragraph that focused on the white South's embedded racism. "Viewed from any angle," he explained, the task of achieving racial reconciliation in the South "is a stupendous one. Little wonder that a southern educator who has read this chapter asks: 'How shall we take these ten millions of shiftless, improvident, unmoral, inefficient child-men of an alien race and convert them into desirable citizens? With individual exceptions, the negro population rests like a great black blight upon the industrial and social life of the South.'" Haworth had extracted this seminal quotation directly from Ramsdell's letter.[10]

The southern professor's regional and racial chauvinism sprang from his youthful experiences in post-Reconstruction Texas. Born in the hill country just north of Austin, Ramsdell was the scion of undistinguished ancestry whose memorials were etched on the bureaucratic lines of the United States Census. "As well as I can tell," he explained to a distant relative, the Ramsdell clan "has been middle-class throughout, neither distinguished particularly nor very low in the social scale." In 1880 Charles H. Ramsdell, his father, was listed in the census as a merchant residing in Bell County along with his wife, Fredonia, and their firstborn, three-year-old Charles W. The Ramsdell lineage originated in New England, along the boundary between New Hampshire and Massachusetts, and only just before the Civil War did a teenage Charles H. appear in Texas. He arrived in time to do service as a private in the Confederate Army, after which at some point before 1877 he and his bride settled in the tiny village of Salado. Apparently the father also engaged in agriculture, for later his son Charles W. recalled, "I lived on a cotton farm as a boy and young man during the terrible days of the eighteen-nineties." The decade's depression swept away the family's comforts and forced the Ramsdells' departure from Salado; shortly before 1900 they had resettled as tenants on a farm near Houston. Twenty-three-year-old Charles W. remained with his family, employed as a schoolteacher.[11]

Charles W. Ramsdell grew up in a community cursed with passionate and negative memories of the disruptive years from 1861 to 1877. The people of Bell County initially supported secession with enthusiasm, but as hardships and disillusionments developed, scores of Union sympathizers and Confederate deserters congregated in its northern region at a place locals referred to as "Camp Safety." At the war's conclusion, the county entered a prolonged period of violence. After the lynching of several Union supporters, blue-clad troops occupied the county seat not only to protect individuals disposed to accept the war's verdict, but also to carry out the administrative policies of the federal judge Hiram Christian. By 1870, however, local Ku Klux Klan–like cabals had succeeded in forcing the removal of Christian and the overthrow of other Reconstruction officials. Bitter, biased memories of that epoch prevailed. A Salado attorney and friend to the Ramsdell family, George W. Tyler, complained that "Judge Christian, backed up by the military, stripped every poor family and every Confederate soldier of the last vestige of property for which any claim could be made of it having technically belonged to the Confederacy." The victims of this and other outrages, he assured all who would listen, "carried the memory of them to their graves."[12]

The historian Ramsdell would devote his life to the study of the Civil

War and Reconstruction, the memories of which had raged among the people of his youth. The intellectual journey to his chosen profession commenced in the village of Salado, progressed at the University of Texas in Austin, and received its polish through participation in stimulating Columbia University seminars; and at each point a dedicated teacher introduced to him the intellectual tools that would craft his scholarship. Samuel J. Jones, who had earned a doctorate from Vanderbilt University, founded Salado's Thomas Arnold High School, recognized in the teenage Ramsdell an appetite for history, and shared with him the large collection of Civil War newspaper articles preserved by his own father. This first experience with primary documents awakened in Ramsdell a lifetime craving to find, to touch, and to reflect on original sources.[13]

At the University of Texas, Ramsdell relished his classes under George P. Garrison, who created the institution's Department of History, who produced a creditable body of scholarship on Texas history, and who was a founder of the Texas State Historical Association and editor of its journal. He became Ramsdell's role model, and his influence spurred the would-be scholar to the challenge of advanced work at Columbia in New York. Garrison first recommended to Ramsdell the Reconstruction epoch as a fertile research field, after which Dunning at Columbia reenforced the desire to fully understand the machinations of the period, provided Ramsdell with the philosophical approach to the topic, and guided him to the successful completion of his dissertation, titled simply "Reconstruction in Texas" (published under the same title in 1910).[14]

The doctoral thesis mirrored Dunning's commitment to scientific history even as it also echoed the mentor's ideological predispositions. This volume showcased the fundamental contradiction of Ramsdell's career. For in it he established his credentials as a "scientific historian," while at the same time he evidenced the cultural values that would color his concept of what constituted objectivity. Completing the Texas study in 1909, the younger scholar acknowledged what he considered self-evident: that in "narrating the process of reconstruction in any of the Southern States, one is naturally drawn into a sympathetic attitude toward the people whose social and political system was being 'reconstructed.' "[15] However much Ramsdell kept faith with the idea of setting Texas within a national context, in the end he presented the Reconstruction decade as an unrelenting travail for the white people of the South in general and the white people of Texas in particular.

Throughout *Reconstruction in Texas* Ramsdell portrayed the postbellum decade as a violent epoch in which Texas whites, subjugated by adversaries of their own race—northern-sponsored reformers and politicians—thwarted a scheme to put the defeated slaveholders under permanent subjection to their former slaves. Though by definition the Texas scholar's commitment to scientific history meant that he forsook the development of a discernable thesis and considered the personal interpretation of facts a violation of professional ethics, he nonetheless developed powerful themes that he assumed were no more than incontrovertible facts. With the destruction of Confederate authority, traditional southern social relationships stood near collapse, he argued. "The immediate and pressing problem was to preserve the normal balance of society, and to provide for the freedman an industrial position in that society such that agricultural interests would suffer the least possible additional shock." Southern whites assumed that "free negro labor would be a failure and that a labor famine was imminent." Subsequent events validated that fear, for to "the child-like negro, concerned only with the immediate present, there was no difference" between working under a labor contract "and his old condition as a slave." The Texas scholar emphasized that, emancipated from restraint, these newly freed people abandoned their former masters, replacing obedience with "vagrancy, theft, vice and insolence"; and where "negroes had made contracts they broke them without cause, often leaving their families for their employers to feed."[16]

Ramsdell lectured that the southern social structure had been inverted by radical reformers who were "serenely unconscious of negro incapacity," northern "carpet-baggers, none of whom showed conspicuous ability," and southern scalawags who cynically exploited the Negroes for their own purposes. Led by Governor Edward J. Davis, this ill-begotten coalition enfranchised the former slaves even as it restricted the suffrage of ex-Confederates; it enrolled black voters into chapters of the Union League, which directed them to keep the Republican Party in power against the wishes of the white majority; and it fostered an unhealthy political environment that removed from the Negro community any sense of shared civic responsibility. By late summer 1868, Ramsdell reasoned, a state of "general disorder and lawlessness" prevailed, the Negroes showing "the effects of the teachings of reckless carpet-baggers and 'scalawags.'"[17]

In Ramsdell's paradigm, Texas whites engaged in a successful resistance that blunted Radical corruption and punished black lawlessness. "The continuous and peculiarly offensive activities of branches of the Union League

. . . among the negroes," he averred, "brought into existence the counter organization of the Ku Klux Klan." The Klan, keenly aware of that
race's natural phobia concerning things supernatural, sent its sheeted spec-
ters everywhere the Union League "had produced recklessness among the
blacks." Sometimes "giant horsemen, shrouded in ghostly white, some of
them headless, passed at midnight through the negro settlements, disarm-
ing and frightening the superstitious freedmen, . . . but otherwise doing
no harm." Nonetheless, whenever "negroes and Radical whites" engaged
in political activities that "made them particularly obnoxious," the Klan
issued stern warnings of ominous consequences, and—if this proved insufficient—"the offender was likely to be . . . whipped, or even murdered."[18]

Emboldened by the Klan, Texas whites focused on the general election of December 1873, resolved to overthrow the Davis administration
and its "radical-carpetbag-negro domination." It "was in a sense a revolution," Ramsdell observed, in which the oppressed majority was justified in
employing extralegal measures. "'Davis negroes' were in many communities ordered to keep away from the polling places, while white men under
age were voted." The uprising succeeded, and all "the new state officials
were Democrats, as were the great majority of the legislators and the county
officers." For nine torturous years the white people of Texas had endured
"the rule of the minority, the most ignorant and incapable of her population
under the domination of reckless leaders." Reconstruction was overthrown,
but in its wake the social pyramid had been turned "upon its apex." Ramsdell concluded in the dissertation that the next generation of Texas leaders would be dedicated to the task of placing the pyramid "upon its base
again."[19]

Ramsdell's *Reconstruction in Texas* played a generative role in the determined crusade to restore Texas's white ruling class to its accustomed place
at the social pyramid's pinnacle. It constituted a professional historian's
affirmation of a tinted version of historical truth already sanctioned by the
South's power elites—a resurgent aristocracy that was determined to restore
its antebellum entitlements and to justify its antidemocratic values to northern reformers, the southern white masses, and oppressed blacks alike. Confederate defeat had made difficult the reassertion of aristocratic hegemony
after the war, as northern reformers introduced into the South democratic
reforms harmful to their interests. But even as the aristocrats' counterrevolution crippled the northern crusade, at Reconstruction's demise southern patricians found their status challenged by a threatening alliance of

238 Fred Arthur Bailey

small farmers—white and black—who were discontented with the southern oligarchy.

From Texas to Virginia this alliance marched under the Populist Party banner and mounted a serious attack on the South's establishment. Menaced patricians responded vigorously, preaching the linked doctrines of class stratification and white supremacy. Blatantly appealing to white fears of black domination, they defeated the Populists in the election of 1896, and, once secure in their control over southern state legislatures, they quickly passed laws to suppress all threats from below. Throughout the South, poll taxes, literacy tests, and all-white Democratic primaries virtually eliminated black suffrage and significantly reduced the rolls of white voters. The southern elites recognized, however, that merely restricting civil rights insufficiently dampened discontent. All southern whites had to be taught to think correctly, to appreciate the virtues of elite rule, to fear the enfranchisement of blacks, and to revere the Confederate cause. History properly presented would perpetuate Old South values into ensuing generations.

Across the South, Confederate patriotic associations—the United Confederate Veterans (UCV), the Sons of Confederate Veterans (SCV), and the United Daughters of the Confederacy (UDC)—rose to the task, castigated "northern-biased" history books, and challenged southern educators to generate narratives more favorable to their cultural assumptions. No longer encumbered by Populist politicians, the Texas legislature followed the associations' lead, passing the South's first uniform textbook law in 1897. It required all cities with populations of fewer than 10,000 to adopt state-mandated books and created a board to review manuscripts, hold open hearings, and select academic works that "shall not contain anything of a partisan or sectarian character." In short order the Confederate societies established themselves as the arbiters of *partisan* and *sectarian*. Since the state textbook board chose only those books "highly censored by the Confederate veterans and the Daughters of the Confederacy," the UDC textbook committee of 1915 declared all history books in Texas schools free from sectional impurity.[20]

These powerful Confederate societies' unrelenting supervision of the historical academy established the parameters of acceptable history, created a climate of both oppression and opportunity for those affected by them, and, deep into the twentieth century, sculptured the careers of southern historians in general and of Charles W. Ramsdell in particular. Even as university-trained historians complained of the Confederate organizations' lack of balance, their censorship of textbooks, and their purging of noncompliant teachers, these same scholars garnered their livelihoods from accommodating schools and colleges and profited from the sale of textbooks targeted to the southern market. Enveloped in a sere intellectual environment, the professors privately voiced their repugnance to the neo-Confederates' assaults on objectivity, at the same time publicly professing a historical perspective congenial to the neo-Confederates' cosmology. Within months of his dissertation's completion, Ramsdell explained to one of his Columbia professors that "a great many southern people are still sensitive to adverse criticism of the south, but the mass of them, I believe, are less so than many politicians seem to think." The principal difficulty "seems to be with the numerous confederate veterans 'camps' and perhaps even with the 'chapters' of the Daughters of the Confederacy. These are militantly patriotic and are supposed to have considerable political influence." Nonetheless, he mused, "I am optimistic enough to believe they do not always represent the sentiments of enlightened southern people."[21] Even though Ramsdell styled himself among the "enlightened southern people," he easily harmonized his career with the intellectual environment generated by the Confederate patriotic societies.

Ramsdell's grand ambition was to write the definitive history of the southern Confederacy, a magnum opus merging into a well-formed whole the elements of constitutional debate, government maneuvers, military strategy, economics, religion, and social dynamics. He commenced the project in the autumn of 1914 and, unfortunately, never brought it to fruition. His was a busy life, one filled with teaching and research and professional honors, but one that also counted the physical act of writing onerous. "I seem terribly slow at writing," he confessed to an old friend in 1940. "Writing is hard work and I don't particularly enjoy it." In truth, he admitted, "I get a great kick out of research. . . . If I had written up all I have dug out, I would have a great many volumes to my credit." In spite of this lament, he left posterity a worthy legacy that included two books, a textbook for the elementary grades, several edited works, and a scattering of respected articles. He enjoyed the positive fellowship of his University of Texas colleagues and was esteemed by his peers, who elected him president of both the Mississippi Valley Historical Association and, of course, the Southern Historical Association. He accomplished all this within the constraints of a university parsimonious in its salary allotments and a larger political environment that restrained creativity and rewarded conformity.[22]

If a symbiotic relationship developed between Ramsdell and the Confederate societies, he was far from an intended ally. His commitment was to the pure discipline of history, to the ideal of the "scientific" approach, and to the practice of his profession without intellectual restraint. And yet he could neither separate himself from his southern roots nor divorce himself from the academic climate that shadowed his world. Reflecting in 1911 on the urgent need for quality textbooks at all levels, Ramsdell emphasized to a prominent publishing house the opportunity for the company to "treat the South sympathetically, not only with a regard" to the Civil War and Reconstruction but also in accord with "the more recent past or present." This did not mean "pandering to sectional prejudice," he stressed; rather, there was a market for any book that gave "relatively greater emphasis and more sympathetic treatment to a large section of the country that needs to know its history better."[23]

Scant months after Ramsdell earned the doctorate, three closely related events solidified the uneasy convergence of the professor's ambitions with the Confederate societies' intentions. His published dissertation echoed the historiographic elements they already insisted on; his ambition to publish influential and profitable textbooks required him to work by the political rules they had already established; and his oversight of the University of Texas's Littlefield Fund for Southern History bound him to both Confederate Major George W. Littlefield's beneficence and to the expressed intent of his largesse. Blended together, these charted his career's balance.

From the 1890s the principal Confederate organizations insisted that all southern historians and public school teachers adhere to "true history" as they defined it, and they exercised particular diligence in their scrutiny of university professors. "Strict censorship is the thing that will bring the honest truth," pronounced one Texas leader in 1915. "That is what we are working for and that is what we are going to have." Fortunately for Ramsdell, not only did his published dissertation meet the essential elements they had laid down, but his position as a professor at the state's premier university lent credence to his place in their intellectual paradigm; they happily added his volume to their lists of sanctioned works. "I have been rereading your *Reconstruction in Texas* and realize more than ever the great importance as a historical record," gushed one of their number. "The present generation knows absolutely nothing of that period in our history, because it is so painful to those who passed through it, that their pens refused to write of it, their tongues were silent from extensive emotion" generated by "its humiliating experiences."[24]

The University of Texas's meager salary allotments merged with the political economy created by the neo-Confederate partisans to create an environment in which the former forced Ramsdell to seek additional sources of income and the latter provided for him the opportunity to supplement that income through the writing of textbooks targeting the southern market. His Columbia University mentor fully appreciated Ramsdell's dilemma along with its potential solution. "No man can acquire" sufficient income "on a professor's salary," Dunning admonished his Texas disciple, "but the flood of wealth that comes from the text-book is the only hope of getting our profession in line with that of Carnegie and Rockefeller."[25]

Basking in the Confederate societies' approval, Ramsdell, along with his coauthors, Eugene C. Barker and Charles S. Potts, determined to enter the lucrative Texas textbook market. They placed their just completed *School History of Texas* before the state textbook board in 1912, arguing that as professionals trained in the "scientific method," they had produced a worthy replacement to Anna J. Pennybacker's venerable *New History of Texas for Schools* (first edition published in 1888). This would be no easy sell; it became a campaign that relied as much on guile as on scholarship. Pennybacker was a powerful leader of the Texas Federation of Women's Clubs who had long mastered the board's byzantine politics. Her book had stood unchallenged since the board first met in 1898, and it was in fact well loved by elementary school teachers, who praised it as reading like "a story or a fairy tale" that caught the "TRUE SPIRIT OF A TRUE TEXAS."[26]

Intent on catching Pennybacker unawares, Ramsdell and his partners cloaked their work with secrecy; carefully crafted their manuscript (Ramsdell handled the chapters on the Civil War and Reconstruction) and, on the advice of a local book agent, contracted with a Chicago publisher Row, Peterson and Company; and then announced their book's nomination only weeks before the board's meeting. To ensure their success, they solicited numerous testimonials from teachers who had once graced their classrooms and even planted an effusive review in the *Southwestern Historical Quarterly*. "The characteristic feature of this book is the success with which it conforms to the newer ideas in history writing," opened the review. "The authors have performed their best service to the State of Texas in supplying . . . a text-book . . . that recognizes throughout the true nature of historical material." In a hardly veiled critique of Pennybacker's volume, the reviewer praised the University of Texas professors for abandoning the "old method of using gubernatorial administrations as the basis of organization" while impressing on elementary schoolchildren "the correct philosophy of history."[27]

Energized by this unanticipated challenge, Pennybacker responded vigorously, appealing to teachers who had long used her book, writing to her base—the powerful Texas women's clubs—and proclaiming her history threatened by "a book put out by northern people." The last panicked Ramsdell and his cohorts. They immediately ordered their Chicago publisher to rebind their textbook in patriotic gray and to reduce its selling price to less than that of their opponent's work. The latter move probably led to their victory, for, as Barker observed, Pennybacker had a well-deserved reputation for "squeezing all the dollars that come into her hands until the 'eagle squeals.'"[28]

Adhering firmly to the legislated mandate that all selected works "shall not contain anything of a partisan or sectarian character," the Texas Textbook Board was particularly impressed by a positive and planted book review that praised the Barker-Potts-Ramsdell work as "appealing to all lovers of truth [presented] in its spirit of fairness and accuracy." And, the author emphasized, "the part of Texas in the Civil War is developed with unusual clearness and fairness, while the period of reconstruction is dealt with in the same broad spirit."[29]

Ramsdell's chapters on the Civil War and Reconstruction conformed to what both the textbook board and the Confederate societies deemed nonpartisan, nonsectarian. Even as Texas soldiers defended the state against the North, the professor explained to schoolchildren, "the slaves remained for the most part faithful to their masters . . . they guarded the homes and protected the defenseless women and children." Their labor, he stressed "went far to support the Confederacy in its struggle against the government which wished to free them." Even so, the South lost the conflict, and the postwar period of Reconstruction was in "many ways . . . more distressing to the white people of Texas than the war had been." Fifth- and sixth-grade students were grounded in the faith that the state was overrun by corrupt "'carpet-baggers' and 'scalawags'" and, even worse, by "bands of idle negroes" who confused freedom with a lack of responsibility. In short order, the Freedmen's Bureau interfered with the South's natural social order by unwisely taking the side of the Negroes in disputes with the white community, by supplying welfare for "the helpless negroes," and, once the agency "gained influence over the negroes," by setting "them against their former owners." Offended by carpetbaggers' alleged corruption, black voting, and armed black militias marching across the countryside, Ramsdell taught, the "conservative white men of the South" formed the Ku Klux Klan to "hold the negroes in check, to prevent them from voting," and to stop them from "making and enforcing the laws." The Klan's successes led to the restoration of white rule. From that point forward, the textbook assured its young readers, the state "entered upon a period of rapid development which has continued without any serious interruption down to the present time."[30]

From the Confederate societies' perspective, both Ramsdell and Pennybacker met their rigorous historiographic criteria, leading the textbook board in 1912 to reward the authors who made the most successful presentation. But Pennybacker was hardly defeated. She and her attorneys pored over the original legislation, discovered that it allowed local districts to adopt her work as a supplemental reading, and so informed superintendents and teachers across the state. Hundreds happily remained loyal to her history, which denied to Barker, Potts, and Ramsdell much of their anticipated profits. The two books competed with each other deep into the 1930s.[31]

For his part, Ramsdell sought additional opportunities to write for the southern market. He engaged in several abortive attempts to coauthor general histories of the United States, but in each case his heavy teaching loads and his distaste for the physical act of composition forestalled the effort. Frustrated by months of his own procrastination, Ramsdell in 1918 admitted to the University of North Carolina's J. G. de Roulhac Hamilton—his friend and would-be coauthor—that "this will be the last 'pot boiler' I shall ever undertake. I would much prefer to go back to the farm and raise pigs."[32]

Even as Barker, Potts, and Ramsdell ushered their elementary history to approval, events in their larger and related world merged the powerful Confederate societies, textbooks unacceptable to them, and University of Texas politics to structure Ramsdell's career and profoundly influence southern historiography. Barker, as head of the Department of History, longed to make the university a center for research in southern studies, and he secured a benefactor in the wealthy banker George W. Littlefield—university regent, late major CSA, and dominant figure in the John Bell Hood Camp, United Confederate Veterans, in Austin. The two men possessed an intense love of history, shared a common view of its proper interpretation, and longed to create a respectable academic infrastructure necessary to perpetuate their ideological model. But though Barker assumed that he approached the past from a scientific perspective unsoiled by ideology, Littlefield consciously commanded that southern history must be taught in conformity with the essential elements of a neo-Confederate interpretation. Unfortunately for Barker, the path that led to the endowment of the Littlefield Fund for the Study of Southern History was far from felicitous.[33]

The series of events that drew together Barker and Littlefield, and eventually Ramsdell, began in a distant part of the South. In February 1911 tiny Roanoke College in Salem, Virginia, became the target of the state's Confederate partisans and like-minded zealots across the South. When a prominent local judge and Civil War veteran discovered that the school's history professor—Herman J. Thorstenberg—required students to read Henry William Elson's *History of the United States of America* (1904), he clamored for the book's immediate removal and demanded that the teacher's lectures be monitored. The Confederate societies considered Elson's textbook thoroughly objectionable because it portrayed the sexual indiscretions of masters with their female slaves, termed the nation-rending conflict a slaveholders' war, and praised Lincoln as "the Providential instrument . . . guiding the nation through the wilderness of threatened disunion." That Elson disparaged Reconstruction and considered Negro citizenship a travesty against the white race hardly mollified enraged apologists for the Lost Cause.[34]

Before Professor Thorstenberg tendered his resignation from Roanoke College and left the South for good, he protested that Elson's history was commonly used throughout the country and in fact had been adopted by at least twenty other southern colleges. This sparked a wave of hysteria as Confederate societies everywhere demanded that their schools and libraries remove "such damnably false literature as this Elson's history." Trinity College (now Duke University), the University of North Carolina, and the University of Georgia purged the offending textbook from their curricula. Much to his consternation, Littlefield learned that the University of Texas's Department of History required its students to read Elson's "damnably false" history.[35]

Prodded by Littlefield, the university's president demanded an explanation from the Department of History chair. Barker immediately acknowledged Elson's analytical shortcomings, but he pointed out that at least his discussion of postbellum events was fair to the South. "Of 'Carpetbaggers' he speaks as contemptuously as they deserve, and he finds no excuse for the Reconstruction governments." He assured the school's chief administrator that he and his department remained faithful to the South. "I beg to remind you, sir, that I am a southern man. I was born, and have lived all my life, in Texas. My grandfathers . . . and several of my uncles fought in the Confederate Army"; and every member of his department shared the same credentials and the same loyalty.[36]

Ramsdell was, of course, a native Texan whose father and grandfathers marched in the Confederate ranks, whose cosmology matched that of the Confederate societies, but who was also guilty of requiring the Elson textbook. He chaffed at the "great howl throughout the South over Elson," complaining to the book's publisher that he had "no sympathy with [it] in so far as it [was] an attack on academic freedom in the choice of text-books," but he then urged the firm to make needful revisions that would "satisfy the jealousy of all our old ex-Confeds. And U.D.C.'s." If the offending passages were edited to their satisfaction, Ramsdell pledged to continue with the textbook. But Littlefield and the Confederate Camps deemed Elson devoid of merit, the hallmark of unacceptable scholarship. Barker, Ramsdell, and their colleagues stilled their academic consciences, resigned themselves to the repressive climate, and quietly deleted Elson's book from their department's reading list. Months later, a Texas UDC official informed her colleagues throughout the South that the University of Texas had belatedly joined the ranks of the righteous.[37]

Carefully and with proper deference to the desires of the Confederate partisans as a whole and to Littlefield in particular, Barker negotiated with the regent an endowment to purchase manuscripts, newspaper files, and books useful in the writing of a "true history" of the South. He submitted his full proposal to Littlefield in March 1913, but before the wealthy philanthropist could respond, the Department of History once again found itself trapped in the vortex of a free-speech controversy. Without warning, the John Bell Hood Camp, United Confederate Veterans, denounced the University of Texas for requiring undergraduates to read the Harvard University professor Edward Channing's *Student History of the United States* (1904). Publishing their protests in the *Austin Statesman*, they excoriated the book as "written by a person thoroughly imbued with sectional hostility and bias against the Southern people, institutions and sentiments." How, they asked, could "any Regent or professor of the University who has a drop of Southern blood in his veins . . . recommend Channing's book—or Elson's either—or teach it to our Southern sons and daughters"?[38]

Fearful for his own employment as well as the fate of his department,

Barker begged for Littlefield's intercession. The regent promised to mollify the veterans, but he also chided Barker, noting that "your explanation now is [the same] that you gave some year or more ago, when there was much talk about Elson's History." The Confederate camp remained adamant, insisting that the university should not "prejudice the minds of the rising generation in our Southland against the action of their parents in the great war of the '60s." Surely, they noted, "there is some way in which we can all work in harmony for a desired end." Indeed there was. A chastened Department of History removed the offending book from its curriculum. The Confederate societies credited their victory to Littlefield's sagacious overseeing of the university. Major Littlefield, boasted the historian of the Texas Division UCV, "is a member of the Board of Regents of our State University and in position to lay the axe to this deadly Upas tree."[39]

When the University of Texas Board of Regents formally announced the creation of the well-endowed Littlefield Fund for the Study of Southern History in April 1914, they revealed nothing of the arm-twisting that had occurred; but in a private memorandum Barker ruefully noted that in the formal discussions, the board "recounted previous difficulties in getting satisfactory text[books] in history—really meaning the difficulty of getting books satisfactory to the Confederate camps." They "thanked Major Littlefield," admitting "the justice of the previous complaints of partisanship" in the Department of History.[40]

Publicly, Barker wrote in the *Nation* magazine for July 2, 1914, that "Major Littlefield's gift is gratifying to historical students as a symptom of the South's dawning consciousness of obligation to its own history. . . . It is no part of Major Littlefield's purpose to promote the partisan study" of the past. Perhaps that was so, but Littlefield specifically stated his "desire to see a history written of the United States with the plain facts concerning the South and her acts . . . since 1860, fairly stated." He intended that "the children of the South may be truthfully taught and persons matured since 1860 . . . be given the opportunity to inform themselves correctly." Littlefield's concept of "plain facts . . . truthfully taught," however, envisioned a pattern of history deliberately crafted to ensure predetermined goals. In short order, Barker placed his younger colleague Charles W. Ramsdell in charge of Littlefield's bequest, tasking him to fulfill the benefactor's mandate.[41]

Given oversight of Littlefield's beneficence, Ramsdell inherited the ideal situation to fund his grand quest of writing the definitive history of the southern Confederacy. Across the next two decades endowment funds underwrote research trips to important repositories and enabled him to ferret out and to purchase for the university rare newspaper files and manuscript collections. From this he amassed a tremendous body of information that he fashioned into informative articles, preludes to his larger goal. With one notable exception, each of these compositions reflected the scientific style of presentation, exercises more closely resembling an antiquarian's precision than a thesis-driven exposition.[42]

Ramsdell chose his presidential address before the Mississippi Valley Historical Association in 1929 to make his one clear departure from the "scientific" style of writing history. Caught in the intellectual pacifism current in the decades between the World Wars, he became the first of a small school of southern historians hypothesizing that the Civil War was a needless conflict, that the South would have ended slavery on its own accord, and that the awful social disruptions of that conflict need never have happened. His paper, "The Natural Limits of Slavery," emphasized that though the "peculiar institution" was economically viable in the 1850s, rational men of thought should have realized that it was on the verge of destruction, that within a generation, perhaps sooner, it would have come to its inevitable end. Absent the Civil War and absent the nation-damaging Reconstruction era, inevitable emancipation would have led to reasonable "codes for the control of free negroes" that would have limited the negative effect of black citizenship and enfranchisement. Those "who wished [slavery] destroyed," he moralized, "had only to wait a little while. . . . It was summarily destroyed at a frightful cost to the whole country and one third of the nation was impoverished" to that day.[43]

Ramsdell's growing stature in the history profession encouraged department chairman Eugene C. Barker to appoint him supervisor of the Littlefield Fund because, in Barker's words, Ramsdell "was the obvious man to take the lead in the writing of any history of the South." Twenty years beyond the fund's endowment, Ramsdell was widely respected across the history profession and acknowledged as one of the leading experts on the late Confederacy, but no cohesive manuscript, certainly no book had appeared. By the mid-1930s the University of Texas's president had grown concerned that Littlefield's expressed wishes remained unfulfilled, and he charged Ramsdell immediately to construct a plan for its execution.[44]

Prodded, Ramsdell developed an outline for an eight-book series, each written by a different, well-respected author, and he reserved the Reconstruction volume for himself. Without his knowledge, Wendell Holmes

Stephenson, then a professor at Louisiana State University, had urged his school's press to undertake a similar project; both men issued invitations within days of each other and several went to the same historians. Given the essential harmony of the two proposals, Ramsdell and Stephenson combined their efforts, settled on a ten-volume format, and searched for authors they considered faithful to a historiographical slant long held by the Confederate partisans. Most notable among them, the University of Georgia's E. Merton Coulter—a scholar deeply committed to the Dunning School's interpretation—had already been promised by Stephenson the Reconstruction era; Ramsdell deferred, accepting instead the commission for the monograph on the Confederacy.[45]

Naively Ramsdell and Stephenson contracted with each author to finish his assignment in no more than three years; in reality the last volume appeared three decades later. The editors had made critical assumptions that proved incorrect, but which in the long run made the series stronger and allowed individual volumes to become major contributions that altered the direction of southern historiography. Both editors presupposed that each book would be premised on extant southern scholarship. But outside the fields of the Civil War and Reconstruction, relatively little secondary work had been published across the span of southern history. Authors, assigned grand periods of the region's past, soon engaged in detailed primary research that required more time than expected; in the process they collected impressive data, and several contemplated new interpretations. They did this even as the crisis of World War II drew the younger historians into national service, suspending their scholarship for the duration.[46]

Ramsdell and Stephenson soon discovered that their pool of worthy scholars proved less loyal to their ideological perspective than anticipated. The respected Duke University historian Charles S. Sydnor, whose earliest writings harmonized with neo-Confederate interpretations, drew the assignment for the pre–Civil War volume. The editors could hardly have bargained for his shifting historiographic views. Sydnor had come to see southern independence as more the nadir than the zenith of the region's historical experience, a position that would hardly have endeared itself to the long-deceased George Washington Littlefield. C. Vann Woodward's *Origins of the New South, 1877–1913* (1951) strayed even further from the intent of the late regent's legacy. Initially the editors had assigned the volume to another scholar who, pleading overwork, recommended Woodward as his replacement. That recommendation pleased neither Ramsdell nor

Stephenson; they saw in Woodward both an author new to the craft and a historian tinged with radicalism. They leaned toward Holland Thompson, a professor of history at the City College of New York, whose post-Reconstruction volume in the Yale Chronicles of America series struck Stephenson as politically reliable. Ramsdell agreed, but he and Stephenson were concerned about Thompson's advanced age and rumored poor health. Thompson's death resolved the issue, and Woodward's prizewinning contribution would not merely challenge the presuppositions of earlier generations, but also excoriate the southern patrician class as a retrogressive force in the region's culture.

Both Sydnor's and Woodward's works appeared at the threshold of the South's civil rights movement and offered a historical perspective congenial to positive social change. By contrast, Coulter's Reconstruction volume was a well-drafted refashioning of the Dunning perspective, untainted by any of the revisionist literature that had begun to appear in the 1930s. The first manuscript completed, it arrived in Ramsdell's office in mid-June 1942.[47]

Ramsdell received Coulter's draft with great satisfaction. It marked a major milestone in the *History of the South,* but it also came at a time of personal concern for the Texas historian. "I haven't had time as yet to do more than open" the package, Ramsdell admitted to Coulter. But "[I] gaze[d] at it with reverent awe, read the Preface, and dip[ped] my toe into the stream at various spots further along. At all these spots it seems good and invites a plunge." Immersion into the document would have to wait, he explained, because he was scheduled to consult a Dallas physician concerning "an enlarged prostate gland" and must have "an operation this summer." Ramsdell died on the surgeon's table on July 3, 1942.[48]

This disciple of William Dunning contributed much and could have contributed more to the foundational literature associated with the discipline of southern history. In the wake of his untimely passing, first Barker and then Coulter engaged in a thorough search of his personal files and found nothing that resembled a Confederate manuscript. By default, the task of writing a "definitive" history of the Confederate States of America fell to the Georgia historian, who also replaced Ramsdell as coeditor of the *History of the South.* Coulter's volume appeared in 1952, a panegyric celebrating the Lost Cause. As he expressed to friends while writing the book, "In my teachings I am still trying to re-establish the Southern Confederacy."[49]

If the University of Texas historian was less effusive than Coulter, he

nonetheless shared congenial views with him. The scholar in Ramsdell held
to the professional ethics of "scientific history," to the belief that the aca-
demician must be informed by and faithful to discovered facts. He thus
remained loyal to the academic grounding he inherited from his mentor,
William A. Dunning. Both preached objectivity and both wrote with a
precision intended to expunge any evidence of bias. Of course this intent
was impossible to fulfill. Like every scholar, every historian, each was the
product of his own heritage, his own time, and his own class. Neither could
separate himself from the zeitgeist that enveloped his world and that cor-
roded his supposed objectivity. By this act of unintentionally interpreting the past, as prompted by the scholar's particular values, the scientific
approach was corrupted. Dunning's and Ramsdell's interpretations of the
Reconstruction epic endorsed contemporary assumptions of race and citizenship and became a scholarly imprimatur that blessed those standards as
the basis of society's future policy.

A product of a volatile South still reeling from the dramatic events
of 1861–77, Ramsdell sermonized as a matter of gospel that the "orgy of
reconstruction kindled" resentments "more enduring than that caused
by the war itself," that racial peace would arrive only when "the Negro
accept[ed] the role of dependent" to the Caucasian, and above all else,
as Ulrich B. Phillips had argued, that "the South should remain 'a white
man's country.' "[50]

Notes

1. Charles W. Ramsdell, "The Changing Interpretations of the Civil War,"
Journal of Southern History 3 (February 1937): 3, 27. For biographical sketches of
Ramsdell see Wendell Holmes Stephenson, "Charles Ramsdell: Historian of the
Confederacy," *Journal of Southern History* 27 (November 1960): 501–25; Wen-
dell Holmes Stephenson, *Southern History in the Making: Pioneer Historians of the
South* (Baton Rouge: Louisiana State University Press, 1964), 184–204; James Sut-
ton Payne, "Texas Historiography in the Twentieth Century: A Study of Eugene
C. Barker, Charles W. Ramsdell, and Walter P. Webb" (Ph.D. diss., University of
Denver, 1972), 139–77.

2. Ramsdell, "Changing Interpretations of the Civil War," 12.

3. William A. Dunning, *Reconstruction, Political and Economic, 1865–1877*
(New York: Harper and Brothers, 1907), xv.

4. Ramsdell, "Changing Interpretations of the Civil War," 12–13.

5. William A. Dunning, "Truth in History," *American Historical Review* 19
(January 1914): 219; Charles W. Ramsdell to Virginia Quitman McNealus, June

26, 1923, Charles W. Ramsdell Papers, Briscoe Center for American History, University of Texas, Austin.

6. Charles W. Ramsdell to R. L. Schuyler, April 15, 1941, Ramsdell Papers.

7. Ramsdell's antipathy toward African Americans is evident in his essay "The Southern Heritage," in *Culture in the South,* ed. W. T. Couch (Chapel Hill: University of North Carolina Press, 1934), 1–23.

8. Paul Leland Haworth, *America in Ferment* (Indianapolis: Bobbs-Merrill, 1915), 148–49.

9. Charles W. Ramsdell to Paul Leland Haworth, September 5, 1914, Ramsdell Papers.

10. Haworth, *America in Ferment,* 156; Ramsdell to Haworth, September 5, 1914, Ramsdell Papers.

11. 1850 U.S. Census, Population Schedule, Cheshire County, New Hampshire, 261B; 1880 U.S. Census, Population Schedule, Bell County, Texas, 310B; 1900 U.S. Census, Population Schedule, Brazonia County, Texas, 86; Charles W. Ramsdell to Cousin Cora, February 5, 1937, Charles W. Ramsdell to Maida W. Carson, August 10, 1941, Charles W. Ramsdell to Sirs [Carnegie Book Shop, New York City], February 7, 1936, Charles W. Ramsdell to T. F. Harwood, March 23, 1928, all in Ramsdell Papers.

12. See "Bell County," "Belton, Texas," and "Tyler, George W.," in *The Handbook of Texas Online,* www.tshaonline.org/handbook (accessed August 22, 2012); George W. Tyler, *The History of Bell County* [ed. Charles W. Ramsdell] (San Antonio, Tex.: Naylor, 1936), 249–50.

13. Charles W. Ramsdell to George P. Garrison, July 18, 1902, December 11, 1904, George P. Garrison Papers, Briscoe Center for American History, University of Texas, Austin; Tyler, *History of Bell County,* 360, 364; Charles W. Ramsdell, *Reconstruction in Texas* (New York: Columbia University Press, 1910), 7–8; H. Y. Benedict, "George Pierce Garrison," *Quarterly of the Texas State Historical Association* 14 (January 1911): 173–75.

14. Benedict, "George Pierce Garrison," 173–75.

15. Ramsdell, *Reconstruction in Texas,* 7.

16. Ibid., 44–46, 49–50, 70, 139.

17. Ibid., 48, 70, 201, 230.

18. Ibid., 192, 232, 233.

19. Ibid., 292, 315.

20. *General Laws of the State of Texas . . . Twenty-Fifth Legislature* (Austin: Ben C. Jones, 1897), 238, 239–43; *Proceedings of the Twentieth Annual Convention of the Texas Division, United Daughters of the Confederacy . . . 1915* (n.p., 1916), 42. As the nineteenth century merged into the twentieth, the Confederate patriotic societies across the South engaged in a virulent effort to sculpt the content of textbooks and other literature into a view of slavery, the Civil War, and Reconstruction favorable to the South's patrician class. "Strict censorship is the thing that will bring the honest truth," proclaimed Mary Margaret Birge, chair of the Textbook

Committee, Texas Division, United Daughters of the Confederacy, in 1915. "That is what we are working for and that is what we are going to have." *Proceedings of the Twentieth Annual Convention of the Texas Division, United Daughters of the Confederacy . . . 1915*, 43.

21. Charles W. Ramsdell to James Robinson, October 25, 1911, Ramsdell Papers.

22. Charles W. Ramsdell to W. Mary Bryant, April 4, 1935, Charles W. Ramsdell to Fred [L. Ramsdell], April 2, 1940, Charles W. Ramsdell to John H. Rose, October 6, 1940, and Eugene C. Barker, "Resolutions in Memory of Professor Charles W. Ramsdell," September 25, 1942, all in Ramsdell Papers.

23. Charles W. Ramsdell to Macmillan Company, June 16, 1911, Ramsdell Papers.

24. Adele B. Looscan to Charles Ramsdell, April 4, 1914, Texas State Historical Society Records, Briscoe Center for American History, University of Texas, Austin; Laura Lyons McLemore, *Inventing Texas: Early Historians of the Lone Star State* (College Station: Texas A&M Press, 2004), 79.

25. Dunning to Ramsdell, December 20, 1912, Ramsdell Papers.

26. Anna J. Hardwicke Pennybacker, *New History of Texas for Schools*, 8 eds. (Tyler, Tex.: Published for Author, 1888–1936); Eugene C. Barker, Charles S. Potts, and Charles W. Ramsdell, *A School History of Texas* (Chicago: Row, Peterson, 1912), 221; W. H. Rushing, recommendation, March 8, 1912, Mrs. Percy V. Pennybacker Papers, Briscoe Center for American History, University of Texas, Austin.

27. Charles W. Ramsdell to Eugene C. Barker, September 5, 1911, Charles W. Ramsdell to Carl Hartman, April 4, 1912, Charles W. Ramsdell to R. Longley, July 16, 1912, Charles W. Ramsdell to J. A. Hill, July 20 and July 27, 1912, Charles W. Ramsdell to L. F. McKay, July 27, 1912, S. J. Jones to Charles W. Ramsdell, April 7, 1912, Eugene C. Barker to Charles W. Ramsdell, August 29, 1912, all in Ramsdell Papers; Eugene C. Barker to Isaac Peterson, March 22, 1912, Eugene C. Barker to [?] Pye, June 18, 1912, Eugene C. Barker to [Adele?] Looscan, July 16, 1912, all in Eugene C. Barker Papers, Briscoe Center for American History, University of Texas, Austin; Charles W. Ramsdell to J. G. de Roulhac Hamilton, J. G. de Roulhac Hamilton Papers, Southern Historical Collection, Wilson Library, University of North Carolina, Chapel Hill; J. A. Hill, review of Eugene C. Barker, Charles S. Potts, and Charles W. Ramsdell, *A School History of Texas*, in *Southwestern Historical Quarterly* 16 (July 1912): 105–6.

28. Charles W. Ramsdell to Leonard M. Dumas, July 3, 1912, Charles W. Ramsdell to H. J. Stark, July 15, 1912, Charles W. Ramsdell to S. H. Moore, July 19, 1912, and Charles W. Ramsdell to R. G. Hall, October 19, 1912, all in Ramsdell Papers; Eugene C. Barker to Row, Peterson and Company, May 17, 1912, [Eugene C. Barker] to Edith [?], July 4, 1912, Eugene C. Barker to [?] Peterson, July 7, July 9, and July 24, 1912, C. D. Kennedy to Eugene C. Barker, May 6, 1912, W. F. Jourdan to Eugene C. Barker, May 21, 1912, and Stuart H. Condron to Eugene C. Barker, July 8, 1912, all in Barker Papers.

29. Hill, review of Barker, Potts, and Ramsdell, *A School History of Texas*, 105–6.

30. Barker, Potts, and Ramsdell, *School History of Texas*, 221, 229, 230, 231, 243.

31. Anna J. Hardwicke Pennybacker to Sir, July 14, 1913, Pennybacker Papers.

32. Charles W. Ramsdell to J. G. de Roulhac Hamilton, January 9, January 20, and February 15, 1917, January 26, February 20, April 4, April 13, May 6, and August 26, 1918, April 28, July 19, and November 12, 1919, March 29, 1921, and March 20, 1922, all in Hamilton Papers.

33. Fred Arthur Bailey, "The Best History Money Can Buy: Eugene Campbell Barker, George Washington Littlefield, and the Quest for a Suitable Past," *Gulf South Historical Review* 20 (Fall 2004): 33–34.

34. Henry W. Elson, *History of the United States of America* (1905; reprint, London: Macmillan, 1920), 558, 624–27, 776; W. W. Moffett to J. A. Morehead, February 23, 1911, Elson Textbook Controversy Papers, Henry H. Fowler Collection, Roanoke College, Salem, Va. Reflecting on conditions in the post-Reconstruction South, Elson declared that the "negro is quite safe and his happiness quite secure under the white man's government. The white man at this time makes every law in every southern state but in no case, aside from those pertaining to the franchise, do the laws discriminate against the black man." Elson, *History of the United States*, 802.

35. Fred Arthur Bailey, "Free Speech and the 'Lost Cause' in the Old Dominion," *Virginia Magazine of History and Biography* 103 (April 1995): 265; David Crenshaw Barrow (chancellor of the University of Georgia) to Nathaniel Harris, [1912], Elson Controversy Papers; George W. Littlefield to Eugene C. Barker, April 15, 1911, Barker Papers.

36. Eugene C. Barker to Edward Mezes, April 12, 1911, Barker Papers.

37. Charles W. Ramsdell to Richard R. Smith, March 15, 1912, Ramsdell Papers; Minutes of the Board of Regents, University of Texas, May 31, 1911, vol. D, p. 138, Office of the Board of Regents, University of Texas, Austin; *Minutes of the Eighteenth Annual Convention of the United Daughters of the Confederacy . . . 1911* (Paducah, Ky.: Paducah Printing Co., 1911), 29.

38. Eugene C. Barker to George Washington Littlefield, April 28, 1913, George Washington Littlefield Papers, Holding Records, Briscoe Center for American History, University of Texas, Austin; *Austin Statesman*, April 28, 1913.

39. George Washington Littlefield to Eugene C. Barker, April 30, 1913, Barker Papers; H. G. Askew, J. M. Brown, and W. B. Warmar to George Washington Littlefield, May 3, 1913, Littlefield Papers; C. C. Cummings, "Annual Report of Historian Texas Division, U.C.V.," *Confederate Veteran* 22 (September 1914): 390.

40. Eugene C. Barker, memorandum, n.d., Littlefield Papers, Holding File; Minutes of Board of Regents, University of Texas, April 28, 1914, vol. D, pp. 377, 380.

41. Eugene C. Barker, "Southern History in the South," *Nation*, July 2, 1914, 15; Eugene C. Barker to Milton R. Gutsch, July 16, 1942, Barker Papers (copy in E. Merton Coulter Papers, Special Collections, University of Georgia Library, Athens).

42. Eugene C. Barker to Milton R. Gutsch, July 16, 1942, Barker Papers; William C. Binkley, untitled obituary of Charles W. Ramsdell, *Mississippi Valley Historical Review* 29 (September 1942): 314–15.

43. Charles W. Ramsdell, "The Natural Limits of Slavery Expansion," *Mississippi Valley Historical Review* 16 (September 1929): 171. For other examples of this line of thought, see Avery Craven, "The Coming of the War between the States: An Interpretation," *Journal of Southern History* 2 (May 1936): 303–22; James G. Randall, "The Blundering Generation," *Mississippi Valley Historical Review* 27 (June 1940): 3–28.

44. Eugene C. Barker to Milton R. Gutsch, July 16, 1942, Barker Papers.

45. Charles W. Ramsdell to Wendell H. Stephenson, November 11, December 12, 1937, October 27, 1938, and October 18, 1941, all in Ramsdell Papers; Wendell Holmes Stephenson to E. Merton Coulter, November 4 and December 17, 1937, both in Coulter Papers; E. Merton Coulter to Fletcher Green, March 1, 1944, Fletcher Melvin Green Papers, Southern Historical Collection, Wilson Library, University of North Carolina, Chapel Hill; Wendell Holmes Stephenson to E. Merton Coulter, July 21, 1942, and June 21, 1952, and E. Merton Coulter to Wendell Holmes Stephenson, August 7, 1942, all in Wendell Holmes Stephenson Papers, Rare Book, Manuscript, and Special Collections Library, Duke University, Durham, N.C. For a discussion of Coulter's historiographic importance, see John David Smith, "E. Merton Coulter, the 'Dunning School,' and *The Civil War and Readjustment in Kentucky*," *Register of the Kentucky Historical Society* 86 (Winter 1988): 52–69; Fred Arthur Bailey, "E. Merton Coulter and the Political Culture of Southern Historiography," in *Reading Southern History: Essays on Interpreters and Interpretations*, ed. Glenn Feldman (Tuscaloosa: University of Alabama Press, 2001), 32–38.

46. E. Merton Coulter to Bruce Fant, January 23, 1969, Coulter Papers.

47. E. Merton Coulter to Charles W. Ramsdell, June 13, 1942, Ramsdell Papers.

48. Charles W. Ramsdell to E. Merton Coulter, June 20, 1942, Ramsdell Papers; *Dallas Morning News,* July 4, 1942.

49. Minutes of the Littlefield Fund for Southern History, September 3, 1942, Barker Papers; E. Merton Coulter to Mr. and Mrs. James Spruill, January 23, 1946, E. Merton Coulter to Bruce Fant, January 23, 1969, and Eugene C. Barker to E. Merton Coulter, July 7, 1942, all in Coulter Papers; Wendell Holmes Stephenson to E. Merton Coulter, July 21, 1942, Stephenson Papers; E. Merton Coulter to Fletcher M. Green, March 1, 1944, Green Papers.

50. Ramsdell, "The Southern Heritage," 9–10. The theme of the South as "the white man's country" was foundational among those Dunning students hailing from the states of the former Confederacy. See, for example, Ulrich B. Phillips's affirmation that the federal government had to acquiesce to the South's racial customs, "that the South shall remain 'a white man's country.'" Ulrich B. Phillips, "The Central Theme of Southern History," *American Historical Review* 34 (October 1928): 43.

9

The Not-So-Strange Career of William Watson Davis's *The Civil War and Reconstruction in Florida*

Paul Ortiz

William Watson Davis's doctoral dissertation, published as *The Civil War and Reconstruction in Florida,* appeared in 1913 on the eve of the semi-centennial of the Battle of Gettysburg. Historians immediately showered it with acclaim. William E. Dodd characterized the study as "a doctoral dissertation of rather extraordinary character." Dodd continued: "It needs hardly to be said that the study is properly documented at every point and that the contentions of the writer are so cogently presented that the reader is not likely to dissent." Though the historian John H. Russell offered a more critical assessment, he concluded that the book's overall thesis was sound: "The results of [Davis's] work do not revolutionize but confirm accepted opinion concerning Reconstruction in general. He finds that for nine years the State was wracked by political wrangling, violence, and mutual suspicion. 'The attempt to found a commonwealth government upon the votes of an ignorant negro electorate proved a failure. It made the Solid South.'" The *Nation's* reviewer was equally enthusiastic about the book: "Professor Davis's work leaves little to be desired. Where the whole is so thoroughly done, comment upon the excellence of particular features is hardly necessary. . . . Never, perhaps, has the course of a great political party suffered such withering condemnation from historians as has that of the Republican party for the twelve years following Appomattox; and Professor Davis's study only confirms the general condemnation." The reviewer for the *Independent* underscored the book's intellectual pedigree, observing that the text "has been prepared 'under the eye' of Prof. William A. Dunning and with the help of Prof. E. R. A. Seligman."[1]

W. W. Davis's 769-page survey of Florida's epoch of secession, war, and "Redemption" dominated Florida historical scholarship for well over half a century. Historians repeatedly cited the book as an authoritative source in essays that appeared in the *Florida Historical Quarterly*, and it remains one of the most frequently cited books in the history of that journal. Davis's book also has been praised through the decades by leading scholars such as James G. Randall, Francis Butler Simkins, and David Herbert Donald. The Federal Writer's Project guidebook on Florida characterized *The Civil War and Reconstruction in Florida* as "a painstaking history of a tragic and sordid era." Fifty years after its initial publication, the Florida Quadricentennial Commission chose *The Civil War and Reconstruction in Florida* as one of twelve books to celebrate the state's four hundredth anniversary in 1964. Governor C. Farris Bryant and his cabinet appeared prominently in the front matter of the newly republished work. Professor Fletcher Green of the University of North Carolina, then a dean among southern historians, composed an introduction for the commemorative edition. In a laudatory treatment, Green wrote, "One is, therefore, safe in saying, as did James Garfield Randall in 1937, that William Watson Davis, *The Civil War and Reconstruction in Florida,* is still the best work on that subject." Top historians continue to consider the volume to be an enduring classic.[2]

Davis's family history and the education he received before he traveled to Columbia to study under Dunning shaped his development as a scholar. Indeed, the evidence suggests that Davis's orientation to the study of the past derived as much from his own upbringing as from the mentoring of Dunning. It is impossible to understand *The Civil War and Reconstruction in Florida* without examining the deep structures of memory that shaped Davis's understanding of history. Furthermore, the longevity of Davis's thesis reveals as much about Jim Crow America as it does about the Civil War and Reconstruction. This monograph was much more than a "product of its times." As a text that stood at the apex of Florida scholarship for generations, the *Civil War and Reconstruction in Florida* helped shape those times.[3]

Writing in 1964 to Fletcher Green, Lane Davis recalled, "My father, William Watson Davis, was born in Pensacola, Florida on February 12, 1884." Davis proudly identified himself as a native Southerner, although his family was not originally from the South. Watson, as family members referred to him, grew to manhood to understand that he had a distinguished heritage. He was the proud descendent of Christian, slave-owning settlers who had forged their own distinctive characters in the fires of three major wars. Davis's elders provided Watson Davis with a heritage, a worldview, and an educational foundation that would help determine his intellectual trajectory in college.

His great-great-grandfather Matthew Davis had served as an officer in the American Revolution and fell at the Battle of Monmouth in 1778. Davis's great-grandfather Matthew Livingston Davis was the grand sachem of the Tammany Society in New York City. He also served as Aaron Burr's second in his infamous duel with Alexander Hamilton. Lane Davis recalled, "Family history has it that although a man of violent temper, he was hardly the soundrelly [sic] son of a bitch that comes out in the *Dictionary of American Biography,* but that is another matter also which you might or might not want to follow up."[4]

John Eayres Davis, Watson's grandfather, moved to Columbus, Georgia, and established himself as a leading member of the community. He fought in the Creek War, married into a prominent slaveholding family, helped establish the local Episcopal church, began a cotton brokerage firm, and fought in the Mexican War. He espoused the extension of American slavery into Latin America. For the better part of two decades the Davis family prospered as slave labor fueled the expansion of Columbus and its hinterlands; the Civil War, however, cost them grievously. Two sons perished in the conflict, and J. E. Davis died shortly after serving as quartermaster of General Paul Jones Semmes's Georgia Brigade at Gettysburg. Much of the Davis fortune evaporated as a result of war and emancipation. Watson's grandmother Sarah Davis moved her children to Pensacola after the war and opened a boardinghouse in an attempt to rebuild her fortunes. Her younger son and Watson's father, Matthew Livingston Davis II, became a partner in a successful lumber business near Pensacola in the 1870s. After the death of his elder business partner, Matthew Davis moved three-year old Watson and the family to Oak Grove, Alabama, to start his own timber operation.[5]

Matthew Davis and his family flourished in Oak Grove. The family lived in a substantial house amid two hundred acres of virgin land. It spared no expense on Watson's education. A governess tutored him in Latin and French, and his family sent him to private educational academies—including the prestigious San Antonio Academy for Boys—in preparation for his matriculation to college. Oak Grove produced in Watson deeply held convictions about the way the world worked as well as an undying love of the South. "I would say that Watson was a decided conservative, politically," his sister Margaret Davis noted. Lane Davis told Fletcher Green that "the relation between my father and the south which he wrote about in the book you are editing grew out of three things: the involvement of the Davis family in the south and the Civil War, my father's youth in the backwoods of southern Alabama, and his education—formal and informal." His son emphasized that Davis learned the history of the Civil War and Reconstruction long before he studied with Dunning. Young Watson "roamed the woods and hunted and fished, and apparently knew everyone who lived in the area and absorbed their stories and their lives like a sponge. There were a number who had lived through the Civil War and knew the reconstruction first hand—and I would say that he knew it nearly first hand too, long before he was ready for college." "Although an unreconstructed southerner," Lane Davis concluded, his father "did not allow this (until perhaps his very last years) to get in the way of his appreciation of the facts of any particular situation."[6]

Davis entered Alabama Polytechnic Institute (later Auburn University) in 1900. He had the good fortune of studying with Professor George Petrie. Revered as "the Father of Alabama Historians," Petrie had earned his Ph.D. at Johns Hopkins University under Herbert Baxter Adams. Petrie was renowned for his rigorous research methods—which included interviewing formerly enslaved African Americans about slavery. He taught his students to argue on the basis of an intensive study of primary documents. He insisted that they bring an analytical framework to the discipline of history. According to his biographer, Petrie also "believed that blacks were inferior and childlike and that they needed the care and guidance of white people." Petrie was "a proud southerner who defended his heritage and wanted fellow southerners to write their own history." In George Petrie, Watson Davis had found the ideal mentor.[7]

Petrie was a charter member of the Alabama Historical Society, and it was under that organization's aegis that Watson Davis published an essay in 1904 titled "Ante-Bellum Southern Commercial Conventions." Though this essay demonstrated Davis's ability to treat the South as a whole, the young scholar increasingly evinced an interest in Florida history, no doubt encouraged by his family relations—particularly cousins and the noted historians P. K. Yonge and his son Julien. After graduation, Davis stayed at

Auburn to earn a master's and served as a librarian and instructor in history and Latin.[8]

Petrie helped Watson gain admission to Columbia University. Another Petrie student, Walter Lynwood Fleming, was finishing his Ph.D. under William Dunning around the same time that Davis arrived in New York. Columbia's newest Alabamian quickly established himself as one of Dunning's most astute pupils. "It was," according to Davis's son, "apparently, a happy and active time for him—he enjoyed New York and always retained a mild affection for it." Named University Fellow, Davis earned his master's degree in history from Columbia in 1906 and received a fellowship from Columbia to study at the University of Paris. There he took seminars with the legendary Marc Bloch and earned a certificate from the Sorbonne.[9]

Davis also served as a research assistant to Dunning, helping in the preparation of his mentor's *Reconstruction, Political and Economic, 1865–1877* (1907). Dunning gave his advisee ample credit for his contributions to the text, writing, "Mr. William Watson Davis, University Fellow in History at Columbia, has rendered invaluable service in reading all the proofs and verifying the references." Dunning listed a book in his bibliography that would play a major role in Davis's dissertation and forthcoming book on Florida: John Wallace's *Carpetbag Rule in Florida* (1888). Professor Dunning characterized the former Florida state senator Wallace's political memoir as a "crude and untrustworthy review of its subject, by a negro who was active as a politician."[10]

Watson Davis received his Ph.D. from Columbia in 1913 after publishing his dissertation on Florida. Three years earlier he had accepted an assistant professorship of American history at the University of Kansas. The *Independent* wryly noted of his arrival that "the whirligig of time brings about some curious changes, but nothing quite so curious as that this particular brand of history should be taught to the sons of the pioneers who first raised the banner for free soil and free men." There is no evidence to suggest that the scholar from Oak Grove felt unwelcome in Lawrence, a onetime bastion of abolitionism. By this time whites in the South and North had negotiated a rapprochement on race relations, as the latter deferred to the former on the best way to deal with what had been reduced to "the Negro Problem." By all accounts, Davis was a popular professor at Kansas, and he was particularly active in the university's athletic association. His students revered him. "A recent poll by the Kansas Alumni Office of alumni opinion of teachers remembered found my father rated in the top group during the teens, twenties and thirties," his son noted proudly.[11]

Like many historians of his generation, Watson Davis served his nation in World War I. He volunteered to work with the Red Cross and was a witness to the bloody trenches of France. The horrors of that conflict made a deep impression on him. Shortly after the Armistice, Davis helped present a resolution to the faculty senate of Kansas that urged President Warren G. Harding to pursue a policy of armament reduction: "Be it Resolved that we, the members of the Senate of the University of Kansas, approve the purpose of the international conference called by President Harding to meet in Washington on November 11, 1921; that we affirm our confidence in the representatives of the United States and of the other nations in the conference; and that we petition them to take positive action toward a reduction of armaments compatible with the maintenance of peace, the assurance of justice and the preservation of the rights of humanity."[12]

Davis later chaired Kansas's Department of History, serving in that capacity until 1949. He taught undergraduate courses on the history of Latin America, a seminar on modern Asia, and a Civil War history course for R.O.T.C. students. He was a longtime member of the American Association of University Professors, and he retired from the university in 1954. The father passed down his love for learning to his son. Edward Lane Davis went on to teach political theory at the University of Iowa. He became one of the "most storied instructors," at Iowa, "loved by generations of Iowa students." In declining health, Davis moved to Iowa to spend his final years with Lane. William Watson Davis passed away in 1960.[13]

Davis opened *The Civil War and Reconstruction in Florida* with an analysis of the controversies that divided Florida in the years leading to disunion. His use of existing sources was impressive. He carefully mined newspapers, congressional records, and the proceedings of the Florida state legislature. Davis also made good use of political broadsides, pamphlets, maps, and private papers. Many of these sources were not yet housed in archival repositories. Therefore, the young historian must have traveled extensively to compile research materials for the book. Perhaps reflecting the influence of George Petrie, Davis also relied heavily on interviews with surviving protagonists of Reconstruction, particularly Governor William D. Bloxham, along with numerous anonymous white sources. The influence of this testimony on Davis's narrative was profound.

Davis insisted that slavery was the foundational cause of the Civil War. Generations of scholars have posited states' rights, the character defects of northern abolitionists, southern fire-eaters, or economic factors for the coming of war. In contrast, Davis concluded that slavery was the paramount force driving secession in Florida. This is not to say that he ignored other important trends that fractured the Union—for instance, sectional political debates, the disintegration of the national Democratic Party, and the issue of the southern debt. Time and time again, however, he emphasized that white plantation owners and leaders in Florida viewed the expansion of slavery into the burgeoning southwest and the enforcement of the Fugitive Slave Act to be nonnegotiable long before the election of Abraham Lincoln to the presidency. In the spring of 1860 Democrats in Jacksonville stated that regardless of who was nominated to run for president, "the amplest protection and security to slave property in the territories owned by the General Government" and "the surrender [of] fugitive slaves when legally demanded" were vital to Florida's interests. If these terms were not met, "then we are of the opinion that the rights of the citizens of Florida are no longer safe in the Union, and we think that she should raise the banner of secession and invite her Southern sisters to join her." The leading society ladies of Broward's Neck informed the *Jacksonville Standard* after the election of 1858, "In our humble opinion the single issue is now presented to the Southern people, will they submit to all the degradation threatened by the North toward our slave property and be made to what England has made white people experience in the West India Islands—the negroes afforded a place on the same footing with their former owners, to be made legislators, to sit as Judges."[14]

By the semicentennial of Gettysburg it was fashionable for historians to minimize slavery as a factor in the coming of the Civil War. Why, then, did Watson Davis choose a different approach? It is likely that his background as the son of a successful businessman—and the grandson of cotton merchants—saved him from falling into abstraction or propaganda when discussing the reasons for Florida's alienation from the United States. Ever the economic pragmatist, Davis insisted, "The material well-being—if not the very existence—of the state depended upon the labor of the slave." He added, "The stupidest man realized the essential point in the great social issue of the war." When the war finally arrived, the maintenance of slavery was more important than ever. Davis quoted a military commander in the state imploring the Confederate secretary of war Leroy Pope Walker to understand that "money is the sinews of war. If the plantations belonging to our Gulf coast are ravaged, to avoid the plunder of the negroes (not to speak of insurrection) the capacity of the country to contribute to the war is at an end." Advocates of the states' rights school of secession thus were greatly disappointed in Davis's *Civil War and Reconstruction in Florida*.[15]

Another major strength of the book is the author's refusal to accept the myth of the united white South, even on the eve of secession. Davis pointed out that many white Floridians were not convinced that leaving the Union was the proper course to take, and he documented the horrific violence that was visited on dissident whites. "Men were dragged from their beds at night, stripped, blind-folded, taken into the woods and whipped." Others were murdered outright, and Calhoun County was declared to be in a state of "insurrectionary war" by state circuit court Judge J. J. Finley. Plantation owners organized vigilance committees across the state to guard against slave insurrections and published severe warnings that the institution of slavery was inviolate: "If any individual is convicted of tampering with our slaves let him die the death of a felon. If they furnish necks, hemp is cheap and oak limbs handy." In such an environment, political pluralism withered rapidly. Whig and Constitutional Union party leaders who argued for more pacific responses to the impending crisis had little chance of success.[16]

After Lincoln's election, Governor Madison S. Perry urged his state to form an independent republic, or else "our fate will be that of the whites in Santo Domingo [Haiti]." *The Civil War and Reconstruction in Florida* explicates the background of Governor Perry's plea. Because of its long history as a battleground among the Spanish, British, and American governments, Florida was unlike any other state in the South. Davis noted that as American settlers moved into the Spanish colony of East Florida in the late eighteenth and early nineteenth centuries, "Florida became more and more the place of retreat for runaway negro slaves, hostile Indians, and lawless white men." Indeed, when enslaved African Americans allied themselves with Seminole Indians, the stage was set for the largest slave rebellion in U.S. history, the Second Seminole War (1835–42). Quartermaster General Thomas Jessup characterized the conflict as "a Negro war." In the first year of the war, hundreds of slaves rose up along the St. Johns River to join forces with Native Americans. The war destabilized slavery on the southeastern perimeter of the United States. Davis's knowledge of the Creek War in Alabama probably helped him grasp this point. As the *Niles' Register* observed in 1836, "The Creeks are said to be encouraged in their war upon the whites by the lamentable issue of the campaign against the Seminoles." In contrast to many of their counterparts in other southern states, when Florida planters invoked the specter of the Haitian Revolution, they knew whereof they spoke.[17]

Davis criticized Florida's leadership in the weeks leading up to secession, and he was especially sharp in his treatment of the railroad magnate and U.S. senator David L. Yulee. After the Civil War, Yulee claimed, "I did not advise or stimulate secession of the State"; he asserted that he had left Washington only when Floridians had independently decided to sunder their ties with the United States. Davis showed Yulee's claim to be false. A careful analysis of the records revealed the duplicitous behavior of both of Florida's U.S. senators—Yulee and Stephen R. Mallory (later the Confederate secretary of the navy)—especially in their efforts to gather information from federal authorities on fortifications at the Pensacola Navy Yard well before they formally resigned from office. Yulee implored Floridians to occupy their state's "forts and arsenals" by force if necessary. Furthermore, Davis questioned what Yulee and other railroad magnates in the South had to gain by Florida's entering the war. *The Civil War and Reconstruction in Florida* notes that Yulee owed substantial debt to New York stockholders for his antebellum railroad ventures. Disunion would mean an abrogation of that debt. Davis highlighted Yulee's motives and behavior to raise a larger question about corporate power and the coming of the Civil War. "In this tragic and complex crisis in the South's history," he asked, "did the selfish and sinister designs of a few Southern and Northern capitalists arouse the passionate and generally honest prejudices of the more than 5,000,000 Americans who promptly answered the long roll?" Davis shied away from pursuing this question, but he deserves credit for posing it in the first place.[18]

In an intriguing chapter titled "Economic Adjustment to the War," Davis established Florida's centrality to the Confederate war effort. He rejected the *New York Herald*'s dismissive suggestion at the war's conclusion that Florida was the "smallest tadpole in the dirty pool of secession." According to Davis, Florida contributed much to the Confederacy's armies in terms of manpower and also in the areas of salt manufacturing and cattle provisioning for the South's troops. In fact, Florida's salt and beef stocks became more crucial to the war effort over time, as these resources became depleted in other states. Davis also continued to dissect the diverse social fabric of Florida. In the midst of the Civil War, the state was rife with refugees, Unionists, bandits, and speculators as well as "shirkers" and ubiquitous "lazy loungers" who claimed to be exempt from Confederate military service.[19]

Davis's *Civil War and Reconstruction in Florida* contrasts the heroism of Florida's infantry regiments with the greed of war profiteers and corrupt Confederate officials who used their offices to enrich themselves. Here Davis made his viewpoint clear: "By Confederate law, salt-makers were exempted from military service. One sickening result of this exemption was the extreme eagerness of many people to be enrolled among the salt-makers." Equally damaging to the Confederate war effort were the "merchants [who] traveled through Florida dishonestly claiming to be Confederate commissary agents with authority to 'impress' supplies or to collect the 'Tithe.' This was plain rascality and is mentioned here because for a time it was prevalent in part of the state." By subterfuge, "preachers, physicians, county officials multiplied and claimed exemption under Confederate law." Florida was anything but a unified state of the Confederacy.[20]

Anticipating later generations of social historians, Davis believed that class was an integral element in the divergent perspectives that white Floridians held during the conflict. He stressed, "The poor white of the South was often disloyal to the Southern republic, because economic and class conditions left his family destitute and isolated when the 'men folks' were in the army." Davis noted that despite their "pathetic poverty," most poor whites backed the cause. He contrasted "the fairly enlightened Southern planter and merchant" who supported the hostilities with "the illiterate back-woodsman—'kasion,' 'cracker,' 'poor white' or 'red-neck' of to-day—almost cut off from the mass of his fellow men, knowing little about the subtler issues of the war, caring little for 'civic' obedience or 'national patriotism,' and interested not one whit in the purely economic question of preserving slavery." Though modern readers may blanch at this description, Davis demonstrated that dissent and disunity lay at the heart of the South's and Florida's Civil War experience. He showed that the internal Civil War between Floridians itself raged as intensively between 1861 and 1865 as the external one.[21]

The scholarly depth and nuance that Davis brought to his study began to crumble when he discussed the role that African Americans played in the Civil War. The *Independent* observed that Davis sketched a caricatured portrait of slavery. "The idyllic picture of slavery and of the society based upon it is painted in serene obliviousness of easily accessible data giving a contrary showing." This was a fair assessment. Davis fell short of accurately portraying the role of African Americans in the Civil War because he was unable to critique impartially an institution that had greatly enriched his own family. On the one hand, Davis depicted a paternalistic system that would have produced little strain or discomfort among its laborers. "The fact is," Davis argued, "that the Southern slave was well-fed, well-housed, well-treated, and lastly, well-watched and controlled; hence the peace about the slave quarters on isolated plantations when the war was raging at no great distance." He also asserted, "The field hands were normally passive under the stress of war because they were semi-barbarous people held in watchful and firm restraint, and well-treated." Davis surely understood that he was on shaky ground here. A few pages later, he quoted Florida's Civil War governor John Milton grappling with the military exemption of plantation overseers. At a moment when the Confederates were desperate for more troops, Milton insisted that " 'the safety of the Confederacy depends on the exemption of overseers for two reasons,' . . . '1. because without them the slaves will not labor in a manner to secure subsistence for the armies in the field. 2. because if left without control of overseers the result will be insubordination and insurrection.' "²²

Because he stressed the passivity and backwardness of enslaved African Americans, Davis could not explain the fact—as he noted in the text—that over a thousand formerly enslaved Floridians risked their lives to serve in the Union Army. Worse, he asserted without evidence that African Americans were poor soldiers. For example, he charged that "the blacks usually gave way under determined attack." He could not square this assertion with the exemplary battlefield performance of most black troops at Florida's largest battle, Olustee, as well as their conduct in dozens of smaller engagements and actions throughout the state. In contrast to his glowing depictions of the actions of white Florida regiments, Davis stated that black Union soldiers were more adept at "plundering" and "thieving" than at fighting. Davis's assertions clashed with the facts. He noted that the Confederacy belatedly authorized the raising of 300,000 black troops to save the South on March 3, 1865. If African Americans made such poor soldiers, why, then, did the Rebels resort to this measure?²³

As Davis closed the book on Florida's Civil War, he attempted to capture the heartbreak of war's end:

> The palpable tragedy of violent death had befallen the family circles of the South's patriotic not merely twice as frequently as

in times of peace, or three times as frequently, or even ten times, but a hundred times as frequently. Within the space of four years was crowded the sorrow of a century. Mourning for more than 250,000 dead on battle-field or on the sea or in military hospitals was the ghastly heritage of the war for the South's faithful who survived. Those 250,000 came mostly from the courageous, positive, idealistic folk of the Southern States. The majority of the dead were young men. Thousands were mere boys. Verily, "a voice was heard in Ramah, lamentation and bitter weeping; Rachel weeping for her children refused to be comforted for her children, because they were not."[24]

Despite such sentimentalism, Davis apparently never pondered whether there would also have been mourning among those who were not the "courageous, positive, idealistic" citizens of the South. Nor did he consider the feelings of African Americans or Florida's substantial population of Unionists or refugees. In reckoning with the appalling costs of war, Davis proved incapable of separating his family history from his scholarship. The book's initial reviewers did not fault him for this lack of objectivity. Certainly, it was not uncommon for professional historians of the era to reiterate the myths of the Lost Cause. Herman J. Thorstenberg, who had once been threatened with mob violence for assigning a text critical of slavery, went so far as to write in the *American Historical Review* that Davis wrote with the perspective of a "dispassionate looker-on." The *Independent* published what may have been the only initial negative review of *The Civil War and Reconstruction in Florida*. "There is no gainsaying the industry performed in its preparation," its reviewer admitted. "It would be, however, of greater interest and value, if instead of professing to be a historical study it frankly confessed the sectional bias in which it is written."[25]

In the book's opening chapters Davis had done a superb job of crafting character sketches of the different protagonists in Florida and in sorting out their reasons for actions. Tellingly, devotion to his Confederate heritage negatively colored the final chapters treating the Civil War. Davis did not attempt to hide his belief in the southern cause; historians, however, generally failed to remark on this element of the book. Again, it was left to the *Independent*'s reviewer to observe: "The South cares very much about these things, and its educated youth write sentimental and partisan history. We wonder, however, what a gallant soldier and impartial chronicler such as

James Longstreet or Edward Porter Alexander would have said of such a work?" In the end Watson Davis's stunted portrayal of African Americans lacked empathy as well as an evidentiary base. These tendencies continued to mark his text as Davis moved into the era of Reconstruction.[26]

In evaluating Davis's book, W. E. B. Du Bois grouped *The Civil War and Reconstruction in Florida* among those works he judged "Standard—Anti-Negro." By this Du Bois meant that "these authors believe the Negro to be sub-human and congenitally unfitted for citizenship and the suffrage." In Jim Crow Florida whites relegated African Americans to the bottom rungs in society, and Davis's book provided a historical explanation for why Caucasians generally considered this the best arrangement for all parties concerned. Davis's dim assessment of African American humanity and agency punctuated almost every page of his chapters on Reconstruction. He variously referred to African Americans as "semi-barbarous people," "slightly above barbarism," "hardly above barbarism," "open-mouthed, thick lipped, insolent, intemperate, offensive, ugly, and incendiary." In his opinion, African Americans had no conception of freedom—except that it exempted them from hard work.[27]

Black Floridians, in Davis's estimation, joined political organizations and the Lincoln Brotherhoods because they satisfied their "longing for some sort of hoodooism." Repeatedly, he described black political rallies as exercises in African superstition. In a typical rendering of one such meeting, Davis narrated the effect of one speaker on his audience: "The spell of Africa was upon him and he spoke with the native eloquence of his race. Most of his auditors, hardly above voodooism, would feel the spell." Even worse, Davis was incredulous that anyone could hold African Americans in esteem: "Strangers in the land—from the North—were heavily impressed with what they saw. Many of them made hasty, optimistic and thoroughly asinine or dishonest generalizations and prophecies about the bright cultural outlook for the negro." Davis, astonished, grumbled, "Such optimism continues to this day."[28]

Davis's approach to Reconstruction stemmed from his beliefs in the sanctity of white conservative leadership and black inferiority, as well as his estimation of northern interlopers (carpetbaggers) and disloyal Southerners (scalawags) as generally lacking in character or at least good judgment. Black citizenship and voting rights were held to be corrosive of the state's health: "The [Fourteenth Amendment] was a political measure meant not only to protect the black," Davis wrote, "but also to help clinch negro suffrage upon the South, to suppress the natural leaders of the Southern people, and thus to strengthen the grip of the national Union-Republican machine." In contrast, he wrote, Florida's postwar Black Codes were a necessary and critical part of "The Problem of Conservative Rule." Under the codes, the flogging of African Americans for certain crimes and the comparatively lesser punishment for whites made sense because " 'to degrade a white man by corporal punishment' then was to make a bad member of society, usually, and a dangerous political agent." In contrast, "to fine and imprison a petty negro offender would mean his withdrawal from work in the fields. To whip him was a more speedily terminated interruption and less damaging to the white planter." Davis agreed with the premise of the Black Codes, and he pointed out that white Floridians designed these statutes to enforce labor discipline and racial inequality. "It is undeniable that these laws put the black in a position inferior to the white. That was in part their object."[29]

Davis sought to show that a general motivation behind the Black Codes was to enforce racial separation. Nowhere did this exercise prove more futile than in the state's attempt to regulate sexual contact between the races. White women were to be severely punished for "cohabitating" with black men. At the same time, "Rape was a statutory crime only when perpetrated on 'white women.' " Yet, Davis wrote, "This legislation contained no reference to the irregular sexual activities of white male and black female—an interesting omission in light of the efforts made to draw clearly the color line." He suggested that white men would not stand for legislation that explicitly protected African American women from their sexual overtures. Indeed, "The law-makers were worldly wise enough to know that some ideas drafted into law would be impossible to enforce and of no practical effect. Nowhere do written laws prove more futile than when applied to some sexual questions." According to Davis, then, black women simply did not merit legal protection against white sexual violence.[30]

As the era of the Black Codes gave way to Florida's 1868 Constitutional Convention and Congressional Reconstruction, Davis found little to celebrate. He did not try to hide his devotion to white conservatism, stating, "The most disturbing factor in the uncertain future for the mass of whites in Florida was the impending fact of negro enfranchisement." Davis found especially unsettling the Freedmen's Bureau because, he explained, "The Bureau was founded in the assumption that the Southern black unaided would not obtain justice from the Southern white. In its operation it affords an example in American history of arbitrary, bureaucratic government from a remote center—a form of political atavism suggestive of ancient Babylonia or modern Russia." Throughout his treatment of Reconstruction Davis blasted black political participation and anyone who supported it. "As the government became Africanized it became weaker," he insisted.[31]

While Davis invoked terms such as *Radical Republicans* and *Radical Reconstruction* to describe people and events in Florida between 1866 and 1877, he in fact failed to establish that Radical Reconstruction or Negro rule had ever occurred in the state. He did note that the 1866 Congressional Civil Rights Bill was not enforced in Florida. More important, Davis wrote that the constitution of 1868 (known subsequently by many as the "radical constitution") "was the joint product of moderate Republicans in the convention and certain native white Conservatives (not Republicans) who had no place there." The constitution's framers gave the executive branch the power to appoint most of the important local offices through the state, which placed much of the government beyond the reach of black Floridians. The constitution also placed a restrictive numerical cap on county representation in Tallahassee. White conservatives took pains to ensure that the more populous black-belt counties of middle Florida would not enjoy political power commensurate with their respective numbers. In other words, the new constitution empowered African Americans to vote, but the strength of their vote was heavily diluted. Davis asserted that the constitution had the "sympathy and support of Governor Walker and the native whites throughout the state. What was of more immediate importance, they had the sympathy of the Federal military commander in Tallahassee." Davis thus acknowledged federal complicity in curbing African American political influence. But he judged the mere fact of black enfranchisement to be a revolutionary and reprehensible step.[32]

Because Davis did not accept the legitimacy of black political participation in Florida, he struggled with the question of political terrorism, because whites directed most of this terrorism at denying African Americans the ballot. At the outset he made clear who were the perpetrators of mayhem: "The Conservative whites, defeated in the elections, were already beginning to physically assault Republicans, black and white, in desperate efforts to break their grip on the ballot-boxes and the government. This meant violence, often of the worst form." Davis in no way sought to minimize the horror of white-on-black violence, stating, "It meant the saddest part of the Reconstruction ordeal—peace sought through means of midnight assassination, riot, and terror."[33]

Though Davis did not equivocate in describing the reign of savagery that white conservatives brought to Florida, he glossed over its depth and severity. After concluding that the 1868 Constitution saved Florida from "Negro domination," he later asserted that "the lawlessness was the effect of establishing a local government dominated by negroes and Radical whites." At times he appeared to blame the victims, stating in one passage that homicidal whites were spurred to action by, among other indignities, the "Africanization of social institutions," and "negro rowdies" who jeered and "crowded away the white voter at the polls." Davis also charged, again without providing evidence, that "The drunken negro in the little towns became insistently insolent and invited killing."[34]

Davis maintained that whites engaged in mob violence because they believed that they would not get fair hearings in the courts. Yet he also acknowledged that these same courts rarely prosecuted whites who engaged in criminal actions. In Jackson County, for instance, where scores of African Americans were assassinated, "the sheriff of Jackson County was unable often to serve warrants during 1868–70 because public sentiment was so strongly and dangerously against him." As Davis noted, "Negro domination" was in fact absent from such bloody episodes. If anything, this was a period shaped by "white domination" and mayhem in Florida.[35]

No doubt influenced by Petrie, Davis incorporated into his narrative a significant amount of oral testimony from persons who had engaged in heinous crimes. That said, he interviewed only whites and also leaned heavily on leading white conservatives. For example, in Davis's chapter "The Outbreak of Lawlessness," that evidence had been drawn "from the Ku Klux testimony and conversation with those who took part in regulating"; he added, "A former Conservative regulator of that locality in conversation with me concluded that probably 175 murders were perpetrated in Jackson County during the entire Reconstruction period." Such testimony greatly increased the visceral effect of his narrative, and Davis was careful to note that these individuals had repeatedly subjected innocent people to brutality in order to uphold white supremacy. Nonetheless, the absence of narratives that challenge the anonymous white perpetrators of violence on their own terms proves most troubling. In fact, extensive African American testimony was available in the congressional documents that Davis mined for evidence of KKK violence.[36]

Davis's unbalanced approach left the impression that he all but endorsed white racial violence. "The Southerner was certainly face to face with negro domination foisted upon him by Federal law," he wrote. "He arose to protect his own unwritten laws in order that his property, his self-respect, and his family might not be injured or destroyed. He resorted to physical violence under cover, in one of the most sinister and interesting contests of modern times. And in this contest for a very necessary supremacy many a foul crime was committed by white against black." Davis thus seems to have suggested that white terror was acceptable because Caucasian leaders believed that they were saving their state from Negro domination—even though such a circumstance was fictitious in the first place.[37]

Though Davis agreed with his mentor on most aspects of Reconstruction, he broke with Dunning over the latter's negative assessment of John Wallace's *Carpetbag Rule in Florida*. Davis used the book extensively. Historians have long debated its authorship and accuracy. (Governor Bloxham told Davis that he had assisted Wallace in the compilation of the book.) Written from the perspective of one of the leading African American politicians during Reconstruction, *Carpetbag Rule in Florida* is a political memoir, a settling of accounts, rife with charges against Wallace's enemies. Wallace denounced the white northern wing of the Republican Party for its incompetence, its alleged graft, and its failure to create a cohesive party unity with African Americans. Perhaps not surprisingly, Davis mined these sections heavily. Significantly, Davis ignored the sections of Wallace's book that praised the conduct of African American soldiers and black people in general.[38]

Davis also ignored another section of Wallace's book, an omission that underscores the central flaw of *The Civil War and Reconstruction in Florida*. During the 1872 legislative session in Tallahassee, the state representatives from Leon County, all of whom were black, appointed Representative John W. Wyatt to give a speech against a measure that would have given corporations greater power in the state. Representative Wyatt's speech in opposition to this bill signifies one of the most remarkable moments in the history of Florida politics. In it he touched on the belief of many African Americans that the southern wing of the Republican Party was deserting them in an effort to woo northern capital. Wyatt countered that railroad companies already had corrupted northern states such as Pennsylvania, and that Floridians should guard against corporate rule. "In the first place," Wyatt argued, "why should corporations desire to consolidate unless by the unity and coalition thus formed they intended to become a vast and extended power, governing the people and exercising an influence, the magnitude of which would appall us?" Floridians, he warned, had to be vigilant against efforts to install corporate rule in their state:

> Capital needs no legislation in order to provide for its use. Capital is strong enough to take care and provide for itself, but corporations are a dangerous power, especially large or consolidated corporations, and the American people fear them with distrust. . . . We want no Tom Scotts, Jim Fisks or Vanderbilts in this State to govern us, by means of which they would influence legislation tending to advance personal interests. The great curse of Florida has been dishonest corporations, rings and cliques, with an eye single to their central interest, and if this bill is suffered to pass this Assembly, in my opinion we may look for a continuation of abuses and a usurpation of the rights of citizens who may be opposed to the evil machinations such as are generally exerted by consolidated bodies.[39]

White Democrats in Tallahassee immediately praised Wyatt for his stance against corporate power. His speech quickly became the linchpin of anti-Bourbon politics in Florida. Davis could not incorporate this example of interracial solidarity into *The Civil War and Reconstruction in Florida* because its argument did not fit with his narrative of ignorant African Americans imposing "Negro rule" on terrified, antiblack whites. Like Dunning, Davis had overgeneralized splits between "native whites" and African Americans. And like other members of the Dunning School, he doubted the possibility of interracial alliances while bolstering southern Democrats who built their financial empires on the bedrock of white supremacy. In truth, many of Florida's "native whites," particularly small farmers, had good reasons to ally themselves with blacks against the growing power of the railroads. Subsequent generations of historians also disregarded these incipient alliances because their interracial character made a mockery of the usual justifications for the imposition of Jim Crow and segregation.[40]

Davis celebrated Redemption because it led to the restoration of white conservative rule, what he termed "the slow but sure tendency for peace since." Yet Florida was anything but peaceful in the years before and after the publication of *The Civil War and Reconstruction in Florida*. African

Americans in the state suffered the highest lynching rate per capita in the South. In 1907 Governor Napoleon Bonaparte Broward recommended to the state legislature that African Americans be expelled from Florida; the upper chamber of that body accommodated him by resolving to abrogate the Fourteenth and Fifteenth amendments to the U.S. Constitution. The state experienced numerous race riots and massacres that culminated in the mass murder of blacks in Ocoee (1920), Perry (1922), and Rosewood (1923). For decades the Ku Klux Klan continued to exert a powerful force in state politics, effectively running entire towns. Numerous political scandals wracked Jim Crow–era Florida, contributing to the state's reputation for governmental corruption that continues today.[41] In placing a scholarly stamp of approval on the denouement of Reconstruction in Florida, Davis helped enable the state's white citizenry avoid the hard questions about how to build democracy in Florida. This is the ultimate failure of *The Civil War and Reconstruction in Florida*.

Unfortunately, historians generally ignored the strongest sections of Davis's book when it appeared in 1913. His thesis on slavery and the coming of the Civil War was overlooked in favor of his polemic on Reconstruction. Most reviewers—North and South—praised the book for its attacks on Radical Republicanism and black political participation. This is unsurprising. In the wake of the defeat of Populism, it became a national truism that politics should be controlled by the elite, and not left in the hands of the mass of the population, certainly not African Americans or immigrants. When civil rights activism blossomed anew in Florida in the 1960s, Davis's book was chosen for special recognition by the Florida Quadricentennial Commission, just as the black freedom struggle began to make inroads against the conservative order that Davis had revered.[42]

Even as Florida's segregationist governor Hayden Burns was feting *The Civil War and Reconstruction in Florida,* a new generation of historians began launching frontal assaults on Davis's analysis of race and Reconstruction. Ralph L. Peek's 1967 essay on the election of 1870 pointedly observed that the idea of Radical Reconstruction in Florida was a myth and that "the beginning of the end of Reconstruction of Florida was marked by the election of 1870. Although the Republicans won the election of 1872, it was then apparent that the Democrats must be consulted in all important matters. . . . Thus, if Reconstruction was characterized by misrule, the Democrats must share the blame." Joe M. Richardson's groundbreaking book, *The Negro in the Reconstruction of Florida* (1965), argued that African

Americans were rational political actors, and that Davis's analysis of the Freedmen's Bureau was terribly flawed. Jerrell H. Shofner's *Nor Is It Over Yet: Florida in the Era of Reconstruction* (1974) took Davis to task for his uncritical reliance on Governor Bloxham's testimony, and it set a new standard for post-emancipation studies in Florida. More recently, Larry Eugene Rivers has demolished Davis's argument on the mild nature of slavery in Florida, whereas Daniel Schafer has rendered a balanced assessment of the performance of African American troops in Civil War Florida.[43]

This scholarship cannot erase the fact that, as Du Bois wrote in 1935, for over half a century the officially sanctioned interpretation of the Civil War and Reconstruction in Florida was marred by a "Standard—Anti-Negro" bias. The power of Davis's *Civil War and Reconstruction in Florida* can be attributed to the ways that its author affirmed the racial status quo that governed Florida and American social and political relations. With the exception of Stetson Kennedy's *Palmetto Country* (1942), Davis's analysis of perhaps the most important period of Florida's history remained largely unchallenged for six decades. If Davis wrote as an "unreconstructed southerner," his readers in the North as well as the South adopted him as a voice of authority—with dire consequences for the better part of the twentieth century.[44]

Notes

I am indebted to the guidance of William H. Chafe, David Colburn, David Chalmers, William Link, Otto Olsen, Larry Rivers, Irvin D. S. Winsboro, and John David Smith in the writing of this essay. Sarah McNamara provided invaluable research assistance and a concise reading of an early draft of the essay. Sheila Payne provided critical editorial feedback every step of the way.

1.William E. Dodd, review of William Watson Davis, *The Civil War and Reconstruction in Florida*, in *Journal of Political Economy* 21 (November 1913): 871–72; John H. Russell, review of Davis, *The Civil War and Reconstruction in Florida*, in *American Political Science Review* 8 (February 1914): 137–38; "Notes," *Nation*, January 22, 1914, 88; Herman J. Thorstenberg, review of Davis, *The Civil War and Reconstruction in Florida*, in *American Historical Review* 19 (October 1913–July 1914): 404–5; review of Davis, *The Civil War and Reconstruction in Florida*, in *Independent Weekly* 75 (September 25, 1913): 745. David W. Blight has evocatively captured the importance of the semicentennial of Gettysburg in American history in *Race and Reunion: The Civil War in American Memory* (Cambridge: Belknap Press of Harvard University Press, 2001), 6–18.

2. For examples of citations of *The Civil War and Reconstruction in Florida* as an authoritative source, see "Documents Relating to Secession in Florida," *Florida Historical Quarterly* 4 (April 1926): 183–91; T. Frederick Davis, "The Disston Land Purchase," *Florida Historical Quarterly* 17 (January 1939): 200–210; George R. Bentley, "The Political Activity of the Freedmen's Bureau in Florida," *Florida Historical Quarterly* 28 (July 1949–April 1950): 28–37; Federal Writer's Project, *Florida: A Guide to the Southernmost State* (New York: Oxford University Press,1939), 144; Fletcher Green, "William Watson Davis: Introduction to the 1964 Edition of William Watson Davis's *The Civil War and Reconstruction in Florida*," in Fletcher Melvin Green, *Democracy in the Old South*, ed. J. Isaac Copeland (Nashville: Vanderbilt University Press, 1969), 264; W. W. Davis, review of A. J. Hanna, *Flight into Oblivion*, in *Florida Historical Quarterly* 17 (January 1939): 227–36; Green, "William Watson Davis," 270.

3. For the importance of historical memory in the South, see Allesandro Portelli, *They Say in Harlan County: An Oral History* (New York: Oxford University Press, 2010); W. Fitzhugh Brundage, ed., *Where These Memories Grow: History, Memory, and Southern Identity* (Chapel Hill: University of North Carolina Press, 2000); William H. Chafe, Raymond Gavins, Robert Korstad, and Paul Ortiz, et al., eds., *Remembering Jim Crow: African Americans Tell about Life in the Jim Crow South* (New York: New Press, 2008).

4. Lane Davis to Fletcher M. Green, February 28, 1964, Fletcher Melvin Green Papers, Southern Historical Collection, Louis Round Wilson Special Collections Library, University of North Carolina, Chapel Hill; "Matthew Livingston Davis," *Dictionary of American Biography,* 20 vols. (New York: Charles Scribner's Sons, 1928–36), 5:138–39; Thomas McAdory Owen and Marie Bankhead Owen, *History of Alabama and Dictionary of Alabama Biography,* 4 vols. (Chicago: S. J. Clarke, 1921), 3:469–70.

5. "Muscogee COUNTY GA Indian Wars Roster—The Columbus Guards," Georgia State Archives–Atlanta, http://files.usgwarchives.net/ga/muscogee/military/indian/roster.txt (accessed December 7, 2010); Lucian Lamar Knight, *Georgia's Landmarks, Memorials and Legends, Complete in Two Volumes* (Atlanta: Byrd Printing Co., 1913), 1:823; *Columbus, Georgia, from Its Selection as a Trading Town in 1827 to Its Partial Destruction by Wilson's Raid in 1865* (Columbus, Ga.: Thos. Gilbert, 1874), 98; "Act of Incorporation, Trinity Episcopal Church," www.trinityepiscopalchurch.com/hst-chtr.htm (accessed March 23, 2011); "Brooks' Riding Crop? Long Island, New York," *History Detectives*, episode 7, 2004, www.pbs.org/historydetectives (accessed March 12, 2012).

6. For a sketch of similar sawmill towns, see William Jones, *The Tribe of Black Ulysses: African American Lumber Workers in the Jim Crow South* (Urbana: University of Illinois Press, 2005), 1; "Big Timber Lands, Big Help to South," *Chicago Record-Herald,* March 29, 1905; Occie Clubbs, "Pensacola in Retrospect: 1870–1890," *Florida Historical Quarterly* 37 (January–April 1959): 377–96; Lane Davis to Fletcher M. Green, February 28, 1964, Margaret Davis to Fletcher Green, Feb-

ruary 26, 1964, and Lane Davis to Fletcher M. Green, February 28, 1964, all in Green Papers. Margaret Davis wrote this letter at the behest of University of Florida professor Rembert W. Patrick to provide Green with biographical details to use in his sketch about Davis in the commemorative edition of *The Civil War and Reconstruction in Florida*. Patrick had studied under Professor Green at Chapel Hill, and he wrote the editorial preface to the 1964 edition of *Civil War and Reconstruction in Florida;* Marjorie Yonge to Rembert Patrick, February 11, 1964, Green Papers.

7. Owen and Owen, *History of Alabama and Dictionary of Alabama Biography*, 3:469–70. Davis was a member of Auburn's chapter of the Kappa Alpha Order, founded in 1883. The order referred to General Robert E. Lee as "our spiritual founder"; Auburn University Kappa Alpha Order, www.auburnka.com/history. php (accessed December 15, 2010). Also see Anthony Donaldson, "The Father of Alabama Historians: Professor George Petrie and His Survey of Slavery," *Alabama Review* 62 (January 2009): 37–58; George Petrie, "Can the History of the United States Be Made Interesting?" *Sewanee Review* 4 (May 1896): 270.

8. M. Yonge to Patrick, February 11, 1964, Green Papers.

9. Owen and Owen, *History of Alabama and Dictionary of Alabama Biography*, 3:469–70.

10. William Archibald Dunning, *Reconstruction, Political and Economic, 1865–1877* (New York: Harper & Brothers, 1907), xvi, 354.

11. Review of Davis, *The Civil War and Reconstruction in Florida*, in *Independent Weekly*, 745.

12. Peter Novick, *That Noble Dream: The 'Objectivity Question' and the American Historical Profession* (New York: Cambridge University Press, 1988); "With the Faculty," *University of Kansas Graduate Magazine* 20 (January 1922): 29. This conference was timed to coincide with Armistice Day and was designed to limit the global proliferation of armaments. See John W. Dean, *Warren G. Harding* (New York: Henry Holt, 2004), 129–35.

13. John S. Nelson, "A Gentleman and a Scholar: A Tribute to Lane Davis," *Poroi* 3 (December 2004); *Bulletin of the American Association of University Professors* 4 (January 1918): 87; *Annual Catalog of the University of Kansas: 1921–1922* (Lawrence: University of Kansas, 1921), 153.

14. Davis, *Civil War and Reconstruction in Florida*, 38–42; Paul Goodman, "David Donald's Charles Sumner Reconsidered," *New England Quarterly* 37 (September 1964): 373–87; Samuel Proctor, ed., "The Call to Arms: Secession from a Feminine Point of View," *Florida Historical Quarterly* 35 (January 1957): 269. The best of the newer generation of Florida scholarship reinforced and expanded Davis's thesis on slavery. See, for example, Daniel L. Schafer, *Thunder on the River: The Civil War in Northeast Florida* (Gainesville: University Press of Florida, 2010), x–xi.

15. Davis, *Civil War and Reconstruction in Florida*, 221–24. For a national trend to minimize slavery as a cause of the Civil War, see Blight, *Race and Reunion*.

16. Davis, *Civil War and Reconstruction in Florida*, 43–45.

17. Ibid., 48, 11; "The Creek War," *Niles' Register,* June 11, 1836; Jane Landers, *Black Society in Spanish Florida* (Urbana: University of Illinois Press, 1999); Larry Eugene Rivers, *Slavery in Florida: Territorial Days to Emancipation* (Gainesville: University Press of Florida, 2009); Larry Eugene Rivers, *Rebels and Runaways: Slave Resistance in Nineteenth-Century Florida* (Urbana: University of Illinois Press, 2012); Claudio Saunt, *A New Order of Things: Property, Power, and the Transformation of the Creek Indians, 1733–1816* (New York: Cambridge University Press, 1999); James M. Denham, *A Rogue's Paradise: Crime and Punishment in Antebellum Florida, 1821–1861* (Tuscaloosa: University of Alabama Press, 2005).

18. Davis, *Civil War and Reconstruction in Florida*, 66–70; Charles Beard and Mary Beard, *The Rise of American Civilization* (New York: Macmillan, 1927).

19. A. J. Hanna, *Flight into Oblivion* (1938; reprint, Baton Rouge: Louisiana State University Press, 1999), 217; Davis, *Civil War and Reconstruction in Florida*, 191–213; Denham, *A Rogue's Paradise*.

20. Davis, *Civil War and Reconstruction in Florida*, 190–204; David J. Coles and Richard J. Ferry, "'The Smallest Tadpole': Florida in the Civil War," Florida Memory: Florida State Library & Archives of Florida, Division of Library & Information Services, http://floridamemory.com/onlineclassroom/floridacivilwar/history/ (accessed April 25, 2013).

21. Davis, *Civil War and Reconstruction in Florida*, 245–46; Wayne Durrill, *War of Another Kind: A Southern Community in the Great Rebellion* (New York: Oxford University Press, 1994); Margaret M. Storey, *Loyalty and Loss: Alabama's Unionists in the Civil War and Reconstruction* (Baton Rouge: Louisiana State University Press, 2004); Noel C. Fisher, *War at Every Door: Partisan Politics and Guerilla Violence in East Tennessee, 1860–1869* (Chapel Hill: University of North Carolina Press, 2000).

22. Review of Davis, *Civil War and Reconstruction in Florida*, in *Independent Weekly*, 745; Davis, *Civil War and Reconstruction in Florida*, 219–23.

23. Davis, *Civil War and Reconstruction in Florida*, 227–34. Confederates frequently mistreated formerly enslaved African American Union soldiers who became prisoners of war. After the Battle of Olustee, some black prisoners were executed. See Schafer, *Thunder on the River*, 188–89, 193; Benjamin Quarles, *The Negro in the Civil War* (Boston: Little, Brown, 1953); Joseph T. Glatthaar, *Forged in Battle: The Civil War Alliance of Black Soldiers and White Officers* (New York: Free Press, 1990).

24. Davis, *Civil War and Reconstruction in Florida*, 320.

25. Review of Davis, *Civil War and Reconstruction in Florida*, in *Independent Weekly*, 745.

26. Thorstenberg, review of Davis, *The Civil War and Reconstruction in Florida*, 404–5. For Professor Thorstenberg's 1910 ordeal, see Gaines M. Foster, *Ghosts of the Confederacy: Defeat, the Lost Cause, and the Emergence of the New South, 1865 to 1913* (New York: Oxford University Press, 1987), 189–90.

27. Davis, *The Civil War and Reconstruction in Florida*, 219, 535, 647, 375, 457, 390.

28. Ibid., 390.

29. Ibid., 416–37.

30. Ibid., 420–21.

31. Ibid., 448, 378, 619, 610. For the inherently conservative character of Florida's first "Carpetbagger" governor, Harrison Reed, and his relationship to former senator David Yulee, see Richard Nelson Current, *Those Terrible Carpetbaggers: A Reinterpretation* (New York: Oxford University Press, 1988).

32. Davis, *Civil War and Reconstruction in Florida*, 512–14. According to Current, Republican governor Harrison Reed "wanted to join with Yulee and other prewar Floridians to form a party that could reconstruct the state in the way that would be best for business. He had no enthusiasm for the Reconstruction Act, with its directive for Negro suffrage. Good Johnson man that he was, he would have preferred to see the state continue under the President's restoration plan." Current, *Those Terrible Carpetbaggers*, 85.

33. Davis, *Civil War and Reconstruction in Florida*, 515–16.

34. Ibid., 587, 588–99, 602. The year after Davis's book appeared, William Stewart Simkins, a professor of law at the University of Texas, initiated a yearly campuswide lecture whereby he regaled students and faculty with his exploits as a cofounder of the Ku Klux Klan in Florida. See Simkins, "Why the Ku Klux," *Alcade* (June 1916): 735–48. For a masterful assessment of Professor Simkins, see Thomas D. Russell, "Keep Negroes Out of Most Classes Where There Are a Large Number of Girls: The Unseen Power of the Ku Klux Klan and Standardized Testing at the University of Texas, 1899–1999," in *Law, Society, and History: Themes in the Legal Sociology and Legal History of Lawrence M. Friedman*, ed. Robert W. Gordon and Morton J. Horwitz (New York: Cambridge University Press, 2011), 309–36.

35. Davis, *Civil War and Reconstruction in Florida*, 603–4; Daniel R. Weinfeld, *The Jackson County War: Reconstruction and Resistance in Post–Civil War Florida* (Tuscaloosa: University of Alabama Press, 2012).

36. Davis, *Civil War and Reconstruction in Florida*, 567, 582.

37. Ibid., 586.

38. James C. Clark, "John Wallace and the Writing of Reconstruction History," *Florida Historical Quarterly* 67 (April 1989): 409–27; Davis, *Civil War and Reconstruction in Florida*, 265; John Wallace, *Carpetbag Rule in Florida: The Inside Workings of the Reconstruction of Civil Government in Florida after the Close of the Civil War* (1888; reprint, Kennesaw, Ga.: Continental Book Co., 1959), 19.

39. Wallace, *Carpetbag Rule in Florida*, 156–57. For a confirmation of African American fears of railroads and corruption specifically involving Fisk and Vanderbilt, see Charles Francis Adams Jr., *Chapters of Erie* (1871; reprint, Long Grove, Ill.: Waveland Press, 2002).

40. Philip R. Muller's observation of Dunning could apply equally to Davis:

"He tended to generalize too facilely about collectivities such as northern public opinion, or white southerners, or blacks, or carpetbaggers." See Muller, "Look Back without Anger: A Reappraisal of William A. Dunning," *Journal of American History* 61 (September 1974): 329–30.

41. Davis, *Civil War and Reconstruction in Florida,* 738; Paul Ortiz, *Emancipation Betrayed: The Hidden History of Black Organizing and White Violence in Florida from Reconstruction to the Bloody Election of 1920* (Berkeley: University of California Press, 2005), 61–84, 205–36; Stephen R. Prescott, "White Robes and Crosses: Father John Conoley, The Ku Klux Klan, and the University of Florida," *Florida Historical Quarterly* 71 (July 1992): 18–40; Michael Newton, *The Invisible Empire: The Ku Klux Klan in Florida* (Gainesville: University Press of Florida, 2001). A recent statewide grand jury declared that "corruption is pervasive at all levels of government" in Florida. "Ethics Law Falls Flat in Legislature," *Gainesville Sun,* May 31, 2011.

42. More balanced appraisals appear in Irvin D. S. Winsboro, ed., *Florida's Civil War: Explorations into Conflict, Interpretations and Memory* (Cocoa: Florida Historical Society Press, 2008). For an assessment of American politics during the early twentieth century, see Lawrence Goodwyn, *The Populist Moment: A Short History of the Agrarian Revolt in America* (New York: Oxford University Press, 1978).

43. Ralph L. Peek, "Election of 1870 and the End of Reconstruction in Florida," *Florida Historical Quarterly* 45 (April 1967): 352–68; Joe M. Richardson, *The Negro in the Reconstruction of Florida, 1865–1877* (Tallahassee: Florida State University, 1965); Jerrell H. Shofner, *Nor Is It Over Yet: Florida in the Era of Reconstruction, 1863–1877* (Gainesville: University Presses of Florida, 1974); Rivers, *Slavery in Florida;* Rivers, *Rebels and Runaways;* and Schafer, *Thunder on the River.* Other important works that have helped present a more balanced history of the period include Jerrell H. Shofner, "A Failure of Moderate Republicanism," in *Reconstruction and Redemption in the South: An Assessment,* ed. Otto Olsen (Baton Rouge: Louisiana State University Press, 1980), 13–46; and David R. Colburn and Jane L. Landers, eds. *The African American Heritage of Florida* (Gainesville: University Press of Florida, 1995).

44. Indeed, Davis's interpretation of Reconstruction continued to resonate throughout Florida long after the wave of newer scholarship had seemingly replaced it. Drawing heavily on *The Civil War and Reconstruction in Florida,* Elizabeth Sims stated in 1986, "The war might be over but the South's troubles were far from over. It would be many years before the bitterness was gone, mainly because of the North's actions after the war, and even today, after one hundred and twenty years, there is still a trace of resentment." Sims, *A History of Madison County, Florida* (Madison, Fla.: Madison County Historical Society, 1986), 79–96.

10

C. Mildred Thompson

A Liberal among the Dunningites

William Harris Bragg

On February 16, 1975, the last surviving student of Professor William A. Dunning's fabled Reconstruction seminar died, only six years short of her hundredth birthday. C. Mildred Thompson left the world where she had entered it: Atlanta, Georgia, whose history was entwined with the subject of her only book, *Reconstruction in Georgia: Economic, Social, Political, 1865–1872*. She had been born in 1881, the year that the last Reconstruction president had left office, and only a few years after America's centennial. Now death had come the year before two other events Thompson would have welcomed: the nation's bicentennial celebration and the election to the U.S. presidency of the first Georgian to hold that office—a southern liberal much like herself. Indeed, Thompson's traditional liberalism would form the truest, most continuous thread in the richly textured tapestry of a long life well and productively lived. Nonetheless, her liberalism, in both life and works, would not prevent her from being most commonly remembered by later academics as a "Dunningite," a member of the "Dunning School" of Reconstruction historiography, a group portrayed by critics as not only illiberal but profoundly racist.[1]

During a lifetime literally "full of years and honors," Thompson worked primarily in the northeast, far from her native city, but not nearly the distance her father, Robert Galbraith Thompson, had traveled. He had arrived in America in 1851, aboard one of the last "famine ships" from Ireland. Anglican, not Catholic, he had by 1861 married Alice Gray Wood, daughter of a tanner and currier of Brooklyn, New York, himself an English immigrant. Though the couple arrived in the South during the 1860s, there is no hint that Robert Thompson ever served in the Confederate army.[2]

One critic (reducing the Dunningites to the southern-born authors of the southern state studies, a common practice) suggested that most of the Dunning scholars were children of the Lost Cause, similar in ancestry, rural background, and outlook. Obviously, Thompson never fit this stereotype. Her parents (an immigrant and a first-generation American) had settled permanently in urban Atlanta's political and commercial center in the late 1860s. While raising six children, the Thompsons made their living operating small businesses, including billiard halls, confectionaries, family restaurants, and, ultimately, a small hotel. Rather than a devotion to the Lost Cause, Robert Thompson had the enterprising immigrant's appreciative love of a land of freedom and opportunity.[3] Nonetheless, where Georgia Reconstruction was concerned, Robert Thompson served as a primary source for his daughter's knowledge. Some of his anecdotes, she later said, formed the core of her book.[4]

As an Atlanta public school girl, Mildred Thompson learned eagerly in an environment reflecting less a preoccupation with the Lost Cause than pride in her birthplace, described by the journalist-orator Henry W. Grady as a "brave and beautiful city," the capital of a reconciled and forward-looking New South. Mirroring on a smaller scale Grady's distinction between the old Atlanta and the new, Thompson distinguished herself not only academically, but personally, through a signal act of self-identification. Christened Clara Mildred (and always known as Mildred to family and friends), she countered the classroom presence of another Mildred Thompson by renaming herself C. Mildred Thompson. From that time until it was carved into her small memorial stone in Atlanta's Oakland Cemetery, this would be her name of record.[5]

After high school graduation in 1899, Thompson, only seventeen, departed for Vassar College, near Poughkeepsie, New York. Already famous for offering a superior education to young women, the college was symbolized by its impressive Main Building, a grand exercise in Second Empire style. During most of the next half century, Thompson would remain happily at Vassar, successively as student, professor, and dean, only an occasional visitor to Atlanta.[6]

Excelling as a Vassar student, Thompson acquired her first mentor, the redoubtable Lucy Maynard Salmon. She introduced Thompson to the historical profession, hardly older than Thompson herself and then represented by the American Historical Association (AHA), founded in 1884, and the *American Historical Review* (*AHR*), established in 1895. "Scientific history" reigned, with its emphasis on creating a factual record based on the truth as ascertained through deep, objective research in the original sources. After Thompson earned her bachelor's degree (Phi Beta Kappa) in 1903, she immediately embarked on several years' secondary school teaching, gaining experience while earning money to help pay for graduate schooling.[7]

In 1906 Thompson began studying for her master's degree at Columbia University in New York City. Though the university would not become fully coeducational until after Thompson's death, women had been admitted to graduate studies programs since the 1880s. At Columbia Thompson was drawn to her second mentor, William A. Dunning, like Salmon prominent in the AHA, and a committed exponent of the organization's recruitment of students from the South. Her degree achieved in 1907, Thompson continued with Dunning for her doctoral degree. Over the next eight years she labored on her dissertation on Reconstruction Georgia, one of the last Dunning School southern state studies of Reconstruction, published by the university press in 1915.[8]

During her time as a Columbia graduate student, Thompson began working as an instructor at Vassar. By 1923 she had graduated to full professor and been appointed dean of the college, a post she would hold for a full quarter century. For Thompson the deanship represented no escape from the classroom; instead, she maintained a punishing schedule to fulfill her passion for teaching. Usually she taught two courses each term: America from the Civil War to the Present and The Contemporary History of the United States, an advanced course. In 1964 one of her appreciative students would anonymously endow in her name an ongoing lecture series.[9]

As dean, Thompson made many progressive additions to the curriculum. In the 1920s she introduced independent studies, and she added interdisciplinary courses in the 1940s. Thompson also conducted a continuous campaign to expand scholarship opportunities. Though she supported racial integration at Vassar (one of the "larger principles of Democracy" at the college), she opposed, as a meritocrat, what would later be called affirmative action. And, as a proponent of "mental hygiene," she inaugurated in 1924 a "formal psychiatric service for students," one of the first of its kind. Moreover, she constantly modeled for her students a life of civic engagement and political commitment.[10]

In her persona of "dean of Vassar," Thompson also became nationally famous, not least because of her close friendship with the Roosevelts of nearby Hyde Park. Widely known as an FDR Democrat, Thompson enthusiastically supported Roosevelt and his New Deal policies. Her political ideology, she stated, had been best expressed by FDR in his 1932 San Francisco campaign speech on progressive government. Also a great admirer of Eleanor Roosevelt, Thompson considered her "First Lady of the World."[11]

Always an outspoken feminist, Thompson worked to promote women in the academy through the Berkshire Conference of Women Historians and otherwise. In the AHA she set a precedent at the 1940 meeting by chairing a landmark panel titled "Some Aspects of the History of Women," a first for the organization. Whether or not it was an aspect of her feminism, Thompson, like Lucy Salmon, never married. Certainly during Thompson's early years at Vassar, marriage and a full professional life were judged incompatible, and women were expected to choose between marriage and a career.[12]

In the 1940s Thompson's celebrity increased through her heightened profile as a speaker and writer, often on women's issues. She appeared on current affairs radio programs such as *Listen: The Women,* as well as the highly popular *Information, Please,* and contributed witty, topical articles to a variety of magazines. In 1948 she was honored as principal speaker at the Washington, D.C., centennial commemoration of the Seneca Falls women's rights convention.[13]

During the same period Thompson earned her reputation as an internationalist. She attended the 1943 Conference of Allied Ministers of Education in wartime London, the sole woman delegate from the United States. The next year she flew again to London with a five-member delegation, chaired by Congressman William J. Fulbright, and participated in the conference that founded the United Nations Educational, Scientific and Cultural Organization (UNESCO). A lifelong supporter of the United Nations, she fervently hoped the organization would promote world peace through education.[14]

Reaching Vassar's retirement age in 1948, Thompson returned to her native state. There she taught for four years at the University of Georgia in Athens, where her department head was E. Merton Coulter, whose *The South during Reconstruction* (1947) would come to be seen as the last major work in the Dunning tradition. Thompson enjoyed her first experience with coeducation, and her students liked and admired her, as did her colleagues. One of them, Robert Preston Brooks, at Georgia since 1901, said of her, "No more distinguished a scholar has ever served the University." When Thompson reached Georgia's retirement age, she initiated her eighth decade of life by traveling to Europe to serve as the dean of women at the College of Free Europe (1952–53) in Strasbourg, France, opposing communism by helping educate young refugees from behind the Iron Curtain.[15]

Thompson returned to Atlanta in 1960 and remained there for the rest of her life, active in civic, political, and cultural affairs until her final years of illness and infirmity. Newspapers from coast to coast noted her death in 1975 and celebrated her achievements; the *New York Times* published a prominent, illustrated obituary. Without exception, Thompson's death notices mentioned her authorship sixty years earlier of *Reconstruction in Georgia*.[16]

In the context of such a remarkably busy and productive life, Thompson's 1915 book on Reconstruction might appear to be no more than a footnote. But she was quite proud of her book and the scholarly praise it had won. Likewise, she had been delighted to learn in 1937 that her fellow Atlantan Margaret Mitchell had considered *Reconstruction in Georgia* her "mainstay" and her "comfort" when writing the last half of *Gone with the Wind*. Moreover, preparing a Reconstruction lecture for a university class in the 1950s, Thompson herself was pleased to find her Reconstruction monograph, almost forty years old, still "interesting" and holding up well.[17]

Thompson's progress toward publication of *Reconstruction in Georgia* began in 1906, when she entered Columbia. Her arrival as one of Lucy Salmon's students, "with a very strong recommendation," had been anticipated. Dunning found Thompson to be an even better scholar than he had expected. As he wrote to Columbia's president Nicholas Murray Butler in mid-1907:

> All that Miss Salmon said of Miss Thompson's ability has been abundantly proved to us in the history department . . . by the performance of Miss Thompson. American history has been her major subject, and she has taken the seminar with me. In this work, the papers which she has presented have manifested a very unusual excellence in respect both to the diligence and rationality of research, and to the clearness of the presentation. . . . She has become interested in certain phases of the Reconstruction time in Georgia, and has not only the ability to work them out, but also very unusual advantages in the way of getting material down there.[18]

Without Thompson's knowledge, Dunning had written to President Butler, with the support of Thompson's other history professors, to arrange a fellowship in American history for her; it was granted. Supporting Dunning's successful request was James Harvey Robinson, who had taught Thompson in his groundbreaking course, "The Intellectual History of Western Europe." Robinson, a devotee of social and intellectual history, along with Charles Beard (a proponent of economic history), represented the "New History," which opposed scientific history's emphasis on political, institutional, and military subjects. The "New Historians" considered history a tool for social reform, not an objective record of the past; indeed, they would ultimately attack the idea of objectivity itself. The New History initiated trends in historiography that would eclipse the scientific historians in general and the Dunningites in particular.[19]

As a graduate student in history, Thompson was distinguished by more than her accomplishments and promise. She had entered an expanding profession, quite well organized and intercommunicative, where her southern birth was at a premium. Moreover, as a woman academic, she belonged to a small and elite group, for of the 543 doctorates of philosophy in history granted by American universities through 1915, only around 10 percent were received by women.[20]

The principal male Dunningites (and Dunning himself) appear to have held Thompson in high esteem. In one important instance Thompson even managed to become one of the Old Chief's "boys," at least in an honorary sense. Of Dunning's women students, Thompson alone was invited to contribute to *Studies in Southern History and Politics*, a Festschrift of fifteen essays presented in 1914 to Dunning by his students in honor of his election to the AHA's presidency. Thompson's contribution, "Carpet-baggers in the United States Senate," effectively surveyed its subject. It drew mainly from the *Congressional Globe* and various government documents, along with periodical articles and the state Reconstruction studies of her fellow Dunningites.[21]

Thompson concluded that the senatorial carpetbaggers (none of whom came from Georgia) "were a mixed lot; some few were quite respectable and able men; several were thoroughly dishonest and corrupt, and the majority mere non-entities." What united them, she asserted, was "their real center of interest . . . the spoils of office," which she demonstrated by showing that most bills they introduced dealt "almost entirely with railroad grants and private claims."[22] Thompson's only other Reconstruction article, "The

Freedmen's Bureau in Georgia in 1865–6: An Instrument of Reconstruction," based in part on material from her dissertation, would not appear until 1921.[23]

In contrast to essay writing, preparation of "Reconstruction in Georgia" as her doctoral dissertation for Dunning would constitute the most challenging scholarly task of Thompson's life. To gain control over the mass of material she had gathered, Thompson organized it both chronologically and topically (highlighting economic, social, and political factors). She logically divided her book into three parts; the first and longest section deals principally with Georgia's period of Presidential Reconstruction, 1865–66, and the second and third parts of the book survey Congressional Reconstruction, 1867–72.[24]

Thompson began part 1 of her book by relating the catastrophic effects the war had worked on Georgia's economy. Emancipation came next, in some of its social aspects, as well as in its effect in changing both labor patterns and land use. In politics she covered the state's evolution from the abrupt end of Joseph E. Brown's tenure as war governor into a brief period of military oversight, and on through the administration of the appointed provisional governor James Johnson. Finally, she surveyed the tenure of the restoration governor Charles Jones Jenkins, the last Reconstruction chief executive chosen by a white electorate.[25]

In the book's second part Thompson described Georgia under military rule, followed by the Republican triumph over the white conservatives with the election of Rufus Bullock as governor. After describing Georgia's initial return to the Union, she recounted the story of Georgia's second Reconstruction, brought on by the expulsion of most of the newly elected black members of the General Assembly. This portentous act, carried out by a coalition of white Democrats and white Republicans, exploited the state constitution's silence on black officeholding rights. There follows an account of the extravagance of the Bullock administration (demonstrated by meticulous comparison with the expenditures of previous state governments), the charges of Republican corruption (documented in detail, but legally unproven—for the most part—by later Democratic investigators), and the ultimate downfall of the Republicans as the Democrats returned to power.[26]

The last part of Thompson's book returns to economic and social matters, including comprehensive surveys of agriculture, industry, commerce, banking, schools, churches, and courts, as her chapter headings promise.

This section consigns the Ku Klux Klan to social rather than political history, since Thompson saw the organization as an attempt by the "conservative whites, the old ruling class," to "bring some order out of social chaos."[27]

In her conclusion Thompson stressed that Reconstruction had brought Georgia "a wider democratization of society." With "emancipation as the central fact," she noted, "a greater social democracy" had been established. Moreover, she asserted, the "greatest constructive achievement of the Civil War was the establishment of the negro in freedom," though during Reconstruction the Republicans had "failed to establish him in permanent equality . . . either in political rights or social privileges."[28]

Reconstruction in Georgia represents Thompson at her scholarly best. Making paramount her historian's responsibility for collecting and critically examining sources, she had carefully conducted bibliographical work that equaled or surpassed the preceding Dunning southern state studies. This was especially true in regard to the earlier Dunning dissertation on her subject, *The Reconstruction of Georgia* (1901) by Edwin C. Woolley of Illinois. Woolley, Thompson noted, had gathered "only the most evident authorities and public documents" for his mainly political study.[29]

In replacing Woolley's brief study with a comprehensive history, Thompson dug deeply and widely in the primary sources on Georgia Reconstruction. The mother lode of original sources lay in Atlanta. Since no separate state archives would exist until 1918, Thompson spent many hours among the official documents, both printed and manuscript, in the state capitol. Several blocks away were the offices of the *Atlanta Constitution*, whose files were opened to her by the paper's owner and editor in chief, Clark Howell. Also in Atlanta were certain troves of private papers to which she was able to gain access, including most critically those of the powerful political shape-shifter Joseph E. Brown.[30]

As for printed sources, Vassar boasted a serviceable library, but that of Columbia was uncommonly rich. It held abundant printed sources, constantly expanding. In particular, the library's staff had lavished much attention on gathering sources for the crucial years 1860–80 and by 1898 held "practically all published material" on that period. Included was "the remarkable Townsend collection of newspaper clippings," which Thompson considered "indispensable" for the Reconstruction period.[31]

Likewise essential to Thompson's analysis of her findings was the mentoring she received from William A. Dunning and Lucy Salmon. Though he famously gave students much leeway as they prepared their dissertations, Thompson's preface would state: "Anything of fairness or wisdom or truth that [this book] may contain must be ascribed to Professor William Archibald Dunning of Columbia University, in whom many students of Reconstruction History have found their guide and inspiration."[32] Thompson also handsomely acknowledged Salmon for her "constant encouragement and helpful criticism," without which *Reconstruction in Georgia* "would not have come to completion." Salmon, who prized independent minds, prided herself on teaching students how to think, not what to think.[33]

Showing she had been recruited to Salmon's expansive view of history, Thompson drafted her book's subtitle to emphasize, in descending order, what she considered the most important factors in Georgia's reconstruction: the economic, the social, and the political—a striking alteration of the title of Dunning's own general study, *Reconstruction, Political and Economic, 1865–1877.* She recorded her considered judgment that the "political results of Reconstruction were, in the long run, the least important . . . in the later history of Georgia." She further asserted that the "'undoing of reconstruction' applie[d] merely to politics, for the social and economic reconstruction of Georgia after the war continues to-day."[34]

Of social reforms, she noted that progress in public education, often an achievement of the Republicans in other southern states, had actually been initiated by Georgia Democrats during Presidential Reconstruction. The Georgia Republicans did indeed address education in the 1868 constitution and through legislative activity, but none of their plans were implemented. Public schools for black and white students awaited the return of the Democrats to power.[35]

In the political realm, Thompson had little to say about the Georgia carpetbaggers, since their numbers were so few. Not so the scalawags, such as Governor Rufus Bullock (northern-born but a Georgian before the war). She found several scalawags to deserve their poor reputations—despite their being unconvicted, forgiven, and in some cases transformed into business partners by the Redeemer Democrats in post-Reconstruction days. Nonetheless, in much of Thompson's discussion she was more likely to speak of the Republicans in terms of Radicals and Moderates than carpetbaggers and scalawags, and she praised Republicans of any sort she considered constructive statesmen, as in the case of Amos T. Akerman, later U.S. attorney general.[36]

It was, however, the man whom white conservatives considered Georgia's Arch-Scalawag, Joseph E. Brown, who engaged Thompson's attention most directly. Woolley's study had given positive treatment to Brown—Democratic war governor of Georgia, Reconstruction Republican, and Redemption Democrat—presumably because of his scanty source material. But as Thompson understood, the two major Brown primary sources in Woolley's bibliography represented the governor's personally arranged printed legacy: Isaac W. Avery's *The History of Georgia* (1881) and Herbert Fielder's *The Life and Times of Joseph E. Brown* (1883). The former is an account by a warm admirer of Brown, the latter the work of a complete Brown sycophant. Thompson's deep research into the original sources—particularly state documents, newspapers, and private correspondence—revealed Brown as a much more compromised figure than Woolley had suspected.[37]

In her account Thompson closely followed Brown each time he switched political parties, discovering much that was suspicious, some that was discreditable. She particularly noted his dramatically changing pronouncements on black officeholding and their consequences. Her candid approach to Brown was a brave if not foolhardy act. The governor had died immensely wealthy and still quite powerful in 1894, and his son, Joseph M. Brown, had served as governor during much of the time Thompson was working on her book (1909–11; 1912–13). The Browns, it came to be known, were not pleased with Thompson's picture of their patriarch.[38]

Regarding the black politicians of the period, Thompson covered in most detail their political debut in the Constitutional Convention of 1867–68. Like later historians, she singled out Henry McNeal Turner as having most distinguished himself. Thompson also followed the later Reconstruction careers of these men—necessarily entangled with their expulsion and restoration to the General Assembly—along with their appearances before congressional committees. On the whole, she found the expulsion of the black legislators "unwise"—no matter "how unsuited negroes were to the important function of making laws for the commonwealth." The white conservatives erred, she asserted, in considering "solely what was best for the white people of Georgia, instead of viewing reconstruction as a national political problem and consulting the pleasure of the Republican leaders in Congress and the effect of Georgia proceedings on public opinion in the North."[39]

In her final analysis, Thompson argued that Congressional Reconstruction had created serious and lasting problems in Georgia. What had been done by the Radicals—the "transaction"—had been a "forced sale and the price extorted, not paid willingly." In particular, the granting of black suffrage had been a mistake, since "emancipation itself [had been] enough to generate race antagonism between some classes of blacks and whites." Consequently, the "most important and enduring contribution of Congressional Reconstruction" was having "extended and intensified the racial antagonism a hundredfold."[40]

When *Reconstruction in Georgia* came to judgment in 1915, the historical community was represented by several professional journals, and various influential magazines and newspapers also evaluated historians' works. To Thompson's great relief, most reviews of her book approached the rhapsodic. And, happily, a particular concern was alleviated early. She had hoped that her measured, objective treatment would not be attacked in Atlanta, particularly by Georgia's most powerful newspaper, the *Atlanta Constitution*, and her hopes were realized. As she wrote to Lucy Salmon, *Reconstruction in Georgia* had been welcomed with "a most roseate review," written by the University of Georgia's Robert Preston Brooks. His admiring evaluation somewhat allayed her fears "that Georgians might hurl anathema" on her "for taking too mild a view of the horrors of Reconstruction."[41]

Professor Brooks, the state of Georgia's first Rhodes Scholar, wrote that Thompson had left "untouched no phase of the history of the period, whether political, social, or industrial," and he ranked her monograph with the best of the similar state studies. Thompson, he continued, had "unearthed a surprising amount of valuable historical material, shown a rare ability in handling it," and presented her findings "in a thoroughly interesting manner." As an aspirant to objectivity, Thompson welcomed Brooks's verdict that although "her attitude throughout the book [was] sympathetic to the conservative point of view," she did not "in the least allow her feeling to manifest itself in biased judgments."[42]

Evaluating Thompson's book for the *American Historical Review*, J. H. T. McPherson, another University of Georgia professor, also contributed a positive assessment. He considered *Reconstruction in Georgia* an "interesting and comprehensive volume" and lauded the "wealth of materials therein," as listed in Thompson's seventeen-page annotated bibliography. McPherson highlighted two of her judgments in particular, one being her final appraisal of Georgia's Republican regime: "On the whole, as far as personnel [were] concerned, the reconstruction administration of Georgia was not entirely bad, was even quite good in some members. This praise, faint as it is, is more than can be given to most of the governments in the other Southern states in 1868." He noted as well her appreciative assessment of Georgia's Freedmen's Bureau, which, although "hotly resented by most Southerners of the day, seems on the whole to be vindicated"[43]

McPherson's major criticism fell on a gap in the book's scholarly apparatus: "unfortunately it lacks an index." This complaint would be repeated in some other reviews and assessments, then and later. As the *AHR*'s long-time editor, J. Franklin Jameson, commented, many critics considered that historians who failed to provide an index proved themselves "ripe for any atrocity." Thompson's omission certainly reduces her book's usefulness as a reference, and it sets it apart from the other southern state studies of the Dunning school, although the books of some other Dunningite authors (Benjamin Kendrick's, for example) also lacked indexes.[44]

The most mixed of the book's many reviews came from Carter G. Woodson's *Journal of Negro History*, then in its first year of publication. The reviewer, most likely Woodson himself, noted that Thompson's "read-able and interesting work" marked "considerable improvement upon histor-ical writing in this field," particularly in dealing not only with the political but also with the economic and social phases" of Georgia Reconstruction. Nonetheless, the journal's critic felt the book could have offered a "more unbiased treatment" where blacks were concerned, despite the author's attempt "to write with restraint and care."[45]

Amid this general chorus of praise, Thompson waited impatiently for the verdict of the liberal weekly the *Nation*. When the review finally appeared in April 1916, it not only met Thompson's hopes, but softened other reviewers' major criticism: "The lack of an index," wrote the reviewer, "is in part made good by a full table of contents." Indeed, it was full, run-ning in detail for six pages of small print.[46]

The *Nation*'s critic mentioned approvingly Thompson's comment that Reconstruction "laid the foundation of a new democracy, in which the negro became for the first time, a part of 'the people.'" The reviewer quoted as well Thompson's assertion (echoing Henry W. Grady) on the effect of emancipation on both races: "While the white man was master of the slave, slavery was the master of the white man. Abolition freed the white as well as the black." Further noted was Thompson's realization that Reconstruction consigned the whites themselves to a kind of political slavery as part of the Solid South, for "by forcing all whites to be Democrats," it "operate[d] to curtail political freedom in the class which actually governed."[47]

There remained a final tribute from the reviewer: "It is too much to expect that even the most scientific historian will be wholly unmoved by such stirring events as the Bullock regime, the backing and filling of Congress on the question of admitting Senators and Representatives, the political exploitation of the railways, the operation of the Freedmen's Bureau, the efforts to maintain white supremacy, and the lawless activities of the Ku Klux Klan; but Miss Thompson shows little disposition to apportion blame beyond what the facts themselves impart."[48]

Thompson had won laurels enough from the reviewers, as had her fellow scholars in the coterie of graduate students who had labored with Dunning. The southern state studies, the special studies of other Reconstruction topics, and Dunning's own works became the historiographical orthodoxy in American education (secondary and collegiate) until the 1960s. Moreover, made more accessible by works of popular history and historical fiction, the Dunning view of Reconstruction continued in great part to dominate the popular mind.[49]

Almost from the first, however, Thompson and the other Dunningites had attracted academic opponents, foremost among them the black historian W. E. B. Du Bois. Arguably, he was the first revisionist, a term that would come to cover a variety of approaches to Reconstruction history, all essentially anti-Dunningite. Though Du Bois was not linked to Atlanta by birth like Thompson, much of his career would be spent there, at historically black Atlanta University, for two lengthy periods, 1898–10 and 1933–44.[50]

His first clarion blast against the Dunningites had come with his 1910 essay "Reconstruction and Its Benefits," cited by Thompson in *Reconstruction in Georgia* along with some of his other works. Then, during his second sojourn in Atlanta, Du Bois published *Black Reconstruction* (1935), a massive history presenting his perspectives on Reconstruction and, as the title indicates, his identification of the era's major actors. Included in the book's back matter was a sort of bibliographical rogues' gallery. It collected most of the Dunningites' works, describing them as "Standard—Anti-Negro." These books, Du Bois argued, showed their authors to "believe the Negro to be sub-human and congenitally unfitted for citizenship and the suffrage." Thompson appeared therein as the author of both *Reconstruction in Georgia* and "Carpet-baggers in the United States Senate."[51]

In *Black Reconstruction*'s last chapter, "The Propaganda of History," Du Bois wrote, "Thompson's 'Georgia' seeks to be fair, but silly stories about Negroes indicating utter lack of common sense are included, and every noble sentiment from white people. When two Negro workers, William and Jim, put a straightforward advertisement in a local paper, the author says that it was 'evidently written by a white friend.' There is not the slightest historical evidence to prove this, and there were plenty of educated Negroes in Augusta at the time who might have written this."[52]

Actually, persuasive historical evidence did exist that the advertisement had been "written by a white friend." The ad had come from Turnwold, a cotton plantation some eighty miles west of urban Augusta, where the number of literate blacks was, to say the least, quite small. Turnwold was owned by a "benevolent master," Joseph Addison Turner, publisher of his own "plantation newspaper," the *Countryman* (from which the Augusta newspaper had excerpted the ad), and mentor of the Georgia journalist and author Joel Chandler Harris. The crystalline prose of the Turnwold advertisement, past the ability of most literate Georgians of the time, white or black, strongly suggests that Turner was helping Jim and William, now freedmen, by crafting a pitch-perfect appeal for business from white customers.[53]

Black Reconstruction's sixteen-page alternative to Thompson's *Reconstruction in Georgia* is not an impressive piece of work. Although vast expanses of text are unsupported by citations, available evidence indicates that the brief passage on Reconstruction Georgia was cobbled together primarily from notes made perfunctorily from a few sources, principally Thompson's book and Edwin C. Woolley's *The Reconstruction of Georgia*, in addition to yeoman service by a third work, "Participation of Negroes in the Government of Georgia, 1867–1870." This 1932 M.A. thesis by Ethel Maude Christler, one of Du Bois's students, runs for only ninety-eight pages, but it does provide uncritical biographical information on its subjects and their political contributions.[54]

Although it would become the urtext of future revisionists, *Black Reconstruction* perplexed some revisionists then and later with its outré attempts at Marxist interpretation, particularly its surprising discovery that the Civil War had been ended by a "General Strike" of slaves. But the book was on solid ground in arguing for a history of Reconstruction that chronicled the activities of the period's freed people and credited them for their achievements. And it also made a stingingly accurate assessment of the problem some of the Dunningites had in dealing with blacks, historically or otherwise: they could not "conceive Negroes as men."[55]

This was hardly the case with Thompson, however. When the black historian Alrutheus A. Taylor conducted his own survey of Reconstruction historians in 1938, he took issue with Du Bois by providing a more positive view of *Reconstruction in Georgia*. Nonetheless, Taylor echoed Du Bois in praising James W. Garner as the most fair of the Dunning scholars. But Vernon Lane Wharton, who revised Garner's *Reconstruction in Mississippi*, later published his own assessment of the Dunningites. He found Thompson, "if anything, even more cautious, judicious and temperate than Garner." Du Bois had gone past allowable criticism in his thinly based, largely undocumented accusations against Thompson.[56]

In attacking the Dunning scholars, Du Bois was not without supporters. Inspired in part by *Black Reconstruction*, Howard K. Beale, "spearhead" of the revisionists, confronted Thompson and the other Dunningites in his 1940 *AHR* article, "On Rewriting Reconstruction History." Beale gave Thompson and some of the other Dunningites credit for "delv[ing] into social and economic life," but he argued that they had not seen "its full implication." He admitted, however, that Thompson herself had "escaped from the restricting frames of reference" of most of the other Dunningites. Nevertheless, Beale asserted, there remained a need to "restudy Reconstruction in each state, freed from preconceptions of the right and wrong of Reconstruction and determined to discover just what lasting influence Reconstruction exerted."[57]

Though Beale identified several historians in the rising cadre of young revisionists, he made special note of one "no longer young," W. E. B. Du Bois, "whose race and philosophy" had given *Black Reconstruction* "freshness." Despite what Beale saw as the book's "Marxian" distortions, he felt that "in describing the Negro's role," the author had "presented a mass of material, formerly ignored, that every future historian must reckon with."[58]

Thompson presented her rebuttal to Beale's critique at a "Round Table on Reconstruction" at the 1940 meeting of the Southern Historical Association, where the revisionist Robert H. Woody, coauthor with Francis Butler Simkins of a 1932 study of South Carolina Reconstruction, moderated.[59] Woody admitted that "no reviewer in the *American Historical Review* [had] found any serious fault with [the Dunning school state studies] because of the authors' racial prejudice." But the revisionists, he continued, "the most extreme being Dr. W. E. B. Du Bois, regarded many such works as 'propaganda' which sought to 'discredit the Negro and demonstrate the supremacy of the white man.'" Nonetheless, Woody conceded, the Dunningites' state studies were by then "so well fixed in American historiography as to be susceptible of challenge only by an abundance of substantial evidence."[60]

When asked how she would revise *Reconstruction in Georgia*, Thompson gave a lengthy and thoughtful response. She suggested among her main points that she would carry her book down to 1890, since Reconstruction's "economic and social influences" endured until around that year. Showing that she had closely read Beale's critique, Thompson quoted his own words in commenting that her revision would "delve more into economic and social materials and their implications."[61]

Nonetheless, she argued against Beale's suggestion of revising the state studies. By 1940, she asserted, the "study by states [had] served its purpose, and served it well, on the whole." Consequently, new studies should examine not states but (perhaps with a nod toward the Chapel Hill regionalists) "the various geographical regions of the South." Regional studies, she thought, were the place to explore topics in need of further study: "the growth of towns and the importance of town classes; the mobility of population and its influences; race relations 'of the more common sort than those made critical by the Ku Klux'; religion and the social activities of churches with the growth of urban life." Most important, she "would want to know more about the part of the Negroes themselves in securing and maintaining their freedom."[62]

Revisionist critiques of the Dunning scholars, particularly in journal articles and reviews, increased during the 1950s and 1960s, and the academic reputation of Thompson and the other Dunningites began to plummet as civil rights fervor increased. Many members of the academic establishment committed themselves deeply to the cause and promoted it in their historical writings. In the 1960s the tenets of the New History reemerged stronger than ever, with an emphasis on social history, race, and political activism. In some quarters the old "scientific history" came to be scorned as a mere descriptive record, and many historians celebrated the new activist, purposive history as an instrument of social justice.[63]

The 1960s would see the death of all the original Dunningites except for Thompson, then in her eighties. For her part, she continued to add to her liberal credentials. Among her activities were working against the antidemocratic county-unit system in Georgia and participating in the battle to keep Georgia's public schools open as enforcement of the *Brown* decision loomed. Unsurprisingly, given her pro-integration record at Vassar, she also supported the 1961 desegregation of the University of Georgia. Thompson saw grassroots efforts in Georgia, coupled with federal legislation, result in her own congressional district having a black incumbent by the end of the decade, along with eight other black politicians in the Georgia General Assembly, one of them a woman. By the year of Thompson's death (1975), Atlanta would have its first black mayor.[64]

In university classrooms during the 1960s (and over the next two decades) Dunning's *Reconstruction* text (last issued in paperback in 1962) was to be supplanted by the revisionist Kenneth Stampp's *The Era of Reconstruction* (1965). Deeply unfavorable to Dunning and his scholars in his initial chapter, "The Tragic Legend of Reconstruction," Stampp also used his "Bibliographical Note" to assail Thompson and the other authors of the state studies as "Anti-Negro and anti-Radical." Nonetheless, he also admitted that the state studies had "not yet been superseded and remain[ed] valuable for factual detail." Stampp's *Era of Reconstruction*, published in paperback for college use (along with a useful paperback anthology of revisionist views of Reconstruction), probably marked the beginning of the end of the Dunningites as a respectable school of historiography within the university.[65]

By the mid-1960s, Thompson's *Reconstruction in Georgia* had attracted revisionist attention. But the British historian Alan Conway's *The Reconstruction of Georgia* (1966) would conform only slightly to Thompson's 1940 blueprint for revision, whereas her original work proved vital enough to be reprinted in 1964, 1971, and 1972.[66]

Conway's revision, produced during a relatively brief research trip to the United States, appeared somewhat halfhearted. Conway admitted that Thompson's book was "a very good piece of work," and, though he did not "agree with many of her opinions," he would in no way try to "denigrate" it. "No attempt," he concluded, "has been made to duplicate in detail what has already been adequately covered. It is largely on points of interpretation we differ."[67]

Though Conway's book does not succeed as a revision, it proves an interesting, occasionally rather madcap companion piece to Thompson's superior work. Alternately riveting and exasperating, erratically vivid in style, *The Reconstruction of Georgia* is seldom dull. And it does seek to expand Thompson's coverage of the black experience. His approach to Du Bois, however, was not as reverential as would be common thereafter. Labeling Du Bois the "great Negro apologist," Conway noted that he had "in Marxist fashion . . . examine[d] the dark underbelly of Reconstruction," but "had redressed the balance so violently in his righteous indignation that all his colored geese became snow-white swans."[68]

Appearing in 1968, Elizabeth Studley Nathans's *Losing the Peace: Georgia Republicans and Reconstruction, 1865–1871* obviously focused more narrowly than Conway's book. But *Losing the Peace* examined much of the ground Thompson had covered, though it offered a more scholarly, comprehensive revision than had Conway's work. Of the three Reconstruction studies available to Nathans—those of Woolley, Thompson, and Conway, Nathans concluded that Thompson's book stood out as most satisfactory. "Moderate and fair-minded in its discussion of the Negro and of the Republican regime," Nathans wrote, "it was one of the most outstanding of the 'Dunning' state studies of Reconstruction and remains the best book on its subject."[69]

Nevertheless, during the last years of Thompson's life, the Dunning school—and by extension Thompson herself—would be deplored more and more frequently, as the academy moved evermore leftward. According to William L. O'Neill, this was a consequence of the New Left (the campus student radicals of the 1960s—at Thompson's Columbia and elsewhere) moving by the 1990s onto university faculties as the Academic Left. Thompson had been the most conspicuous liberal of the southern authors of the Dunning school state studies, but the increasingly "politically correct" campuses of the 1990s and beyond would have considered Thompson's views as unfashionable as her customary pince-nez: anticommunist, anti–affirmative action, traditionally patriotic, and "completely a product of the Western cultural tradition, which provided her frame of reference and principles for action."[70]

In 1963 W. E. B. Du Bois died an exile's death an ocean away in Ghana. In a sense, the Dunningites could not be brought down until their great antagonist's *Black Reconstruction* had been raised to the heights they once occupied. Kenneth Stampp, though radical enough by his own admission, was not the man for this task. To him the "Marxian interpretation" of *Black Reconstruction* had been "at best naïve."[71]

Eric Foner proved to have the requisite qualifications to elevate Du Bois and dethrone the Dunningites. As Foner's *Reconstruction: America's Unfinished Revolution, 1863–1877* (1988) supplanted Stampp's *Era of Reconstruction,* the academic repudiation of the Dunningites neared completion. Once again a Columbia professor was the acknowledged colossus of Reconstruction history, but now the black experience had been made central, and Du Bois's "Marxian" ideas were no longer a concern. Foner denounced the Dunning School in both the preface and epilogue of his book, although he didn't purge all the Dunningite works from his bibliography. Foner's *Reconstruction* was widely praised and soon pronounced definitive, although David Donald confessed in reviewing Foner's book that it was "hard to think of any general history of [Reconstruction] . . . more worth reading than William Archibald Dunning's old, prejudiced, but nevertheless informative *Reconstruction: Political and Economic.*"[72]

Thus far, some twenty-first-century books on Reconstruction have been even more severely critical than Foner of Thompson and the other Dunning scholars. For example, Michael Fitzgerald's *Splendid Failure: Postwar Reconstruction in the American South* (2007) reduced them to caricature in his book's brief survey of sources. Fitzgerald provided a stern three-sentence dismissal: "In briefly describing the scholarly literature on the Reconstruction Era, one is tempted to refer readers to the works of William A. Dunning and his students, if only to highlight the racist enormities of early twentieth-century historians. The older literature rationalized black disfranchisement and Jim Crow, and sometimes even lynching. Think of themes of the silent film *Birth of a Nation*, repeated in various states with footnotes."[73]

Perhaps an even worse fate was visited on the Dunningites as serious historians in 2010 with the publication of *The Great Task Remaining before Us: Reconstruction as America's Continuing Civil War*. Edited by Paul A. Cimbala and Randall M. Miller, this collection of Reconstruction essays, organized in large part around the various southern states (including Georgia), neither mentions nor uses any of the works of Dunning and his scholars.[74]

But, surprisingly enough, 2012 brought a qualified defense of the Dunning School (in particular Thompson and her "excellent analysis of postwar southern agriculture"), as well as a support for their assertion that the "grant of black suffrage" had been a mistake. The historian involved was no reactionary, but rather Adam Fairclough, an esteemed British historian of the American civil rights movement. It remains to be seen whether Fairclough's argument represents an interesting footnote to post–Civil War historiography or the thin edge of a wedge that might shatter a quarter century of Reconstruction orthodoxy.[75]

In any case, Thompson and her fellow historians deserve a spirited defense. Their work underlies all Reconstruction studies since their time, foundations dug deep and wide and laid with care, whether visible (or acknowledged) or not. Their scholarship, typified by meticulous footnotes, extensive bibliographies, and thorough explorations of a wide variety of subjects (most divorced from race), should command academic respect. Thompson, like the other Dunningites, attempted to follow the "noble dream"—the "disinterested search for objective historical truth"—and thus to prevent history from becoming nothing but "an instrument of entertainment, or of social control." As had traditionalist historians before her, she labored to create a reliable record of the past, not to forge a tool for transforming the present and the future. As many Reconstruction-era politicians proclaimed as their consolation, she has nothing to fear from the "judgment of impartial history."[76]

Notes

1. There is no book-length biography of C. Mildred Thompson. A lengthy, detailed biographical sketch is found in *The National Cyclopedia of American Biography* (Clifton, N.J.: James T. White, 1982), s.v. "Thompson, C[lara] Mildred." Briefer sketches are in David C. Roller and Robert W. Twyman, eds., *The Encyclopedia of Southern History* (Baton Rouge: Louisiana State University Press, 1979), s.v. "Thompson, Clara Mildred"; Jennifer Scanlon and Shaaron Cosner, *American Women Historians, 1700s–1900s: A Biographical Dictionary* (Westport, Conn.: Greenwood Press, 1996), s.v. "Thompson, Clara Mildred"; *The New Georgia Encyclopedia*, s.v. "C. Mildred Thompson (1881–1975)," www.georgiaencyclopedia.org/nge/Article.jsp?id=h-3162; and *Vassar Encyclopedia*, s.v. "C. Mildred Thompson," http://vcencyclopedia.vassar.edu/alumni/c-mildred-thompson.html. Valuable memoirs are Elizabeth Studley Nathans, "C. Mildred Thompson: Scholar," *Vassar Quarterly* (Winter 1976): 44, 46–48; and Caroline Ware, "C. Mildred Thompson: Activist," *Vassar Quarterly* (Winter 1976): 45, 48–50. The major collections of manuscripts and printed materials relating to Thompson's life and career are held by the Atlanta Historical Society, Atlanta (hereinafter cited as AHS), and Vassar College Archives and Special Collections, Poughkeepsie, N.Y. Smaller collections are in the Hargrett Rare Book and Manuscript Library, University of Georgia Libraries, Athens (hereinafter cited as UGA), and the Franklin D. Roosevelt Presidential Library, Hyde Park, N.Y.

2. The various Thompson collections contain practically no information on the Thompson family. Family information in the above and following paragraphs is drawn principally from U.S. Census records on the Thompson and Wood families (1860–1910) and, for the Thompson businesses and residences, Atlanta City Directories and Sanborn Insurance Maps (1868–1910).

3. Bernard A. Weisberger, "The Dark and Bloody Ground of Reconstruction Historiography," *Journal of Southern History* 25 (November 1959): 446; "Robert G. Thompson Is Claimed by Death," *Atlanta Constitution*, October 28, 1911; Nathans, "C. Mildred Thompson: Scholar," 46.

4. "Robert G. Thompson Is Dead at Old Home," *Atlanta Georgian and News*, October 28, 1911; Nathans, "C. Mildred Thompson: Scholar," 46.

5. Frank Daniel, "She Found Teaching Is Friendship," *Atlanta Journal*, March 18, 1963; Rebecca Franklin, "South's Women Helpless? Fiction, Says Vassar Dean," *Atlanta Journal*, March 22, 1946; Harold E. Davis, *Henry Grady's New South: Atlanta, a Brave and Beautiful City* (Tuscaloosa: University of Alabama Press, 1990), 17–18; Henry W. Grady, *The New South: Writings and Speeches of Henry Grady* (Savannah: Beehive Press, 1971), 10.

6. "C. Mildred Thompson Memorial Minute," October 22, 1975, p. 1, folder 14, Thompson, C. Mildred, Collection, Vassar College Historical Biographical Files, Vassar College Archives and Special Collections, Vassar College, Poughkeepsie, N.Y. (hereinafter cited as Thompson Biographical Files, the location as VCA).

7. Ibid.; John Higham, *History: Professional Scholarship in America*, new ed. (Baltimore: Johns Hopkins University Press, 1989), 6–11; W. Stull Holt, *Historical Scholarship in the United States and Other Essays* (Seattle: University of Washington Press, 1967), 17–18.

8. Robert A. McCaughey, *Stand, Columbia: A History of Columbia University in the City of New York, 1754–2004* (New York: Columbia University Press, 2003), 164–68; Barbara Miller Solomon, *In the Company of Educated Women: A History of Women and Higher Education in America* (New Haven: Yale University Press, 1985), 84; Thompson, C. Mildred, File, folder 8, box 307, Historical Biographical Files, Columbia University Library (hereinafter cited as CUL); Bill W. Santin, Office of the Registrar, Columbia University, e-mail message to author, August 17, 2010; C. Mildred Thompson, *Reconstruction in Georgia: Economic, Social, Political, 1865–1872* (New York: Columbia University Press, 1915), 4a–4b. "Columbia's Summer School," *New York Times*, August 5, 1906; C. Mildred Thompson to Lucy Maynard Salmon, March 3, 1907, folder 11.7, Salmon Papers, VCA; David D. Van Tassel, "The American Historical Association and the South, 1884–1913," *Journal of Southern History* 23 (November 1957): 469–70; Wendell Holmes Stephenson, *The South Lives in History: Southern Historians and Their Legacy* (Baton Rouge: Louisiana State University Press, 1955), 5.

9. Collegiate and Professional Education Record (ca. 1952), folder 2, box 1, C. Mildred Thompson Collection (hereinafter cited as CMT Collection), AHS; "C. Mildred Thompson Memorial Minute," p. 2, Thompson Biographical Files, VCA; "Goodbye, Messrs. Chips," *Time*, June 21, 1948, 59.

10. C. Mildred Thompson, retirement announcement, Office of Public Relations, Vassar College, July 1, 1947, folder 2, box 1, CMT Collection, AHS; C. Mildred Thompson to Sarah Gibson Blanding, June 11, 1956, folder 6, box 1, CMT Collection, AHS; C. Mildred Thompson, "Non-discrimination at Vassar," June 28, 1956, folder 6, box 1, CMT Collection, AHS; Joan Marie Johnson, *Southern Women at the Seven Sister Colleges: Feminist Values and Social Activism, 1875–1915* (Athens: University of Georgia Press, 2008), 53; "C. Mildred Thompson Memorial Minute," pp. 1–2, Thompson Biographical Files, VCA.

11. C. Mildred Thompson, "FDR—A Recollection and Appraisal" (type-script), p. 5, folder 1, box 2, CMT Collection, AHS; Elizabeth Adams Daniels, "FDR, ER, and VC," *Vassar Quarterly* (Spring 1992): 24, 26–27. FDR's San Francisco speech is in *The Public Papers and Addresses of Franklin D. Roosevelt*, comp. Samuel I. Rosenman, 13 vols. (New York: Random House, 1938–50), 1:742–56.

12. Solomon, *In the Company of Educated Women*, 137–38; Johnson, *Southern Women at the Seven Sister Colleges*, 111; Julie des Jardins, *Women and the Historical Enterprise in America: Gender, Race, and the Politics of Memory, 1880–1945* (Chapel Hill: University of North Carolina Press, 2003), 40; Katherine H. Adams and Michael L. Keene, *After the Vote Was Won: The Later Achievements of Fifteen Suffragists* (Jefferson, N.C.: McFarland, 2010), 87; "Program of the Fifty-fifth Annual Meeting, Held in New York City, December 27–30, 1940," *Annual Report of the American Historical Association for the Year 1950* (Washington, D.C.: U.S. Government Printing Office, 1941), 19; Rosalind Rosenberg, *Changing the Subject: How the Women of Columbia Shaped the Way We Think about Sex and Politics* (New York: Columbia University Press, 2004), 115–16.

13. "Spent Crusade," *Time*, June 21, 1948, 59; C. Mildred Thompson to Eloise Ellery, August 15, 1956, Eloise Ellery Papers (hereinafter cited as Ellery Papers), VCA; "C. Mildred Thompson Memorial Minute," p. 3, Thompson Biographical Files, VCA; Martin Grams Jr., *Information, Please* (Boalsburg, Pa.: BearManor Media, 2003), 158, 175, 183.

14. C. Mildred Thompson to Lucy Maynard Salmon, July 16, 1921, folder 11.8, Salmon Papers, VCA; Anna T. Kitchel, "Dean Thompson," *Vassar Alumnae Magazine* (October 1947): 15; Fernando Valderrama, *A History of UNESCO* (Paris: UNESCO Publishing, 1995), 20; "Vassar Dean Sees Education as Pathway to World Peace," unidentified newspaper clipping, March 26, 1946, Thompson Biographical Files, VCA. The United Nations Educational, Scientific, and Cultural Organization Papers, Ms. 2182, UGA, comprises a collection of Thompson's materials relating to UNESCO; included are Thompson's UNESCO–related correspondence (1944–46), minutes, clippings, and various printed materials.

15. C. Mildred Thompson, "To [the Vassar Senior Class of] 1923," typescript, June 7, 1955, folder 6, box 1, CMT Collection, AHS; "C. Mildred Thompson Memorial Minute," p. 4, Thompson Biographical Files, VCA; Joe Gray Taylor, "The White South from Secession to Redemption," in *Interpreting Southern History: Historiographical Essays in Honor of Sanford W. Higginbotham*, ed. John B. Boles and Evelyn Thomas Nolen (Baton Rouge: Louisiana State University Press, 1987), 182; Robert Preston Brooks, *The University of Georgia under Sixteen Administrations, 1785–1955* (Athens: University of Georgia Press, 1956), 223; Margaret Shannon, "Atlanta Educator Helping DPs Patch Up School Lives," *Atlanta Journal-Constitution*, October 26, 1952; *Free Europe University in Exile* (New York: National Committee for a Free Europe, 1953), 8.

16. "Mildred Thompson, Historian, Vassar Dean Emeritus, Is Dead, *New York*

Times, February 17, 1975, and numerous other obituary clippings, folder 2, box 1, CMT Collection, AHS.

17. Nathans, "C. Mildred Thompson: Scholar," 47; Mrs. John Marsh to C. Mildred Thompson, February 9, 1937, C. Mildred Thompson Papers, Ms. 606, UGA; Thompson to Eloise Ellery, February 19, 1956, folder 6.19, Eloise Ellery Papers, VCA.

18. William A. Dunning to Nicholas Murray Butler, May 23, 1907, George Foster Peabody Collection, CUL.

19. Ibid.; Thompson to Lucy Salmon, October 21, 1906, folder 11.7, Salmon Papers, VCA; Higham, *History,* 104, 110–14; Michael Kraus, *The Writing of American History* (Norman: University of Oklahoma Press, 1953), 367–68; William A. Dunning, *Truth in History and Other Essays by William A. Dunning,* ed. J. G. de Roulhac Hamilton (New York: Columbia University Press, 1937), 163; Ernst A. Breisach, *American Progressive History: An Experiment in Modernization* (Chicago: University of Chicago Press, 1993), 79, 100; Fritz Stern, ed., *The Varieties of History from Voltaire to the Present* (Cleveland: World, 1956), 256–57, 265; Peter Novick, *That Noble Dream: The "Objectivity Question" and the American Historical Profession* (New York: Cambridge University Press, 1988), 100–101.

20. Van Tassel, "The American Historical Association and the South," 469–70; Stephenson, *The South Lives in History,* 1; William B. Hesseltine and Louis Kaplan, "Women Doctors of Philosophy in History," *Journal of Higher Education* 14 (May 1943): 255; William B. Hesseltine and Louis Kaplan, "Doctors of Philosophy in History," *American Historical Review* 47 (July 1942): 772–73.

21. Hamilton, *Truth in History,* xxvi; James W. Garner, preface to *Studies in Southern History and Politics, Inscribed to William Archibald Dunning . . . by His Former Pupils the Authors* (New York: Columbia University Press, 1914), v; C. Mildred Thompson, "Carpet-baggers in the United States Senate," in *Studies in Southern History and Politics,* 161–76.

22. Thompson, "Carpet-baggers in the United States Senate," 162, 169, 174, 165, 168.

23. C. Mildred Thompson, "The Freedmen's Bureau in Georgia in 1865–6: An Instrument of Reconstruction," *Georgia Historical Quarterly* 5 (March 1921): 40–49.

24. Thompson, *Reconstruction in Georgia,* 5–10.

25. Ibid., 13–167.

26. Ibid., 171–275.

27. Ibid., 279–401, 388.

28. Ibid., 400, 401.

29. Ibid., 402; Edwin C. Woolley, *The Reconstruction of Georgia* (New York: Columbia University Press, 1901).

30. Theodore H. Jack, "The Preservation of Georgia History," *North Carolina Historical Review* 4 (July 1927): 246; Thompson, *Reconstruction in Georgia,* 4a; Nathans, "C. Mildred Thompson: Scholar," 47.

31. Karen van Lengen and Lisa Reilly, *Vassar College: An Architectural Tour* (Princeton, N.J.: Princeton Architectural Press, 2004), 64–65; Barry Bergdoll, *Mastering McKim's Plan: Columbia's First Century on Morningside Heights* (New York: Miriam and Ira Wallach Art Gallery, Columbia University, 1997), 44–45; "The Department of History in Columbia University," *Columbia University Bulletin* 20 (June 1898): 191.

32. J. G. de Roulhac Hamilton, introduction to Dunning, *Truth in History and Other Essays*, xviii–xix; Thompson, *Reconstruction in Georgia*, 4a–4b.

33. Thompson, *Reconstruction in Georgia*, 4a; Chara Haeussler Bohan, *Go to the Sources: Lucy Maynard Salmon and the Teaching of History* (New York: Peter Lang, 2004), 6–7.

34. Thompson, *Reconstruction in Georgia*, 399–400.

35. Ibid., 334–38.

36. Ibid., 5–10, 189–95, 216, 222, 240, 297, 365–66, 390 (carpetbaggers), 189, 370 (scalawags), 272–75 (Bullock), 192, 257 (Akerman); C. Vann Woodward, *Origins of the New South, 1877–1913* (Baton Rouge: Louisiana State University Press, 1951), 16–17.

37. Thompson, *Reconstruction in Georgia*, 223–24; Woolley, *Reconstruction of Georgia*, 10, 11, 11n2, 13, 14, 52n2, 87, 112; Joseph H. Parks, *Joseph E. Brown of Georgia* (Baton Rouge: Louisiana State University Press, 1977), 580; Thompson, *Reconstruction in Georgia*, 4a, 413 (Brown sources), 37, 145n1, 155n2, 161, 172–74, 176, 197, 211–12, 218–19, 223–24, 250–52, 266, 354, 360, 386 (Brown's activities).

38. Thompson, *Reconstruction in Georgia*, 172–73, 197, 215, 359–60; Parks, *Joseph E. Brown*, 574–75; Numan V. Bartley, *The Creation of Modern Georgia*, 2nd ed. (Athens: University of Georgia Press, 1990), 164–66; Nathans, "C. Mildred Thompson: Scholar," 47.

39. Thompson, *Reconstruction in Georgia*, 190–91, 257, 211–15.

40. Ibid., 401, 399.

41. Thompson to Salmon, July 22, 1915, folder 11.7, Salmon Papers, VCA.

42. R. P. Brooks, "Miss C. Mildred Thompson's 'Reconstruction in Georgia' a Georgia Woman's Work," *Atlanta Constitution*, July 17, 1915.

43. J. H. T. McPherson, review of C. Mildred Thompson, *Reconstruction in Georgia*, in *American Historical Review* 21 (October 1915): 162–64.

44. Ibid., 164; J. Franklin Jameson, *The History of Historical Writing in America* (Boston: Houghton, Mifflin, 1891), 151; Benjamin B. Kendrick, *The Journal of the Joint Committee of Fifteen on Reconstruction* (New York: Columbia University Press, 1914).

45. Review of C. Mildred Thompson, *Reconstruction in Georgia*, in *Journal of Negro History* 1 (1916): 418.

46. Thompson to Salmon, July 22, 1915, folder 11.7, Salmon Papers, VCA; *Nation*, April 20, 1916, 441.

47. *Nation*, April 20, 1916, 441.

48. Ibid.

49. Vernon L. Wharton, "Reconstruction," in *Writing Southern History: Essays in Historiography in Honor of Fletcher M. Green,* ed. Arthur S. Link and Rembert W. Patrick (Baton Rouge: Louisiana State University Press, 1965), 295–96. Harper Torchbooks released a paperbound version, in the original typography, of Dunning's *Reconstruction, Political and Economic, 1865–1877* in 1962 and his *Essays on the Civil War and Reconstruction* in 1965, the latter with an introduction by David Donald.

50. David Levering Lewis, *W. E. B. Du Bois: Biography of a Race* (New York: Henry Holt, 1993), 198, 386; David Levering Lewis, *W. E. B. Du Bois: The Fight for Equality and the American Century, 1919–1963* (New York: Henry Holt, 2000), 303–5, 493.

51. Lewis, *W. E. B. Du Bois: The Fight for Equality and the American Century,* 304, 359–76; W. E. B. Du Bois, *Black Reconstruction in America* (1935; reprint, New York: Free Press, 1992), 731 (Thompson), 731–37 (bibliography).

52. Du Bois, *Black Reconstruction,* 720; Thompson, *Reconstruction in Georgia,* 56. The advertisement was printed in *Reconstruction in Georgia* as follows: "Work wanted—We have established a shop at Turnwold where we are prepared to do all manner of wood and iron work—wagon making and repairing included. We have not turned fools because we are free, but know we have to work for our living, and are determined to do it. We mean to be sober, industrious, honest, and respectful to white folks, and so we depend on them to give us work. (signed) William & Jim." Thompson's transcription from the original (*Augusta Chronicle & Sentinel,* April 17, 1866) is exact.

53. Paul M. Cousins, *Joel Chandler Harris: A Biography* (Baton Rouge: Louisiana State University Press, 1968), 42–43, 152, 177.

54. Du Bois, *Black Reconstruction,* 495–510 (Reconstruction Georgia), 524 (source notes); Ethel Maude Christler, "Participation of Negroes in the Government of Georgia, 1867–1870" (master's thesis, Atlanta University, 1932), 76–79 (bibliography of some forty sources).

55. Du Bois, *Black Reconstruction,* 55–83 (General Strike), 726; David Levering Lewis, *W. E. B. Du Bois: The Fight for Equality and the American Century,* 371–72, 375–76.

56. A. A. Taylor, "Historians of the Reconstruction," *Journal of Negro History* 23 (1938): 28–29, 27; Wharton, "Reconstruction," 301.

57. Fletcher M. Green, introduction to William Watson Davis, *The Civil War and Reconstruction in Florida* (1913; reprint, Gainesville: University of Florida Press, 1964), xxxi; Howard K. Beale, "On Rewriting Reconstruction History," *American Historical Review* 45 (July 1940): 808–9, 823.

58. Beale, "On Rewriting Reconstruction History," 809.

59. Albert B. Moore, "The Sixth Annual Meeting of the Southern Historical Association," *Journal of Southern History* 7 (February 1941): 66.

60. Ibid.

61. Ibid., 67–68.

62. Ibid.

63. Larry Kincaid, "Victims of Circumstance: An Interpretation of Changing Attitudes toward Republican Policy Makers and Reconstruction," *Journal of American History* 57 (June 1970): 61–62; Gertrude Himmelfarb, *The New History and the Old: Critical Essays and Reappraisals* (Cambridge: Belknap Press of Harvard University Press, 1987), 13–15; Oscar Handlin, *Truth in History*, 2nd ed. (New Brunswick, N.J.: Transaction, 1998), 409.

64. Thompson to Ernest Vandiver, governor of Georgia, September 26, 1959, folder 6, box 1; Horace Montgomery to Thompson, June 12, 1961, folder 6, box 1; Thompson to Arthur Schlesinger Jr., May 21, 1961, folder 6, box 2, all in Thompson Collection, AHS; Albert B. Saye, *Georgia: History and Government* (Austin, Tex.: Steck-Vaughn, 1982), 231–40; Frederick Allen, *Atlanta Rising: The Invention of an International City* (Atlanta: Longstreet Press, 1996), 180–81.

65. Kenneth M. Stampp, *The Era of Reconstruction, 1865–1877* (New York: Alfred A. Knopf, 1965), 3–23, 217–18, 224–25; Kenneth M. Stampp and Leon F. Litwack, eds., *Reconstruction: An Anthology of Revisionist Writings* (Baton Rouge: Louisiana State University Press, 1969), 3–21.

66. Alan Conway, *The Reconstruction of Georgia* (Minneapolis: University of Minnesota Press, 1966), v; Colin Brown, "Alan Arthur Conway, 1920–2003," *University of Canterbury Chronicle* [Christchurch, New Zealand], April 17, 2003, 2; Mills Lane, *The First Twenty-five Years of the Beehive Press* (Savannah, Ga.: Beehive Foundation, 1995), 9–11. The 1964 and 1971 reprints of *Reconstruction in Georgia* were offered by Peter Smith Publisher and the Cherokee Publishing Company, respectively. Since the Beehive edition was produced in a different format and typeface, its pagination does not match that of Thompson's book as originally published or reprinted.

67. Conway, *Reconstruction of Georgia*, v.

68. Ibid., 20n73, 50, 52, 53n53, 57n65, 131n36, 146, 149n46, 161nn87–88, 165n10, 166, 167n24, 172, 185n86, 195n32, 199n49 (the foregoing represent Conway's extended notices of Thompson or particular passages of her book in his text). In addition to these mentions of Thompson, Conway provided simple citations to her work a like number of times); 41n2 (Du Bois).

69. Elizabeth Studley Nathans, *Losing the Peace: Georgia Republicans and Reconstruction, 1865–1871* (Baton Rouge: Louisiana State University Press, 1968), 233–54 (bibliographical essay), 247.

70. William L. O'Neill, *The New Left: A History* (Wheeling, Ill.: Harlan Davidson, 2001), 106–9, 80; Ware, "C. Mildred Thompson: Activist," 50. For liberal and conservative views, respectively, of the changing nature of the historical profession from the 1930s into the twenty-first century, see Oscar Handlin's *Truth in History*, esp. 3–24, and Forrest McDonald, *Recovering the Past: A Historian's Memoir* (Lawrence: University Press of Kansas, 2004).

71. Lewis, *W. E. B. Du Bois: The Fight for Equality and the American Century,*

567–70; Stampp, *The Era of Reconstruction*, 218. At the same page Stampp divides the Revisionists into "Marxian" and "non-Marxian."

72. Eric Foner, *Reconstruction: America's Unfinished Revolution, 1863–1877* (New York: Harper & Row, 1988), xix, xxii, 608–10; David Donald, review of Eric Foner, *Reconstruction: America's Unfinished Revolution, 1863–1877*, in *New Republic*, August 1, 1988, 41.

73. Michael W. Fitzgerald, *Splendid Failure: Postwar Reconstruction in the American South* (Chicago: Ivan R. Dee, 2007), 213.

74. Paul A. Cimbala and Randall M. Miller, eds., *The Great Task Remaining before Us: Reconstruction as American's Continuing Civil War* (New York: Fordham University Press, 2010).

75. Adam Fairclough, "Was the Grant of Black Suffrage a Political Error? Reconsidering the Views of John W. Burgess, William A. Dunning, and Eric Foner on Congressional Reconstruction," *Journal of the Historical Society* 12 (June 2012): 155–88, 158. For critiques of Fairclough's essay see *Journal of the Historical Society* 12 (September 2012): 241–70, and Fairclough's rebuttal, "Congressional Reconstruction: A Catastrophic Failure" (his title itself is a rebuttal to Du Bois's "splendid failure"), on 271–82.

76. Theodore Clarke Smith, "The Writing of American History in America, from 1884 to 1934," *American Historical Review* 40 (April 1935): 449.

Acknowledgments

The editors acknowledge with gratitude the encouragement that they received in conceptualizing and executing this book from Anne Dean Watkins, their editor at the University Press of Kentucky; the press's director, Stephen M. Wrinn; and Bailey Johnson, acquisitions assistant. Ann Twombly copyedited the manuscript superbly. We also thank the two anonymous readers for the press who critiqued the manuscript thoroughly and offered useful suggestions that strengthened the volume considerably. Eric Foner generously agreed to write the book's foreword. Tara C. Craig helped us identify the dust jacket image in the Dunning Papers at Columbia University. Peter Coclanis and Adam Fairclough kindly sent us material on the recent debate over the broad historiographical meaning of the Dunning School. Leigh Robbins, Department of History, University of North Carolina at Charlotte, provided expert office support. Finally, we wish to thank the eight historians whose essays, in addition to our own, make up *The Dunning School: Historians, Race, and the Meaning of Reconstruction*.

Contributors

Fred Arthur Bailey is emeritus professor of history at Abilene Christian University, Abilene, Texas. He is the author of two books—*Class and Tennessee's Confederate Generation* (1987) and *William Edward Dodd: The South's Yeoman Scholar* (1997)—and more than forty articles in professional journals and anthologies.

William Harris Bragg recently retired from Georgia College at Milledgeville, where he was director of the Center for Georgia Studies. The author of five books and numerous articles and reviews, he is a recipient of the Georgia Historical Society's E. Merton Coulter Award for Excellence in the Writing of Georgia History and its Presidential Citation for "distinguished contributions" to his field.

Michael W. Fitzgerald is professor of history at St. Olaf College in Minnesota. He is the author of numerous articles and three books: *The Union Movement in the Deep South: Politics and Agricultural Change during Reconstruction* (1989), *Urban Emancipation: Popular Politics in Reconstruction Mobile, 1860–1890* (2002), and *Splendid Failure: Postwar Reconstruction in the American South* (2007).

Eric Foner, the DeWitt Clinton Professor of History at Columbia University, is the author of many books on the Civil War and Reconstruction era. These include *Free Soil, Free Labor, Free Men: The Ideology of the Republican Party before the Civil War* (1970) and *The Fiery Trial: Abraham Lincoln and American Slavery* (2010). Foner's *Reconstruction: America's Unfinished Revolution, 1863–1877* (1988) remains the standard work. It received the *Los Angeles Times* Book Award for History, the Bancroft Prize, and the Parkman Prize. Foner received the Pulitzer Prize in 2011 for *The Fiery Trial*.

James S. Humphreys is an associate professor of history at Murray State University in Murray, Kentucky. He is the author of *Francis Butler Simkins: A Life* (2008). Humphreys also edits, along with Brian D. McKnight, the Interpreting American History series published by Kent State University Press.

J. Vincent Lowery is assistant professor of humanistic studies and history at the University of Wisconsin–Green Bay. He completed his dissertation, "Reconstructing the Reign of Terror: Popular Memories of the Ku Klux Klan, 1887–1921," at the University of Mississippi. He is currently working on a biography of the Wilmington, North Carolina, businessman Hugh MacRae.

Shepherd W. McKinley is a senior lecturer in history at the University of North Carolina at Charlotte. He is the coauthor (with David Brown) of *North Carolina: New Directions for an Old Land* (2006) and the author of the forthcoming *The Origins of "King" Phosphate in the New South: Workers, Managers, and Entrepreneurs in South Carolina's Phosphate and Fertilizer Industries, 1865–1884.* He is also coeditor (with Steven Sabol) of the multimedia project "North Carolina in the First World War, 1914–1922."

Paul Ortiz serves as director of the Samuel Proctor Oral History Program and associate professor of history at the University of Florida. He is the author of *Emancipation Betrayed: The Hidden History of Black Organizing and White Violence in Florida from Reconstruction to the Bloody Election of 1920* (2005) and coeditor of *Remembering Jim Crow: African Americans Tell about Life in the Segregated South* (2008). He is currently finishing *Our Separate Struggles Are Really One: African American and Latino Histories,* which will be published by Beacon Press.

John Herbert Roper Sr. is the Richardson Professor of American History at Emory & Henry College, Emory, Virginia, and author of eight books about southern history, most recently *The Magnificent Mays: A Biography of Benjamin Elijah Mays* (2012).

John David Smith is the Charles H. Stone Distinguished Professor of American History at the University of North Carolina at Charlotte. He has written and edited many books, including *Black Voices from Reconstruction, 1865–1877* (1996), *Black Judas: William Hannibal Thomas and "The American Negro"* (2000), *An Old Creed for the New South: Proslavery Ideology and Historiography, 1865–1918* (3rd ed., 2008), *Seeing the New South: Race and Place in the Photographs of Ulrich Bonnell Phillips* (2013) (with

Patricia Bellis Bixel), and *A Just and Lasting Peace: A Documentary History of Reconstruction* (2013).

W. Bland Whitley is an assistant editor for *The Papers of Thomas Jefferson.* He previously worked as a historian for the Valentine Richmond History Center and as an assistant editor of the *Dictionary of Virginia Biography.* Whitley earned his Ph.D. from the University of Florida, where he completed the dissertation "Precious Memories: Narratives of the Democracy in Mississippi, 1865–1915."

Index

315

Burgess, John W. *(cont.)*
51, 57; criticism, 32, 34, 58–62,
69–71; on Reconstruction, 19–20,
53, 61–64, 66; relationship with
William Archibald Dunning,
20, 25, 26, 49, 65–69; and
Teutonism, 49, 52, 56, 57, 69,
70. *See also* Columbia University;
William Archibald Dunning;
Dunning School; German
influences on American historians;
Reconstruction; scientific method
—PUBLICATIONS: *The Administration
of President Hayes* (1916), 54; *The
Civil War and the Constitution,
1859–1865,* 2 vols. (1901), 19,
53, 60, 66, 69; *The Foundations
of Political Science* (1933), 52; *The
Middle Period, 1817–1858* (1897),
19, 53, 58–60, 69; *Political Science
and Comparative Constitutional
Law,* 2 vols. (1890, 1893), 19,
52, 57–58, 60; *Recent Changes in
American Constitutional Theory*
(1923), 54; *The Reconciliation of
Government with Liberty* (1915), 54;
*Reconstruction and the Constitution,
1866–1876* (1902), 19, 20, 53,
61–62, 64, 65, 66, 67, 68, 218
Burns, Hayden, 273
Burton, Orville Vernon, 181
Burrows Brothers Publishing
Company, 209
Butler, Marion, 185
Butler, Nicholas Murray, 70, 285–86

Caldwell, R. J., 90
Carnegie Institution, 140
Carpenter, William H., 137
"carpetbaggers," 3, 30, 62, 63, 92,
122, 135, 136, 163, 242–43, 267
Chadsey, Charles E., 44n86
Chamberlain, Daniel H., 135, 211

Channing, Edward, 84, 245
Chapman, Anne M., 16, 78
Chase, Harry Woodburn, 180
Chesnutt, Charles W., 228n48
Christler, Ethel Maude, 294
Church, W. F., 12
Cimbala, Paul A., 299
Clark, John Bates, 19
Clarke, James Freeman, 11–12
Cleveland, Grover, 110
Clews, Henry, 135
Coker, Francis W., 113
Cole, Arthur C., 1
Columbia University, 35, 81, 230, 235;
Columbia University Press, 136;
School of Political Science, 19, 51,
57; Studies in History, Economics
and Public Law, 20, 137
Commager, Henry Steele, 2
Compromise of 1877: election of 1876,
210–12; Electoral Commission,
209, 212; Rutherford B. Hayes,
210; historiography, 210–12;
Samuel J. Tilden, 213; Wormley
Conference, 212, 213
Connor, Robert Digges Wimberly,
193–94, 196
Conway, Alan, 297–98
Copeland, Isaac, 195, 196
Couch, William Terry, 192, 195
Coulter, E. Merton, 21, 36, 44n87, 69,
284
Cox, James M., 80
Cox, LaWanda, 70
Craven, Avery, 44n86, 69
Croly, Herbert, 221
Cromwell, John W., 31
Crowell, Edward P., 50
Current, Richard, 123

Davis, Jefferson, 53, 61
Davis, William Watson: biography,
256–59; on the Civil War,

Phillips, Ulrich B. *(cont.)*
at the Carnegie Institution, 140;
on the "central theme" of southern
history, 133, 147–48, 250, 254n50;
education, 138–40; on the Ku
Klux Klan, 150; historians on
Phillips, 134, 150–51; and Charles
McCarthy, 146; on the Old South,
145, 150; on Reconstruction, 134,
135, 152n10; on slavery, 143, 144,
145–47; on the "Solid South," 38,
136; at Tulane University, 134,
146–47; and Frederick Jackson
Turner, 90, 138, 140, 142, 144;
at the University of Georgia, 134,
142; at the University of Michigan,
134, 147, 150; at the University of
Tennessee's Summer School of the
South, 144–45; at the University of
Wisconsin, 134; at Yale University,
134. *See also* William Archibald
Dunning; Dunning School
—PUBLICATIONS: *American Negro
Slavery* (1918), 133, 150;
contribution to *Studies in Southern
History and Politics* (1914), 94, 114,
140–41; contribution to *The South
in the Building of the Nation* (1909),
145; *The Correspondence of Robert
Toombs, Alexander H. Stephens, and
Howell Cobb* (1913), 147; *Georgia
and State Rights* (1902), 138,
142–44; *History of Transportation
in the Eastern Cotton Belt to 1860*
(1908), 146; *Life and Labor in the
Old South* (1929), 133–34, 135; *The
Life of Robert Toombs* (1913), 147;
*Plantation and Frontier Documents:
1649–1863*, 2 vols. (1909), 147;
reviews of on Edwin Woolley's *The
Reconstruction of Georgia*, 137
Pike, James Shepherd, 13, 211
Plessy v. Ferguson (1896), 6

Polakoff, Keith Ian, 210, 212
Pollard, Edward A., 135–36
Populism, 159, 238
Porter, George H., 44n86, 113
Potts, Charles C., 241, 242
Powers, Ridgley C., 114, 120
Progressive era and Progressivism,
5–6, 10, 80, 110, 150, 218;
Progressive ("New") Historians,
190, 195, 204, 285. *See also* James
Wilford Garner; Paul Leland
Haworth

Rabinowitz, Howard N., 3, 6
race riots, 187–88, 190, 197, 210, 211,
273
Ramsdell, Charles W., 21, 69, 97,
227n46; academic freedom and
Edward Channing's *Student
History of the United States*
(1904), 245–46; Confederate
patriotic societies, 238–40,
251n20; Henry William Elson's
*History of the United States of
America* (1904), 244–45, 253n34;
biography, 233–35; education, 235;
correspondence with Paul Leland
Haworth, 215, 220, 232–33;
president of the Mississippi Valley
Historical Association, 239, 247;
presidential address, Southern
Historical Association (1936), 229;
on Reconstruction, 236–37, 243;
at the University of Texas, 230–31,
238–42, 244–49. *See also* William
Archibald Dunning; Dunning
School; Paul Leland Haworth
—PUBLICATIONS: contribution
to *Studies in Southern History
and Politics* (1914), 94, 141;
Reconstruction in Texas (1910),
235–36; *School History of Texas*
(1912), 240–43

Turner, Frederick Jackson, 85, 90, 138, 144, 190, 195, 204, 232
Turner, Henry McNeal, 290
Turner, Josiah, 189, 190
Tuskegee Institute, 171, 219

Union League, 64, 164, 236–37

Vance, Zebulon, 14, 190
Van Tyne, Claude H., 141
Vardaman, James K., 124, 157
Vest, G. G., 14
Villard, Oswald Garrison, 157–58

Waldrep, Christopher, 26–27
Walker, Clarence E., 34
Walker, Leroy Pope, 261–62, 269
Wall, Bennett Harrison, 193
Wallace, Carolyn, 195, 196
Wallace, John, 259, 271
Washington, Booker T., 125, 170, 219, 220
Watterson, Henry, 21, 213–14, 226n26
Watts, Trent A., 5–6
Weatherly, Ulysses S., 205
Weisberger, Bernard A., 70
Weyl, Walter E., 221

Wharton, Vernon L., 4, 9, 67, 91–92, 95, 123
Wiggins, Sarah, 159, 161
Williamson, Joel, 180, 181, 184
Wilson, D. L., 169
Wilson, Henry, 11–12, 16
Wilson, Woodrow, 26, 58, 70
Wilmington Race Riot (1898), 187–88, 190, 197
Wineburg, Sam, 10–11
Wish, Harvey, 19
Woolley, Edwin C., 44n86, 85, 97, 137, 141, 166, 288, 290, 294, 298
Woodburn, James A., 143–44, 205
Woodman, Harold D., 70
Woodson, Carter G., 32, 176n53, 292
Woodward, C. Vann, 7, 8, 9, 13, 70, 185, 193, 195, 196
Woody, Robert, 96–97, 295
Woolsey, Theodore, 58
World War I, 52, 90, 109, 148–50, 262
World War II, 30, 98, 151
Wormley Conference, 212, 213
Wyatt, John W., 271–72

Yerger, William L., 117
Yulee, David L., 263

CPSIA information can be obtained at www.ICGtesting.com
Printed in the USA
BVOW03*1831050215

386443BV00002B/3/P